ON
THE NIGHTMARE

BY

ERNEST JONES, M.D.

LIVERIGHT

NEW YORK

Originally published in 1951 by Liveright Publishing Corp. Printed in Great Britain by Lund Humphries, London & Bradford. All rights reserved.

Liveright Paperbound Edition 1971
SBN: 87140-052-9
LCC: 70-149625

CONTENTS

PART I

PART II

PART III

PART IV

PREFACE

THE history of this book is as follows. Only Part I. has appeared hitherto in English, in the *American Journal of Insanity*, January 1910. Part II. is a translation from a booklet entitled *Der Alptraum in seiner Beziehung zu gewissen Formen des mittelalterlichen Aberglaubens*, which was published in 1912 as Heft XIV. of the *Schriften zur angewandten Seelenkunde*. Part III. was being prepared for publication when the War broke out, and pressure of other work has laid it aside till now. Part IV., now marked off separately, was the Conclusion to *Der Alptraum*. Most of the book was thus written in the years 1909 and 1910. In revising it for English publication I have freely re-arranged the material, especially in Part III. Some confirmatory material of which I have jotted down notes from time to time has been added, but anything substantially post-dating the original is enclosed in square brackets. Professor Priebsch has read through the chapter on etymology (Part III. Chapter V.), but while grateful to him for his kindly criticism I do not wish to hold him responsible for the views there expressed. To the courtesy of Professor Ganz of Basle I owe both the permission to reproduce the plate of Fuseli's celebrated picture and also practical assistance in making this possible. To my wife, Dr. Katherine Jones, I am deeply indebted for much expert criticism and suggestion and for unfailing encouragement and help in what in the circumstances of my life was an arduous labour.

The question may naturally arise why, in a study advancing so rapidly as psycho-analysis is, one should think it worth while to publish work done more than twenty years ago. The answer lies only partly in the numerous requests that it should be made accessible. A more compelling reason will be discovered in the following considerations.

For the true significance of the Nightmare to be properly appreciated, first by the learned professions and then by the general public, would in my opinion entail consequences, both scientific and social, to which the term momentous might well be applied. What is at issue is nothing less than the very meaning of religion itself. In this book I have brought forward reasons why an intensive study of the Nightmare and the beliefs held about it makes it hard to avoid the conclusion that religion is in its essence one of the means—hitherto perhaps the most valuable—of helping mankind to cope with the burden of guilt and fear everyone inherits in his unconscious from the deepest stirrings of mental life, the primordial conflict over incest. Other workers, notably Freud and Reik, have confirmed and amplified this conclusion, which the world will one day have seriously to take into its reckoning.

January 1931

PREFACE TO THE SECOND EDITION

IT would seem inartistic to revise a book written for the most part some forty years ago, besides which I cannot find that it stands in need of any revision. Since its publication, however, some subsequent reflections have occurred to me that I would now adumbrate.

Were I writing the first chapter now I should lay stress on the bisexual nature of nightmare experiences; although, it is true, this is emphatically predicated later on in the book. (p. 247.)

Detailed examination of the theme of the book proved of unexpected interest in two respects. It is not likely that any better example exists of the *impasse* reached in the conflict between the spiritual outlook—in its supernatural sense—and what I would call the pseudo-materialistic one than is presented by the explanations they respectively give of the Nightmare. It is, here and perhaps elsewhere, to be resolved only by recognising that, opposite as they may appear, they agree in ignoring the psychological, with all the burden of personal responsibility that its admission would entail. It is indeed hard to avoid the conclusion that the emotional attachment to them owes its strength mainly to the very fact that such responsibility can be thus evaded. When clerical belief ascribed nightmares to evil spirits and medical to bodily disturbances they both absolved the subject's personality from any share in bringing them about. In modern language one would say simply that they represent alternative defences against admission of the unconscious. What is curious is that, having this common aim, the two should maintain such intense hostility to each other. But then we have seen a similar state of affairs between rival dictatorships in our own time, however much they may agree in opposing democracy and individual liberty. Apparently belief in salvation by panaceas tends to follow a mono-idealistic pattern.

The second source of interest is more profound and will in time be of similar importance to recognition of the unconscious, since it concerns the origin and significance of religious beliefs.

Investigation shows that the underlying meaning of nightmare experiences is cognate with that of the various elements of folk belief which the Catholic Church fused for three centuries into the unity known as devil worship or, alternately, the witchcraft epidemic. This the Church evidently regarded as a form of heresy, and conversely did its best to prove that all heresies were in essence devil-worship. To the Church the independent judgement of the individual conscience so characteristic of all heresy betokened not only disobedience to authority and the apparently unrestrained clamour to do whatever one likes, but even more danger of reverting to ungovernable primitive behaviour which it is the main function of the Church, and indeed of all religions, to curb. The phrase 'primitive behaviour' is well exemplified in the maleficium and satanic orgies of the witches and can be more precisely defined as the reproduction, in direct or distorted forms, of the hatreds and perversions that, as Freud has shown, accompany the beginnings of life, derive from the conflicts centering around the incestuous phantasies of the infant, and persist in the unconscious mind of adults.

Religious leaders naturally take the view that any such primitive aspect of man needs to be checked or suppressed and that he should be guided by a quite different set of motives, moral ones inspired by various religious beliefs. It never occurs to him that what they offer as a substitute may not be something foreign, but the same thing refined, civilised and disguised beyond recognition. Yet psycho-analysis has been able to produce much evidence indicating that the highest forms of religious belief are sublimated and spiritualised expressions of the very impulses they so condemn.* There was, however, one feature of the devil-worship that evoked the most intense horror in the breasts of believers and doubtless explains the bitterness of the persecutions. That was the obvious caricature of Christian beliefs displayed throughout the orgiastic rituals (black mass, etc.). The two things were uncomfortably close. Devil-worship seemed to be a rebellious and hostile reaction against Christianity, but it would be truer to describe it as a regression to the primitive levels from which Christianity had itself emerged; it was an intolerable exposure of the buried origins of the most sacred beliefs. Not devil-worship, but Christianity, was the reaction.

The data extant are so confusing and one-sided that it is extraordinarily difficult to ascertain how much basis of devil-worship actually existed. Margaret Murray has attempted to prove that in the case of Scotland there were 'covies' of witches and sorcerers who not only indulged in orgies but were devotees of a pre-Christian religion. Pagan beliefs of course survived extensively, and do so still, but it is very doubtful if there was much

* See my Essays in Applied Psycho-Analysis, vol. ii, 1951

definite organisation of them in religious form. The Church itself ascribed the most outrageous practices to all heretics, even to the ultra-moral Albigenses. Of the various heresies themselves, culminating in Protestantism, we have ample records. It is plain that they originated in dissatisfaction with the moral salvation offered by the official Church, especially in the days of its obvious decadence. Characteristically they sought for a purer and more spiritual code with a morality that tended to become increasingly harsh as the strain on the individual conscience proved hard to bear. That they were later exploited by selfish interests, with spoliation of the Catholic Church's possessions, is familiar ground. How far the spiritual distress that led to these divarications was grounded in the social miseries of the Middle Ages and in the economic disturbance induced by the Black Death, is a question that belongs to the province of the historian.

December 1950 E.J.

PART I

PATHOLOGY OF THE NIGHTMARE

So on his Nightmare, through the evening fog,
Flits the squat fiend o'er fen, and lake, and bog ;
Seeks some love-wilder'd maid with sleep oppress'd,
Alights, and grinning sits upon her breast—
    Such as of late, amid the murky sky,
Was marked by Fuseli's poetic eye ;
Whose daring tints, with Shakspeare's happiest grace,
Gave to the airy phantom form and place—
Back o'er her pillow sinks her blushing head,
Her snow-white limbs hang helpless from the bed ;
While with quick sighs and suffocative breath
Her interrupted heart-pulse swims in death.

ERASMUS DARWIN

PATHOLOGY OF THE NIGHTMARE

No malady that causes mortal distress to the sufferer, not even seasickness, is viewed by medical science with such complacent indifference as is the one which is the subject of this book. Textbooks, both on bodily and on mental disorders, may in vain be ransacked for any adequate description of the phenomenon, and still less satisfying is the search for anything more than the most superficial consideration of the pathogenesis of it. The clinical aspects of the malady are commonly ignored except for some desultory remarks on the frequency of bad dreams in certain affections, particularly mitral disease, of which condition indeed they are sometimes alleged to be a diagnostic indication.[1] On the rare and embarrassing occasions on which a physician's aid is sought the consolation offered usually takes the form of irrelevant advice on matters of general hygiene, coupled perhaps with the administration of such potent remedies as silica and cinnibar[2] or with a half-jocular remark concerning the assimilable capacity of the evening meal. The relief afforded to the sufferer does not surpass that obtainable in ages when the treatment in vogue consisted in scarifying the throat and shaving the head,[3] in bleeding at the ankle,[4] or in the administration of wild carrot, Macedonian parsley[5] and the black seeds of the male peony.[6]

The reasons for this state of affairs are manifold, but the central one can be hinted at. It is not often realised that most descriptions of Nightmare given by its victims

[1] Artiques, *Essai sur la valeur séméiologique du rêve*. Thèse de Paris, 1884, No. 99. M. A. Macario, *Du sommeil, des rêves et du somnambulisme*, 1857, etc.
[2] Marggraf, *Die Schlaflosigkeit, Schlafsucht, das Alpdrücken und nervöse Herzklopfen*, 1905, S. 12.
[3] A. Caelius, *Tard. Pass.*, 1618, i. 3.
[4] Rhases, *Ad. Mansor*. ix. 12. Contin. i.
[5] Paulus Aegineta, *Sydenham Transactions*, vol. i. p. 388.
[6] Andrew Bell, *Nocturnal Revels, or a General History of Dreams*, 1707, Pt. i. p. 14.

are an inarticulate and feeble echo of the dread reality. This is one result of the general human tendency to shun deep emotions whenever possible, leading to an imperfect appreciation of the intensity of mental suffering. Another manifestation of this tendency is the still prevailing materialistic attitude towards the origin and nature of mental symptoms in general, and of dreams in particular, which are regarded by physicians as being produced by unaccountable alimentary and circulatory vagaries and as having no serious import. It is significant in this connection that earnest consideration of the malady has as a rule been offered only by actual sufferers, such as Bond,[1] Hodgkin, Boerner, Fosgate, Waller, Macnish, Boschulte, and others.

Even from a physical standpoint, however, it is questionable if the condition is so negligible. When it is remembered that the occurrence of a cerebral hæmorrhage probably always takes place at a moment when the blood pressure is above the average for that of the individual, it would seem to follow that the number of attacks occurring during sleep must be small. Some years ago I was able to show,[2] on the contrary, that the pro-

---

[1] J. Bond, *An Essay on the Incubus, or Nightmare*, 1753. In the preface he states that his was the first book written expressly on the subject. Before his date, however, had appeared the following works: W. Schmidt, *De Ephialte sive Incubone*, Rostock, 1627. Teichmeyer, *De Incubo*, Jena, 1640. Welsch, *De Incubo*, Leipsic, 1643. A. Wanckel, *De Incubo*, Witteberg, 1651. G. F. Aeplinius, *Diss. sistens aegrum incubo laborantem*, Jena, 1678. J. P. Jorolis, *De Incubo*, Ultrajeckti, 1680. D. C. Meinicke, *De Incubo*, Jena, 1683. J. Muller, *De Ephialte seu Incubo*, Leipsic, 1688. C. G. Wenzlovius, *De Incubo*, Frankfort, 1691. G. S. S. Herzberg, *De Incubo*, Traj. ad Rhenum, 1691. C. L. Göckel, *De Incubo ex epitome praxeos clinicae*, Jena, 1708. J. M. Rosner, *De Incubo*, Erfodiae, 1708. C. B. Hagedorn, *De Incubo*, Kiel, 1730. Huisinga, *Diss. sistens incubi causas praecipuas*, Lugd. Bat., 1734. M. Chardulliet, *De Incubo*, Argentorati, 1734. D. Textoris, *De Incubo*, Jena, 1740.

In the next hundred years appeared, apart from the many works cited elsewhere in this book, Kok, *De Incubo*, Louvain, 1795. J. F. E. Waechter, *De Ephialte*, Halle, 1800. J. Unthank, *De Incubo*, Edinburgh, 1803. L. Dubosquet, *Dissertation sur le cauchemar*, Paris, 1815. S. Simpson, *De Incubo*, Bonn, 1825. H. J. Wolter, *De Incubo*, Berlin, 1827. J. C. F. Adler, *De Incubo*, Berlin, 1827. F. Dony, *De Incubo*, Berlin, 1829. C. D. F. Hainlin, *De Incubo*, Göttingen, 1830. C. G. Kühn, *Pr. inert. Caelii Aureliani de incubo tractatio*, Leipsic, 1830. A. Castellano, *Dello incubo commentario medico*, Venice, 1840. J. Kutsche, *De Incubo ejusque medela*, Berlin, 1842.

[2] Ernest Jones, 'The Onset of Hemiplegia in Vascular Lesions', *Brain*, 1905, vol. xxviii. p. 533.

tection against cerebral hæmorrhage afforded by sleep is decidedly less than might have been supposed, and one cannot help thinking that the rise of blood pressure that must accompany the violent agonies of many bad dreams, and especially of Nightmares, is probably related to this fact. Vaschide and Marchand[1] have found that the blood pressure rises 25 mm. during an *Angst* attack in the waking state, and this, though clinically and patho-genetically akin to it, is much less severe than a Nightmare attack. Kornfeld's[2] observations led him to conclude that the rise of blood pressure constitutes the chief symptom of an *Angst* attack, and that the extent of this rise is the most accurate measure of the intensity of the attack. [The evidence for the rise of blood pressure during sleep disturbed by Nightmare dreams has been considered at length by MacWilliam.[3]] Thus the unanimous opinions of the older authors, from Paulus Aegineta[4] and Avicenna[5] to Boerhaave,[6] Bond,[7] Macnish,[8] Arbuthnot,[9] Forbes Winslow,[10] Hammond[11] and Foville,[12] concerning the important part played by Nightmares in the causation of apoplexy may well have had a very considerable backing of truth.

On the mental side, the frequency with which attacks of Nightmare precede or accompany the development of hysteria and insanity has been noted by the majority of

---

[1] N. Vaschide and Marchand, 'Contribution à l'étude de la psycho-physiologie des émotions à propos d'un cas d'éreuthophobie', *Revue de Psychiatrie*, juillet, 1900, t. iii. p. 193, and 'Ufficio che le condizioni mentali hanno sulle modificazioni della respirazione e della circolazione periferica', *Revista sperimentale di freniatria*, 1900, vol. xxvi. p. 512.

[2] Kornfeld, *Centralblatt f. d. ges. Therapie*, 1902, No. 11, u. 12.

[3] J. A. MacWilliam, 'Blood Pressures in Man under Normal and Pathological Conditions', *Physiological Review*, 1925, vol. v. p. 303.

[4] Paulus Aegineta, *op. cit.* p. 388.

[5] Avicenna, cited by Motet in S. Jaccoud's *Nouveau Dictionnaire*, 1867, t. vi. Art. 'Cauchemar'.

[6] H. Boerhaave, *Aph.*, 1709, No. 1020.

[7] Bond, *op. cit.* pp. 64, 65, 69.

[8] R. Macnish, *The Philosophy of Sleep*, 1834, p. 138.

[9] J. Arbuthnot, *On the Nature and Choice of Aliments*, 1731.

[10] Forbes Winslow, *On Obscure Diseases of the Brain and Disorders of the Mind*, 1860, p. 611.

[11] W. A. Hammond, *Sleep and its Derangements*, 1869, p. 149.

[12] Foville, cited by T. Hodgkin, *Brit. Med. Jour.*, May 16, 1863, p. 502.

writers on the subject.[1] Consideration of the actual relation of it to these affections will be postponed until some conclusion has been reached on more preliminary questions. Before entering on a discussion of the pathogenesis of the condition it will be well to consider in some detail its clinical characteristics and to define its essential features.

Striking descriptions of the condition have been given by Psellus,[2] Hammond,[3] Radestock[4] and many others. As the most graphic accounts, impossible to surpass, have been given by self-sufferers I will quote from some of the more interesting of these sources and will then attempt to summarize the most salient of the characteristics there described. Bond,[5] a century and a half ago, tersely described the chief features of the condition as follows: 'The Nightmare generally seizes people sleeping on their backs, and often begins with frightful dreams, which are soon succeeded by a difficult respiration, a violent oppression on the breast, and a total privation of voluntary motion. In this agony they sigh, groan, utter indistinct sounds, and remain in the jaws of death, till, by the utmost efforts of nature, or some external assistance, they escape out of that dreadful torpid state. As soon as they shake off that vast oppression, and are able to move the body, they are affected with a strong Palpitation, great Anxiety, Languor, and Uneasiness; which symptoms gradually abate, and are succeeded by the pleasing reflection of having escaped such imminent danger.'

[1] P. Chaslin, *Du rôle du rêve dans l'évolution du délire*, 1887, pp. 40, 44, 46, 54. D. Cubasch, *Der Alp*, 1877, S. 8. J. E. D. Esquirol, *Des maladies mentales*, 1832, t. ii. ch. xxi. P. Janet, *Névroses et idées fixes*, 1898, t. i. ch. ii. et iv. etc. G. Kelle, *Du sommeil et ses accidents en général et en particulier chez les épileptiques et chez les hystériques.* Lhomme, 'Rapport médico-légal sur l'état mental du Gendarme S . . .', *Annales médico-psychologiques*, 1863, 4e série, t. ii. p. 338. M. E. Escande de Messières, *Les rêves chez les hystériques.* Thèse de Bordeaux, 1895. Sante de Sanctis, *I sogni, studi psychologici e clinici di un alienista*, 1899, pp. 140-172. N. Vaschide et Meunier, *Revue de Psychiatrie*, fév., 1901, p. 38. J. Waller, *A Treatise on the Incubus, or Nightmare*, 1816, p. 7.
[2] M. C. Psellus, *Opus medicum. Carmen de re medica*, 1741 ed.
[3] Hammond, *op. cit.* pp. 183, 184.
[4] P. Radestock, *Schlaf und Traum*, 1879, S. 126, 127.
[5] Bond, *op. cit.* p. 2.

The picture painted by Macnish[1] is so vivid in its colouring as to deserve reproduction if only for its literary interest. 'Imagination cannot conceive the horrors it frequently gives rise to, or language describe them in adequate terms. They are a thousand times more frightful than the visions conjured up by necromancy or *diablerie*; and far transcend everything in history or romance, from the fable of the writhing and asp-encircled Laocoon to Dante's appalling picture of Ugolino and his famished offspring, or the hidden tortures of the Spanish Inquisition. The whole mind, during the paroxysm, is wrought up to a pitch of unutterable despair; a spell is laid upon the faculties, which freezes them into inaction; and the wretched victim feels as if pent alive in his coffin, or overpowered by resistless and unmitigable pressure.

'The modifications which nightmare assumes are infinite; but one passion is almost never absent—that of utter and incomprehensible dread. Sometimes the sufferer is buried beneath overwhelming rocks, which crush him on all sides, but still leave him with a miserable consciousness of his situation. Sometimes he is involved in the coils of a horrid, slimy monster,.whose eyes have the phosphorescent glare of the sepulchre, and whose breath is poisonous as the marsh of Lerna. Everything horrible, disgusting or terrific in the physical or moral world, is brought before him in fearful array; he is hissed at by serpents, tortured by demons, stunned by the hollow voices and cold touch of apparitions. A mighty stone is laid upon his breast, and crushes him to the ground in helpless agony: mad bulls and tigers pursue his palsied footsteps: the unearthly shrieks and gibberish of hags, witches, and fiends float around him. In whatever situation he may be placed, he feels superlatively wretched: he is Ixion working for ages at his wheel: he is Sisyphus rolling his eternal stone: he is stretched upon the iron bed of Procrustes: he is prostrated by inevitable destiny beneath the approaching wheels of the Car of Jugger-

[1] Macnish, *op. cit.* pp. 122-125.

naut. At one moment he may have the consciousness of a malignant demon being at his side: then to shun the sight of so appalling an object, he will close his eyes, but still the fearful being makes its presence known; for its icy breath is felt diffusing itself over his visage, and he knows that he is face to face with a fiend. Then, if he looks up, he beholds horrid eyes glaring upon him, and an aspect of hell grinning at him with even more than hellish malice. Or, he may have the idea of a monstrous hag squatted upon his breast—mute, motionless and malignant; an incarnation of the evil spirit—whose intolerable weight crushes the breath out of his body, and whose fixed, deadly, incessant stare petrifies him with horror and makes his very existence insufferable.

'In every instance, there is a sense of oppression and helplessness; and the extent to which these are carried, varies according to the violence of the paroxysm. The individual never feels himself a free agent; on the contrary he is spellbound by some enchantment, and remains an unresisting victim for malice to work its will upon. He can neither breathe, nor walk, nor run, with his wonted facility. If pursued by any imminent danger, he can hardly drag one limb after another; if engaged in combat, his blows are utterly ineffective; if involved in the fangs of any animal, or in the grasp of an enemy, extrication is impossible. He struggles, he pants, he toils, but it is all in vain: his muscles are rebels to the will, and refuse to obey its calls. In no case is there a sense of complete freedom: the benumbing stupor never departs from him; and his whole being is locked up in one mighty spasm. Sometimes he is forcing himself through an aperture too small for the reception of his body, and is there arrested and tortured by the pangs of suffocation produced by the pressure to which he is exposed; or he loses his way in a narrow labyrinth, and gets involved in its contracted and inextricable mazes; or he is entombed alive in a sepulchre, beside the mouldering dead. There is in most cases an intense reality in all that he sees, or hears, or feels. The aspects of the hideous phantoms

which harass his imagination are bold and defined; the
sounds which greet his ear appallingly distinct; and when
any dimness or confusion of imagery does prevail, it is of
the most fearful kind, leaving nothing but dreary and
miserable impressions behind it.'

A more accurate and no less graphic account is given
by Motet.[1] 'Au milieu du sommeil, le dormeur est pris
tout à coup d'un profond malaise, il se sent suffoqué, il
fait de vains efforts pour inspirer largement l'air qui lui
manque, et il semble que tout son appareil respiratoire
soit frappé d'immobilité. Ce qui pour le rêveur est le
plus pénible, c'est le sentiment de son impuissance. Il
voudrait lutter contre ce qui l'opprime, il sent qu'il ne
peut ni se mouvoir ni crier. Des ennemis menaçants
l'enveloppent de tous côtés, des armes s'opposent à sa
fuite, il entrevoit un moyen de salut, il s'épuise en vains
efforts pour l'atteindre. D'autres fois il se sent entraîné
dans une course rapide; il voudrait s'arrêter, un gouffre
béant s'entrouve sous ses pas, il est précipité, et le sommeil s'interrompt après une violente secousse, comme
celle que produit, dans la veille, une chute, un faux pas.
Tout ce que l'esprit peut inventer de dangers, tout ce
qu'il y a de plus effrayant, se présente dans le cauchemar.
La sensation la plus habituelle, est celle d'un corps lourd
qui comprime le creux épigastrique. Ce corps peut
prendre toute sorte d'aspects; ordinairement c'est un
nain difforme qui vient s'asseoir sur la poitrine et re-
garde avec des yeux menaçants. Chez quelques person-
nes la sensation pénible est, pour ainsi dire, prévue. Le
cauchemar commence par une véritable hallucination;
l'être qui va sauter sur la poitrine (éphialte) est aperçu
dans la chambre, on le voit venir, on voudrait pouvoir
lui échapper, et déjà l'immobilité est absolue; il bondit
sur le lit, on voit ses traits grimaçants, il s'avance et
quand il a pris sa place accoutumée, le cauchemar arrive
à son summum d'intensité. A ce moment le corps est
couvert de sueur, l'anxiété est extrême; parfois s'échap-
pent des cris, des gémissements, et enfin un réveil

[1] Motet, *ibid.*

brusque, accompagné le plus souvent d'un mouvement violent, termine cette scène de terreur.'

From these and other descriptions we may say that the three cardinal features of the malady are (1) agonizing dread; (2) sense of oppression or weight at the chest which alarmingly interferes with respiration; (3) conviction of helpless paralysis. Other accessory features are commonly present as well, but they will be discussed after the triad just mentioned has been considered in more detail.

The dread that occurs in Nightmare and in other unpleasant dreams is best denoted by the German word *Angst*, for there is in English no term that indicates the precise combination of fearful apprehension, of panic-stricken terror, of awful anxiety, dread and anguish that goes to make up the emotion of which we are treating. The striking characteristic of it in pronounced cases of Nightmare is its appalling intensity. That Shakespeare well appreciated this is shown by Clarence's outburst on awaking from such a dream.[1]

> As I am a Christian faithful man
> I would not spend another such a night,
> Though 'twere to buy a world of happy days,
> So full of dismal terror was the time.

After describing the experience that was the cause of so much misery he continues:[2]

> I trembling waked, and for a season after
> Could not believe but that I was in hell,
> Such terrible impression made my dream.

Bond[3] is equally emphatic: 'I have often been so much oppressed by this enemy of rest, that I would have given ten thousand worlds like this for some Person that would either pinch, shake, or turn me off my Back; and I have been so much afraid of its intolerable insults, that I have slept in a chair all night, rather than give it an opportunity of attacking me in an horizontal position.'

---

[1] *King Richard the Third*, Act i. Sc. 4, l. 4.
[2] *Op. cit.* l. 61.   [3] Bond, *op. cit.* p. 71.

Macnish,[1] in the more distended style that is his wont, says: 'There is something peculiarly horrible and paralyzing in the terror of sleep. It lays the energies of the soul prostrate before it, crushes them to the earth as beneath the weight of an enormous vampyre, and equalizes for a time the courage of the hero and the child. No firmness of mind can at all times withstand the influence of these deadly terrors. The person awakes panic-struck from some hideous vision; and even after reason returns and convinces him of the unreal nature of his apprehensions, the panic for some time continues, his heart throbs violently, he is covered with cold perspiration, and hides his head beneath the bedclothes, afraid to look around him, lest some dreadful object of alarm should start up before his affrighted vision. Courage and philosophy are frequently opposed in vain to these appalling terrors. The latter dreads what he disbelieves; and spectral forms, sepulchral voices, and all the other horrid superstitions of sleep arise to vindicate their power over that mind, which, under the fancied protection of reason and science, conceived itself shielded from all such attacks, but which, in the hour of trial, often sinks beneath their influence as completely as the ignorant and unreflecting hind, who never employed a thought as to the real nature of these fantastic and illusive sources of terror. The alarm of a frightful dream is sometimes so overpowering, that persons under the impression thus generated, of being pursued by some imminent danger, have actually leaped out of the window to the great danger and even loss of their lives.'

The *second cardinal feature* in the attack is the sense of stifling oppression on the chest as of an overpowering weight that impedes the respiration often to the extreme limit of endurance. Radestock[2] regards this inhibition of respiration as the central symptom of the attack: 'Steigert sich die Athembeklemmung zur Athemnoth, welche im Wachen als beschwerliches Athemholen empfunden wird, so entsteht das vielgefürchtete Alp-

---

[1] Macnish, *op. cit.* p. 68.   [2] Radestock, *op. cit.* S. 126.

drücken.' ('If the interference with breathing increases to the point of suffocation, felt in the waking state as a great difficulty in drawing breath, then there comes about the greatly dreaded Nightmare.') Erasmus Darwin,[1] on the other hand, maintained that there cannot exist any actual difficulty of breathing, since the mere suspension of volition will not produce any, the respiration going on as well asleep as awake; he, therefore, doubted the observation. Waller[2] pertinently remarked to this that 'any person that has experienced a paroxysm of Night-mare, will be disposed rather to give up Dr. Darwin's hypothesis than to mistrust his own feelings as to the difficulty of breathing, which is by far the most terrific and painful of any of the symptoms. The dread of suffocation, arising from the inability of inflating the lungs, is so great, that the person, who for the first time in his life is attacked by this "worst phantom of the night", generally imagines that he has very narrowly escaped death, and that a few seconds more of the complaint would inevitably have proved fatal.'

The *third typical feature* of the malady is the utter powerlessness, amounting to a feeling of complete paralysis, which is the only response of the organism to the agonizing effort that it makes to relieve itself of the choking oppression. Many writers, such as Kelle,[3] Hodgkin,[4] etc., put this in the forefront of the picture, and Macnish[5] considers it a diagnostic feature in distinguishing Nightmare from other forms of unpleasant dreams. He writes: 'In incubus, the individual feels as if his powers of volition were totally paralyzed; and as if he were altogether unable to move a limb in his own behalf, or utter a cry expressive of his agony. When these feelings exist, we may consider the case to be one of nightmare: when they do not, and when, notwithstanding his terror, he seems to himself to possess unrestrained

[1] Erasmus Darwin, *Zoonomia*, 1796, vol. i. Sect. xviii. 3, p. 205.
[2] Waller, *op. cit.* p. 13.
[3] Kelle, *op. cit.* p. 23.
[4] T. Hodgkin, *Brit. Med. Journ.*, May 16, 1863, p. 501.
[5] Macnish, *op. cit.* p. 73.

muscular motion, to run with ease, breathe freely, and
enjoy the full capability of exertion, it must be regarded
as a simple dream.' Erasmus Darwin,[1] indeed, held the
view that the malady was nothing more than too deep
a sleep; 'in which situation of things the power of volition,
of command over the muscles, of voluntary motion, is
too completely suspended; and that the efforts of the
patient to recover this power constitute the disease we
call Night-mare'. This paralysis is perhaps most characteristic with the voice. To quote Macnish[2] again: 'In
general, during an attack, the person has the consciousness of an utter inability to express his horror by cries.
He feels that his voice is half choked by impending
suffocation, and that any exertion of it, farther than a
deep sigh or groan, is impossible. Sometimes, however,
he conceives that he is bellowing with prodigious energy,
and wonders that the household are not alarmed by his
noise. But this is an illusion: those outcries which he
fancies himself uttering, are merely obscure moans,
forced with difficulty and pain from the stifled penetralia
of his bosom.'

The relation to one another of the members of this
triad of symptoms is admirably portrayed by Cubasch[3]:
'zu einer beliebigen Stunde der Nacht fühlt der Traü-
mende plötzlich, oder nach und nach, dass die Respiration behindert ist; irgend ein Wesen, meistens ein zottiges
Thier, oder eine hässliche menschliche Gestalt stemmt
sich dem Schläfer auf die Brust, oder schnürt ihm die
Kehle zu, und sucht ihn zu erwürgen; die Angst wird mit
der Athemnoth immer grösser, jede Gegenwehr ist unmöglich, denn wie durch Zauberkraft sind alle Glieder
gelähmt; der Unglückliche sucht zu fliehen—umsonst,
er ist wie angewurzelt an die Stelle; die Gefahr, die Angst
wird immer grösser, da endlich überwindet eine letze
furchtbare Kraftanstrengung das feindliche Wesen, eine
heftige Bewegung erweckt den Träumenden aus seinem
Schlafe und—Alles ist vorüber, nur der kalte Schweiss

---

[1] Darwin, cited by Waller, *op. cit.* p. 12.
[2] Macnish, *op. cit.* p. 140.   [3] Cubasch, *op. cit.* S. 8.

auf dem ganzen Körper, ein laut hörbares Herzklopfen erinnert den Erwachten an den verzweifelten Kampf auf Leben und Tod, an die grässliche Todesangst, die er soeben zu überstehen hatte. Dieses sind in Kürze die Erscheinungen des Alps; nie fehlende Symptome sind die Athemnoth und die mit ihr vergeschwisterte Angst, das Gefühl eines schweren Körpers auf der Brust, das Unvermögen, irgend welche Gegenwehr zu leisten, oder irgend eine Bewegung zu machen.' ('At any particular hour of the night the dreamer feels, either suddenly or gradually, that his respiration is impeded. Some kind of Being, most often a shaggy animal, or else a hideous human form presses on the sleeper's breast, or pinions his throat and tries to strangle him. The terror increases with the suffocation, every effort at defence is impossible, since all his limbs are paralysed as though by magical power. The unhappy person seeks to escape, but in vain, for he is rooted to the spot. The danger, the terror, becomes ever greater, and then at last a final frightful effort overcomes the adverse Being, a vigorous movement wakens the dreamer from his sleep, and all is over —only the cold sweat over the whole body and a loudly audible beating of the heart serve to remind the waking person of his desperate life and death struggle, of the horrible and deathly terror he has just had to endure. These are in short the signs of Nightmare: invariable symptoms are the suffocation and the dread accompanying this, the sensation of a heavy body on the breast and the impossibility of offering any defence or of making any sort of movement.')

At the culmination of the attack there are commonly present many accessory evidences of the effort with which the patient, in a mortal panic, has escaped; such are, an outbreak of cold sweat, convulsive palpitation of the heart, singing in the ears, sense of pressure about the forehead, a terror - stricken countenance. Many writers, including Bond,[1] Waller,[2] Motet[3] and Fos-

---

[1] Bond. See quotation above.
[2] Waller, *op. cit.* p. 55.   [3] Motet, *loc. cit.*

gate,[1] lay especial stress on the exhaustion and malaise that immediately follow. Throughout the next day it is common for the patient still to suffer from malaise, heaviness, depression, dread, lack of confidence, pains in the head and weakness in the lower extremities. In cases of recurrent attacks the dread of the coming night may be so great that the patient avoids going to bed, and sometimes spends night after night in a chair. Bond[2] relates the case of a gentleman who was bled and purged by way of treatment until he was too weak to endure more. 'He, therefore, was obliged to sleep in a chair all night, to avoid Night-mare. But one night he ventured to bed, and was found half dead in the morning. He continued paralytic for two years; and after taking the round of Bath and Bristol to no purpose, he died an Idiot.' The signs that indicate to the patient that he is in danger of the attack recurring are well narrated by Waller[3] as 'a weight and great uneasiness about the heart, requiring often a sudden and full inspiration of the lungs. If I sit down to read I find my thoughts involuntarily carried away to distant scenes, and that I am in reality dreaming, from which state I am only aroused by a sense of something like suffocation, the unpleasant sensation before mentioned about the heart. I am relieved for the moment by a sudden and strong inspiration or by walking it off, but there is present a strong inclination to sleep, which if followed inevitably results in Incubus.'

Though the agonizing struggle usually subsides very soon after waking, it is not rare for the attack to continue for some time in spite of clear consciousness. In the second quotation from Macnish given above there is a graphic description of this, and it may further be illustrated by the following sketch drawn by Waller[4]: 'The uneasiness of the patient in his dream rapidly increases, till it ends in a kind of consciousness that he is in bed, and asleep; but he feels to be oppressed with some

[1] B. Fosgate, 'Observations on Nightmare', *American Journal of the Medical Sciences*, 1834, vol. xv. p. 81.   [2] Bond, *op. cit.* p. 65.
[3] Waller, *op. cit.* pp. 56, 57.   [4] Waller, *op. cit.* pp. 22, 23.

weight which confines him upon his back, and prevents his breathing, which is now become extremely laborious, so that the lungs cannot be fully inflated by any effort he can make. The sensation is now the most painful that can be conceived; the person becomes every instant more awake and conscious of his situation: he makes violent efforts to move his limbs, especially his arms, with a view of throwing off the incumbent weight, but not a muscle will obey the impulse of the will: he groans aloud, if he has strength to do it, while every effort he makes seems to exhaust the little remaining vigour. The difficulty of breathing goes on increasing, so that every breath he draws, seems to be almost the last that he is likely to draw; the heart generally moves with increased velocity, sometimes is affected with palpitation; the countenance appears ghastly, and the eyes are half open. The patient, if left to himself, lies in this state generally about a minute or two, when he recovers all at once the power of volition.'

We have now to consider a few points concerning the circumstances under which the attack takes place. Some writers, such as Cubasch,[1] Waller,[2] etc., emphatically maintain that it can arise only during sleep, and indeed only during exceptionally deep sleep. We saw above that Darwin made this the basis of his explanation of the condition. There can be no doubt, however, that attacks in every way indistinguishable from the classical Nightmare not only may occur but may run their whole course during the waking state. Rousset's thesis is based mainly on the study of such an attack, which he rightly considers[3] to be of the same nature as the ordinary Nightmare. Macnish, in relating a self-observation,[4] says: 'The more awake we are, the greater is the violence of the paroxysm. I have experienced the affection stealing upon me while in perfect possession of my faculties, and have undergone the greatest tortures, being haunted by

[1] Cubasch, *op. cit.* S. 7, 9.   [2] Waller, *op. cit.* p. 21.
[3] César Rousset, *Contribution à l'étude du cauchemar*, 1876, p. 24:
[4] Macnish, *op. cit.* p. 132.

specters, hags, and every sort of phantom—having, at the same time, a full consciousness that I was labouring under incubus, and that all the terrifying objects around me were the creation of my own brain.' In another place[1] he devotes a chapter to this condition, which he designates 'Daymare'; Still,[2] using a kindred term, has given an excellent description of a similar condition in children. It is however probable, as was long ago indicated by Fosgate,[3] that it is chiefly or perhaps exclusively recurrent attacks, of the nature of a relapse, that occur during the waking state, and that a person who for some time has been free from the malady will be again attacked only during sleep.

The most likely times for Nightmare to appear are either within the first two or three hours of sleep, or else in the morning in the torpid state that so often supervenes after an over-long or over-deep sleep. Motet[4] and Pfaff[5] state that it generally occurs in the first half of the night; Waller[6] says that it is almost always produced by sleeping too long, frequently by sleeping too soon, and that in his own case indulging in sleep too late in the morning is an almost certain method of bringing on an attack. I have noticed that the attack tends to recur at about the same time in the same subject, and have the impression that it more frequently appears in the early part of the night than in the morning. Macnish[7] states that dreams of all kinds occur more frequently in the morning than in the early part of the night, but this is a kind of fact that is not easily established and more modern observations lend it but little support.

It has always been a generally accepted opinion that Nightmare is more likely to attack a person who is sleeping on his back, and this view is strongly maintained by

[1] Macnish. op. cit. ch. vi. p. 142 et seq.
[2] G. F. Still, 'Day Terrors (Pavor diurnus) in Children', Lancet, Feb. 3, 1900, p. 292.
[3] Fosgate, loc. cit.
[4] Motet, loc. cit.
[5] E. R. Pfaff, Das Traumleben und seine Deutung, 1873, S. 37.
[6] Waller, op. cit. p. 110.
[7] Macnish, op. cit. p. 47.

among others, Burton,[1] Lower,[2] Bond,[3] Macnish[4] and
Rousset.[5] To avoid the supine posture in sleep has commonly been a therapeutic recommendation, and we shall
presently see that the observation has been made to
play an important part in several hypotheses concerning
the malady. On the other hand Fosgate[6] and Hammond[7]
find the posture assumed in sleep to be of little importance in relation to the onset of Nightmare, and Splittgerber[8] modified the usual view by saying the attack
generally occurs in persons lying either on the back or
on the left side. Waller[9] has pointed out that, on account
of the feeling in the chest as of some weight pressing him
down, the sufferer is often deceived about his original
position, especially as during his struggle he tends in
any case to assume the supine posture. Boerner[10] and
Cubasch[11] consider even that the prone posture is com-
moner in attacks than is the supine. In my experience
the supine posture is decidedly the more frequent of the
two, as is generally believed. I have never known of an
instance of true Nightmare occurring when the patient
was in a lateral position, though presumably in very exceptional cases this may be so, for Macnish[12] has given
clear accounts of attacks that he has suffered in every
position, even when sitting in a chair.

We now come to the vexed problem of the pathogenesis of the malady, and the temptation is great to
follow the example of Cubasch,[13] who avoids discussion
of previous opinions by saying: 'Ich übergehe die verschiedenen Erklärungen, die von medicinischer Seite aus
versucht wurden, die sich aber alle nicht beweisen lassen,
oft sogar geradezu unmöglich sind.' ('I pass by the

---

[1] Robert Burton, *The Anatomy of Melancholy* (1621), 1826 ed., pp. 134, 434.
[2] R. Lower, *Tractatus de Corde*, 1669, p. 145.
[3] Bond, *op. cit.* pp. 71, 74, etc.
[4] Macnish, *op. cit.* pp. 139, 272.   [5] Rousset, *op. cit.* p. 41.
[6] Fosgate, *loc. cit.*   [7] Hammond, *op. cit.* p. 186.
[8] F. Splittgerber, *Schlaf und Tod*, 1866, S. 166.
[9] Waller, *op. cit.* pp. 73, 74.
[10] J. Boerner, *Das Alpdrücken, seine Begründung und Verhütung*, 1855, S. 8, 9, 27.
[11] Cubasch, *op. cit.* S. 22.
[12] Macnish, *op. cit.* p. 128.   [13] Cubasch, *op. cit.* S. 17.

various medical explanations that have been proffered, since they are all unproven and often even absolutely impossible.') The criticism passed on medical views of Nightmare by Waller,[1] that 'in all probability every one of them is wrong, so that it can be of little utility to inquire into them', would be as true to-day as when it was written nearly a century ago if it were not for the epoch-making work of one man—Professor Freud—on the psychogenesis of dreams and the relation of them to the neuroses.

It would be a laborious and certainly unprofitable task to review most of the hypotheses on the subject that at various times have been put forth, and the only reason why some of the chief ones will be enumerated is that in my opinion there is a kernel of truth in all of them, however widely they may at first sight seem to diverge from the view here to be sustained. As a preliminary remark one may say that, from the very multiplicity and protean nature of the 'causes' to which the malady has been attributed—ranging from an elongated uvula[2] to the ingestion of West Indian alligator pears,[3] which is said to be an infallible recipe for the production of a Nightmare—the prediction might be ventured that writers have in general mistaken for the true cause of the malady factors that play a part, of varying importance, in the evocation *of a given attack*. In other words there is an *a priori* probability that there is an underlying abnormal condition, which may be regarded as the predisposition to the affection, and that there is a large number of superficial factors which may be concerned in eliciting the manifestations that we call attacks of Nightmare. It has previously been held that this predisposition is of relatively slight importance in comparison with what may be termed the exciting causes—just as we commonly regard it to be with such diseases as scarlet fever, where our attention is focussed on the external

[1] Waller, *op. cit.* p. 69.
[2] J. H. Rauch, 'Case of Nightmare caused by elongation of the uvula', *American Journal of the Medical Sciences*, 1852, N.S., vol. xxiii. p. 435.
[3] Waller, *op. cit.* p. 105.

factor—so that for instance Waller[1] could state that the malady will attack any person whatever, provided he gets indigestion. On the contrary, the view here maintained is that the predisposition is of cardinal importance, and that when this is developed to a pronounced extent an attack of Nightmare can be elicited by the most insignificant external factor or may occur even in the absence of any external factor whatever. Attention therefore will here be concentrated on the nature and pathogeny of the predisposition, though something will also be said on the subject of the connection between this predisposition and the external exciting factors to which previous writers have attributed so much significance.

Of the eight principal systems of the body four have almost always been selected as being the ones incriminated in the production of Nightmare: the alimentary, the respiratory, the circulatory and the nervous. Many of the hypotheses emitted are now of only historical interest and need be no more than mentioned; such are for instance Lower's[2] view that the condition is due to a collection of lymph in the fourth ventricle of the brain, Willis'[3] that incongruous matter from the blood mixes with the nervous fluid in the cerebellum, Fosgate's[4] that it is an affection of the anterior column of the spinal marrow and the nerves arising therefrom, Bailey's[5] that it is a distemper caused by undigested humours stopping the passage of the animal spirits, so that the body cannot move, Hohnbaum's[6] that it is produced by poisonous gases or miasmata, Splittgerber's[7] that it occurs at certain phases of the moon, and Baillarger's[8] that it is due to primary congestion of the brain. Boschulte's[9] curious

[1] Waller, op. cit. p. 64.   [2] Lower, loc. cit.
[3] T. Willis, De anima brutorum, 1672, Cap. 6. p. 127
[4] Fosgate, op. cit. p. 83.
[5] N. Bailey, English Dictionary, 1789. Art. 'Nightmare'.
[6] Hohnbaum, Psychische Gesundheit und Irresein in ihren Übergängen, 1845, S. 38, 41.   [7] Splittgerber, loc. cit.
[8] J. Baillarger, 'De l'influence de l'état intermédiare à la veille et au sommeil sur la production et la marche des hallucinations', Mém. de l'Acad. roy. de Méd., 1846, t. xii. p. 476.
[9] Boschulte, 'Eine Mittheilung über Alpdrücken', R. Virchow's Arch. f. pathologische Anatomie und Physiologie, 1881, Bd. lxxxv. S. 371.

hypothesis, although of comparatively recent date, must
also be classed in the same group. He writes: 'Wir sehen
also durch Stockung in den peripherischen Gefässen
einen Druck auf die peripherischen Theile der Empfin-
dungsnerven veranlasst, dadurch aber, vermöge des me-
chanisch-chemisch-physikalischen Prozesses, die Emp-
findungen zwar parästhetisch erregt, aber in einem
Theile des Centralnervensystems oder des Reflex-ap-
parats die gebundene motorische Kraft nicht wirksam
genug afficirt, während darauf der Reiz des Schellentons,
in seiner proportionalen Stärke wirkend auf die speci-
fische Energie des Gehörnerven, jene bis zum völligen
Erwachen entfesselt.' ('We thus see how stagnation in
the peripheral vessels sets up a pressure on the peripheral segments of the sensory nerves of such a kind
that, although sensations are, by means of the mechanical, chemical and physical process, paræsthetically
aroused, the motor power bound in some part of the
central nervous system or the reflex apparatus does not
adequately function; whereupon the stimulation of vi-
bratory tones, working on the specific energy of the
auditory nerves in proportion to its strength, thunder-
ously arouses them to the point of awakening.') The
only modern writer who makes the nervous system responsible for the primary change is Rousset.[1] He attributes the malady to an active congestion of the brain,
brought about by fearful or excitable ideas of the preceding evening.

The earliest, and still the most popular, medical hypothesis of the origin of Nightmare was that it arose from
gastric disturbances. This view was originally brought
forward by Galen,[2] was elaborated by Paulus Aegineta[3]
and is given as the orthodox medical one in the latest
editions of *Chambers's Encyclopædia,*[4] and of the *Imperial Dictionary,*[5] where full accounts of it may be

[1] Rousset, *op. cit.* pp. 36, 37.
[2] Galen, *Comment. ad aph. Hipp.*, Ed. Kühn, xvii. 2, S. 628 u. 747.
[3] Paulus Aegineta, *loc. cit.*
[4] *Chambers's Encyclopædia,* 1902, vol. iv. p. 89.
[5] *Imperial Dictionary of the English Language,* 1883, vol. iii. p. 260.

found. Practically all writers accept it, but so far as I am aware the only one who does so quite empirically is Binz,[1] all others adding some hypothesis concerning the mode of operation of the gastric disorder. As we shall presently see, there is a certain amount of truth in the empirical observation, but the commonly accepted hypotheses have little relation to what probably is the actual explanation of it. Two explanations have been offered, (1) that an over-full stomach presses on the diaphragm and thus mechanically impedes the circulation through the heart and lungs, and (2) that the presence of undigested food in the stomach acts as a peripheral source of irritation to the nervous system. That the former of these views, which has been maintained by Paulus Aegineta,[2] Bond,[3] Burton,[4] Floyer,[5] Macnish,[6] Hodgkin,[7] Scholz,[8] Hammond,[9] Herbert Spencer,[10] Motet[11] and many others, is not the inclusive explanation it is often supposed to be was very convincingly demonstrated by Waller's[12] self-observations. He says: 'I religiously abstained, for many years, from eating anything after dinner, and took dinner also at as early an hour as two o'clock. It was during this period that I suffered most from the disease.' No one can accuse Waller, therefore, of not having put the over-full stomach hypothesis to adequate experimental proof, and he is unequivocal about the results of his investigation. Both Macnish and Hodgkin strongly maintain the improbability of a full stomach interfering with the action of the heart to such an extent as seriously to embarrass the circulation, though they hold that it acts by mechanically impeding the respiration; according to Macnish the stomach causes pressure on the

[1] C. Binz, Über den Traum, 1878, S. 28.   [2] Paulus Aegineta, loc. cit.
[3] Bond. op. cit. p. 51.
[4] Burton, op. cit. vol. i. Pt. 2, Sec. 2, Mem. 5, p. 434.
[5] Sir James Floyer, quoted by Latham, A Dictionary of the English Language, 1882, vol. i. p. 1240.
[6] Macnish, op. cit. p. 134.   [7] Hodgkin, loc. cit.
[8] F. Scholz, Schlaf und Traum, 1887, S. 30.
[9] Hammond, op. cit. pp. 185, 187.
[10] Herbert Spencer, Principles of Sociology, 1885, vol. i. p. 133.
[11] Motet, loc. cit.
[12] Waller, op. cit. pp. 11, 70, 75.

diaphragm and torpor of the intercostal muscles, with consequent hindering of the pulmonary circulation.

The second explanation, which has been maintained by Paulus Aegineta,[1] Waller,[2] Barclay,[3] Splittgerber,[4] Radestock,[5] Chambers[6] and Maudsley,[7] is to the effect that indigestible or undigested food in the stomach acts by producing irritating afferent impulses, which on reaching the brain are transformed into feelings of terror. Strahl[8] describes the afferent impulses as being not of a nervous nature but as consisting of stomach gases which are carried to the brain and disturb its repose. The precise kind of indigestible food that is most efficacious in this connection is often described, for instance by Waller,[9] with a fulness of detail that betokens a confidence of belief only too incommensurate with the value of the evidence on which it is founded. It is plain that this explanation is even harder to sustain than the last, for at the best it is obvious that there are gaps of considerable extent in the description of the mode of action of the morbid process.

Distension of the stomach is not the only way in which the circulation has been supposed to get embarrassed. Strümpell,[10] Radestock[11] and others have attributed to a similar mechanism the frequency of Nightmares in cases of heart disease. Albers[12] holds that 'determination of the blood to the chest', from whatever source, is the essential cause of Nightmare. A constrained posture has frequently been invoked as the active agent in bringing about this state of embarrassment, for instance by Hammond,[13] Radestock[14] and Scholz[15]; Radestock holds that the

[1] Paulus Aegineta, loc. cit.   [2] Waller, op. cit. pp. 65, 75, 96, 98.
[3] J. Barclay, Universal English Dictionary. Revised by Woodward, 1851, p. 564.
[4] Splittgerber, loc. cit.
[5] Radestock, op. cit. S. 129.   [6] Chambers's Encyclopædia, loc. cit.
[7] H. Maudsley, The Pathology of Mind, 1879, p. 32.
[8] Strahl, Der Alp, sein Wesen und seine Heilung, 1833.
[9] Waller, op. cit. pp. 105, 106, 109.
[10] L. H. Strümpell, Die Natur und Entstehung der Träume, 1874, S. 116.
[11] Radestock, op. cit. S. 130.
[12] Albers, quoted by Ernst von Feuchtersleben, 'The Principles of Medical Psychology', Sydenham Transactions, 1847, p. 198.
[13] Hammond, op. cit. p. 186.
[14] Radestock, op. cit. S. 118, 125.   [15] Scholz, loc. cit.

abnormal posture causes embarrassment of the heart directly, Hammond and Scholz that it does so only by impeding the circulation. Kant[1] formulated the remarkable opinion that Nightmare was a beneficent process the function of which was to wake the individual and so warn him of the danger to which he was exposed from the effect of the constrained posture of his circulation. As we shall presently learn, Freud also sees a teleological function, though of a vastly different kind, in the waking from Nightmare.

The supine posture even, normal and unconstrained, has been incriminated by some writers as the efficient agent in the production of Nightmare. This view was greatly elaborated by Bond,[2] who founded on the basis of it a most complicated hypothesis concerning the mechanism of the circulation, and ascribed all sorts of harmful results to the dangerous practice of lying on the back. He asks,[3] as Kant did, 'Are not these monstrous dreams intended as a stimulus to rouse the sentient principle in us, that we might alter the position of the body, and by that means avoid the approaching danger?' Splittgerber[4] and Rousset[5] also consider the supine position is in itself harmful, though the latter ascribes to it only a predisposing rôle in that it sets up a passive congestion of the brain which allows active congestion to supervene and originate the attack. Waller,[6] on the other hand, held that the importance of posture as a cause of embarrassment of respiration or of the circulation had been greatly overestimated, on the ground that he personally had repeatedly suffered from Nightmare in every position, even when sleeping with his head leaning forwards on a table.

Of late years there has been a reaction against the views that placed in the foreground the circulatory troubles, and that culminated in Maury's[7] work, where the varying state of the cerebral circulation was made to

---

[1] I. Kant, *Anthropologie*, 1798, Sec. 34, S. 105.
[2] Bond, *op. cit.* ch. ii.
[3] Bond, *op. cit.* p. 23.
[4] Splittgerber, *loc. cit.*
[5] Rousset, *op. cit.* pp. 38, 39.
[6] Waller, *op. cit.* p. 69.
[7] L. F. A. Maury, *Le sommeil et les rêves*, 1865.

account for most of the phenomena of sleep and dreams. As the result mainly of the work of Boerner,[1] attention has been more and more concentrated on the respiratory embarrassment as a chief factor in the production of Nightmare. Although the respiratory symptoms had long been noticed they had generally been thought, in the way expounded for instance by Rousset,[2] to be secondary to the circulatory disturbance. Gradually, however, it was recognized that this might be produced by a primary respiratory trouble, as mentioned by Radestock[3] in the case of asthma, and Cubasch[4] indeed holds that with Nightmare this is invariably so. Binz,[5] following Boerner, has developed what he calls a toxic theory of Nightmare, which he attributes to the poisoning of the brain by carbon dioxide. Prout[6] also takes this position, and explains the frequency with which Nightmare occurs at midnight by the fact, he declares to have established, that the percentage of carbon dioxide in the blood is greatest at that time.

According to these observers, then, gastric disturbances would play only a very subsidiary rôle, and the views of Scholz,[7] that Nightmare always arises from a disorder of either the respiratory or circulatory systems, or of Motet,[8] who gives a long list of 'causes' which, however, he says all act by impeding the circulation and giving a supply of bad blood to the brain, fairly represent a large number of writers on the subject.

In this brief review of the different hypotheses we thus see that they fall fairly distinctly into two groups. On the one hand sources of peripheral irritation, which consist almost exclusively of various indigestible foods, are made to play the chief part in the production of the malady; on the other various mechanical sources of embarrassment to the circulation and respiration, principally a distended stomach and a constrained posture,

---

[1] Boerner, *op. cit.*
[2] Rousset, *op. cit.* p. 37.
[3] Radestock, *op. cit.* S. 130.
[4] Cubasch, *op. cit.* S. 17, 18.
[5] Binz, *op. cit.* S. 27, 28.
[6] Prout, cited by Radestock, *op. cit.* S. 129.
[7] Scholz, *op. cit.* S. 27.
[8] Motet, *loc. cit.*

are asserted to be the efficient agents and to act by bringing about a supply to the brain of non-aerated blood.

So far as I am aware, the first writer to point out the insufficiencies of these physical factors was Moreau[1] of Tours. He laid such stress on the psychological side of the problem as to call forth from Rousset[2] the shocked protest: 'Il admet bien une excitation comme point de départ des troubles psychiques, mais avec tant de réserve, qu'on se demande si, réellement, il fait intervenir le système circulatoire dans la production des désordres cérébraux.' The heresy of Moreau was, however, soon surpassed by that of Splittgerber,[3] who not only expressed dissatisfaction with the adequacy of the physical explanations but went on to trace the origin of the mental distress in Nightmare to hidden tendencies in the mind and the agonies of an evil conscience, thus lightly foreshadowing the modern psychological view of the malady. Before discussing these matters he says in reference to the physical explanations: 'Es führen uns aber gerade diese letzten Bemerkungen von selbst darauf, dass wir nun auch noch den eigentlichen und tiefsten Grund aller Verwirrung des Seelenlebens im Traum aufdecken; denn alle turbirende Einwirkung auf die in sich selbst zurückgezogene Seele von aussen her, sei es dass sie von der weiteren Aussenwelt oder von dem sie enger umschliessenden körperlichen Organismus herrührt, reicht doch nicht hin, um die Turba des Traumlebens überhaupt nach ihrer ganzen Tiefe und Ausdehnung zu erklären. Oder woher kommt es denn, dass in den phantastischen Gebilden des Traums gerade so wie in unserm wirklichen Leben mehr Ängstlichkeit als Heiterkeit des Gemüths, mehr Unfriede als Friede des Gewissens, mehr Unreinheit als Keuschheit des Herzens, mehr Sorge als kindliches Gottvertrauen heimisch sind?' ('These last remarks, however, lead us to discover the real and deepest

---

[1] J. J. Moreau, 'De l'identité de l'état de rêve et de la folie', *Annales médico-psychologiques*, 1855, p. 361.
[2] Rousset, *op. cit.* p. 13.   [3] Splittgerber, *op. cit.* S. 170.

cause of all disturbance of mental life that takes place in dreams; for none of the external interferences acting on the mind withdrawn into itself, whether they proceed from the distant outer world or from the bodily organism that encloses it more nearly, is adequate to explain the turmoil of dream life in its whole depth and extent. Or else whence comes it that in the phantastic imagery of our dreams, just as in our waking life, anxiety is more at home than joyousness of spirit, uneasiness than peace of mind, impurity than chastity of heart, care than childlike trust in God?')

This penetrating query of Splittgerber's well reveals the wide gap between the agents operative according to the physical explanations and the predominating features actually observed in the attack. In reality, to regard the discovery of any conceivable modification of the quantity or quality of the cerebral circulation as a satisfactory and final explanation of such a phenomenon as a sudden and mortal dread of some assaulting monster displays such a divergence from the principles of psycho-physiology as to leave no common ground on which the subject can be discussed.

We need not further consider, however, *a priori* probabilities, for on the purely observational side we find that what at once strikes anyone who begins to study the malady uninfluenced by previous views is the singular lack of correlation between the alleged causes and the actual attacks. In other words, the most damaging criticism of all the hypotheses mentioned above is the simple observation of the frequency with which on the one hand the alleged factors occur without being followed by Nightmare, and with which on the other hand given attacks of Nightmare occur without having been preceded by any of the alleged factors. Let us take any one of them as an example, for instance gastric disorders. As a plain fact it may be observed that only a minority of individuals who suffer with Nightmare also suffer from gastric troubles, while on the other hand the percentage of patients with gastric ulcer, carcinoma ventriculi, or any other form of gastric disorder—except possibly the so-called nervous dyspepsia that is found in patients suffering from *Angst* neurosis—who are subject to Nightmare is correspondingly small. Take again the question of posture; is there the slightest reason to believe either that the sufferers from Nightmare are peculiarly apt to sleep in constrained attitudes, or that their cerebral circulation is specially liable to be disorganized by the adoption of a supine posture? As to the over-full stomach hypothesis, how many patients who dread the Nightmare, or for the matter of that, how many other people, so distend their stomachs just before retiring to rest as to set up an embarrassment of the heart and lungs enough to cause acute poisoning with the carbon dioxide of non-aerated blood? On the other hand, healthy individuals who are in reality thus poisoned or who are suffocated in any kind of way, from immersion under water, from the choke-damp of colliery explosions or from the leak of a gas stove, may pass through various distressing experiences and may suffer from many mental symptoms, but they hardly ever undergo an attack at all resembling that of Nightmare.

Any sceptical inquiry, therefore, immediately reveals two facts. *First*, that all the alleged causes of Nightmare often occur, both alone and in combination, in persons who never show any symptom of Nightmare; a patient whose stomach is half destroyed with cancer may commit all sorts of dietary indiscretions, including even indulgence in cucumber—the article of food that is most looked askance at in relation to Nightmare—he may even sleep on his back, and still will defy medical orthodoxy in not suffering from any trace of Nightmare. *Secondly*, that a habitual sufferer from Nightmare may be scrupulously rigorous in regard to both the quality and quantity of all that he eats, may in fact develop a *maladie de scrupule* in this direction, that he may martyr himself with elaborate precautions to avoid these and other 'causes' of the malady, and by means of a contrivance of spikes ensure against ever lying—let alone sleeping—on his back, but despite all his endeavours he will have to endure as many and as severe attacks as before.

Thus, apart from any theoretical considerations, purely empiric observation compels the conclusion that any part played by the factors we have mentioned above must be an exceedingly subordinate one, and that what we have called the predisposition of the individual must be a factor of overwhelming importance. My own experience has convinced me that in individuals healthy in a certain respect presently to be defined it is impossible by any physical or mental agent to evoke any state resembling that of Nightmare, while in other individuals unhealthy in this respect nothing will prevent the recurrence from time to time of Nightmare attacks, and further that these can be elicited in them by the most insignificant of morbid incidents.

This is the reason why all attempts to base on experimental evidence the physical hypotheses concerning Nightmare have had to be carried out on persons who habitually suffered from the malady; such are, for example, the oft-quoted experiments of Boerner,[1] who succeeded in evoking Nightmares by covering the nasal passages and otherwise obstructing the breathing of sleeping individuals, and of Radcliffe,[2] Hoffmann,[3] Macnish[4] and Waller,[5] all of whom employed various ill-digestible articles of diet. Such methods notoriously fail when applied to individuals who are not already subject to Nightmare.

It is therefore evident that some quite different standpoint is needed from which the problem, and especially the question of predisposition, can be attacked anew. This, it seems to me, is best obtained by considering the phenomena themselves in a more direct and less theorizing way than before.

---

[1] Boerner, *op. cit.*
[2] A. Radcliffe, cited by H. Spitta, *Die Schlaf- und Traumzustände der menschlichen Seele*, 1882, S. 237.
[3] E. Th. Hoffmann, cited by Spitta, *op. cit.* S. 238.
[4] Macnish, *op. cit.* p. 133.   [5] Waller, *op. cit.* pp. 105, 106, 109.

Looked at quite simply, the prominent manifestations of Nightmare are seen to be an overmastering dread and terror of some external oppression against which all the energies of the mind appear vainly to be fighting. They are thus pre-eminently mental manifestations, the central one being a morbidly acute feeling of *Angst*. We have therefore to enquire into the nature and origin of this emotion in general.

It may at once be said that *Angst*, when developed to anything approaching the morbid extent present in Nightmare, is altogether a pathological phenomenon, and in fact forms the cardinal feature of the well-defined malady known as *Angst* neurosis. It is interesting to note in this connection that many years ago Sauvages[1] and Sagar[2] pointed out the kinship of Nightmare and what was then called panophobia (an important clinical type of *Angst* neurosis). Long prior even to this, Burton,[3] in his discursion of Symptomes of Maids, Nuns, and Widows' Melancholy had given an excellent description of *Angst* neurosis and had remarked 'from hence proceed . . . terrible dreams in the night'. He further pointed out that the symptoms were cured by marriage, an observation which in a modified sense contains a considerable nucleus of truth.

Many hypotheses have at different times been framed concerning the nature of *Angst*; thus Arndt[4] attributed it to an abnormal functioning of the heart, Wille[5] to irritation of the brain centres, Roller[6] to irritation of the medulla oblongata, Krafft-Ebing[7] to cramp of the cardiac arteries, and Meynert[8] to impoverishment of the cortex induced by the vascular contraction following on stimulation of the cortical vasomotor centres. The sub-

[1] F. Boissier de Sauvages de la Croix, *Synopsis nosologiae methodicae*, 1763, vol. iii. p. 337.
[2] J. B. M. Sagar, *Systema morborum symptomaticum*, 1776, vol. ii. p. 520.
[3] Burton, *op. cit.* vol. i. Pt. i. Sec. 3, Mem. 2, Subsect. IV. p. 302.
[4] Arndt, Wille, Roller, R. Krafft-Ebing, cited by Th. Puschmann, *Handb. der Geschichte der Medizin.*, Bd. iii., 1905, S. 717.
[5] *Ibid.*   [6] *Ibid.*   [7] *Ibid.*
[8] Th. Meynert, *Psychiatrie*, 'Klinik der Erkrankungen des Vorderhirns', 1884.

ject, however, remained in total obscurity until Freud[1] published his now classical papers on *Angst* neurosis, in which he established the nosological independence of the affection and stated his conclusions on its nature and ætiology. In these papers he pointed out how important a part is played in the generation of this malady by various abnormalities in the functioning of the sexual activities of the individual. The association in general between the sexual instinct and the emotions of fear and dread is a very intimate[2] one; it is, however, impossible here to enter into a discussion of the exact relationships of the two, the more so as it is proposed later to deal fully with the subject in another paper.[3] Suffice it to say that the type of emotion designated as *Angst* is in general closely connected with sexual emotion, and in particular with pathological 'repression' of it or with unsatisfactory functioning of what may broadly be called the psycho-sexual system of activities. Since Freud's writings it has gradually become recognized how important is this factor in the production of *Angst* neurosis. Stekel[4] has recently published an impressive array of evidence in support of this view, and to anyone with any experience in the psycho-analytic method of psychotherapy the remark is a mere truism. The same conclusion has also been reached along other routes by workers, such as Strohmayer,[5] Warda,[6]

[1] Sigm. Freud, 'Über die Berechtigung, von der Neurasthenie einen bestimmten Symptomenkomplex als "Angstneurose" abzutrennen', *Neurolog. Centralbl.*, 1895, S. 50. 'Zur Kritik der "Angstneurose" ', *Wiener klinische Rundschau*, 1895. A translation of both papers is reprinted in Freud's *Collected Papers*, 1924, vol. i. p. 76.

[2] [When this essay was first published (1909) the shocked printer changed this word to 'distant', and, in spite of my correcting it in the proof, saw to it that 'distant' was the word that appeared on publication.]

[3] 'The Pathology of Morbid Anxiety', *Journal of Abnormal Psychology*, 1911, vol. vi., reprinted in my 'Papers on Psycho-Analysis'.

[4] W. Stekel, *Nervöse Angstzustände und ihre Behandlung*, 1908.

[5] W. Strohmayer, 'Zur Characteristik der Zwangsvorstellungen als "Abwehrneurose" ', *Centralbl. f. Nervenheilk. u. Psychiatr.*, 15 Mai, 1903, Bd. xxvi., and 'Über die ursächlichen Beziehungen der Sexualität zu Angst- und Zwangszuständen', *Journ. f. Psychol. u. Neur.*, Dez., 1908, Bd. xii. S. 69.

[6] W. Warda, 'Über Zwangsvorstellungspsychosen', *Monatsschr. f. Psychiatr. u. Neur.*, 1902, Bd. xii. S. 1, and 'Zur Pathologie und Therapie der Zwangsneurose', *Monatsschr. f. Psychiatr. u. Neur.*, 1907, Bd. xxii. Ergänzungsheft, S. 149.

PATHOLOGY OF THE NIGHTMARE

Loewenfeld[1] and many others, who do not perform psycho-analyses.

A word must here be said about the modern psychological theory of dreams, which we also owe entirely to Freud.[2] Detailed analysis of many thousand dreams, performed by his free association method, convinced Freud that, without exception, every dream represents the fulfilment in the imagination of some desire on the part of the patient, a desire that has either been 'repressed' in the waking state or else could not for some reason or other come to expression. In most of the dreams of adults, where the dream appears on the surface to contain no evidence of any desire, the operative desire is one that is unacceptable to the subject's consciousness and has therefore been 'repressed'. This repressed desire can now be allowed to attain imaginary gratification only when it is not recognizable by the subject, so that it appears in another form by becoming distorted, perverted and disguised. The mechanisms by means of which this concealment of the original desire takes place have been formulated into precise laws by Freud, and of course cannot here be even enumerated. This exceedingly epitomized statement of the theory, however, will perhaps serve to indicate the outstanding fact that in most cases the dream as related by the subject bears superficially no likeness to the mental processes to which it owes its origin. One or two corollaries also may be mentioned. It is a general law that the more intense is the 'repression', in other words the greater is the conflict between the repressed desire and the conscious mind, the more distorted will be the dream that represents the fulfilment of that desire, and the less recognizable and likely will seem to the subject the interpretation of it. Broadly speaking, there is an inverse relationship between the amount of distortion present in the ideas themselves (condensation, symbolism, etc.) and the

---

[1] L. Loewenfeld, *Die psychischen Zwangserscheinungen*, 1904, S. 470, and *Sexualleben und Nervenleiden*, 4e Aufl., 1906, S. 258 *et seq.*
[2] Sigm. Freud, *Die Traumdeutung*, 1900.

amount of *Angst* present. Thus a repressed wish for a particular sexual experience may be represented in a dream by imagery which, though associatively connected with them in the unconscious, is very dissimilar in appearance to the ideas of that experience: or, on the other hand, the ideas may appear in the dream, but accompanied by such a strong emotion of dread that any notion of their representing a wish is completely concealed from consciousness. In practice one finds in fear dreams all admixtures of these two mechanisms, and it is instructive to observe how the analysis of either type leads to the same conclusions about the underlying content of the dream.

When the distortion of the wish-fulfilment is insufficient to conceal from consciousness the nature of the repressed desire, in other words when the conflict is so great that no compromise can be arrived at, then the sleep is broken and the subject wakes to his danger.[1] When the desire shows such vehemence as to threaten to overpower the repressing force exercised by consciousness, and at the same time is of such a nature as to be in the highest degree unacceptable, then we have present the conditions for the most violent mental conflict imaginable. Conflict of this fierce intensity never arises except over matters of sexuality, for on the one hand the sexual instinct is the source of our most resistless desires and impulses, and on the other no feelings are repressed with such iron rigour as are certain of those that take their origin in this instinct. The mere dimly realized possibility of becoming against his will overmastered by a form of desire that the whole strength of the rest of his mind is endeavouring to resist is often sufficient to induce in a given person a state of panic-stricken terror. These intense conflicts never take place in consciousness, for if the desire is repressed it definitely passes out of consciousness, so that the subject is not aware of either the source or the nature of them.

The subject raised by these reflexions is so extensive

[1] Sigm. Freud, *Die Traumdeutung*, 2e Aufl., 1909, S. 358.

that it is only possible here to state, in what may appear an over-categorical way, a few conclusions, the evidence in support of which must be considered elsewhere. The considerations brought forward above, cursory as they are, may however serve to introduce the main thesis of this essay, namely that *the malady known as Nightmare is always an expression of intense mental conflict centreing about some form of 'repressed' sexual desire*. This conclusion, however, is probably true of all fear dreams, and we can carry it a step further in the particular Nightmare variety. In this dread reaches the maximum intensity known, in either waking or sleeping state, so that we should not be surprised if the source of it lies in the region of maximum 'repression', *i.e.* of maximum conflict. There is no doubt that this concerns the incest trends of the sexual life, so that we may extend the formula just given and say: *an attack of the Nightmare is an expression of a mental conflict over an incestuous desire*.

The definite proof of this conclusion is best obtained by the psycho-analysis of a number of cases. Those who have employed this method know that every case thus studied can be traced to repressed desire, and that the translation of this desire into consciousness is followed by permanent cessation of the malady. The object of this essay, however, is not to discuss psycho-analysis but to point out that in the conflict theory of Nightmare we have a view that better than any other is able to generalize the known facts of the condition. For this reason I shall confine my attention to the facts and observations collected and recorded by writers who were uninfluenced by any inkling of the psychological theory, and shall attempt to show how harmoniously on this theory the diverging views and observations can be reconciled.

The view just advanced may at once be illustrated by considering the description of a case recorded by Bond[1] a century and a half ago. 'A young Lady, of a tender, lax habit, about fifteen, before the Menses appear'd, was

[1] Bond, *op. cit.* Case I. p. 47.

seiz'd with a fit of this Disease, and groan'd so miserably that she awoke her Father, who was sleeping in the next room. He arose, ran into her chamber, and found her lying on her Back, and the Blood gushing plentifully out of her Mouth and Nose. When he shook her, she recover'd and told him, that she thought some great heavy Man came to her bedside, and, without farther ceremony, stretched himself upon her. She had been heard moaning in sleep several nights before; but, the next day after she imagin'd herself oppress'd by that Man, she had a copious eruption of the Menses, which, for that time, remov'd all her complaints.'

The explanation of such an occurrence, put very simply, is that what the young lady both desired and dreaded actually came to pass in her imagination. The struggle between the two conflicting emotions was so intense, and her dread of the unacceptable desire so lively, that the resulting distress was correspondingly great. That erotic feeling is in most cases more ardent during the days preceding the catamenial period is of course well known, and may be illustrated by another case taken from the same author.[1] 'A robust servant Girl, about eighteen years old, was severely oppress'd with the Nightmare, two or three nights before every eruption of the Menses, and used to groan so loudly as to awake her Fellow-servant, who always shook or turn'd her on her Side; by which means she recover'd. She was thus afflicted periodically with it, 'till she took a bed-fellow of a different sex, and bore Children.' At a time when Nightmares were attributed to evil spirits Paracelsus[2] stated that the menstrual flux engendered phantoms in the air and that therefore convents were seminaries of Nightmares.

The description of the attack may, however, not be so transpicuous as in these cases, especially when the 'repression' is more energetic than it probably was there. The oppressing agent will then seem to be not a member

[1] Bond, *op. cit.* p. 49.
[2] Paracelsus, quoted by J. Delassus, *Les incubes et les succubes*, 1897, p. 49.

of the opposite sex but some being having certain attributes thereof, *e.g.*, strength, energy, determination, force. The individual then feels herself assailed by an embracing bear, a wolf, a monster, or even a vague indefinable 'something' that lies on her breast and produces the oppression described above.

It has long been recognized that even in the most terrifying Nightmares the *Angst* often has a distinctly traceable voluptuous character. This can of course be more readily observed by subjects capable of accurate introspection. More than a thousand years ago Paulus Aegineta[1] wrote: 'Persons suffering an attack experience incapability of motion, a torpid sensation in their sleep, a sense of suffocation and oppression, as if from one pressing them down, with inability to cry out, or they utter inarticulate sounds. Some imagine often that they even hear the person who is going to press them down, that he offers lustful violence to them but flies when they attempt to grasp him with their fingers.' Waller[2] notes as a frequent symptom, 'Priapismus interdum vix tolerabilis et aliquamdiu post paroxysmi solutionem persistens', and curiously attributes it[3] to engorgement of the pudic arteries caused by the palpitation of the heart. Loewenfeld[4] also remarks on seminal emissions as a feature of *Angst* dreams. Boerner[5] writes: 'Bisweilen ist mit dem Gefühle der Angst das der Wollust gepaart, namentlich bei den Weibern, welche oft glauben, der Alp habe an ihnen den coitus geübt (Hexenprocesse). Männer haben durch den auf die Genitalien ausgeübten Druck analoge Sensationen und meistens Samenergüsse.' ('Sometimes voluptuous feelings are coupled with those of *Angst;* especially with women, who often believe that the night-fiend has copulated with them (as in the Witch trials). Men have analogous sensations from the pressure exerted on the genitals, mostly followed by seminal emission.')

[1] Paulus Aegineta, *loc. cit.*   [2] Waller, *op. cit.* p. 25.
[3] Waller, *op. cit.* p. 55.
[4] L. Loewenfeld, *Sexualleben und Nervenleiden*, 4e Aufl., 1906, S. 206. See also 'Über sexuelle Träume', *Sexual-Probleme*, Okt., 1908, Jahrg. iv. S. 592.
[5] Boerner, *op. cit.* S. 27.

Cubasch[1] similarly finds that the majority of Nightmares manifest erotic features; after describing the symptoms of an attack he adds: 'Häufig gesellen sich bei Männern noch unwillkührliche Samenverluste hinzu. Bei Frauen ist der Alp meistens liebenswürdigerer Natur: er stürzt sich nicht plötzlich auf sein Opfer, sondern tritt oft ganz gemächlich in die Stube, und steigt dann ebenso gemächlich auf das Lager, um sich der Träumerin als Beischläfer zuzugesellen.' ('With men they are often accompanied by losses of semen. With women the Bogey (*Alp*) is for the most part more gallant: he does not suddenly throw himself on his victim, but often enters the room gently and just as gently climbs on to the couch, so as to become a love partner of the sleeper.') The description given by Delassus[2] is equally unequivocal: 'Une angoisse immense étreint l'être qui sent l'approche de l'Incube ou du Succube. La gorge se serre; un commencement de suffocation se produit, en même temps toutes les muqueuses sont caressées par des titillements voluptueux. Il semble qu'un amant extraordinairement expert vous enveloppe, vous pénètre, se fond en vous. La jouissance alors est insensée, la dépense nerveuse terrible.' Madame Blavatsky,[3] in a series of thrilling delineations, gives a vivid account of the lustful violence manifested by the threatening being. 'A young girl, almost a child, was desperately struggling against a powerful middle-aged man, who had surprised her in her own room, and during her sleep. Behind the closed and locked door I saw listening an old woman, whose face, notwithstanding the fiendish expression upon it, seemed familiar to me, and I immediately recognized it: it was the face of the Jewess who had adopted my niece in the dream I had at Kioto. She had received gold to pay for her share in the foul crime, and was now keeping her part of the covenant. . . . But who was the victim? O horror unutterable! Unspeakable horror!—it was my own child-niece. . . . I fastened upon him, but the man heeded it not, he seemed

---

[1] Cubasch, *op. cit.* S. 8.   [2] Delassus, *op. cit.* p. 50.
[3] H. P. Blavatsky, *Nightmare Tales;* 1892, pp. 47, 48.

not even to feel my hand. The coward, seeing himself resisted by the girl, lifted his powerful arm, and the thick fist, coming down like a heavy hammer upon the sunny locks, felled the child to the ground.

'I could hardly shut my eyes without becoming witness of some horrible deed, some scene of misery, death or crime, whether past, present or even future. . . . Scenes of wickedness, of murder, of treachery and of lust fell dismally upon my sight, and I was brought face to face with the vilest results of man's passions, the most terrible outcome of his material earthly cravings.'

The erotic character may be so evident that the oppressing agent, however hateful at first, becomes more or less suddenly transformed into a most attractive being of the opposite sex. This type of Nightmare, which is not very rare, was recognized over sixty years ago by Macario,[1] who gave the following graphic description of it: 'Il est une variété de cauchemar dans lequel les monstres horribles, une femme vieille et hideuse, s'approchent de vous, s'appuient sur votre poitrine de tout le poids de leur corps. L'infortunité éprouve alors des angoisses inexprimables; la sueur ruisselle de tous ses pores, toutes les fibres de son être frémissent d'horreur, et puis tout à coup, comme par enchantement, ces monstres, cette vieille sorcière, se transforment quelquefois en une jeune et jolie personne; les organes de la génération sont alors excités par cet objet imaginaire; ils entrent en action et la crise a lieu.'

Hallucinations of exactly the same nature as those described above are extremely common in many forms of mental disorder, and almost every asylum contains patients who bitterly complain of the attentions forced on them by various nightly visitors. Simon,[2] in speaking of erotic hallucinations, points out the same alternation between hateful and attractive visitations that we have just mentioned in connection with Nightmare. He says:

[1] M. A. Macario, 'Des rêves considérés sous le rapport physiologique et pathologique', Annales médico-psychologiques, 1847, p. 38.
[2] M. Simon, Le monde des rêves, 1882, pp. 183, 184.

'Tantôt le spectre hallucinatoire est de forme agréable: c'est un mari, un amant, une femme aimée et, dans ces cas, la sensation éprouvée par l'halluciné est voluptueuse. Plus souvent, peut-être, l'hallucination visuelle est repoussante: il s'agit du démon, de quelque être difforme, d'une vieille femme à l'aspect hideux dont les embrassements sont pour l'aliéné un objet d'horreur; d'images dégoûtantes qui poursuivent le malade et qui l'obsèdent. Dans ces cas, l'hallucination génitale consiste en une impression douloureuse, à tout le moins, pénible ou désagréable.' Chaslin[1] relates an interesting case in which the one type of hallucination appeared in *Angst* attacks in the waking state, and the other during dreams. The case well illustrates how much more effective is the 'repression' during the waking state, so that when the inhibitions of consciousness have been to some extent abrogated, as during sleep, the desire may be gratified without any concealment. The patient was a woman of twenty-three. 'Les attaques d'hystérie sont précédées d'une hallucination: un homme se précipite sur la malade avec un couteau. Grande frayeur. Rêves fréquents de l'homme au couteau n'amenant jamais d'attaques, mais quelquefois le réveil en sursaut. Rêves voluptueux dans lesquels elle voit un homme imaginaire, *mais toujours le même*. Jamais d'autres rêves pénibles.' It is important in this connection to remember how frequent is a voluptuous trait in the *Angst* attacks of the waking state; indeed this often passes on to actual emission during the attack, a phenomenon to which attention was first drawn by Loewenfeld[2] in the case of men, and by Janet[3] in the case of women.

It is clear that the great rarity with which Nightmare attacks persons who are sleeping in any other posture than the supine or prone one is readily explicable on the psychological view here maintained, for these are the postures in which the love embrace is normally consum-

[1] Chaslin, *op. cit.* p. 54.
[2] L. Loewenfeld, 'Zur Lehre von den neurotischen Angstzuständen', *Münch. med. Wochenschr.*, 1897, No. 24, 25.
[3] P. Janet, *Les obsessions et la psychasthénie*, 1903, tome i. p. 222.

mated. Burton's[1] observation, then, concerning those who are 'troubled with incubus, or witch-ridden (as we call it): if they lie on their backs, they suppose an old woman rides and sits so hard upon them, that they are almost stifled for want of breath', needs no detailed elucidation. In significant accord with this explanation is the well-known fact that most sleepers experience voluptuous dreams far more often when in the supine posture than when in any other.[2] Paulus Aegineta[3] laid great stress on this in the treatment of satyriasis and allied conditions.

In exactly the same way may be explained the mode of operation of all the other physical factors besides posture, namely as external stimuli which evoke a body of feeling that is already present and very ready to be evoked. It has generally been supposed that they actually create this feeling, a view well expounded for instance by Rousset:[4] 'Qu'une sensation isolée telle que celle d'un poids pesant au creux épigastrique, sensation que donne la gêne croissante de la respiration, que cette sensation, dis-je, parvienne à ébranler le sensorium ainsi assoupi; aussitôt elle fera naître l'idée d'un objet dont la forme sera en rapport avec l'espoir, la crainte, le mysticisme, le sensualisme, en un mot avec les idées habituelles ou dominantes de l'individu à l'état de veille; ce sera un chat, un singe, une vieille femme, une sorcière, un monstre hideux, un revenant ou bien enfin un amant redouté ou désiré, qu'il s'appelle le diable ou qu'au contraire il porte un nom moins terrible.' On the contrary it is here maintained that these sensations will arouse the emotions in question only in persons in whom the emotions are already present and, as it were, lying near the surface. What we have called the predisposition is thus the all-important essential in the production of the

[1] Burton, *op. cit.* vol. i. Pt. I. Sec. 2, Mem. 3, Subsect. 2, p. 134.

[2] The prevalence of the supine posture over the prone even among males is to be accounted for by the passive part played by the sleeper, who yields—often against his will—to a desire that is felt to be of external origin, something forced on him: this attitude is closely akin to the feminine and masochistic components of the sexual instinct.

[3] Paulus Aegineta, *op. cit.* pp. 594, 596.   [4] Rousset, *op. cit.* p. 50.

attack; the external stimuli are of minimal significance. We thus have the key to the easily verifiable observation that these external 'causes' can bring about an attack only in persons who are subject to the malady, and that on the other hand the most scrupulous avoidance of all these alleged 'causes' will not prevent attacks with those in whom the predisposition is sufficiently pronounced. It is probable that most of the causes that have been given by various writers in this connection may play some slight part in the manner we have indicated, though I am convinced that the significance of them has in the past been greatly exaggerated. For instance, that a heavy repast is apt to be followed by an accession of erotic desire is an observation acted on by every *roué*; that it, like alcohol, tends to dull the activity of the conscious inhibitions of the waking state and so release suppressed mental trends is so well known as to make it comprehensible that it may occasionally play some part in the evocation of Nightmare; *Sine Cerere et Baccho friget Venus*. A full stomach may also act by arousing the sensation of a heavy weight lying in, and therefore on, the abdomen. The relation of diet in general to erotic dreams is fully dealt with by Spitta.[1] Again, in considering the effect of respiratory obstruction as an inciting cause of Nightmare, one has to remember the important, though commonly ignored, connection between stimulation of the upper air passages and erotic excitation. That these passages constitute an erotogenic zone of varying intensity was first pointed out by Sir Morell Mackenzie[2]; the subject has been fully discussed since by Endriss among many other writers. This connection holds good in disorders as well as in health, so that pathological irritation or obstruction is apt to arouse various partial, *i.e.* perverse combinations of the sexual instinct. Thus the observations made in

[1] H. Spitta, *Die Schlaf- und Traumzustände der menschlichen Seele*, 1882, S. 252.
[2] Sir Morell Mackenzie, 'Irritation of the Sexual Apparatus as an etiological factor in the Production of Nasal Disease', *The American Journal of the Medical Sciences*, 1884, p. 4.

this connection by the older writers almost always contain a certain modicum of truth, although the explanations of them offered have been wide of the mark in attributing to physical factors ninety-nine per cent of importance in the production of Nightmare, whereas in reality less than one per cent should be so attributed.

We have last to say something about the clinical significance of Nightmare. I shall take the definition of Nightmare in its strict sense, as a distressing dream necessarily showing, amongst other features, the three cardinal ones that were described above. A large variety of distressing dreams, equalling in intensity the classical Nightmare attack but not having the sense of direct physical oppression characteristic of this, will thus be excluded.

It is impossible to reach even an approximate estimate of the frequency of the malady. Jewell's[1] finding from questionnaire work that they are the most frequent of all dreams is obviously based on an unduly wide conception of Nightmare. Waller's[2] statement that there are few affections more universal among all classes of society is certainly untrue if the definition just given is adhered to, for true Nightmare is beyond doubt much rarer than the more complex forms of *Angst* dreams. Waller[3] and Macnish[4] both state that men are more subject to it than women, and of these unmarried women more than the married. In judging from my own experience I would say that the second statement is true; as to the first, I have no decisive evidence, though I would agree with Cubasch[5] when he says that the manifestations of Nightmare are generally more stormy and vehement among men, and the agony correspondingly greater. Waller[6] and Macnish[7] also state that sailors are of all men most subject to Nightmare, the former attributing this to their coarse unwholesome food; there is, however, a clue to

[1] J. R. Jewell, 'The Psychology of Dreams', *American Journal of Psychology*, 1905, vol. xvi. p. 4.
[2] Waller, *op. cit.* p. 14.
[3] Waller, *op. cit.* p. 68.
[4] Macnish, *op. cit.* p. 134.
[5] Cubasch, *op. cit.* S. 8.
[6] Waller, *op. cit.* p. 66.
[7] Macnish, *loc. cit.*

another explanation in Macnish's remark, made in the days when long voyages were common, that the attacks more often occurred at sea than on shore. Bond[1] quaintly observes that 'Melancholy persons, profound Mathematicians, and fond pining Lovers, are most subject to this affection', and Bell, a still earlier writer,[2] says that it affects those who 'are Melancholly, of few and gross Spirits and abounding with Phlegm'.

In subjects who pass as being mentally normal, Nightmares never occur as isolated morbid phenomena; on investigation it will always be found that other manifestations of *Angst* neurosis are present, with or without evidences of hysteria. In short, Nightmare may in such a subject be regarded as a symptom of this affection, and should be treated accordingly. This fact was partly realized nearly a century ago by Waller[3] when he wrote that 'Nightmare may be considered only as a symptom of great nervous derangement or hypochondriasis'. I may add that in my experience 'repression' of the feminine or masochistic component of the sexual instinct rather than of the masculine is apt to engender the typical Nightmare, a fact which probably explains why the malady is usually more severe, and possibly even more frequent, in men, with whom this component is more constantly and more intensely repressed than with women.

In subjects who deviate still more from the normal, more alarming evidences of a lack of harmonious control of the psycho-sexual activities may be present, such as satyriasis or nymphomania, as in a case recorded by Ribes.[4] This, however, is decidedly uncommon. Also, as was previously mentioned, the affection is frequently met with in various forms of mental alienation, particularly manic-depressive insanity and dementia præcox, and especially during the early stages of the disease.

We may summarize the conclusions reached in the

---

[1] Bond, *op. cit.* p. 27.   [2] Andrew Bell, *op. cit.* p. 13.
[3] Waller, *op. cit.* p. 7.
[4] F. Ribes, ' Observation d'un cauchemar causé par la nymphomanie', *Mém. et observ. d'anat., de phys., etc.,* 1845, t. iii. p. 127.

statement that Nightmare is a form of *Angst* attack, that
it is essentially due to an intense mental conflict centreing around a repressed component of the psycho-sexual
instinct, essentially concerned with incest, and that it may
be evoked by any peripheral stimuli that serve to arouse
this body of repressed feeling; the importance, however,
of such peripheral stimuli in this connection has in the
past been greatly over-estimated as a factor in producing
the affection.

PART II

THE CONNECTIONS BETWEEN THE NIGHT-MARE AND CERTAIN MEDIÆVAL SUPERSTITIONS

INTRODUCTION

THE attempt is made in this book to estimate the part that Nightmare experiences have played in the production of certain false ideas. These ideas—incubus, vampire, werewolf, devil and witchcraft—have a great deal in common. For three hundred years, from about 1450 to 1750, they were fused together and reached their acme of importance; they are still accepted by many in their original form, and by far more in their essential elements. The deepest source of them is identical with all, and they have all been responsible for an incalculable amount of human suffering. These sources are still active in human nature even though the expression of them has changed in the last couple of centuries, so that interest in the subject is far from being a purely antiquarian one.

My attention has been directed not so much to the historical aspects of the ideas in question as to their deeper psychological significance, but—in contrast to some members of the so-called historical school of modern ethnology—I have adopted the position that these two studies are not independent of each other. In order to obtain a clearer view of the material I have been several times obliged to leave the main theme itself, though I have avoided doing so more than was necessary. Lange[1] remarks 'im geschichtlichen Zusammenhange der Dinge schlägt ein Tritt tausend Fäden, und wir können nur einen gleichzeitig verfolgen. Ja, wir können selbst dies nicht immer, weil der gröbere sichtbare Faden sich in zahllose Fädchen verzweigt, die sich stellenweise unserem Blicke entziehen'. ('In historical connections a turn of the spindle moves a thousand threads, and we can follow only one at a time. Indeed, we cannot always do this, because the coarser visible thread ramifies into numerous filaments which at places escape from sight.')

[1] R. Lange, *Geschichte des Materialismus*, 1866, S. 282.

CHAPTER I

DREAMS AND BELIEFS

THE interest men have at all ages taken in dreams and the far-reaching significance that has been attributed to them make it very probable that the phenomena there experienced have greatly influenced the forming of waking thoughts. If this, as I have shown elsewhere,[1] can still happen among educated people, it must have done so on a far more extensive scale in past ages when the general importance attaching to dreams was much greater than to-day.

The vividness of dreams is so intense at times that even educated people may find it hard or actually impossible to distinguish them from real events.[2] I have, for example, mentioned the case of a physician whose mistaking a dream for a real memory led to disagreeable consequences.[3] In fact, this confusion with reality characterizes all intense emotional experiences, not only in dreams, but also in other rarer expressions of the imagination such as ecstatic trances, visions and so on. Johannes Müller[4] remarks in this connection: 'Eigentümlich diesen krankhaften Zuständen ist es, dass die Objektivität der Erscheinungen zuverlässig anerkannt wird. In dem Glauben eines sichtbaren Umganges mit dem Teufel besteigt der Angeklagte den Scheiterhaufen, ein Opfer seiner eigenen Phantasie. Je nachdem die Vision die Gestalt eines guten oder bösen Geistes annahm, wurde der Dämonische als heilig verehrt oder als Zauberer verbrannt. Was bei dem Unbefangenen das Eigenleben der Sinnlichkeit, das Spiel einer dichtenden Phantasie, was

---

[1] 'Some Instances of the Influence of Dreams on Waking Life', *Journal of Abnormal Psychology*, vol. vi. April 1911, p. 11.

[2] See J. Ennemoser, *Geschichte der Magie*, 1844, S. 113. F. Fischer, *Geschichte des Somnambulismus*, 1839, Bd. i. S. 12. A. Lehmann, *Aberglaube und Zauberei*, Zweite deutsche Auflage, 1908, S. 493. H. Rau, *Die Verirrungen in der Religion*, 1904, S. 237. [3] *Op. cit.* p. 15.

[4] Johannes Müller, *Über die phantastischen Gesichtserscheinungen*, 1826, S. 68. 69.

allen Menschen im Traume nicht mehr wunderbar
erscheint, wird in der Geschichte verflucht und verehrt
nach der Natur seiner Objekte. Das Gespenst und die
Dämonen aller Zeiten, die göttliche Vision des Asketen,
die Geistererscheinung des Magikers, das Traumobjekt
und das Phantasiebild des Fiebernden und Irren sind
eine und dieselbe Erscheinung. Nur der Gegenstand ist
verschieden nach der Richtung einer exzentrischen Phantasie, eine göttliche Vision dem religiösen Schwärmer,
dem furchtsamen ein furchtbares Phantasma, dem aber-
glaübisch buhlerischen Weib der Teufelsspuk, dem
traümenden Egmont die Erscheinung der Freiheit, dem
Künstler ein himmlisches Idol, nach dem er längst
gerungen. Der Zeitgeist leiht diesem plastischen Ein-
bilden andere Objekte.' ('What is peculiar to these morbid states is that the objectivity of the phenomena is
accepted with complete assurance. In the belief of having
had visible relations with the Devil the accused mount
the scaffold, victims of their own phantasy. According as
the vision assumed the guise of a good or an evil spirit
the dæmonically inspired person was revered as holy or
burned as a magician. What to the unsophisticated appears as his own sensuousness, the play of an imagin-
ative phantasy, what to everyone in their dreams seems
nothing wonderful, is in history condemned and revered
according to the nature of the objects. The ghost and the
demons of all ages, the divine vision of the ascetic, the
conjured-up spirits of the magician, the object of dream
and phantasy in the feverish and deluded, are all one
and the same phenomenon. Only the object is different
in accord with the direction of an eccentric phantasy, a
divine vision for the religious enthusiast, a frightful
phantasm for the fearful, an apparition of the Devil for
the superstitious lascivious woman, the manifestation
of freedom for a dreaming Egmont, for the artist a long-
sought-after celestial image. The spirit of the age lends
this plastic imagery other objects.') We may also quote
a passage from Hobbes[1] which is peculiarly apposite to

[1] T. Hobbes, *Leviathan*, 1651, ch. xii.

the theme of the present book: 'From this ignorance of how to distinguish Dreams and other strong fancies from Vision and Sense did arise the greater part of the religion of the Gentiles in times past that worshipped Satyres, Faunes, Nymphs, and the like; and nowadays the opinion that rude people have of Fayries, Ghosts, and Goblins, and of the power of Witches.'

This difficulty in distinguishing dreams from the experiences of waking life is naturally greater in less tutored minds, such as those of children and savages. Numerous observers have remarked on the extra-ordinary clearness with which dreams impose themselves on the minds of savages as indubitable reality. Herbert Spencer[1] lays special stress on this point and adduces a mass of material in illustration of it. Im Thurn[2] gives many striking examples of it at the present day: one Indian threatened to leave the traveller because the latter, so he said, had inconsiderately made him work all night dragging his canoe up a series of difficult cataracts; another nearly killed a comrade on the ground that his master had ordered him to inflict a severe chastisement on him (it turned out that he had dreamt this).

That dreams must have exercised a considerable influence in moulding men's beliefs needs, therefore, no further demonstration, and there is also in several important respects unanimity on the further questions of the extent of this influence and the details of the process itself. The first question will be discussed when we come to the form of dream with which we are here concerned, namely the Nightmare. The second question resolves itself into a study of individual beliefs and fancies. Two of the more general of these will next be mentioned; others will be met with later where they more suitably belong.

The first, and in some respects the most important,

---

[1] Herbert Spencer, *The Principles of Sociology*, third edition, 1890, vol. i. ch. x. pp. 132-142.
[2] Sir Everard F. Im Thurn, *Among the Indians of Guiana*, 1883, pp. 344-346.

example of the significance of dreams concerns beliefs
about the soul. Tylor's[1] description of this idea among
savage peoples has hardly been bettered. According to
it the soul is 'a thin, unsubstantial human image, in its
nature a sort of vapour, film, or shadow; the cause of life
and thought in the individual it animates; independently
possessing the personal consciousness and volition of its
corporeal owner, past or present; capable of leaving the
body far behind, to flash swiftly from place to place;
mostly impalpable and invisible, yet also manifesting
physical power, and especially appearing to men waking
or asleep, as a phantasm separate from the body of
which it bears the likeness; continuing to exist and
appear to men after the death of that body; able to
enter into, possess, and act in the bodies of other men,
of animals, and even of things.' The primitive conceptions of the soul may be divided, following Wundt, into
two: those relating to the 'bound soul', the activating
principle of various internal organs and external objects,
and the 'free soul' or psyche. The latter itself has two
roots, according to which may be distinguished the
Hauchseele (Breath-Soul) and the *Schattenseele* (Shadow-
Soul). The idea of the Breath-Soul, mainly taken—as its
name implies—from the phenomenon of breathing and
the cessation of this after death, has shown itself the
better adapted for the higher religious conceptions, but
that of the Shadow-Soul has played the more extensive
part in all ages, and it is evidently the one with which
we shall be mostly concerned in considering the various
spirits and goblins that are associated with the emotion
of fear.

Most authorities[2] agree that the idea of the Shadow-
Soul owes its origin almost exclusively to the experi-

---

[1] E. B. Tylor, *Primitive Culture*, third edition, 1891, vol. i. p. 429.
[2] Ed. Clodd, *Myths and Dreams*, 1891, p. 170. J. Fiske, *Myths and Myth-Makers*, 1872, pp. 78, 220. J. G. Frazer, *The Belief in Immortality*, 1913, p. 27. Lehmann, *op. cit.* S. 494. E. H. Meyer, *Germanische Mythologie*, 1891, S. 61. E. Mogk, *Germanische Mythologie*, 1906, S. 32. J. Moses, *Pathological Aspects of Religion*, 1906, p. 6. Herbert Spencer, *op. cit.* pp. 135, 136; and *Recent Discussions in Science*, 1871, p. 36. E. B. Tylor, *op. cit.* p. 430.

ences of dream life. Wundt,[1] for instance, writes: 'Das ursprünglichste und häufigste Motiv dieser primären Vorstellung der Schattenseele ist unzweifelhaft das Traumbild . . . (Sie) hat allem Anscheine nach in Traum und Vision ihre einzige Quelle.' ('The deepest and most frequent motive of this primary idea of the shadow-soul is undoubtedly the dream image . . . and so far as we can see its sole source is in dreams and visions.') Perhaps the only well-known writer who dissents from this conclusion is Crawley,[2] and the arguments he uses are so intellectualistic as not to commend themselves to any psychologist; I thus see no reason for not accepting the generally received opinion on this matter. The idea of the 'shadow-soul' has throughout preserved the characteristics (visibility, fugitiveness and fantastic changeability) of its visual components. Into the various problems about which is the most primitive form of belief in the soul,[3] the relations between magic and religion, and so on, it is unnecessary to enter here. What is for us of essential importance is the conclusion that dream experiences have furnished significant contributions to the developing conception of the soul, whether of the individual or of supernatural beings, and especially to its characteristics of existence apart from the body (transportation through space, capacity for transformation, etc.).

Dreams of the dead have played an important part in fashioning various religious ideas, their influence being all the greater because they so often bring back the figures of lost loved ones. To begin with they strengthen, as Wundt[4] expounds, the conception—founded on dreams in general—of the 'other self', of the soul that can live and move apart from the body; they constitute further, as Herbert Spencer[5] has shown in detail, an

---

[1] W. Wundt, *Völkerpsychologie*, Zweiter Band, *Mythus und Religion*, Zweiter Teil, 1906, S. 86, 87.
[2] A. E. Crawley, *The Idea of the Soul*, 1909, pp. 13-15.
[3] See, for instance, Irving King, *The Development of Religion*, 1910, ch. vi., and R. R. Marett, 'Pre-animistic Religion', *Folklore*, 1900, vol. xi. p. 198, on the conflict between the old animistic and the younger animatistic hypotheses.
[4] Wundt, *op. cit.* S. 90.
[5] Herbert Spencer, *The Principles of Sociology*, pp. 182, 201, etc.

important source of the belief in immortality and in the existence of another realm which the soul enters after the death of its owner. Again, they are the chief source of the belief that the dead can once more visit the scenes of their previous life, of the widespread idea of returning souls or *revenants*,[1] an idea that composes one of the chief traits of the mediæval superstitions with which we are here concerned. It is seldom a matter of no consequence for the spirits of the departed to visit the living in dreams: to savages it is sometimes of good, oftener of evil, omen, and in the latter event the spirits have to be propitiated in various ways.[2]

The fact that so many of these *revenants* are the spirits of deceased parents is of fundamental importance in this connection, as will be evident to anyone familiar with the subject of psycho-analysis. The attitude of awe and fear in respect of dream visitors from the dead has been thought to be one of the main sources of ancestor-worship. The two are certainly related, but it is more likely that they both proceed from a common source than that one is the source of the other. The parallelism is none the less of interest, for, although Herbert Spencer's[3] view that ancestor-worship was the basis of all religions can no longer be maintained in its original form,[4] still the intimate connection between ancestor-worship and religious motivation has been shown by recent psycho-analytic research to be a fundamental one.

A second class of belief in the formation of which dreams are supposed to have played a prominent part is that in transformation or interchangeability, *i.e.* the idea that a human spirit can pass into the body of another person or of an animal and that the reverse process can also happen. This was and is one of the most widely-spread superstitions of the world; among

[1] See, for instance, F. S. Krauss, *Slavische Volksforschungen*, 1908, S. 110, 111.
[2] See, for instance, A. W. Howitt, *The Native Tribes of South-East Australia*, 1904, p. 434, and H. Ling Roth, *The Natives of Sarawak and British North Borneo*, 1896, vol. i. p. 232.
[3] Herbert Spencer, *op. cit.* p. 281 *et seq.*
[4] See Wundt, *op. cit.* S. 346, 347.

uncivilized peoples it still holds full sway,[1] and even in
Europe it is to be found not merely in the superior guise
of metempsychosis, rebirth and the like, but also in its
crude original forms. In the Middle Ages it was accepted
by many exponents of Roman Catholic doctrine, and,
largely for this reason, played an essential part in the
construction of the superstitious beliefs we are about to
consider. In folklore[2] and mythology metamorphosis has
always been a favourite theme. Even in educated circles
we still find interesting traces of it, such as when animals are used as national emblems, in armorial bearings,
as masks in carnivals and on the stage, as nicknames,
etc. Of especial interest in connection with our theme is
the fact that metamorphosis was so extensively and so
intimately associated with the worship of animals[3] that
we are compelled to infer an inherent relationship between the two ideas. There can be little doubt that the
idea of metamorphosis has important sources in dream
experiences, for here the actual transformation of the
figure of a human being into that of an animal and the
occurrence of composite beings, half animal, half human,
so often takes place directly before the eyes of the
dreamer.[4]

When the untutored mind takes for reality dream
experiences in which he sees himself carried to distant
places, or speaks with someone whom he knows in his
waking state to be far away, he must infer that the
journey has actually taken place, and in an incredibly
short space of time.[5] The similarity between the swift
flight of birds and his own dreams of flying, which, as
Wundt[6] has shown, must have yielded important contributions to the conception of winged beings (angels,
etc.), served to evoke the belief in the night flights which

[1] E. S. Hartland, *Primitive Paternity*, 1909, vol. i. ch. iii. pp. 156-252.
[2] Marian Roalfe Cox, *An Introduction to Folklore*, second edition, 1904, ch. ii.
pp. 85-129.
[3] Herbert Spencer, *op. cit.* pp. 322-346.
[4] This was pointed out by Guillaume de Paris in 1230. Cited from J. Hansen,
Zauberwahn, Inquisition und Hexenprozess im Mittelalter, 1900, S. 138.
[5] Herbert Spencer, *op. cit.* p. 136.
[6] Wundt, *op. cit.* S. 113.

exercised considerable influence on various mediæval ideas.

The conclusions reached up to the present are as follows: in the first place, dreams have played an important part in the genesis of beliefs in a soul that can live and move apart from the body, in fabulous and supernatural beings, in the continued existence of the soul after death —with its power of returning from the grave and visiting the living, especially by night—in the connection between this idea and the spirits of departed ancestors (leading to the worship of these), in the possibility of human beings being transformed into other persons or into animals, in the identity of the spirits of animals with those of ancestors, and in night flights through the air. In the second place, the various conceptions just enumerated are closely associated with one another. The explanation of this strange connection between ideas apparently so remote from one another has always been impossible until Freud's discovery of psycho-analysis provided an adequate instrument for the investigation of the deeper processes of the human mind. In the course of this book the significance of this important connection will become clearer.

Earlier investigations into the problem of what part dreams have played in the genesis of various kinds of superstition and myths were confined to consideration of the superficial content of dreams. Freud's epoch-making[1] revelation of the 'latent' content lying behind the 'manifest' content, i.e. behind the dream as directly perceived, enables us to make important progress in this investigation and throws a clear light on many problems that were previously quite obscure. At the same time as this discovery Freud further pointed out the intimate relation between the structure of myths and of dreams, and his hints have since been interestingly developed by Riklin,[2] Abraham[3] and Rank.[4] These writers have shown

[1] Sigm. Freud, *Die Traumdeutung*, 1900.
[2] F. Riklin, *Wunscherfüllung und Symbolik im Märchen*, 1908.
[3] Karl Abraham, *Traum und Mythus*, 1909.
[4] Otto Rank, *Der Mythus von der Geburt des Helden*, 1909.

that there is an astonishing similarity between dreams
and myths in respect of the unconscious mechanisms at
work, the relation of both to repressed infantile wish-
fulfilments, and even, to a considerable extent, to the
nature of the symbolism at work in both. The gist of
the matter is contained in the following sentences: 'So
ist der Mythus ein erhalten gebliebenes Stück aus dem
infantilen Seelenleben des Volkes und der Traum der
Mythus des Individuums';[1] ('The myth is thus a part of
the infantile mental life of the people that has survived,
and the dream the myth of the individual'); and 'Der
Mythus enthält (in verschleierter Form) die Kindheits-
wünsche des Volkes'[2] ('The myth contains (in disguised
form) the childhood wishes of the people'). We shall see
that this can be shown to be also true of certain superstitious ideas.

This finding, of the substantial identity of individual
dreams and of what may be called folk-dreams, raises,
however, in a new way the old problem of how far the
phenomena of dreams have actually been operative in
providing material for the building up of myths. It makes
this problem harder, since one can no longer—as writers
have often done—regard the problem as solved as soon
as one has simply noted the similarity between dreams
and certain myths or kinds of superstition. Our knowledge that the unconscious meaning of both may be
identical opens the possibility that both may be manifestations of the same underlying forces: a myth may be
a collateral of the dream rather than a lineal descendant.
It is a problem very similar to that of the relationship
between dreams and psychoneurotic symptoms.[3] We
know that both of these arise from very similar mechanisms, from similar sources, and have similar meanings
when interpreted; it is further known that the actual
occurrence of some symptoms may date from particular
dream experiences. In other words, even though both

---

[1] Karl Abraham, *op. cit.* S. 71.   [2] Karl Abraham, *op. cit.* S. 36.
[3] See my paper, 'The Relationship between Dreams and Psychoneurotic
Symptoms', *American Journal of Insanity*, 1911, vol. lxviii. [Reprinted in
Papers on Psycho-Analysis.]

may have a common cause, the symptom may sometimes arise *via* a dream, and this is the only sense in
which a neurotic symptom may properly be held to have
arisen from a dream. In what sense, now, can it be said
that a given myth or superstitious belief owes its origin,
partly or wholly, to dream experiences?

The difficulty in answering this question may be expressed thus. First, a sufficient similarity between the
belief in question and typical dream experiences must
exist to warrant supposition that the two may be
genetically related. Previously this would have been the
sole evidence available, but with our increased knowledge
we cannot be satisfied with any conclusion drawn from
it alone and can regard it only as a suggestive stimulus
to further investigation; in fact, the most important
problems only begin at this point. Secondly, psycho-
analytic comparison of the two phenomena must reveal
an essential identity between the latent content, *i.e.* the
unconscious meaning, of both. Even this, however, is not
sufficient in itself, since, as was remarked above, both
may represent separate manifestations of the same
underlying source. Thirdly, the belief in question must
contain definite features peculiar to, or at least highly
characteristic of, dreams. Only when these three criteria
are satisfied can we infer with confidence that dream
experiences must have helped to build up the superstitious belief.

For the features characteristic of dream processes the
reader is referred to works on that subject, particularly
to Freud's *Die Traumdeutung*. I will merely recall here
their predominantly visual imagery, the extensive use
made of condensation and displacement mechanisms,
the recurrence of certain 'typical' dreams (inhibition
dreams, examination dreams, exposure dreams, etc.),
and the predominance of sexual symbolism. Thus, to
take one or two examples, if we came across a belief that
such and such a supernatural occurrence is followed by a
state of mental paralysis, we should be justified in suspecting that it had been influenced by dream experiences;

the same would be true for beliefs in impossible creatures obviously compounded of two or more animals, and so on.

We may now consider from this point of view some dreams that have been generally supposed to influence various superstitious beliefs. Naturally this can be true only of dreams common to a great number, if not the majority, of mankind. Now the more 'typical' a dream is, *i.e.* the more stereotyped its occurrence with a great number of people, the more surely will its latent content be found to be of a sexual nature, and we must therefore be prepared to find that the same may be true of any superstitious beliefs derived, partly or wholly, from them.

Dreams of people who are dead occur most frequently, and are most heavily charged with emotion when the dead person represents the father or mother. They are concerned with the deepest conflicts of love and hate, and originate ultimately in incest motives repressed from consciousness in childhood. This astonishing statement has been extensively confirmed in actual psychoanalytic investigations of the unconscious mind, which are taken as the basis for the present study.

In respect of those dreams in which figures of animals play a prominent part the reader should first be reminded that for the untutored mind, *e.g.* children and savages, the gulf we perceive between human beings and animals is much less apparent. As Hartland[1] says: 'The lines we draw between the lower animals and the vegetable and mineral kingdoms on the one hand and human beings on the other hand are not drawn in the lower culture.' Fiske[2] writes similarly: 'Nothing is more characteristic of primitive thinking than the close community of nature which it assumes between man and brute. The doctrine of metempsychosis, which is found in some shape or other all over the world, implies a fundamental identity between the two. . . . The recent researches of Mr. McLennan and Mr. Herbert Spencer have served to connect this feeling with the primeval worship of

[1] E. S. Hartland, *op. cit.* p. 250.
[2] Fiske, *op. cit.* p. 74.

CH. I DREAMS AND BELIEFS 69

ancestors and with the savage customs of totemism.'
Even educated people can still feel this relationship in
a varying measure, a fact which is often made use of for
literary purposes.[1] How recent our present attitude towards animals is may be judged by remembering that
until the past few centuries human responsibility was
legally ascribed to them.[2] They used to be formally tried,
and at times condemned to the gallows as murderers.[3]
At Basle in 1474, for instance, a cock was tried on the
devilish charge of having laid an egg and, though its
lawyer pleaded that there was no record of the Devil
ever having made a pact with an animal and that, in any
case, the laying of an egg was an involuntary act, his
client was condemned to death and solemnly burned at
the stake as a sorcerer in disguise. A Court of Law held
at Troyes in 1516 solemnly admonished caterpillars that
had laid waste the district, and made an order that they
were to leave the neighbourhood within a given number
of days under pain of banishment and excommunication.[4] It was only in 1846 that the English law of Deo-
dand was rescinded, according to which any animal that
had injured someone was declared the property of the
Crown and sold for the benefit of the poor.

Naturally it is in spheres where the dominant interests
are of a kind common to human beings and animals that
the distinction between these is less sharply defined than
elsewhere; this is the reason why children and primitive
peoples are much more impressed by the resemblance between them than are poets and philosophers. Doubtless
the feature of animals that most attracts a personal
interest of untutored minds is the freedom they display
in openly satisfying needs, particularly those of a sexual
and excremental order, which with human beings have
often to be restrained; in fact, the expression 'animal

[1] [One may recall, for instance, the success attending David Garnett's *Lady into Fox*.]
[2] See E. P. Evans, *Criminal Prosecution and Capital Punishment of Animals*, 1906.
[3] R. M. Lawrence, *The Magic of the Horse-shoe*, 1899, pp. 308-311.
[4] E. Martinengo-Cesaresco, *Essays in the Study of Folk-Songs*, 1886, p. 183.

passions' is generally employed to denote sexual impulses. Children often owe their first experience of sexual activities to the sight of animal copulation, and every psycho-analyst knows how important the influence of this can be. Animals therefore lend themselves to the indirect representation of crude and unbridled wishes. Analytical experience has shown that the occurrence of animals in a dream regularly indicates a sexual theme, usually an incest one, a typical example being the maiden's dream of being pursued or attacked by rough animals.

In numerous myths the sexual meaning of the transformation of human being into animal is quite clear. There is, for instance, a large class of fairy tales in which the wonderful prince appears first in the guise of a frog, snake, bear, bird or any other animal, to disclose his true nature at the appropriate moment. Riklin[1] has clearly shown how the gradual overcoming of the resistance to sexuality is represented by the releasing from the spell in these stories, *i.e.* the release from guilt and disgust. In many variants the prince is an animal by day and resumes his own personality by night, as was so with the son of Indra,[2] the prototype of the class. In Greek mythology this disguise was a favourite aid adopted by the gods during their love adventures. One thinks at once of Zeus' seduction of Europa in the form of a bull, of Leda in that of a swan and of Persephone in that of a snake; this last disguise was also employed by Apollo on his visit to Atys, while at other times he masqueraded as a tortoise. To imitate the gods in this respect became indeed at times a religious rite, as when the women in Mendes 'submitted themselves nude and openly to the embraces of the sacred goat, which represented the incarnation of the procreative deity.'[3] The 'Alp' (bogey) of the Middle Ages often appeared in the guise of a cat, a pig or other animal,[4] and an episode is described at a

---

[1] Riklin, *op. cit.* S. 41-46.
[2] Sir Richard Burton, *Adaptation of 'Vikram and the Vampire'*, 1893, preface, p. 15.
[3] Quoted from Moses, *op. cit.* p. 26.
[4] W. Hertz, *Der Werwolf*, 1862, S. 73.

Cologne nunnery where a lecherous dog was assumed to be a lewd demon.[1]

I would again call attention here to the connection alluded to earlier between animal dreams and animal worship. There can be no doubt that the explanation of animal worship must lie in the equation between animal and ancestor, and psychologically ancestor means parent. Herbert Spencer[2] was of opinion that primitive man was led to identify animals with his ancestors in the following three ways: first, the stealthy way in which both enter houses at night when the inmates are asleep; secondly, the presence of animals in the neighbourhood of corpses and graves; and thirdly, the confusion arising through primitive language. We know now that there are more significant associations between the two ideas. As the result of our dream studies we cannot fail to be struck by the observation that the associations from the equated (symbolical) animal and parent diverge into two exactly opposite directions and lead to the most revered and most despised ideas of which the human mind is capable, those of God and of genital organ respectively. We are thus faced with the riddle not merely of phallic religions, but probably with that of religion altogether. This train of thought alone—and it is one supported by many other convergent trains—would suggest that the secret of religion is to be sought ultimately in the relation of the child to its parents. This theme is implicit throughout the present work: we shall be concerned with what might be called a parody of religion—incubi instead of angels, devil instead of God and witches instead of Goddesses—and it is in these negative aspects of religion that the underlying incestuous motives can most plainly be demonstrated. [Shortly after this book was first published there appeared Freud's celebrated *Totem and Tabu*, in which this theme of the relations between the idea of animals and of gods on the one hand, and between those of the idea of animals and of sexuality on

---

[1] E. Laurent u. P. Nagour, *Okkultismus und Liebe*, 1903, S. 108.
[2] Herbert Spencer, *op. cit.* pp. 345, 346.

the other are faithfully dealt with. The rich contents of this work are by now too well known to need recapitulation here; among them is a welcome confirmation and amplification of the chief ideas presented in this chapter.]

CHAPTER II

THE NIGHTMARE

WE have set ourselves the task of showing that similar connections exist between dreams and superstitious beliefs as other psycho-analysts have shown to exist between dreams and myths, and further, that with the former at least dreams have also exercised a certain genetic influence. Before Freud's time a similar attempt to the present one was once made in respect of myths, and interestingly enough the starting point was the same as that here employed, namely the Nightmare. I refer to Laistner's[1] remarkable book published in 1889. In it he took the clinical characteristics of the Nightmare and with extraordinary ingenuity traced them through a very large series of myths. There was of course at that time no knowledge of the unconscious layers of the mind, so that to-day the chief value of his work is a casuistic one. Partly because of certain philological difficulties Laistner's work was unduly neglected by mythologists, though before Freud's it should be counted as perhaps the most serious attempt to place mythology on a naturalistically intelligible basis.

It is generally recognized that the Nightmare has exercised a greater influence on waking phantasy than any other dream.[2] This is especially true of the origin of the belief in evil spirits and monsters. Clodd,[3] for instance, speaks of 'the intensified form of dreaming called "nightmare", when hideous spectres sit upon the breast, stopping breath and paralysing motion, and to which is largely due the creation of the vast army of nocturnal demons that fill the folk-lore of the world, and that, under infinite variety of repellent form, have had place

[1] L. Laistner, *Das Rätsel der Sphinx.*
[2] E. H. Meyer, *Germanische Mythologie*, 1891, S. 10, 61, 76-79. W. Wundt, *Völkerpsychologie*, Zweiter Band, *Mythus und Religion*, Zweiter Teil, 1906, S. 118-122.
[3] E. Clodd, *Myths and Dreams*, 1891, p. 171.

in the hierarchy of religions'. Some mythologists even trace the belief in spirits in general to the experiences of the Nightmare. Thus Golther[1] states: 'Der Seelenglaube beruht zum grossen Teil auf der Vorstellung von quälenden Druckgeistern. Erst allmählich entstand weiterhin der Glaube an Geister, die den Menschen nicht nur quälten und drückten. Zunächst aber ging der Gespensterglaube aus dem Alptraum hervor.' ('The belief in the soul rests in great part on the conception of torturing and oppressing spirits. Only as a gradual extension of this did the belief arise in spirits that displayed other activities than torturing and oppressing. In the first place, however, the belief in spirits took its origin in the Nightmare.')

All this is not surprising when we remember that the vividness of Nightmares far transcends that of ordinary dreams. Waller[2] says: 'The degree of consciousness during a paroxysm of Nightmare is so much greater than ever happens in a dream, that the person who has had a vision of this kind cannot easily bring himself to acknowledge the deceit. . . . Indeed I know no way which a man has of convincing himself that the vision which has occurred during a paroxysm of Nightmare is not real, unless he could have the evidence of other persons to the contrary who were present and awake at the time.'

As Macnish[3] insists: 'The illusions which occur are perhaps the most extraordinary phenomena of nightmare; and so strongly are they often impressed upon the mind, that, even on awaking, we find it impossible not to believe them real. . . . In many cases, no arguments, no efforts of the understanding will convince us that these are merely the chimeras of sleep.'

Before we discuss the part that the Nightmare has played in giving rise to superstitious ideas we must first say something about the Nightmare itself. The three cardinal features of a typical Nightmare are: (1) agon-

---

[1] W. Golther, *Handbuch der germanischen Mythologie*, 1895, S. 75.
[2] J. Waller, *A Treatise on the Incubus, or Nightmare*, 1816, pp. 28, 29.
[3] R. Macnish, *The Philosophy of Sleep*, 1836, p. 143.

izing dread; (2) a suffocating sense of oppression at the chest; and (3) a conviction of helpless paralysis. Less conspicuous features are an outbreak of cold sweat, convulsive palpitation of the heart, and sometimes a flow of seminal or vaginal secretion, or even a paralysis of the sphincters. The explanations of this condition still current in medical circles, and which ascribe it to digestive or circulatory disturbances, are probably farther from the truth than any other medical views, and show as little knowledge of the pathogenesis of the condition as was shown in regard to the infection of wounds before Lister's day, or to tuberculosis before Koch's. This is all the stranger since medical practitioners of earlier centuries were well-informed about the sexual origin of the condition. It is one more illustration of how the advance of medicine in the material field during the past century or two has led to the forgetting of much valuable knowledge in the psychopathological field; the sexual origin of Nightmares had to be re-discovered anew in the twentieth century just as did that of Hysteria.

In a previous essay on the subject[1] I have objected to the current medical hypotheses (a) that from their very nature they are incapable of explaining the essential features of the condition; (b) that the noxious factors invoked frequently occur in patients who do not suffer from the Nightmare and are usually absent in patients who do suffer from it. These factors can therefore at most be operative as incitements, not as the cause itself; the latter one reaches by concentrating on the central symptom of deathly fear. After pointing out how Freud had demonstrated the essential dependence of morbid anxiety on repressed Libido I summarized the conclusions of the essay in the statement that Nightmare is a form of anxiety attack, that it is essentially due to an intense mental conflict centreing around some repressed component of the psycho-sexual instinct, characteristi-

[1] 'On the Nightmare', *American Journal of Insanity*, 1910 [Part I. of this volume].

cally re-activation of the normal incest wishes of infancy, and that it may be evoked by any peripheral stimuli that serve to arouse associatively this body of repressed feeling; the importance, however, of such peripheral stimuli as factors in producing the affection has in the past been greatly over-estimated. I added that repression of the feminine, masochistic component of the sexual instinct rather than that of the more masculine is apt to engender the typical Nightmare, a view to which Adler[1] has also subscribed. The latent content of a Nightmare consists of a representation of a normal act of sexual intercourse, particularly in the form characteristic for women; the pressure on the breast, the self-surrender portrayed by the feeling of paralysis, and the genital secretion directly indicate its sexual nature, and the other symptoms, the palpitation, sweating, sense of suffocation, etc., are merely exaggerations of manifestations commonly experienced in some degree during coitus when fear is present.

Special emphasis should be laid on the circumstance that wishes fulfilled in this way always belong to the most powerfully repressed ones. This explains two significant facts: in the first place, that the same person may experience on one occasion a voluptuous dream, on another a Nightmare. This depends principally on the object of the wish, so that with a Nightmare the object is always a person whom the inhibiting forces of morality exclude from the erotic sphere. It is therefore comprehensible that the psycho-analysis of such dreams regularly shows them to relate to a near relative, most usually a parent. In the second place, as I have elsewhere[2] illustrated, an important matter constantly overlooked by modern physicians in discussing the pathogenesis of the Nightmare is that clinically all gradations may be observed between the most extreme form of this on the one hand and erotic dreams on the other. When

---

[1] Alfred Adler, 'Der psychische Hermaphroditismus im Leben und in der Neurose', *Fortschritte der Medizin*, 21 April 1910, S. 492.
[2] *Op. cit.* pp. 411-413.

the repression is slight, so that its effect is practically nullified by the inhibition of the endopsychic censorship that occurs during sleep, an erotic desire, perhaps one which would be suppressed in waking moments, can come to imaginary fulfilment in a dream. When the repression is greater the dream contains a mixture of pleasurable sensation and of discomfort or fear. When the repression is greater still the fear may overshadow the voluptuous feeling, and in the extreme case of the typical Nightmare it entirely replaces it. This circumstance, that an admixture of erotic and apprehensive emotions may be found in all degrees, we shall see to be extensively paralleled by the various myths and superstitious beliefs connected with the Nightmare theme.

We have mentioned above the vividness and the impression of reality characteristic of the Nightmare. It is therefore not astonishing that in all countries and in all ages except the present it has been attributed to the presence of actual strange beings. Thus we have the Greek Ephialtes, the Latin and Mediæval Incubus, the German Alp, the Old-German Mara, the Bohemian Mora, the Swiss Schratteli, the Scottish Leamain Sith, the Russian Kikimara, the Arcadian Kiel-uddakarra, the Mexican Ciuateteo, the Assyrian Ardat,[1] the Malay Langsuior,[2] the Tasmanian Evil-Spirit,[3] the Australian Mrart,[4] and the Autu[5] of Borneo. A striking confirmation of the conclusions enunciated above is the circumstance that all these oppressing spirits are characteristically lewd demons. Even the scientific terms used to designate the Nightmare, namely Incubus and Ephialtes, originally signified a lewd demon.[6] In other words,

[1] F. Lenormant, *Chaldean Magic*, English translation, 1877, p. 38.
[2] F. A. Swettenham, *Malay Sketches*, 1895, p. 198.
[3] J. West, *The History of Tasmania*, 1852, vol. ii. p. 90.
[4] A. W. Howitt, *The Native Tribes of South-East Australia*, 1904, p. 439.
[5] H. Ling Roth, *The Natives of Sarawak and British North Borneo*, 1896.
[6] See, for instance, Bayley, *English Dictionary*, 1785. Art. Incubus: 'The Nightmare, a Disease when a Man in his Sleep Supposes he has a great Weight lying upon him: a Devil who has Carnal Knowledge of a Woman under the Shape of a Man'. Robert Burton, *Anatomy of Melancholy*, Pt. I. Sec. 2, Mem. 3, Subsect. 2: 'and in such as are troubled with incubus, or witch-ridden (as we call it): if they lie on their back, they suppose an old woman rides and sits so hard on them, that they are almost stifled for want of breath'.

with the sole exception of modern physicians, people have constantly regarded the Nightmare as a sexual assault on the part of a lewd demon. We have seen that this folk belief had a certain justification. The view that the process is essentially a sexual one was quite correct; but the unconscious wishes giving rise to it were projected from the subject on to the outer world, as Freud[1] has shown characteristically happens in superstitions. Science, therefore, in setting aside the popular belief rejected the truth as well as the error; the observations of the people were, as usual, correct, but their explanations, as usual, false.

The reason why the object seen in a Nightmare is frightful or hideous is simply that the representation of the underlying wish is not permitted in its naked form, so that the dream is a compromise of the wish on the one hand, and on the other of the intense fear belonging to the inhibition. Maury[2] remarks with but little exaggeration: 'Le dormeur s'imaginait être lutiné par un esprit, oppressé par les impurs embrassements d'un démon incube ou succube. . . . L'origine de cette croyance s'explique par le fait qu'une sensation voluptueuse en rêve est presque toujours accompagnée d'un sentiment désagréable.' Nashe,[3] who more than three hundred years ago wrote on 'The Terrors of the Night', seems also to have had a prevision of the same explanation: 'When Night in her rustie dungeon hath imprisoned our ey-sight, and that we are shut seperatly in our chambers from resort, the divell keepeth his audit in our sin-guilty consciences, no sense but surrenders to our memorie a true bill of parcels of his detestable impietis. The table of our hart is turned to an index of iniquities, and all our thoughts are nothing but texts to condemn us. The rest we take in our beds is such another kinde of rest as the weerie traveller taketh in the coole soft grasse in summer, who thinking there to

[1] Sigm. Freud, *Zur Psychopathologie des Alltagslebens*, Dritte Auflage, 1910, S. 133.   [2] L. F. Alfred Maury, *La magie et l'astrologie*, 1860, p. 254.
[3] *The Works of Thomas Nashe*, 1594, edited by R. B. McKerrow, 1904, vol. i. pp. 345, 386.

lye at ease, and refresh his tyred limmes, layeth his fainting head unawares on a loathsome neast of snakes.[1]
. . . Therefore are the terrors of the night more than of
the day, because the sinnes of the night surmount the
sinnes of the day.'

To Laistner's interesting attempt to follow the traces
of the Nightmare *motif* through a large group of myths
Wundt[2] has raised an objection which appears logical,
but which consideration shows to be not important: it is
that he does not sufficiently distinguish between the
Nightmare and other forms of anxiety dreams. It is
therefore necessary to say something about this relationship. The Nightmare is only one variety of anxiety
dream, and the features it has in common with the other
kinds (dreams of grimacing beings, dreams of being examined, pursued, etc.) are more important than those in
which it differs. The essential difference is that its latent
content is highly specific and stereotyped. In all cases of
anxiety dreams the latent content represents the fulfilment of a repressed sexual wish, usually an incestuous
one, but, whereas in the Nightmare this always relates to
the normal sexual act, various perverse sexual wishes
come to expression in the other forms of anxiety dream.
An example of the latter would be a dream of a frightful
attacking animal, expressing the algolagnic combination of lust with brutality or cruelty. Referring to the
myths built on the same basis, Laistner[3] writes: 'Hier
kommt es uns darauf an, ein für allemal anzudeuten,
dass auch dieser Zug der Alpsagen durchaus den Erfah-
rungen des Alptraums entspricht und dass es guten
physiologischen Grund hat, wenn die Sage die bekannte
Verbindung der Grausamkeit mit der Wollust den Mit-
tagsgeistern zuschreibt.' ('Here we are concerned to
point out once for all that this feature also of the *Alp*
sagas quite corresponds to the experiences of the Night-

---

[1] Psycho-analytical readers will observe the interesting Oedipus symbolism
here.
[2] W. Wundt, *Völkerpsychologie*, Zweiter Band, *Mythus und Religion*, Zweiter
Teil, 1906, S. 122.
[3] L. Laistner, *Das Rätsel der Sphinx*, 1889, Bd. i. S. 45.

mare and that there is a good physiological reason for the saga which attributes to the midday spirits the well-known combination of cruelty with voluptuousness.')

As was pointed out in the previous chapter, the different conceptions of impossible monsters are very suggestive of a source in the experiences of anxiety dreams. This group of ideas is very extensive.[1] The belief in the real existence of such monsters has held its own well into modern times and cannot yet be said to have died out, even amongst civilized nations.[2]

Dreams of grimacing figures (*Fratzenträume*) are more than any others a rich source for the creation of fantastic human caricatures and the half-human, half-animal figures so prominent in mythology. Wundt[3] writes: 'Wer kann in dem Zwerg das Abbild der vielen Traumfratzen mit gewaltigem Kopf und Angesicht, wer in den grinsenden Tiermasken vieler Völker und schliesslich noch in dem Gorgonenangesicht der ältesten griechischen Kunst die Ähnlichkeit mit den Gesichtsverzerrungen der Reizträume verkennen? Dass diese Gattung der Träume eine Quelle neben anderen, und dass sie in Anbetracht der durch alle Einflüsse der Traumvision bezeugten intensiven psychischen Wirkung der Träume nicht die unbedeutendste ist, kann daher als im höchsten Grade wahrscheinlich gelten.' ('Who can fail to recognize in dwarfs the image of the many distorted dream figures with enormous heads and countenances, or in the grinning animal masks of many countries, and finally in the Gorgon face of the oldest Greek art the similarity with the facial distortions of the dreams due to irritation? It is therefore highly probable that this class of dream furnishes one source among others, and that, in view of the intense psychical effect of these dreams, this source is not the least important.')

We may now summarize the features that constitute evidence of ideas originating in anxiety dreams. In the

[1] See, for example, Meyer, *op. cit.* S. 97.
[2] C. Gould, *Mythical Monsters*, 1886. See especially ch. ix. 'The Sea-Serpent'.
[3] Wundt, *op. cit.* S. 116.

first place the occurrence of anxiety itself accompanying a mythical or superstitious conception should at least make one think of the possibility of such an origin, for although anxiety, of course, occurs elsewhere than in dreams still it rarely—if ever—attains there the grade of intensity so common in dreams; further, those subject to continual dread are pretty sure to suffer also from anxiety dreams. Then the occurrence of transformation, especially from human into animal form, makes it very probable that the ideas have their source in anxiety dreams. This is notably so when we find the transformation of a very attractive into an extremely repellent object, a situation frequently met with in both myths and dreams. This combination of the two extremes of attraction and repulsion, of beauty and hideousness, naturally represent the two conflicting forces of wish and inhibition. The inadequacy of the view that refers such dream experiences to variations in gastric activity is here particularly evident; as Fiske[1] well says, 'indigestion doesn't account for beautiful women in key-holes'.

Finally, the combination of anxiety with incestuous themes would lead one to suspect a relationship of the ideas with the experiences of Nightmares, since these contain little else. The sadistic view of sexual functions which so many children hold explains why the parent so often appears in the dream in the symbolic guise of an aggressive animal or monster. The remarkably close connection, mentioned earlier, between totemism and ancestor-worship, between the ideas of animal descent and the interchangeability of human and animal personalities becomes more comprehensible through psychoanalytical knowledge of the symbolism of unconscious repressed wishes.

[1] J. Fiske, *Myths and Myth-Makers*, 1872, p. 95.

CHAPTER III

INCUBUS AND INCUBATION

W E have already commented on the interesting circumstance, so significant for our sexual theory of the Nightmare, that the scientific name for this condition in the Middle Ages also denoted a lewd demon who visits women at night, lies heavily on their chest and violates them against their will. These visitors of women were called Incubi (French *follets*; Spanish *duendes*; Italian *folletti*; German *Alpen*); those of men were called Succubi (French *soulèves*). As it runs in Caxton's Cronycle (Descrypcion of Wales)[1]:

> That fende that goth a nyght,
> Wymmen full oft to gyle,
> Incubus is named by ryght:
> And gyleth men other whyle,
> Succubus is that wyght.

The historical roots of this particular conception are too numerous to allow of their being traced here. It must suffice to say that the central idea itself, the belief that sexual intercourse can occur between mortals and super-natural beings, is one of the most widespread of human beliefs.[2] It is to be found in most religions, from the Zoroastrian to modern spiritism; perhaps the most familiar examples are the amours of the Greek gods. Various renowned people, such as Robert, the father of William the Conqueror, Luther, Merlin (born from an incubus and a nun, the daughter of Charlemagne), Caesar, Alexander the Great, Plato, Scipio Africanus, and the whole race of Huns were supposed to have been born from such unions,[3] and the whole island of Cyprus

[1] Quoted from J. G. Dalyell, *The Darker Superstitions of Scotland*, 1835, p. 682.
[2] Numerous instances of it in different countries and ages may be found in H. Freimark, *Okkultismus und Sexualität*, S. 342-348. P. Gener, *La Mort et le Diable*, 1880, p. 340, etc.
[3] Gener, *op. cit.* pp. 403, 521. R. G. Latham, *A Dictionary of the English Language*, 1882, p. 1240. P. Sinistrari, *Demoniality or Incubi and Succubi* (seventeenth century), English translation, 1879, p. 55.

to have been populated from the offspring of incubi.[1] At
the end of the seventeenth century the belief was still
rife in Scotland,[2] and it has by no means yet died out in
many parts of Europe. In certain mystical[3] and spirit-
istic[4] circles, particularly in France and America, it has
received a new lease of life; the most modern form of it
would appear to be the notion of conception from the
fourth dimension.

The particular form the belief assumed in the Middle
Ages was mainly due to theological influence, which
moulded it to its purposes as it did other popular superstitious beliefs. An astonishing amount of the literature
of this period was taken up with detailed discussions
concerning the precise activities of these evil spirits. The
general conception of them was closely connected with
that of the Devil and his army, so that the subject is
really a chapter of devil-lore. The Church, following St.
Augustin,[5] in his famous passage on 'Silvanos et Faunos,
quos vulgo incubos vocant', regarded Incubi essentially
as fiends of hell whose function it was to tempt frail
humanity; in the elaboration of this idea St. Thomas
Aquinas[6] played an important part. An interestingly
unorthodox departure was made in the seventeenth century by Peter Sinistrari,[7] who maintained that Incubi
were not demons, but higher beings intermediate between men and angels; they degraded themselves but
honoured mankind by human contact.[8] Exorcism had
no influence on them, which was one of the respects in
which they differed from evil fiends. Sinistrari ingeniously
reconciled this view with the pronouncements of the

[1] J. Hansen, *Zauberwahn, Inquisition und Hexenprozess im Mittelalter*, 1900,
S. 141.
[2] R. Kirk, *Secret Commonwealth*, 1690, p. 35.
[3] See books like Jules Bois, *La Satanisme et la magie*, 1895. S. De Guaita,
Temple de Satan, 1891. Des Mousseaux, *Les hauts phénomènes de la magie*.
J. K. Huysmans, *Là-bas*, 1890, and *En Route*, 1895, etc.
[4] Freimark, *op. cit.* S. 335, 364, 368-369, 385. Peixoto, *Archivos Brasileires
de Psychiatrie*, 1909, pp. 74-94.
[5] Augustini Hipponensis Episcopi *De Civitate Dei*, 1825 ed., lib. xv. ch. xxiii.
[6] Thomas Aquinas, *Summa theologica*, Pt. I. Quest. 51, Art. 3-6.
[7] Sinistrari, *op. cit.* pp. 129, 223.
[8] That actually they were derived from the idea of *revenants*, of souls who
could not rest in their grave, will be shown in the succeeding chapter.

Church on the sin of such relations by suggesting that those who did not know the true nature of Incubi, but believed them to be devils, sinned just as grievously as though these spirits really were devils. He was evidently of opinion that the essence of sin lay in the belief in the sinfulness of the act committed.

Women seem to have been troubled by these nightly visitors more than men, and widows and virgins, more particularly nuns,[1] more than married women. Cloisters were especially infected by Incubi, and many instances have been recorded of epidemics of such visitations.[2] The theological teachings about the reality of Incubi evidently permitted manifestations that otherwise would have had to find some other means of expression; Freud[3] has pointed out how the religious beliefs prevailing in the environment must affect the form taken by manifestations of the unconscious, e.g., in hysterical symptoms. A favourite guise assumed by Incubi was the clerical. Thus Hieronymus relates the story of a young lady who called for help against an Incubus whom her friends then found under her bed in the guise of the Bishop Sylvanus; the Bishop's reputation would have suffered had he not been able to convince them that the Incubus had assumed his shape.[4] Reginald Scot[5] comments sceptically on this: 'Oh excellent peece of witchcraft wrought by Sylvanus!' Chaucer, in 'The Wife of Bath's Tale', says slyly that in his day Incubi had become much rarer since the orders of mendicant friars, who, he hints, had replaced them, had been introduced:

> For there as wont to walken was an elf,
> There walketh now the limitour[6] himself,
> .   .   .   .   .   .

---

[1] Freimark, op. cit. S. 349. Gener, op. cit. S. 519.

[2] E. Murisier, Les maladies du sentiment religieux, 1909, p. 49. Ch. Pezet, Contribution à l'étude de la démonomanie, 1909, p. 18.

[3] See Sigm. Freud, Zentralblatt für Psychoanalyse, Jahrg. i. S. 7 [Sammlung kleiner Schriften zur Neurosenlehre, 1913, 3e Folge, S. 296, Gesammelte Schriften, Bd. vi. S. 34. Collected Papers, vol. ii. p. 293.]

[4] H. Institoris and J. Sprenger, Malleus Maleficarum, 1487, Part II. Question I. Kap. 11.

[5] Reginald Scot, The Discoverie of Witchcraft (1584), 1886 edition, p. 62.

[6] Begging friar.

Women may now go safely up and down;
In every bush, and under every tree,
There is no other incubus than hee,
And he ne will dou them no dishonour.

In the reports of the actual examples of visits by Incubi[1] there appears in the most unambiguous way a feature which has special significance for the present discussion. It is that every possible gradation is to be observed between the pleasurable excitement of voluptuousness on the one hand and extreme terror and repulsion on the other. This variation, and the impossibility of demarking it at any point, shows again the intimate connection between libido and morbid dread. It forcibly reminds one of exactly the same gradation that can be observed clinically between erotic dreams and Nightmares. Simon[2] shows that the same interchange between pleasurable and repellent visions is to be found with erotic hallucinations: 'Tantôt le spectre hallucinatoire est de forme agréable; c'est un mari, un amant, une femme aimée et, dans ces cas, la sensation éprouvée par l'halluciné est voluptueuse. Plus souvent, peut-être, l'hallucination visuelle est repoussante: il s'agit du démon, de quelque être difforme, d'une vieille femme à l'aspect hideux dont les embrassements sont pour l'aliéné un objet d'horreur; d'images dégoûtantes, qui poursuivent le malade et qui l'obsèdent. Dans ces cas, l'hallucination génitale consiste en une impression douloureuse, à tout le moins, pénible ou désagréable.'

Höfler's[3] conclusion, therefore, that the belief in demons originated in Nightmares, and that in Incubi in erotic dreams, is quite intelligible, but it must be remembered that, just as the two kinds of dream pass into each other, so—as we shall presently see—are the beliefs in Devil and Incubus inextricably intertwined.

In the following passage by Goerres[4] we have a picture

[1] See, for example, the accounts quoted by P. L. Jacob, *Curiosités infernales*, pp. 85-97.
[2] P. M. Simon, *Le monde des rêves*, 1882, p. 183.
[3] M. Höfler, 'Medizinischer Dämonismus', *Zentralblatt für Anthropologie*, 1900, Bd. v. S. 1.
[4] J. J. von Goerres, cited by J. Delassus, *Les incubes et les succubes*, 1897, p. 34.

of Incubus experiences taken from opposite ends of the scale just described: 'Tantôt ce sont les angoisses de l'étouffement, de la paralysie, tantôt, au contraire, c'est une surexcitation violente des organes sexuels avec la sensation du dégagement du système musculaire, quelque chose comme le vertige de la vitesse.' The resemblance of this passage to a description of dream experiences, or rather the identity of the two, hardly needs to be pointed out. The following account of the unpleasant variety would well pass for a description of a Nightmare; it is taken from Laurent-Nagour[1]: De Nogent related that his mother had because of her great beauty to sustain the onslaught of Incubi. During a sleepless night the demon 'whose habit it was to invade hearts torn with grief' appeared in person and, though slumber had not yet closed her eyes, almost crushed her with his stifling weight. The poor lady could not move or groan or even breathe. The servants found their mistress blenched and trembling, and she told them of the danger she had been threatened by, the traces of which were all too plain. The descriptions of the opposite, pleasurable kind of visit are common in the accounts of Incubi and need not be related in detail; as might be expected, the wooing Incubus often assumed the guise of the sleeper's lover, or of the absent or missing mate.[2] Most of the reports contain an admixture of voluptuous and repellent features; pain and disgust also occur often enough. An excellent example of the underlying attraction exerted by a wicked Incubus is related with fine psychological insight by Goerres[3]; it reminds one of the resistance we encounter nowadays on endeavouring to get neurotic patients to renounce their symptoms: 'En 1643, je fus chargé par mes supérieurs d'aller exorciser une jeune fille de vingt ans qui était poursuivie par un Incube. Elle m'avoua sans détour tout ce que l'esprit impur faisait avec elle. Je jugeai, d'après ce qu'elle me dit, que malgré

[1] E. Laurent und P. Nagour, *Okkultismus und Liebe*, 1903, S. 109.
[2] Brognoli (1650), cited by Delassus, *op. cit.* p. 20. Freimark, *op. cit.* S. 352. J. Michelet, *La Sorcière*, 1863, 3me édition, p. 108.
[3] Goerres, *op. cit.* p. 21.

ses dénégations, elle prêtait au démon un consentement indirect. En effet, elle était toujours avertie de ses approches par une surexcitation violente des organes sexuels; et alors, au lieu d'avoir recours à la prière, elle courait à sa chambre et se mettait sur son lit. J'essayai d'éveiller en elle des sentiments de confiance envers Dieu; mais je n'y pus réussir, et elle semblait plutôt craindre d'être délivrée.'

It is interesting that the doctrines of the Church appear to take into account the same alternation of fearful and voluptuous feelings on the occasion of the visits of Incubi, for they are concerned with the various attitudes on the part of the subjects towards these visits, particularly in respect of the strength of the resistance they manifest. The discussions on this point resemble very much a modern juristic investigation into a case of rape. The authors of the *Malleus Maleficarum*, for instance, divide such subjects into three classes: '(1) Those who voluntarily submit to Incubi, as witches do; (2) those whom witches have brought together with Incubi or Succubi against their will; and (3) a third class, to which certain virgins in particular belong, who are plagued by Incubus demons entirely against their will.'

We may make an interesting contrast between these pleasant and unpleasant experiences, with all their intermediate types, from several points of view. Psychologically the matter is, thanks to Freud's investigations, very simple. His doctrine of intrapsychic repression gives us the full explanation. As was pointed out in the preceding chapter, the wishes culminating in unpleasant experiences differ from those of the opposite kind merely in being subject to internal repression or condemnation, so that they are unconscious. Another way of putting this is to say that the erotic wishes in question may be compatible with the standards of the subject's ego, and therefore accepted by it, or not. [In more recent terminology one would say that such wishes may be either ego-syntonic or ego-dystonic.] The gradual evolution of insight into this state of affairs provides a curious study in human nature, to which we shall now turn.

It has been necessary to lay stress on the gradualness in the distinction between these two types of wishes, or of the experiences they give rise to respectively, and, although we have said that certain of these wishes are acceptable to the ego, this is, strictly speaking, never completely true. That is to say, all erotic wishes without exception that disturb sleep have to overcome a certain amount of internal opposition, some being, of course, more heavily censured than others. Even at the present day it is customary for nocturnal emissions to be ascribed rather to some 'natural' physical activity on the part of the sexual apparatus rather than to any actual wishes that set this apparatus in operation. The tendency has thus always been to avoid any personal responsibility for nocturnal erotic wishes, even those most lightly censured, and to ascribe them to some other agency. In the history of mankind we can clearly distinguish two stages in this respect. To begin with, the dream experiences were ascribed to the action of external personal agents, such as lewd demons; the wishes were, as a psychiatrist would say, projected outwards on to other beings. The second stage consisted in projecting the wishes on to various bodily processes, non-mental and non-sexual. We are even yet only beginning to emancipate ourselves from this form of projection, and the medical world in particular shows the greatest timidity in making this step. It will further become plain that this evolution proceeded earlier in the case of those dream wishes that are relatively acceptable to the ego than in the case of strongly repressed ones; in consequence, superstitious causes — demons or indigestion, according to the epoch — continued to be invoked in explanation of the unpleasant experiences later than for the pleasurable and evidently sexual experiences.

We read that 'presque tous les peuples de l'Orient ont recouru aux incubes et aux succubes dans l'explication qu'ils ont donnée des rêves d'amour et des pollutions nocturnes'.[1]

By the time the Middle Ages were reached, however, the opinion was beginning to gain ground, particularly among physicians, that nocturnal pollutions had a purely physical origin. Gervasius of Tilbury, for instance, quotes this as the approved medical view in 1214, though he himself appears to believe at the same time both in this ætiology and in the existence of lewd Succubi.[2] Later the curious compromise was reached that up to the year 1400 Incubi were supposed to have had intercourse with human beings only against the will of the latter, but that after this date the appearance of a race of lecherous witches led to people giving themselves voluntarily to the Incubi.[3] It is apparent that, just when people were beginning to emancipate themselves from the belief in hallucinated beings in connection with erotic dreams and retaining the belief only in connection with Nightmares, a theological elaboration of the Incubus concept re-animated the ancient belief that the partner in a sexual dream was an actual being.

A neat description of the conflict, with more than a hint of dawning insight, may be quoted from an old play of the early seventeenth century.[4] In it Ursula speaks: 'I have heard you say that dreames and visions were fabulous; and yet one time I dreamt fowle water ran through the floore, and the next day the house was on fire. You us'd to say hobgoblins, fairies, and the like, were nothing but our owne affrightments, and yet o' my troth, cuz, I once dream'd of a young batchelour, and was ridd with the night-mare. But come, so my conscience be cleere, I never care how fowle my dreames are.'

Even the bigoted royal author, King James I, at a still earlier date shows signs of a certain amount of

[1] Gener, *op. cit.* p. 520.
[2] Cited by J. Hansen, *op. cit.* S. 138, Gervasius of Tilbury, *Otia imperialia*, SS. rerum Brunsvicensium i. 897 *et seq.* and lib. iii. cap. 93.
[3] Reginald Scot, *op. cit.* p. 58.
[4] W. Sampson, *The Vow-Breaker, or The Fair Maide of Clifton*, 1636, Act 3, Scene 1.

insight[1]: '*Philomates*: Is it not the thing which we call the *Mare*, which takes folkes sleeping in their beds, a kinde of these spirits, whereof ye are speaking?

'*Epistemon*: No, that is but a naturall sickenesse, which the Mediciners have given that name of *Incubus* unto, *ab incubando*, because it being a thicke fleume, falling into our breast upon the heart, while we are sleeping, intercludes so our vitall spirits, and takes all power from us, as makes us think that there were some unnaturall burden or spirit, lying upon us, and holding us downe.'

At one of the meetings of the *Bureau d'adresse*[2] in 1656 the view was taken by several physicians that the belief in Incubi was merely a product of a voluptuous imagination; according to one, Incubi were 'produites par l'abondance ou la qualité de la semence, laquelle, envoyant son espèce dans la phantaisie, elle se forme un objet agréable, remue la puissance métrice, et celle-ci la faculté expulstrice des vaisseaux spermatiques'. De Saint-André,[3] Louis XV's physician, considered their origin to be partly in the supposed imagination, partly in invented excuses for illicit relations: 'L'incube est le plus souvent une chimère, qui n'a pour fondement que le rêve, l'imagination blessée, et très souvent l'imagination des femmes. . . . L'artifice n'a pas moins de part à l'histoire des incubes. Une femme, une fille, une dévote de nom, etc., débauchée, qui affecte de paraître virtueuse, pour cacher son crime fait passer son amant pour un esprit incube qui l'obsède.' Later writers have confirmed this, and have pointed out in addition the psychopathic nature of the belief. According to Dalyell[4] 'the presence of the Incubi and Succubi denotes amorous illusions only'. Delassus,[5] who insists on the sexual nature of the whole subject, says that the morbid appearance of an Incubus demonstrates 'la victoire de Lilith et de

[1] King James I., *Daemonologie*, Third Book, chap. iii. 'The description of a particular sort of that kinde of following spirit, called Incubi and Succubi.'
[2] *Recueil général des questions traités et conférence du Bureau d'adresse.*
[3] De Saint-André, *Lettres au sujet de la magie, des maléfices et des sorciers*, 1725.
[4] J. G. Dalyell, *The Darker Superstitions of Scotland*, 1835, p. 599.
[5] Delassus, *op. cit.* pp. 39, 41, 51.

Nahemah, les reines des Stryges, sur les imprudents qui ont voulu rester chastes, qui ont voulu mépriser les vérités éternelles du lingam'.

Later authors have laid stress on the morbid nature of the phenomenon. Macario[1] writes: 'Les succubes et les incubes sont des malades atteints d'hallucinations de la sensibilité génitale.' Morel,[2] in 1860, states: 'C'est dans cette catégorie de malades hystérico-religieuses que l'on observe particulièrement les idées délirantes à propos d'obsessions démoniaques, de succubes et d'incubes, le terme *hyperesthesia psychica sexualis* semble particulièrement leur convenir.' Dagonet,[3] in 1876, describes the subject under the term erotomania. Leuret,[4] nearly a hundred years ago, clearly saw the analogy between these beliefs of the Middle Ages and the hallucinations of the insane. He illustrated this by a detailed comparison of one of his patients at the Salpêtrière with a woman from whom St. Bernard exorcised evil spirits: 'Les hallucinations ont entre elles une si grande analogie, que les êtres créés par elles diffèrent seulement dans les accessoires; les descriptions qu'en donnent actuellement nos aliénés ressemblent aux descriptions que donnaient autrefois les saints et les possédés; . . . les noms seuls diffèrent. Ainsi, pour savoir tout ce qui concerne les incubes, il suffit d'écouter un de ces malades qui se plaignent de les recevoir pendant la nuit. Les incubes sont et font encore tout ce qu'ils étaient et faisaient jadis.'

It will be noted that in contrast to the other superstitious ideas here being treated, the idea of transformation plays no part in the Incubus idea. The reason for this is very simple and shows very well the artificial nature of the whole conception. The idea of transformation is to be found in the Middle Ages, both in the theological concept of the Devil and in the popular idea of lewd demons (German *Alp*), but the Church artificially

[1] M. A. Macario, 'Études cliniques sur la démonomanie', *Annales médico-psychologiques*, 1843, t. i. p. 441.
[2] Morel, quoted by Pezet, *op. cit.* p. 54.
[3] H. Dagonet, quoted by Pezet, *op. cit.* p. 54.
[4] F. Leuret, *Fragments psychologiques sur la folie*, 1834, pp. 258, 261-264.

defined an Incubus as a demon in human form. When he
appeared as an animal he was another kind of devil and
no longer an Incubus. The popular equivalent of the
Incubus and Succubus, however, *e.g.*, the *Alp* and *Mara*,
constantly appeared in animal guise.

*   *   *   *   *

The most perfect manifestation of the erotic wishes
that have been most fully brought into harmony with
the standards of the ego is where the nightly visitor was
believed to be not merely not an evil spirit but actually
a divine being. It is comprehensible that such experiences, to which we have already referred in Chapter I,
should be both approved and sought after. In this connection special mention may be made of the interesting
practice known as Incubation or Temple-Sleep (*incu-
batio*, ἐγκοίμησις), for, although this was not a peculiarly mediæval idea, still it lasted throughout the Middle
Ages, and it affords an instructive counterpart to the
Incubus belief. In fact, as Wundt[1] truly remarks, the
very similarity of the terms Incubus and Incubation
point to an inherent relationship between the two conceptions. The subject has an additional value for our
present purpose through its close association with ancestor worship and the idea of animal transformation.

The procedure of Incubation has been most extensively investigated in relation to Greece and Rome, but
it is a world-spread practice. Thus it has been found in
Central America,[2] North Africa,[3] Australia,[4] Borneo,[5]
China,[6] India,[7] Persia,[8] etc. Several different practices
have been included under the designation Incubation.

[1] W. Wundt, *Völkerpsychologie*, Bd. ii. Teil ii. 1906, S. 110.
[2] Antonio de Herrera, *Historia general de los hechos de los Castellanos en las islas y terra firma del Mar Oceane*, 1730, vol. iv. ch. iv.
[3] G. Nachtigal, *Sahara und Sudan*, 1889, Bd. iii. S. 477.
[4] Sir George Grey, *Journals of Two Expeditions of Discovery in North-West and Western Australia*, 1841, vol. ii. p. 336.
[5] H. Ling Roth, *The Natives of Sarawak and British North Borneo*, 1896, vol. i. p. 185.
[6] O. Stoll, *Suggestion und Hypnotismus in der Völkerpsychologie*, Zweite Auflage, 1904, S. 51, 52.
[7] J. A. Dulaure, *Die Zeugung in Glaube, Sitte und Brauch der Völker*, 1908, S. 45, 50, 80.
[8] *Voyages d'Ibn Batoutah*, traduction française, 1873, t. i. p. 418.

The most typical is the union of a person with a god or goddess during sleep in the sacellum of the temple, a custom of which the main source seems to have been in Egypt. Others are union with a departed being during sleep on his grave, *Gräberschlaf*, or with various spirits during sleep near holy wells or springs, a custom chiefly developed in Greece.

Several functions were subserved by the practice. From the idea of close connection with the Godhead developed the custom of assuring divine protection either through the union of men with goddesses, as, for example, with Isis in Egypt and Rome,[1] with Seraphis in Egypt, Rome and Canopaea,[2] with Diana in Ephesus,[3] and with Ino in Sparta,[4] or through the sacred prostitution of women to the gods, as to Vishnu in India,[5] to Bel[6] and Shamash[7] in Babylon, to Ammon in the Egyptian Thebes,[8] and elsewhere.

It is probable that the inner meaning of the practice always was the wish to secure sexual capacity and fertility among those in need of it. It characteristically presents itself, therefore, as a device for remedying impotence or sterility, or the innumerable afflictions that symbolize these. This meaning is plain to see in connection with the most renowned of all the Incubation cults, that of Aesculapius. Towards the end of its vogue his cult had spread from its source in Epidauros to some three hundred and twenty sites. The cure of sterility was one of the central features of this cult. Thus to cite only two well-known examples: Andromache of Epirus visited Epidauros on account of sterility; in a

---

[1] Alice Walton, 'Cornell Studies in Classical Philology', Number 3, *The Cult of Asklepios*, pp. 63, 74.
[2] L. Preller, *Berichte ü. d. Verhandl. d. Königl. Sächs. Gesell. d. Wissenschaften zu Leipzig*, 1854, S. 196.
[3] Th. Puschmann, *Handbuch der Geschichte der Medizin*, 1901.
[4] Pausanias, *Attika*, cap. 21.
[5] Dulaure, *loc. cit.*
[6] Cullimore, *Oriental Cylinders*, Numbers 71, 76, 109. J. G. Frazer, *Lectures on the Early History of the Kingship*, 1905, p. 170.
[7] C. H. W. Johns, 'Notes on the Code of the Hammurabi', *American Journal of Semitic Languages*, 1903, vol. xix. p. 98.
[8] Cullimore, *loc. cit.* Frazer, *loc. cit.*

dream the god lifted up her dress and touched her abdomen, an experience that resulted in the birth of a son.[1] Andromeda of Chios in the same circumstances was visited by the god in the form of a snake who lay on her; she bore five sons.[2]

The connection between Aesculapius and serpent worship was exceedingly close. Serpents were not only sacred in his temples, but actually represented the god[3]; in the year 293 B.C. an enormous snake was brought to Rome as an indication that Aesculapius had extended his patronage to the city. Many famous men were born of the serpent-god, e.g., Aratus of Sicyon, Alexander the Great, Augustus (the snake here represented Apollo, the father of Aesculapius), Aristomenes, Publius Scipio the Elder, etc.[4] It is well known that the Serpent God is one of the commonest objects of worship over the whole world.[5] Even the gods of more cultivated societies often make their appearance in this form, especially when engaged on love adventures; thus Apollo seduced Atys as a serpent (leaving in memory of his visit a corresponding mark on her body), just as Zeus seduced Persephone and Odin Gunnlodh. The circumstances in which the gods assumed this guise provide us with the key for the understanding of snake symbolism and that this is a phallic one is too well attested to need dwelling on here.[6]

It is of especial interest that the serpent symbolizes not simply the male member in general, but particularly the male member of the father. One of the most widely spread superstitions in the whole world is to the effect that snakes are the incarnation of deceased an-

[1] Mary Hamilton, *Incubation, or the Cure of Disease in Pagan Temples and Christian Churches*, 1906, p. 25.
[2] Mary Hamilton, *op. cit.* p. 27.
[3] See especially Puschmann, *op. cit.* S. 169. Alice Walton, *op. cit.* pp. 13-16, 65, 91.
[4] L. Deubner, *De Incubatione*, 1900, S. 33.
[5] Compare J. B. Deane, *The Worship of the Serpent*, 1883. H. C. Du Bose, *The Dragon, Image and Demon*, 1886. J. Fergusson, *Tree and Serpent Worship*, Second Edition, 1872. C. Howard, *Sex Worship*, 1902, ch. viii. 'The Serpent and the Cross'. G. Staniland Wake, *Serpent Worship*, 1888.
[6] F. Riklin, *Wunscherfüllung und Symbolik im Märchen*, 1908, S. 40-44. A. J. Storfer, *Zur Sonderstellung des Vatermordes*, 1911, S. 30, 31.

cestors,[1] a fact which in itself brings snake-worship and ancestor-worship into close association. A product of it is the belief in individual house snakes which desert the house when its male members—particularly the father —die.[2] The idea is closely connected with the belief that the soul leaves a sleeper in the form of a snake which escapes through the mouth.[3] This symbolism and the recognizably chthonic origin in general of such gods as Aesculapius[4] form a connecting link between the ideas of snakes and graves, snake worship and ancestor worship, and the practices of sleeping in temples or on graves.

Incubation thus became an important method of curing sterility, and Aesculapius' gift in this respect was inherited later by a number of Christian saints, notably the Archangel Michael, St. Damien and St. Hubert[5]; the activity of the last mentioned is to be traced in the Ardennes as late as the seventeenth century. This cure of disease by Incubation—known as oneiromancy—was practised in Scotland[6] and Ireland[7] to an even later date, and it is interesting to note that here the person slept in the skin of a sacrificed sheep, just as the worshippers of Ammon did in Thebes,[8] or those of Amphiarus in Attica.[9] In a Welsh church in Monmouthshire recourse was still had to this practice in the nineteenth century.[10]

---

[1] J. G. Frazer, *The Golden Bough*, Third Edition, Part iv. (*Adonis, Attis, Osiris*, second edition), 1907, pp. 76, 77. E. S. Hartland, *Primitive Paternity*, 1909, vol. i. p. 169 *et seq*. Wundt, *op. cit.* S. 61-64.

[2] Andrew Lang, *Myth, Ritual and Religion*, vol. i. p. 57. E. H. Meyer, *Germanische Mythologie*, 1891, S. 63, 64, 73. C. L. Rochholtz, *Deutscher Glaube und Brauch*, 1867, Bd. i. (Deutscher Unsterblichkeitsglaube), S. 146, 147. A. Wuttke, *Der deutsche Volksaberglaube der Gegenwart*, 1900, S. 51.

[3] J. Grimm, *Deutsche Mythologie*, Vierte Ausgabe, 1876, Nachtrag S. 247, 312. B. Thorpe, *Northern Mythology*, 1851, vol. i. p. 289.

[4] Puschmann, *op. cit.* Bd. i. S. 170.

[5] L. F. A. Maury, *La magie et l'astrologie*, 1860, pp. 247, 248, 251.

[6] Th. Pennant, *A Tour in Scotland and Voyage to the Hebrides in* 1772, vol. i. p. 311, in John Pinkerton's 'Voyages and Travels', vol. iii. M. Martin, *A Description of the Western Islands of Scotland*, p. 3, in John Pinkerton's *op. cit.* vol. iii.

[7] J. Richardson, *The Folly of Pilgrimages*, 1727, p. 70.

[8] Herodotus, ii. par. 42.

[9] Pausanias, i. cap. 34.

[10] Howell Rees, 'The Cure of Disease by Incubation', *British Medical Journal*, Oct. 30, 1909, p. 1317.

In the Middle Ages three changes were gradually introduced into the practice of Incubation: (1) Union in sleep was replaced by prayers to the God, Goddess or Saint. (2) More importance was attached to holy wells and springs to which the pilgrimage took place than to the simpler sacred places, groves, etc. This change was doubtless determined by the close unconscious connection between the ideas of water and childbirth.[1] Up to the present day holy wells are the object of adoration throughout Scotland[2] and in many other parts of Europe. (3) The cure of impotence or sterility has been generalized to that of other defects, particularly such as are associated with these ideas in the unconscious (paralysis, blindness, lameness, etc.). The modern pilgrims of Lourdes would be astonished to know how much their pilgrimages have to do with ideas dating from the incestuous wishes of the Ancient Greeks.

Finally, Incubation was practised as a means of divining the future or of procuring inspiration. A well-known example of the latter was the inspiration of a tragedy that Aeschylus received from Bacchus in a dream. In Ireland the choice of a king depended on the intimations received during Incubation.[3]

The connection between the Nightmare and Incubation, particularly in its original form, is too clear to need any lengthy discussion. Wundt[4] writes: 'In der Tat lassen sich alle diese, der Inkubation im weitesten Sinne zugehörigen Tatsachen auf zwei einander in mancher Beziehung verwandte Ausgangspunkte zurückverfolgen; auf den Angsttraum und auf den Krankheitsanfall.' ('Actually all these facts to do with Incubation can be traced to two starting-points which have much in common: to anxiety dreams and to attacks of illness.') It is to be noted, however, that the dreams exercising the greatest influence in this direction must have stood in the middle between pure Nightmares and pure erotic dreams, *i.e.*

---

[1] See Otto Rank, *Der Mythus von der Geburt des Helden*, 1909, S. 69, 70.
[2] Sir Arthur Mitchell, *The Past in the Present*, 1880, p. 276.
[3] E. O'Curry, *On the Manners and Customs of the Ancient Irish*, 1873, vol. ii. p. 199.   [4] Wundt, *loc. cit.*

dreams containing an admixture of anxious and pleasurable feelings.

The prominent part taken by serpents in the original Incubation may be adduced in favour of this conclusion, since snake symbolism is highly characteristic of dream processes. Artemidoros seems to have had an inkling of its significance in his saying, 'When a snake pursues anyone during sleep he should be on his guard against wicked women'.[1] This may be compared with the Brandenburg proverb, 'Wenn man eine Schlange mit ins Bett nimmt, hat man viel Glück' ('If one takes a snake with him to bed he will be very lucky'), or the Oldenburg[2] saying: 'Wenn Schlangen in den Leib eines Menschen hineingehext werden, so drücken sie das Herz.' ('When snakes are bewitched into someone they press on the heart.') Incubation is by no means the only example of a belief that takes its origin from the occurrence of snakes in anxiety dreams. Laistner[3], for example, in one of the chapters he has devoted to 'Die Alpschlange' has considered in detail the part played by these snakes in those Teutonic myths and superstitious ideas originating in the Nightmare.

In conclusion, we may say that in the Incubus-Incubation group of ideas we have an excellent example for a set of beliefs that have not merely acquired their outer guise from the experiences of the Nightmare, but the latent content of which is also identical with that of the Nightmare: that is to say, it consists of an imaginary fulfilment of certain repressed wishes for sexual intercourse, especially with the parents. The beliefs in question are evidently determined by attempts to ward off the sense of guilt accompanying these wishes (*i.e.* by projecting them on to the Incubus) or the resulting punishment [*e.g.*, by curing impotence through the isopathic principle[4] of Incubation.]

---

[1] Wuttke, *op. cit.* S. 115.   [2] Wuttke, *op. cit.* S. 116.
[3] L. Laistner, *Das Rätsel der Sphinx*, 1889, Bd. i. Kap. 17, S. 83-108.
[4] [Ernest Jones, 'Fear, Guilt and Hate', *International Journal of Psycho-Analysis*, vol. ix. footnote p. 386.]

CHAPTER IV

THE VAMPIRE

NONE of the group of beliefs here dealt with is richer or more over-determined than that in the Vampire, nor is there one that has more numerous connections with other legends and superstitions. Its psychological meaning is correspondingly complicated, and in the analysis of it we shall proceed from its most typical form. It may be said at the outset that the latent content of the belief yields plain indications of most kinds of sexual perversions, and that the belief assumes various forms according as this or that perversion is more prominent.

Webster's *International Dictionary* defines a Vampire as: 'A blood-sucking ghost or re-animated body of a dead person; a soul or re-animated body of a dead person believed to come from the grave and wander about by night sucking the blood of persons asleep, causing their death.' The *Century Dictionary* describes a Vampire as: 'A kind of spectral body which, according to a superstition existing among the Slavic and other races on the Lower Danube, leaves the grave during the night and maintains a semblance of life by sucking the warm blood of men and women while they are asleep. Dead wizards, werewolves, heretics and other outcasts become vampires, as do also the illegitimate offspring of parents themselves illegitimate, and anyone killed by a vampire.' According to Horst[1]: 'Ein Vampyr-Gespenst ist eine verstorbene, im Grab fortlebende Person, welche des Nachts aus dem Grab hervorgeht, um den Lebendigen das Blut auszusaugen, wodurch sie ihren in der Erde liegenden Körper im Wachstum und bei vollkommenem Wohlseyn erhält und vor der Verwesung beschützt'. ('A Vampire is a deceased person who continues

[1] G. C. Horst, *Zauber-Bibliothek*, 1821, Erster Theil, S. 252.

to live in the grave; which he leaves, however, by night for the purpose of sucking the blood of the living; he is thereby nourished and maintained in good condition, and is thus preserved from decomposition.')

The two essential characteristics of a true Vampire are thus his origin in a dead person and his habit of sucking blood from a living one, usually with fatal effect. It will be expedient to treat them first separately.

Interest of the living in the dead, whether in the body or in the spirit, is an inexhaustible theme, only a small part of which can be considered here. A continued relation between the living and dead may be regarded in two ways, and each of these from the obverse and reverse. On the one hand it may be desired, and this may result either in the living being drawn to the dead or in the dead being drawn back to the living; on the other hand it may be feared, which may also have the same two effects. In the Ghoul idea a living person visits the body of the dead; the Vampire idea is more elaborate, for here the dead first visits the living and then draws him into death, being re-animated himself in the process.

We shall see that several different emotions—love, guilt and hate—impel towards a belief in the idea of reunion with the dead and in the idea with which we are particularly concerned, that of the return of the dead from the grave. The simplest case of all is where someone longs for the return of a dear lost one, but the greater part of our present problem is taken up with various motives that are supposed to actuate a dead person to return to the living. This latter group is so firmly bound up with the point of view of the corpse that it sometimes needs an effort to remember that they can only represent ideas projected on to him from the minds of the living. In this process, as so commonly with projection, the mechanism of identification is mostly at work; it is as though the living person whose unconscious wishes have been exemplified by the life and conduct of the recently deceased felt that if *he* were dead he would not be able to rest in his grave and would be impelled by various motives to return.

We shall divide into two broad groups the motives urging to re-union, and particularly to return from the grave: they may be called love and hate respectively.

That *Love* should concern itself with the re-union of parted lovers, even when the parting has been brought about by death, is natural enough. The derivatives of this theme, however, prove on examination to be unexpectedly complex. To begin with, the wish for the re-union may be expressed directly on the part of the living or it may be ascribed by projection to the dead. We shall consider first the former of these. The simplest expression of this is the aching longing to meet once more the lost one, a wish commonly gratified in dreams, which reaches its greatest intensity between lovers, married partners or children and parents. Turning from everyday life, we can at once think of various derivatives of this fundamental wish. There are the numerous incantation practices for conjuring up the dead which are to be found in all parts of the world, and again the extensive part this theme plays in mythology, of which we may cite as an example the legend of Orpheus bringing back Eurydice from the underworld. In modern times the wish, or belief, has often assumed a more abstract form, such as, for example, re-union with the departed by means of telepathy or through a medium. Incidentally it is of interest to observe in the present connection that Goerres,[1] in a special chapter on his subject of Christian Mysticism, ascribes Vampirism to occult exteriorization and telepathy.

As has been said, the wish for re-union is often ascribed to the dead by the mechanism of projection. It is then believed that they feel an overpowering impulse to return to the loved ones whom they had left. The deepest source of this projection is doubtless to be found in the wish that those who have departed should not forget us, a wish that ultimately springs from childhood memories

---

[1] J. J. von Goerres, *Die christliche Mystik*, 1836–42.

CH. IV THE VAMPIRE IOI

of being left alone by the loved parent. The belief that
the dead can visit their loved ones, especially by night,
is met with over the whole world.[1] It has always been a
fruitful theme for mythology and literature; one thinks,
for instance, of the various versions of the Lenore legend
or of Goethe's Bride of Corinth—of which Hock[2] has
made the interesting suggestion that it was evoked by
a childhood memory—and of endless other examples, of
which I will quote a short poem by Heine[3]:

> Mir träumte von einem Königskind',
> Mit nassen, blassen Wangen;
> Wir sassen unter der grünen Lind',
> Und hielten uns liebumfangen.
>
> 'Ich will nicht deines Vaters Thron,
> Und nicht sein Zepter von Golde,
> Ich will nicht seine demantene Kron',
> Ich will dich selber, du Holde'.
>
> 'Das kann nicht sein', sprach sie zu mir,
> 'Ich liege ja im Grabe,
> Und nur des Nachts komm' ich zu dir,
> Weil ich so lieb dich habe'.

> (A king's child in my dream I see,
> On her cheeks are her tears' traces.
> We sit under the linden tree
> Locked close in love's embraces.
>
> 'I do not want your father's throne
> Nor his sceptre, his crown or his treasure.
> I want but thee and thee alone,
> For I love thee beyond measure'.
>
> 'That cannot be', she said to me,
> 'For I'm dead and the earth is my cover,
> And but at night I come to thee
> Because I love my lover'.)

[1] Numerous examples are quoted by S. Hock, *Die Vampirsagen und ihre
Verwertung in der deutschen Literatur*, 1900, S. 10 ; and P. L. Jacob, *Curiosités
infernales*, pp. 312-331.　　　　　[2] Hock, *op. cit.* S. 69-81.
[3] Compare Z. Werner: 'Liebe bannt des Todes Not' ('Love banishes the pain
of death'), *Sämtliche Werke*, Bd. viii. S. 164, and F. Hebbel, 'Jeder Tote ist
ein Vampir, die ungeliebten ausgenommen' ('All dead are vampires, except
the unloved ones'), *Tagebücher*, 1887, Bd. ii. S. 73.

‚e evidently have here a reason why Vampires
‚ıways visit relatives first, particularly their married
partners, a feature on which most descriptions dwell.[1]
Widows can become pregnant as the result of such
visits.[2] This happened, for example, in the celebrated
Meduegya epidemic,[3] and the possibility is still believed
in, e.g., in Albania. It was, in fact, the custom in a Vampire epidemic to institute the first enquiries with the
widow of whoever was thought to be the Vampire.[4]
Krauss[5] tells us: 'Es hat sich der Fall schon sehr oft
ereignet, dass bei einem grösseren Sterben im Dorf das
Weib eines kürzlich verstorbenen Mannes von den Dorf-
bewohnern misshandelt wurde, bis sie eingestand, dass
ihr Mann sie besuche und sie das Versprechen gab, sie
werde ihn bestimmen, die Leute nicht zu morden.' ('The
case has often happened that after a number of deaths in
a village the wife of a recently deceased man has been
maltreated until she confessed that her husband was
visiting her and promised to persuade him not to murder
people.') The resemblance to the Incubus belief is striking, even to the detail of the event being believed to
depend on the woman's wishes.

Plainly there must be a reason why the wish for re-
union should here be expressed by the circuitous method
of projection instead of quite simply. The evidence goes
to show that this reason is a sense of guilt on the part of
the living. This also is projected on to the dead. It is believed that certain dead people cannot rest in the grave.
As we shall see, there are several grounds for this, but
we are at the moment concerned only with the one of
sexual guilt. It is felt that because of this the dead person cannot rest in the grave and is impelled to try to
overcome it by the characteristic method of defiantly

[1] Numerous examples are cited by Hock, op. cit. S. 24, 37, 43. See also
J. N. Sepp, Orient und Occident, 1903, S. 268.
[2] J. J. Hanush, 'Die Vampyre', Zeitschrift für deutsche Mythologie und
Sittenkunde, Jahrg. iv. S. 200.
[3] Horst, op. cit. S. 277.
[4] B. Stern, Medizin, Aberglaube und Geschlechtsleben in der Türkei, 1903,
Bd. i. S. 364, 365.
[5] F. S. Krauss, Slavische Volksforschungen, 1908, S. 130.

demonstrating that he can commit the forbidden acts. We are, of course, speaking of an unconscious guiltiness, which, paradoxically enough, is most acute in the presence of what is socially and legally the most permitted love object, the married partner, manifesting itself here in the form of marital unhappiness or even actual impotence. Psycho-analysis has shown unequivocally that this unconscious guiltiness owes its origin to infantile incestuous wishes that have been only imperfectly overcome in the course of development, and we shall presently indicate an interesting feature in the Vampire superstition which confirms this conclusion.

The idea of the dead not being able to rest has become inextricably bound up with the belief that such bodies cannot decompose, and this has played a most important part in the various practices to do with Vampires. It was, and is, firmly held that if the grave in question is opened the presence of a Vampire can be recognized by finding the body in a state of disorder, with red cheeks, tense skin, charged blood-vessels, warm blood, growing hair and nails, and with the left eye open;[1] in the worst cases the grave itself is bespattered with blood, doubtless from the last victim. Some of these features, such as that concerning the hair and nails, are common after death. The others relate to cases of delayed decomposition that occur in various circumstances and which are familiar enough to medical jurisprudence; the causation is a purely medical question into which I do not propose to enter here. Unfortunately the Greek Orthodox Church—it is said in a spirit of opposition to the Roman Catholic pronouncement that the bodies of saints do not decompose—supported the dogma that it is the bodies of wicked, unholy, and especially excommunicated, persons which do not decompose. Just as the Roman Catholic Church taught that heretics could be turned into Werewolves, the Greek Orthodox Church taught that heretics became Vampires after death. It seems probable, however, that the connection between

[1] A. Wuttke, *Der deutsche Volksaberglaube der Gegenwart*, 1900, S. 479.

the ideas of decomposition and innocence is a more
ancient and deeply seated one. Successful decomposition, and the reduction of the corpse to a state of sim-
plicity and purity, signified that the dead person was at
rest in the earth and that his soul was at peace; in psycho-
analytical language, the incestuous re-union with the
Mother Earth is permitted only when purified of sin.
Endless ties bind the relatives to the dead person until
this consummation is achieved, for which the Greek
Church fixed the artificial period of forty days; the best
known are those to do with providing food and drink
for the corpse. Now it is of special interest that not only
was the dead person unable to rest in a guilty state, but
the Earth herself refused to receive him and cast him
forth. Agathias, in his *Historia*, even relates a story
where the dead person himself explained why the earth
had refused to receive his body by admitting that he
had committed incest with his mother. We know that
actual incest is rare enough, but that the wish for it is
the primordial sin from which all others are derived.
[Even to-day in Greece many of the usual imprecations
refer to this belief. The following selection is quoted from
Summers, as also the passage afterwards: 'May the earth
not receive him'; 'May the ground not consume him';
'May the earth not digest thee'; 'May the black earth
spew thee up'; 'Mayest thou remain incorrupt'; 'May the
earth not loose thee'; which is to say may the body not
decompose; 'May the ground reject thee'; 'Mayest thou
become in the grave like rigid wood'; 'May the ground
reject him wholly'. . . . Since even the curse uttered by
a man in moments of anger and impatience may have
such terrible effects, in Greece it is necessary that there
should be some expedient which may dissipate and dis-
pel the forces to which these words have given an im-
petus capable of producing the most serious and horrible results. Accordingly at a Greek death-bed there is
carried out a certain ritual to attain this end. A vessel
of water is brought to the bedside and he throws into it
a handful of salt, and when this is dissolved the sick man

sprinkles with the lymph all those who are present, saying: 'As this salt dissolves so may my curses dissolve.'
This ceremony absolves all persons whom he may have
cursed in his lifetime from the evil of a ban which after
death he would no longer be able to revoke.]

Guilty sexual wishes are not the only ones that are
projected on to the dead, nor are they the only reason
for the supposed unrest in the grave. We shall therefore
have to return to this important theme later to gain a
more complete picture of it after dealing with the other
reasons for the unrest. Before doing this, however, we
have to consider some further derivatives of the wish
for re-union based on love.

In contrast with the wish for re-union with the dead
there is the equally pronounced dread of such a contin-
gency, and this indeed is much the more familiar of the
two attitudes. The thought of meeting a ghost evokes
apprehension far more readily than curiosity or interest.
As Hock[1] very truly says: 'Allen Menschenrassen gemeinsam ist die Furcht vor ihren Toten.' ('Fear of their
dead is common to all races of mankind.') There has in
consequence been developed a quite extraordinary number of rituals in connection with burial the object of
which is to prevent such possibilities, and many of these
are still employed at the present day.[2] Many of these,
which will be mentioned later, are devised with the
specific prophylactic purpose of preventing the dead
returning in Vampire form.

Now fear of the dead has two deep sources both of
which originate in childhood. The first, with which we
are concerned at present, is derived from love, the second
from hate. As these two emotional attitudes so often
occur together, even in respect of the same person, it is
not always easy to distinguish between the manifestations of them. Love itself does not give rise to fear when
it is free and fully accepted by the ego. It gives rise to

[1] Hock, *op. cit.* S. 1.
[2] M. D. Conway, *Demonology and Devil-Lore*, 1879, vol. i. pp. 52, 53. Hock,
op. cit. S. 1. Wuttke, *op. cit.* S. 480.

fear, however, when it is guilty and repressed: one of the most important of Freud's discoveries was that morbid dread always signifies repressed sexual wishes.[1] Further, we know from psycho-analysis that the replacement of repressed sexuality by fear is a process brought about by the persistence in the unconscious of the unsolved incest conflicts of infancy. This also explains the constant association of sadism and fear in such beliefs, dreams, etc., for the infantile conception of sexuality is always sadistic in nature. Three changes thus take place in the original wish: (1) love reverts to sadism, (2) the event is feared instead of desired, and (3) the individual to whom the wish relates is replaced by an unknown being. Even the idea of Death itself may be used to represent this unknown being: dying is often depicted as an attack by a ruthless person who overpowers one against one's will. The sexual idea itself may or may not appear in the conscious belief or fear; it is often concealed by a general apprehension that the creature may throttle one or do some vaguely dreadful thing to one. We are thus led to a large group of myths and superstitious ideas in which the *revenant* inflicts various injuries, and to a still larger group in which the attack proceeds not necessarily from a *revenant*, but from any kind of evil spirit (*Alp* and *Luren* sagas). The presence of the sadistic feature increases the difficulty of distinguishing the elements of love and hate, of sexuality and hostility; a typical example of this would be the Apollonius-Menippus story which Keats has so beautifully elaborated in his Lamia poem. A further complexity is introduced by the beliefs in which the Vampire-like spirit emanates not from a dead but from a still living person. Stern[2] says, for instance, that the Thessalians, Epirotes and Wallachians still believe in such somnambulists who wander about at night and tear people to pieces with their teeth. The

---

[1] See Ernest Jones, 'The Pathology of Morbid Anxiety', *Journal of Abnormal Psychology*, vol. vi. 1911, pp. 81-106. [Reprinted in my *Papers on Psycho-Analysis*, and also Part I. of the present volume.]

[2] Stern, *op. cit.* S. 360. See also B. Schmidt, *Volksleben der Neugriechen*, 1871, Bd. i. S. 166.

Portuguese Bruxsa may also be mentioned here: Andrée[1] describes her as follows: 'Nachts erhebt sie sich von ihrem Lager und fliegt dann in der Gestalt irgend eines riesigen Nachtvogels weit von der Heimat weg. Die Bruxen halten Zusammenkünfte mit ihren teuflischen Liebhabern, entführen, ängstigen und peinigen die einsamen Wanderer; wenn sie von ihrer nächtlichen Lustfahrt heimkehren, saugen sie den eigenen Kindern das Blut aus.' ('At night she leaves her resting-place and flies far from home in the form of some kind of gigantic night-bird. The Bruxsas keep tryst with their diabolical lovers and seduce, terrify and torment lonely wanderers. On returning from their nocturnal journey of pleasure they suck the blood of their own children.')

The considerations brought forward in previous chapters on the transformation of incestuous *revenants* into animals makes it comprehensible that Vampires may appear in a variety of animal guises.[2] Some of these are specially frequent in different countries: thus female cats in Japan,[3] pigs in Servia,[4] etc. Of especial interest is the widespread belief that the Vampire can appear in the form of a snake, of a butterfly[5] or an owl,[6] for these were originally figurative symbols of departed souls, particularly of the parents. Creatures that fly by night will occupy us in a future chapter, but the theme has a number of connections with the Vampire belief. When, for instance, one has anything to do with the body of a Vampire, one has to take special care to watch whether a butterfly flies away from it; if so, it is important to catch and burn it. As to owls, there is the popular belief that they suck at the udders of cows and the breasts of children, just like a real Vampire.[7] Laistner[8] finds associ-

---

[1] R. Andrée, *Ethnographische Parallelen und Vergleiche*, 1878, S. 87. See also H. B. Schindler, *Aberglauben des Mittelalters*, 1858, S. 30.
[2] Andrée, *op. cit.* S. 80, 89.
[3] D. Brauns, *Japanische Märchen und Sagen*, 1885, S. 397.
[4] Krauss, *op. cit.* S. 128.
[5] F. Kanitz, *Donaubulgarien und der Balkan*, 1875, Bd. i. S. 80.
[6] H. Freimark, *Okkultismus und Sexualität*, S. 326.
[7] L. Laistner, *Das Rätsel der Sphinx*, 1889, Bd. ii. S. 258.
[8] Laistner, *op. cit.* S. 257.

ation between a butterfly and an owl on the one hand and the ghostly bird-like spirit that sucks goats' udders (*Habergeiss*) on the other. Henne am Rhyn[1] even regarded the Roman fly-by-night Strigas as the ancestors of the European Vampires, though it is generally held that they were only to a small extent responsible for the belief in the latter.

So far we have been considering one manifestation of the love *motif*, the wish or the fear that the dead should return to the living. We have next to mention its expression in the idea of the living joining the lost one in death, and in so doing we begin to pass into the realm of the definitely pathological. This *motif* of the living being drawn by his love into death, where the two parted ones are for ever united, occurs in a great number of narratives, dramas and poems as well as in actual beliefs. In the present context it is chiefly found in the form of projection on to the dead person, for the Vampire almost always takes the life of the living person he visits. It is probable, however, that the motive here ascribed to the Vampire originates far more in hate than in love, so that we shall deal with it rather in that connection.

Grief for the loved person, however, explains only a part of the peculiar power of attraction that the idea of death exercises. This is evident from the fact that many feel this power who have never themselves experienced the loss of one dear to them. With some the idea is connected with that of a Beyond, the mysterious land of boundless possibilities where all phantasies are realized and all secrets revealed—that land beside whose wondrous treasures even the highest attainable earthly bliss is without value. Shelley in his 'Adonais' expresses this feeling:

> Life, like a dome of many-coloured glass,
> Stains the white radiance of Eternity,
> Until Death tramples it to fragments.

How much more attractive these possibilities of the future can be to those whose life contains little but misery is shown by the use religions have at all times made of them.

[1] O. Henne am Rhyn, *Der Teufel- und Hexenglaube*, 1892, S. 20.

Apart, however, from the attraction death offers as an escape into the promised happiness of another world, there is reason to think that with many people the act of dying itself exercises a curious fascination, one which psycho-analysis has shown to be closely akin to maso-chism. This is one of the reasons why the combination of the two *motifs* Love and Death have preoccupied poets like Heine, Shelley, Swinburne, Werner, etc., who have been so plunged in suffering.

We have next to mention a still more remarkable per-version of the love-instinct, namely, the wish to die to-gether with the person one loves. With some people, of which the poet Heinrich von Kleist was a notable ex-ample, this longing becomes a veritable passion and the whole of their love is concentrated in the idea. The sources of this wish are, as might perhaps be expected, very complicated, and I propose to say only a little about them here.[1] The clearest of them is the sure feeling of definiteness and permanence that death offers: what one has in death one has for ever. This ardently coveted de-sideratum of all lovers is nowhere more wonderfully expressed than in the numerous passages on the Liebes-tod in Wagner's *Tristan and Isolde*, such as:

'So stürben wir, um ungetrennt,
ewig einig, ohne End',
ohn' Erwachen, ohn' Erbangen,
namenlos in Lieb' umfangen,
ganz uns selbst gegeben,
der Liebe nur zu leben.'

('So should we die
that ne'er again
our souls might suffer
parting's pain,—
that unawakened,
unforbidden,
for reach of name
too deeply hidden,
our beings we might blend
in love without an end.')

[1] For further details see Ernest Jones, 'Zum Problem des gemeinsamen Sterbens', *Zentralblatt für Psychoanalyse*, Jahrg. i. S. 563 *et seq.* [Reprinted in *Essays in Applied Psycho-Analysis*, 1923, ch. ii.]

Psycho-analysis[1] has shown that this feature of insatiability and of insistence on exclusive possession is particularly urgent with those who have not succeeded in emancipating themselves from the infantile desire to make a test case of their first love problem, that of incest with the mother and rivalry with the father. Death, which so often in infancy means little more than departure,[2] can then come to signify simply setting forth with the loved mother away from the disturbing influence of the hated father.

This love *motif* can, however, especially when in a state of repression, regress to an earlier form of sexuality, particularly to the sadistic-masochistic phase of development. It was remarked above that the masochistic side of a personality tends to regard the idea of Death as an aggressive onslaught, and the same is even truer of the idea of a dead person. A dead person who loves will love for ever and will never be weary of giving and receiving caresses. This insatiability of the dead was well described by Heine in his dedication to Dr. Faust; the returning Helena says:

> Du hast mich beschworen aus dem Grab
> Durch deinen Zauberwillen,
> Belebtest mich mit Wollustglut—
> Jetzt kannst du die Glut nicht stillen.
>
> Press deinen Mund an meinen Mund,
> Der Menschen Odem ist göttlich!
> Ich trinke deine Seele aus,
> Die Toten sind unersättlich.
>
> (Thou hast called me from my grave
> By thy bewitching will;
> Made me alive, feel passionate love,
> A passion thou canst never still.
>
> Press thy mouth close to my cold mouth;
> Man's breath is god-like created!
> I drink thy essence, I drink thy soul,
> The dead can never be sated.)

[1] See, for example, J. Sadger, *Heinrich von Kleist: Eine pathographisch-psychologische Studie*, 1910, S. 60 *et seq.*
[2] Sigm. Freud, *Die Traumdeutung*, Dritte Auflage, 1911, S. 184.

On the other hand the dead being allows everything, can offer no resistance, and the relationship has none of the inconvenient consequences that sexuality may bring in its train in life. The phantasy of loving such a being can therefore make a strong appeal to the sadistic side of the sexual instinct. Necrophilia, or love for the dead, occurs in two well-marked forms. The more normal of the two appears to be little more than an extension of the part played by love in mourning, the frantic aversion against accepting the event and parting for ever from the loved being. This form was well known to the ancients, both in fact and in legend. Herodotus narrates several examples of it, including that of the Tyrant Periander who continued to have sexual relations with his wife Melissa after her death. King Herod was said to have slept with the corpse of his wife Marianne for seven years after her death, and similar stories were told of King Waldemar IV[1] and Charlemagne.[2] The theme has been widely exploited in modern literature, *e.g.* in Heinrich von Kleist's *Marquise von O*, Otto Ludwig's *Maria*, Heine's *Beschwörung*, Zacharias Werner's *Kreuzesbrüdern*, Brentano's *Romanzen von Rosenkranz*, Marquis de Sade's *Justine*, and, still more, in his *Juliette*, le Vylars Souvestre's *Le Vampire*, and Baudelaire's *Le Vampire*.

The other, more gruesome, form of necrophilia ranks as perhaps the most extreme imaginable perversion of the love instinct. In it the person obtains gratification with any corpse, not that of a loved object, and he does so either by performing some kind of sexual act on the corpse or, more characteristically, by biting, tearing and devouring its decaying flesh. It evidently signifies a reversion to the most primitive aspects of sadism, both of the oral and anal kind; the latter is indicated by the close association that is often found in the unconscious between the ideas of fæces (or the babies supposed to arise from them) and of any kind of decomposing material, particularly human corpses. In superstition

---

[1] Singer, *Bibliothek des literarischen Vereines*, clxxxv. Sect. xvi.
[2] Conway, *op. cit.* vol. ii. p. 396. H. Steffens, *Novellen*, 1837, Bd. i. S. 19.

necrophilia is more correctly represented by the idea of the Arabian ghoul, but this is in many ways connected with that of the Vampire itself. Vampires are, for instance, commonly believed to devour the bodies of neighbouring corpses before they are driven to seek living flesh, and the person he drags into death then does the same. The admixture of the two ideas of Ghoul and Vampire is well illustrated by an Oriental tale where the being in question is a *revenant*, devours corpses, and sucks the blood of his wife.[1] It is not without significance that the expression 'Vampirism' was (inaccurately) used to describe the two best-known cases of necrophilia in the nineteenth century, namely, 'Le vampyre de Paris' for M. Bertrand[2] and 'Le Vampyre du Muy' for Ardisson.[3]

We divided the motives impelling to re-union with the dead into two, those concerned with Love and with *Hate* respectively, and we have now to turn our attention to the second of these two groups. Though it is at least as important as the other motive, there is less to be said about it for the simple reason that it is far less complex. The mechanism is the same as that of the terrors of childhood, *i.e.* the fear of retaliation for wrong-doing or for wicked thoughts. Someone who has a repressed hatred—not an ordinary, conscious one—is apt to have bad dreams, or even a dread of ghosts, indicating his fear of being appropriately punished by the person to whom he had wished ill. These evil wishes play an enormously important part in the unconscious mind and ultimately emanate from the hostile 'death-wishes' nourished by the child against the disturbing parent or other rival. The guilty conscience resulting from such wishes against those who are otherwise objects of affection naturally brings the thought that if they really died, and the evil wishes were thus fulfilled, they would surely return from the grave to haunt and torture their 'murderer'. It is largely because such wishes are so common in

[1] Gholes, *Histoire des Vampires*, 1820, p. 106.
[2] L. Lunier, 'Examen médico-légal d'un cas de monomanie instinctive: affaire du sergent Bertrand', *Annales médico-psychologiques*, 1849, p. 353.
[3] M. Belletrud et E. Mercier, *L'Affaire Ardisson*, 1903.

the unconscious that the prevailing attitude towards the supernatural is one of fear or even terror. We have here another reason, in addition to the one formerly adduced, why a Vampire is so prone to visit his nearest relatives; in a celebrated case, for instance, that was reported by the Count de Cadreras in 1720, and which led to a Commission of Inquiry being instituted by the Emperor Charles VI, a man returned from the grave after sixteen years and caused the death of his two sons by sucking their blood.

As is intelligible from daily experience, traces are plainly to be found in this set of beliefs of endeavours to shift the sense of guilt arising from repressed hostility. The most typical method is to displace it by projection on to the dead person himself, who is supposed to be unable to rest in peace because of his uneasy conscience. A person who is cursed—see above for examples—is believed to become a Vampire after death, the assumption being that he would not have been cursed had he not been a wicked person, so that the person cursing was fully justified in doing so. That is probably why the most effective curses and bans are those of a person of respect such as a father or godfather, above all those of a priest. In spite of these endeavours, however, the psychological fact remains and must be faced, that the person who dreads the Vampire is the person really afflicted by guilt. There is little doubt that we have here a second motive, and probably much the more important one, for the bond described above between the living and the dead and for the numerous ritualistic performances that are intended to appease the dead and allow of peaceful decomposition. One of the most typical of these is the custom, common in all regions of the world, of lacerating one's body until blood flows copiously. It is often accompanied by shaving of the head (*i.e.* symbolic castration), so that the mourner obviates the need of the dead man to inflict the terrible punishment by doing it himself in a milder manner.

This theme of guiltiness leads us to the perception that the two fundamental motives of love and hate, *i.e.* the sexual and hostile impulses, meet at this nodal point. To put the matter simply, love leads to hate and hate leads to guilt. This reproduces the primordial triangular situation through which every individual has to pass in infancy, typically loving the parent of the opposite sex and hating that of the same sex. In the present context both of these emotional attitudes are projected on to the Vampire, whose sense of guilt is then supposed to impel him to allay it by glutting them in the way we have seen described.

Let us now listen to the popular beliefs on this subject. The common people hold that there are two reasons why a departed spirit is moved to leave the grave and to return to the living, according as he does this voluntarily or involuntarily. In the former case his motives are supposed to be those already considered above: love, hate (desire to avenge an old wrong) or his conscience (desire to complete an unfinished task, to settle an unpaid debt, to right a wrong, etc.). The reasons why a spirit is prevented from resting in peace and forced to wander to and fro against his will may lie in his destiny, in his own misdeeds or in interference on the part of those left behind him. The Roman Catholic Church has elaborated this group into a complete dogma; masses are said for those in purgatory. The involuntary activity of the dead often wins the sympathy of the living, who abstain from all manner of things that might increase his unrest.[1]

All these considerations apply to the Vampire belief itself, for, although someone may become a Vampire after death in a great many different ways,[2] still it is easy to distinguish two groups according as he is responsible for the event or not. Sometimes the two types carry different names. Stern[3] tells us: 'Die Vampire der Dalmatiner sind in zwei Arten eingeteilt, in schuldlose und schuldbeladene. Die eine Art heisst Denac, die andere Orko.' ('In Dalmatia Vampires are divided into two

---

[1] See Wuttke, *op. cit.* S. 481, where a number of examples are given.
[2] Hock, *op. cit.* S. 21-23. Stern, *op. cit.* Bd. i. S. 351-369.
[3] Stern, *op. cit.* Bd. i. S. 360.

kinds, into innocent and guilty. The one is called Denac, the other Orko.') Hock[1] lists a number of sins that may lead to this fate after death; they include working on Sundays, smoking on holy days, and having sexual intercourse with one's grandmother.

There are several causes of Vampirism in the innocent. He may be predestined from birth to this fate by being born on an unlucky day or by coming of a family in which there is an hereditary tendency to Vampirism. These congenital causes, like the doctrine of 'original sin', are, of course, connected with parental sin. A clear example of this is the belief in Greece—one, incidentally, which contradicts the old English rhyme on the same topic—that children born on Christmas Day are doomed to become Vampires in punishment of their mother's sin of being so presumptuous as to conceive on the same day as the Virgin Mary. During their lifetime such children are known as Callicantzaros, and in order, if possible, to obviate further developments it is customary to burn the soles of their feet until the nails are singed and so their claws clipped. The other congenital group concerns such features as red hair, blue eyes, pallid countenance, plentiful hair, and strong and precocious teeth: it is noteworthy that this description exactly corresponds with the popular conception of an over-sexual person, one which runs through a great deal of folklore. Even after death this fate may be brought about by an unclean bird or other animal (particularly dogs and cats) settling on his grave, leaping over his dead body, or creeping under his coffin, acts which are evidently connected with the idea of insufficient respect or care for the dead. The animal here is a symbol in the unconscious of the hating person, so that the custom, still prevalent in the North of England, of at once killing it has its psychological sense, as also is the belief that such an animal will *blind* the next person he caresses after leaving the corpse.

After the diagnosis of Vampirism has been made the treatment prescribed is of a very varied kind. The

[1] Hock, *op. cit.* S. 22.

simplest consists of measures calculated to afford the dead some comfort, rest, or at least a peaceful occupation.[1] More active is the practice of drinking his blood[2] or eating his flesh,[3] one which again shows the reciprocal talion nature of the relationship between dead and living. When matters get so far as this, however, it is customary to take even sterner measures. One begins by driving a stake through the heart, and it is important that this should be done with a single blow, for two or three would restore it to life—a belief to be found in many allied fields of folklore.[4] It is then desirable to strike off the head—again with a single stroke—and to place it between the feet, to boil the heart in oil, and to hack the body to pieces. It is noteworthy how closely these correspond with the punishment meted out, especially in the East, to peculiarly atrocious murderers. The one infallible measure, however, when all else fails, is to burn the corpse utterly and to scatter the ashes under appropriate precautions.

*　　*　　*　　*　　*

We pass now to the second essential attribute of the Vampire, namely *Bloodsucking*. Here we find a great many predecessors of the Vampire proper. In general it may be said that the habit of sucking living blood is throughout connected with ideas of cannibalism on the one hand and the Incubat-Succubat, two facts which alone reveal the sexual origin of the belief. The Assyrian and Babylonian Lilats,[5] the Eastern Palukah,[6] the Finnish Lord of the Underworld,[7] the Bohemian Mora,[8] the German Alp:[9] all suck human blood. The Ludak of the Laplanders appears in the form of a bug and sucks blood through an iron tube.[10] The Malayan Molong, as well as

---

[1] Hock, *op. cit.* S. 27, 28. Stern, *op. cit.* Bd. i. S. 351-369.
[2] W. Mannhardt, *Die praktischen Folgen des Aberglaubens*, 1878, S. 13.
[3] W. J. A. Tettau und J. D. H. Temme, *Volkssagen Ostpreussens*, 1837, S. 275.
[4] E. S. Hartland, *The Legend of Perseus*, 1896, vol. iii. p. 23.
[5] C. Binet-Sanglé, *La Folie de Jésus*, t. ii. 1910, p. 91.
[6] Stern, *op. cit.* Bd. i. S. 359.
[7] M. A. Castren, *Vorlesungen über die finnische Mythologie*, 1853, S. 131.
[8] J. V. Grohmann, *Sagen aus Böhmen und Mähren*, 1864, Bd. i. S. 24.
[9] Laistner, *op. cit.* Bd. i. S. 61.
[10] J. C. Poestion, *Lappländische Märchen*, 1886, S. 132.

the Penangelam of Indo-China, visit women at night
and live on the human blood they suck.[1]

The sexual nature of the act is plainly indicated in the
following examples. Heinrich von Wlislocki,[2] in his researches into Roumanian superstitions, tells us: 'Der
Nosferat saugt nicht nur schlafender Menschen Blut,
sondern stiftet auch als Inkubus-Succuba Unheil. Der
Nosferat ist das totgeborene uneheliche Kind zweier
Leute, die beide ebenfalls uneheliche Kinder sind. Kaum
wird das von solcher Mutter und solchem Vater stam-
mende uneheliche und totgeborene Kind in der Erde
verscharrt, so erwacht es zum Leben, entsteigt seinem
Grabe und kehrt nicht mehr dahin zurück. Als schwarze
Katze, als schwarzer Hund, als Käfer, Schmetterling
oder auch blos als Strohhalm besucht es nachts die Menschen; wenn es männlichen Geschlechts ist: die Frauen;
wenn es weiblichen Geschlechts ist: die Männer. Mit
jungen Leuten treibt es geschlechtliche Vermischung,
bis sie krank werden und an Auszehrung sterben. In
diesem Falle kommt es auch als schöner Jüngling oder
als schönes Mädchen, während die Opfer halb wach
liegen und widerstandlos sich ihm fügen. Oft geschieht
es, dass Weiber von ihnen geschwängert werden und
Kinder gebären, die durch ihre Hässlichkeit und dadurch
erkennbar sind, dass sie am ganzen Leibe Haare haben.
Die werden dann sicher wieder Hexen, gewöhnlich
Moroiu. Der Nosferat erscheint bei Bräutigam und Braut
und macht sie impotent und unfruchtbar.' ('The Nosferat not only sucks the blood of sleeping people, but also
does mischief as an Incubus or Succubus. The Nosferat
is the still-born, illegitimate child of two people who are
similarly illegitimate. It is hardly put under the earth
before it awakes to life and leaves its grave never to
return. It visits people by night in the form of a black
cat, a black dog, a beetle, a butterfly or even a simple
straw. When its sex is male, it visits women; when
female, men. With young people it indulges in sexual

---

[1] R. A. Davenport, *Sketches of Imposture, Deception and Credulity*, 1861,
pp. 73, 75.   [2] Quoted by Stern, *op. cit.* Bd. i. S. 357, 358.

orgies until they get ill and die of exhaustion. In this case it also appears in the form of a handsome youth or a pretty girl, while the victim lies half awake and submits unresistingly. It often happens that women are impregnated by the creature and bear children who can be recognized by their ugliness and by their having hair over the whole body. They then always become witches, usually Moroiu. The Nosferat appears to bridegrooms and brides and makes them impotent and sterile.') The Chaldeans believed in the existence of spirits who had intercourse with mortals in their sleep, devoured their flesh and sucked their blood;[1] a complete Jack the Ripper phantasy. The Vedic Gandharvas are bloodthirsty lewd demons who visit women in their sleep.[2] Similar to them are the Indian Pisâchas, who lust after flesh and indulge their cruel pleasure on women when these are asleep, drunk or insane.[3] Other beings of the same kind devote their attention rather to men; thus the Ruthenian Upierzyca when the moon is full seeks youths in their bed[4] and consumes them in kisses and embraces.[5] Freimark[6] writes: 'Die griechisch-römischen Lamien sind zugleich Buhlteufelinnen und Vampire. Sie suchen schöne, kräftige Jünglinge in sich verliebt zu machen und zur Verehelichung mit sich zu bringen. Haben sie sie so weit, so töten sie den Jüngling, indem sie ihm das Blut aussaugen.' ('The Greek and Roman Lamias are at the same time lewd demons and Vampires. They try to get handsome strong youths to fall in love with them and to marry them. Having succeeded in this, they kill them by sucking their blood.') Finally, one may remark that the present-day use of the word, particularly current since the War, speaks in the same direction: a film Vampire is a beautiful woman who uses her sexual charms for anal-sadistic purposes.

[1] J. Menant, Ninive et Babylone, p. 271.
[2] E. W. A. Kuhn, Zeitschrift für vergleichende Sprachforschung, Jahrg. xiii. S. 118.
[3] A. W. von Schlegel, Indische Bibliothek, 1823, Bd. i. S. 87.
[4] Just like the Montenegrin Vampires, Stern, op. cit. Bd. i. S. 361.
[5] F. von Hellwald, Die Welt der Slaven, Zweite Auflage, 1890, S. 367.
[6] Freimark, op. cit. S. 278, 279.

Blood is not the only vital fluid extracted from the victim, though the Vampire proper generally confines himself to it. The German *Alp* sucks the nipples of men[1] and children,[2] and withdraws milk from women[3] and cows[4] more often than blood. The Drud also sucks the breasts of children,[5] while the Southern Slav Mora sucks blood or milk indifferently.[6] In India, the Churel, after spending a night with a handsome young man sucks his very 'life' out.[7]

The explanation of these phantasies is surely not hard. A nightly visit from a beautiful or frightful being, who first exhausts the sleeper with passionate embraces and then withdraws from him a vital fluid: all this can point only to a natural and common process, namely to nocturnal emissions accompanied with dreams of a more or less erotic nature. In the unconscious mind blood is commonly an equivalent for semen, and it is not necessary to have recourse, as Hock[8] does, to the possibility of 'selbst zugefügten Kratzwunden während eines wollüstigen Traumes' ('wounds inflicted on oneself by scratching during a voluptuous dream').

Many myths and legends afford strongly confirmatory evidence of this conclusion. To begin with, the Accadian Gelal and Kiel Galal, the Assyrian Sil and Sileth, who are equivalent to the European Incubus and Succubus, are demons whose special function it was to bring about nocturnal emissions by nocturnal embraces.[9] According to Quedenfeldt,[10] south of the Atlas mountains there prevails the belief that there are old negresses who at night suck blood from the *toes* of those asleep. The Armenian mountain spirit Dachnavar similarly sucks blood from

[1] Grohmann, *loc. cit.*
[2] H. Ploss, *Das Kind im Brauch und Sitte der Völker*, 1884, Bd. i. S. 298.
[3] Laistner, *loc. cit.*   [4] Laistner, *op. cit.* Bd. ii. S. 82.
[5] F. X. von Schönwerth, *Aus der Oberpfalz—Sitten und Sagen*, 1858, Bd. i. S. 201, 211.
[6] Krauss, *op. cit.* S. 147, 148.
[7] Compare Laurence Hope's poem 'Lalla Radha and the Churel' in *Stars of the Desert*, 1909.
[8] Hock, *op. cit.* S. 5.
[9] F. Lenormant, *Chaldean Magic*, English translation, 1877, p. 38.
[10] M. Quedenfeldt, cited by Stern, *op. cit.* Bd. i. S. 359.

the *feet* of wanderers,[1] while Meyer[2] mentions ghostly mothers who suck out the *eyes* of their children. As is well known,[3] toes, feet and eyes are in folklore and mythology, as well as in dreams and psychoneurotic symptoms, frequently recurring phallic symbols. The nervous system, particularly the spinal cord, often has the same symbolic meaning as blood (vital substance), which is the reason why sufferers from excessive nocturnal emissions so often develop the dread of softening of the spine with paralysis. The Roman Strigas, for instance, used to suck, not only the blood of children, but also their spinal marrow.[4] The idea that moral delinquency, essentially masturbation, leads to weakness of the spine is extremely widespread. On the first page of Zschokke's *Die Zauberin Sidonia*, written in 1798, there occurs the following line: 'Die Faulheit saugt uns mit ihrem Vampyrenrüssel Mark und Blut ab' ('Laziness with its vampire snout sucks away our marrow and blood'). This may be compared with Jaromir's speech in Grillparzer's *Ahnfrau*:

> Und die Angst mit Vampirrüssel
> Saugt das Blut aus meinen Adern,
> Aus dem Kopfe das Gehirn.

('And terror, with its vampire snout, sucks the blood from out my veins, the brain from out my head'.)

It is evident that in the Vampire superstition proper the simple idea of the vital fluid being withdrawn through an exhausting love embrace is complicated by more perverse forms of sexuality, as well as by the admixture of sadism and hate. When the more normal aspects of sexuality are in a state of repression there is always a tendency to regress towards less developed forms. Sadism is one of the chief of these, and it is the earliest form of this—known as oral sadism—that plays such an important part in the Vampire belief. The still

---

[1] A. von Haxthausen, *Transkaukasien*, 1856, Bd. i. S. 170.
[2] E. H. Meyer, *Indogermanische Mythen*, 1883, Bd. ii. S. 528.
[3] See Aigremont, *Fuss- und Schuh-Symbolik und -Erotik*, 1909; and S. Seligmann, *Der böse Blick und Verwandtes*, 1910.
[4] G. Roskoff, *Geschichte des Teufels*, 1869, Bd. i. S. 147.

earlier stage, the simple sucking that precedes biting, is
more connected with the love side we have discussed
earlier, the sadism more with the element of hate. The
act of sucking has a sexual significance from earliest
infancy[1] which is maintained throughout life in the form
of kissing; in certain perversions it can actually replace
the vagina itself.

From the earliest times myths and legends about
Vampires have existed in Europe; a typical example is
the Wallachian belief that red-haired men appear after
death in the form of frogs, beetles, etc., and drink the
blood of beautiful girls.[2] Further, there have come down
to us from the earliest Middle Ages reports of the custom
—existing in most European countries—of digging up,
piercing with a stake or burning the corpse of those
spirits who torment the living and suck their blood.[3] As
has already been pointed out, this belief is spread over
the whole world: for example, the modern Pontianaks of
Java, who emanate from corpses, have the habit of sucking blood,[4] and the Assyrian Vampire, called Akakharu,
has on the other hand the most ancient lineage.[5] Our
fullest knowledge of the belief in Europe, however, we
owe to the Balkan peninsula, where it has evidently
been greatly influenced by Turkish superstitions.[6] In
England we have several complete and typical accounts
related by William of Newburgh[7] in the twelfth century,
but since that date hardly a trace of the belief is to be
found. In ancient Ireland the Vampire, under the name
of the Dearg-dul, 'red blood-sucker', played a considerable part among popular dreads, but he likewise seems
to have vanished at an early date.

The epidemics of Vampirism, which had been frequent
enough before, reached their highest point in the south-

---

[1] Sigm. Freud, *Drei Abhandlungen zur Sexualtheorie*, Zweite Auflage, 1910,
S. 40. [*Gesammelte Schriften*, Bd. v. S. 54.]
[2] Andrée, *op. cit.* S. 87.
[3] Hock, *op. cit.* S. 30-34.   [4] Davenport, *op. cit.* p. 72.
[5] Conway, *loc. cit.*
[6] Krauss, *op. cit.* S. 124.
[7] William of Newburgh, *Historia Rerum Anglicarum*, Book V. ch. xxii.-
xxiv.

east of Europe during the eighteenth century[1] and lasted
well on into the nineteenth.[2] The most alarming took
place in Chios in 1708,[3] in Hungary in 1726,[4] in Meduegya
and Belgrade in 1725 and 1732,[5] in Servia in 1825,[6] and
in Hungary in 1832.[7] In the year 1732 there appeared in
Germany alone some fourteen books on the subject,[8]
which evoked general horror and drew wide attention
to the problem. It did not escape Voltaire's satire, who
in his discussion of it in his *Dictionnaire philosophique*
wrote: 'La difficulté était de savoir si c'était l'âme ou le
corps du mort qui mangeait: il fut décidé que c'était
l'un et l'autre; les mets délicats et peu substantiels,
comme les meringues, la crème fouettée et les fruits
fondants, étaient pour l'âme; les ros-bif étaient pour le
corps.' We are not concerned here with the actual causes
of these fatal epidemics, which is a purely medical problem. Hock[9] remarks that they occurred chiefly when
plague was rife, and it is certain that the association of
stench is common to the two ideas. Bearing in mind the
anal-erotic origin of necrophilia, commented on above,
we are not surprised to observe what stress many writers
on the subject lay on the horrible stink that invests the
Vampire. One example of this will suffice: Allacci[10] describes a Greek Vampire called the Burculacas, 'than
whom no plague more terrible or more harmful to man
can well be thought of or conceived. This name is given
him from vile filth. For βοῦρκα means bad black mud,
not any kind of mud but feculent muck that is slimy and
oozing with excrementitious sewerage so that it exhales
a most noisome stench. λάκκος is a ditch or a cloaca in

[1] See especially A. Calmet, *Dissertation sur les apparitions des anges, des démons et des esprits, et sur les revenants et vampires de Hongrie, de Bohème, de Moravie, et de Silésie*, 1746.
[2] Compare *Gartenlaube*, 1873, Nr. 34, 'Der Vampir-Schrecken im neunzehnten Jahrhundert'.
[3] Sepp, *op. cit.* S. 269.   [4] Sepp, *loc. cit.*
[5] Horst, *op. cit.* Erster Teil, S. 251; Fünfter Teil, S. 381. This is the epidemic that has been most often described.
[6] Sepp, *op. cit.* S. 270.   [7] Sepp, *loc. cit.*
[8] Horst, *op. cit.* Erster Teil, S. 265, 266; Fünfter Teil, S. 383.
[9] Hock, *op. cit.* S. 31, 49.
[10] L. Allacci, *De quorundam Graecorum opinationibus*, 1645, p. 142.

which foulness of this kind collects and reeks amain.'
Plagues, in their turn, have always been associated in
the popular—and to some extent in the medical—mind
with the notion of stench, particularly from decomposing sewage. The Vampire of Alnwick Castle, whose story
is narrated by William of Newburgh,[1] was actually believed to have caused an extensive plague through the
evil odours he spread, and it ceased when his corpse was
adequately dealt with. The association of ideas explicit
in this story was doubtless implicit on countless other
occasions. In the Middle Ages there was a close correlation between visitations of the Black Death and out-
breaks of Vampirism, and even as late as 1855 the
terrible cholera epidemic in Dantsic revived such a widespread belief in the dead returning as Vampires to claim
the living that, according to medical opinion, the fears
of the people greatly increased the mortality from the
disease.

The Vampire superstition is still far from dead in
many parts of Europe. In Norway, Sweden and Finland
it lasted until quite recently.[2] Krauss[3] reports that at
the present day the peasants in Bosnia believe in the
existence of Vampires as firmly as in that of God, and
the same is hardly less true of the Servian peasant.[4] The
belief is still rife in Greece, and Lawson[5] in 1910 says:
'Even now a year seldom passes in which some village of
Greece does not disembarrass itself of a *vrykolakas* by
the traditional means, cremation.' In Bulgaria in 1837 a
stranger, suspected of being a Vampire, was tortured
and burned alive.[6] In 1874, in Rhode Island, U.S.A., a
man exhumed the body of his own daughter and burned
her heart in the belief that she was endangering the life
of other members of the family, and about the same
time in Chicago the body of a woman who had died of

[1] *Ibid.*
[2] O. von Hovorka und A. Kronfeld, *Vergleichende Volksmedizin*, 1908, Bd. ii.
S. 425.   [3] Krauss, *op. cit.* S. 124.
[4] *Idem.* 'Vampyre im südslavischen Volksglauben', *Globus*, 1892, Bd. lxi.
S. 326.
[5] J. C. Lawson, *Modern Greek Folk Lore and Ancient Greek Religion*, 1910,
P. 374.   [6] Stern, *op. cit.* Bd. i. S. 362.

consumption was dug up and the lungs burned for the same reason.[1] In 1889 in Russia the corpse of an old man, suspected of being a Vampire, was dug up, at which many of those present stoutly maintained they saw a tail attached to his back.[2] In 1899 Roumanian peasants in Krassowa dug up no fewer than thirty corpses and tore them to pieces with the object of stopping an epidemic of diphtheria.[3] Two further instances occurred as recently as 1902, one in Hungary,[4] one in Bucharest,[5] and in 1909 a castle in South Transylvania was burned by the populace, who believed that a Vampire emanating from it was the cause of a sudden· increase in the mortality of their children.[6] In 1912 a farmer in Hungary who had suffered from ghostly visitations went to the cemetery one night, stuffed three pieces of garlic—note the homeopathic smell factor in the treatment—and three stones into the mouth, and fixed the corpse to the ground by thrusting a stake through it in the approved fashion.[7]

The word 'Vampire' itself, introduced into general European use towards the end of the first third of the eighteenth century, is a Southern Slav word. Its derivation has been much disputed, but the greatest authority, Miklosich,[8] considers the most likely one to be the North Turkish *uber*, a witch. The other Slavonic variants are: Bulgarian and Servian, *vapir*; Polish, *upier;* Russian, *vopyr*. The word has acquired various secondary meanings which are not without interest as showing what significations the conception has for the popular mind. The earliest extension—first made by Buffon[9]—was to designate certain bats which were thought to attack animals and even human beings in sleep. The old idea of a baleful night-flight is plain here. The two chief meta-

[1] Conway, *op. cit.* p. 52.
[2] A. A. Löwenstimm, *Aberglaube und Strafrecht*, Deutsche Übersetz., 1897, S. 101.   [3] *Neue Freie Presse*, Nov. 8, 1899.
[4] Stern, *op. cit.* Bd. i. S. 370.   [5] *Ibid.*
[6] *Neues Wiener Journal*, June 10, 1909.
[7] *Daily Telegraph*, February 15, 1912.
[8] F. Miklosich, *Etymologisches Wörterbuch der slavischen Sprachen*, 1886, S. 374.
[9] G. L. le Clerc de Buffon, *Hist. natur. gén. et part.*, 1762, t. x. p. 55.

phorical connotations of the word are: (1) a social or
political tyrant who sucks the life from his people;[1] this
was used in English as early as 1741;[2] (2) an irresistible
lover who sucks away energy, ambition or even life for
selfish reasons; the latter may be of either sex, either
male, as in Torresani's fascinating cavalry captain,[3] or
female, as in Kipling's Vampire poem and in the daily
speech of Hollywood.

The Vampire superstition is evidently closely allied
to that of the *Incubus* and *Succubus*. Freimark[4] writes:
'Denn man kann, wenn auch nicht als Regel, so doch
in den meisten überlieferten Fällen konstatieren, dass
Frauen stets von einem männlichen, Männer hingegen von
einem weiblichen Vampir heimgesucht werden. . . . Das
sexuelle Moment charakterisiert den Vampirglauben als
eine andere, allerdings gefährlichere Form des Inkubus-
und Sukkubusglaubens.' ('Though it is not an absolute
rule, still it can be observed that in most cases women
are constantly visited by male Vampires, and men by
female ones. . . . The sexual features characterize the
Vampire belief as another form of the Incubus-Succubus
belief—it is true, a more dangerous one.') Zimmermann[5]
and Laurent and Nagour[6] are of the same opinion, and
this is convincingly confirmed by our newly gained
knowledge of the symbolism of such processes. Just as
Incubi suck out vital fluids and thus exhaust the victim
(see above), so do Vampires often lie on the breast and
induce suffocation. The Hebrew Lilith, whom Johannes
Weyer called the princess who presided over the Succubi,
came from the Babylonian Lilîtu, who was definitely a
Vampire; incidentally, the name is now thought to be
derived from *lulti*, 'lasciviousness', and not, as the Rabbis
used to maintain, from the Hebrew Laîlah, 'night'. The

---

[1] See Hock for examples, *op. cit.* S. 56, 57, 61.
[2] C. Forman, *Observations on the Revolution in* 1688, 1741, p. 11.
[3] C. Torresani, *Aus der schönen, wilden Leutnantzeit*, 1894, Bd. ii. S. 141.
[4] Freimark, *op. cit.* S. 331, 332.
[5] Zimmermann, *Die Wonne des Leids*, 1885, S. 113.
[6] Laurent und Nagour, *op. cit.* S. 146.

similarity with the *Alp* belief, which in the popular mind takes the place of that in Incubi, is even more striking; just like the Vampire, the *Alp*, as also the *Mara*, is often the spirit of the recently deceased,[1] and can suck blood during sleep, with the same fatal consequences.[2] Among the Southern Slavs it is believed that when a Mara (there called Mora) once tastes a man's blood she falls in love with him and can never more leave him, plaguing him night after night; she is particularly found of sucking children's breasts, which then exude a thin fluid.[3] The most extensive connection, however, is that subsisting in the details of the two beliefs, particularly those concerning the causes and cure of the evil impulse that moves them to their ruthless deeds. By this I mean such details as the idea that both *Alp* and Vampire sometimes act on their own initiative, sometimes are compelled against their will—the reasons being identical in the two cases; both attack wanderers who answer their questions, or who ask them where they come from, etc., etc. The methods of releasing those condemned by spells are again similar, but to discuss these would be to embark on the complicated, though fascinating, theme of 'release' in folklore, and unfortunately that would take us too far from our topic: it must suffice here to say that of the long list of methods collected by Wuttke[4] by means of which returning or wandering souls, *i.e.* those prone to be Vampires, may be 'released' (or 'saved') the majority are identical with those efficacious in the 'release' of the *Alp* from his condition; Laistner,[5] for example, explains the belief mentioned above that the illegitimate children of illegitimate parents become Vampires as a variant of the 'releasing' *motif*, for when an illegitimate *Mara* begets an illegitimate child she is herself 'released'. Further, the idea of travelling or flying by night is an important point of connection between the Vampire belief and the numerous

---

[1] Laistner, *op. cit.* Bd. i. S. 63.   [2] Laistner, *op. cit.* Bd. i. S. 61.
[3] Krauss, *op. cit.* S. 148.   [4] Wuttke, *op. cit.* S. 480-481.
[5] Laistner, *op. cit.* Bd. i. S. 273.

Alp and *Mahre* myths in which it occurs; for instance, that of the Roman Striga or the Montenegrin Wjeschti- tza, 'ein weiblicher Geist mit feurigen Flügeln, der den Schlafenden auf die Brust steigt, sie mit ihren Um- armungen erstickt oder wahnsinnig macht' ('a female spirit with fiery wings who mounts on to the breast of sleepers and stifles them with her embraces or drives them mad').[1]

The incest complex, which underlies the Incubus belief, shows itself equally in the Vampire one. We have shown above that the whole superstition is shot through with the theme of guilt, and we know from psycho- analysis that this is not only generated in the incest conflicts of infancy, but throughout life depends on them. The very fact that the Vampire is a *revenant* is decisive here, for we have already traced this conception to the in- cest complex. The appearance of the Vampire in animal form, particularly in that of a butterfly or snake[2]—two of the commonest Oriental representatives of the father, is one of the many characteristic features of this origin, as again is the fact that his activities are altogether characterized by every possible infantile perversion.

We have finally to discuss the connections between the Vampire superstition and the experiences of anxiety dreams, particularly the Nightmare. Wundt[3] says on this point: 'Als nächtliche Spuksgestalt, die den Schläfer um- klammert, um ihm das Blut auszusaugen, ist er sichtlich ein Produkt des Alptraumes.' ('As a nocturnal spirit who embraces a sleeper to suck his blood from him, he is evidently a product of the Nightmare.') He adds, how- ever, with justice that the idea of a spirit keeping alive by drinking blood comes from other and more general sources. Hock[4] distinguishes between the true blood- sucking Vampire and the hungry dead that tears his shroud and so draws his family to him merely through sympathy: 'Hat jene Tradition in der Traumvorstellung

[1] Stern, *op. cit.* Bd. i. S. 356.   [2] Krauss, *op. cit.* S. 129.
[3] W. Wundt, *Völkerpsychologie*, Bd. ii. Teil ii. 1906, S. 120.
[4] Hock, *op. cit.* S. 23.

ihre sichere Grundlage, so sind die Sagen von den "schmatzenden und kauenden" Toten offenbar im Hinblick auf tatsächlich erlebte Ereignisse nach dem entsetzlichen Vorbilde eines im Grabe zu spät erwachten Scheintoten gebildet.' ('The former tradition is firmly based on dream ideas, but the legends of the dead person "smacking his lips and chewing" are evidently constructed from actual experiences of people who awakened too late from a death-like trance.')

While Hock admits that the idea of the Vampire proper is derived from dream life, he adduces the experience of finding people buried alive to explain one minor type of the species. Other writers, on the other hand, have used the dread of this experience to solve the whole riddle of the Vampire; this explanation is usually ascribed to Mayo,[1] though Weitenkampf[2] had already proffered it early in the eighteenth century. Medical opinion on the point would certainly be that the occurrence is too rare—at all events when established with surety—to account for any such widely held belief, but I mention the idea at this point because it gives me the opportunity of saying something about the respective parts played by phantasy and reality in the forming of superstitious beliefs. Oddly enough, this is the only psychological explanation of the Vampire superstition that has ever been put forward; other explanations have mostly regarded the belief as a true one and have merely tried to show why it is true. This paucity of psychological explanation in itself shows that essential factors must have been overlooked hitherto, and it is hoped that the present study will contribute something to our understanding of them. There are two other facts of reality that have also been adduced to explain, or rather to justify, the Vampire belief: they are the occurrence of epidemic mortality, especially in association with the idea of foul smell, and the fact that in various circum-

[1] H. Mayo, *On the Truths contained in Popular Superstitions*, 1851, p. 30.
[2] Weitenkampf, *Gedanken über wichtige Wahrheiten aus der Vernunft und Religion*, 1735, Theil i. S. 108 *et seq.*

stances decomposition after death can be very much delayed. Now a general popular tendency may readily be remarked to rationalize all superstitions by explaining them in terms of reality, though the slightest investigation shows that such explanations always leave the essentials unexplained. For instance, to say that the notion of its being unlucky to walk under a ladder simply proceeds from the observation that something may be dropped on to one so doing neither accounts for the distribution of the fear—for it cannot be supposed that only those who have the fear are the only people who have made this observation; on the contrary, it is more often quoted by those who are free from the fear—nor for the demonstrable association between this fear and that of passing through holes in general. And in the present case the three facts just mentioned—burial alive, epidemic mortality and delayed decomposition—in no way in themselves explain why a dead body should change into an animal, fly through the air and commit sexual excesses with sleeping people. Other factors must obviously be at work, and these we maintain are the essential ones. Psycho-analysis, both of superstitious beliefs—general or individual—and of other similar mental processes, shows that the essential factors are much more dynamic than mere observation of external phenomena. The unconscious tendencies at work in the construction of these beliefs simply fortify and justify them by any rationalistic means they can seize on. It is the capacity for immediate and intuitive insight into this way in which the mind functions that distinguishes a psychological mentality from others.

The motives of love and hate discussed at length in this chapter show what extremely complex and what fundamental emotions are at work in the construction and maintenance of the Vampire superstition. It is one more product of the deepest conflicts that determine human development and fate—those concerned with the earliest relationships to the parents. These come to their intensest expression in anxiety dreams, and in the present set of beliefs there is a number of features that point unequivocally to the conclusion that the terrible experiences there must have played an important part in moulding the beliefs in question. Such are: the occurrence of the supposed events during sleep, the evident relation of the events to nocturnal emissions resulting from sexual—particularly perversely sexual—experiences, the Vampire's capacity for transformation, his flight by night, his appearance in animal form and, finally, the connection between the belief and that in the return of dead relatives. The belief is, in fact, only an elaboration of that in the Incubus, and the essential elements of both are the same—repressed desires and hatreds derived from early incest conflicts. The main differences are that hate and guilt play a far larger part in the Vampire than in the Incubus belief, where the emotions are almost purely those of desire and fear.

[Since this chapter was written two works on the subject have appeared in English. One, *Vampires and Vampirism*, by Dudley Wright, is a popular account of the matter; the other, two volumes entitled *The Vampire, His Kith and Kin*, and *The Vampire in Europe*, by Montague Summers, is a learned, though not comprehensive, study which unfortunately is written from the point of view of occultism and so contributes nothing directly to the psychology of the belief.]

CHAPTER V

THE WEREWOLF

THE conception of the Werewolf is one of the most developed examples of the belief in the transformation of men into animals, the sources of which were considered in the first chapter of this book. The other most important elements in this superstition are flight by night and cannibalism.

The wolf belongs to the group of savage animals which have been extensively employed in mythology and folklore for the portrayal of cruel and sadistic phantasies. To the same class as Werewolves belong the men-hyenas of Abyssinia,[1] the men-leopards of South Africa,[2] the men-tigers of Hindustan,[3] the men-bears of Scandinavia,[4] in whose existence, according to Mogk,[5] the Norwegian peasants still believe.

The allegorical significance of the wolf is easy to recognize. Hertz[6] writes: 'Betrachten wir nun speziell den Wolf, so erscheint er,—das unersättlich mordgierige, bei Nacht und zur Winterszeit besonders gefährliche Raubtier,—als das natürliche Symbol der Nacht, des Winters und des Todes. . . . Der Wolf ist aber nicht allein das raubgierigste, er ist auch das schnellste, rüstigste unserer grösseren vierfüssigen Tiere. Diese seine Rüstigkeit, seine wilde Kühnheit, seine grausame Kampf- und Blutgier verbunden mit seinem Hunger nach Leichenfleisch und seinen dadurch angeregten nächtlichen Besuchen der Totenfelder und Walstätten macht den Wolf zum Begleiter und Gefolgmann des Schlachtengottes.' ('If we now consider the wolf in particular, that insatiably

---

[1] *The Life and Adventures of Nathaniel Pierce*, edited by Halls, 1831, vol. i. p. 287.
[2] Marian Roalfe Cox, *An Introduction to Folklore*, 1904, p. 127.
[3] Ed. Clodd, *Myths and Dreams*, 1891, p. 85. Marian Roalfe Cox, *loc. cit.*
[4] Clodd, *loc. cit.* Marian Roalfe Cox, *loc. cit.*
[5] E. Mogk, *Germanische Mythologie*, 1906, S. 34.
[6] W. Hertz, *Der Werwolf, Beitrag zur Sagengeschichte*, 1862, S. 14, 15.

murderous beast of prey, especially dangerous at night and in winter, he would appear to be the natural symbol of *night*, of *winter* and of *death*. . . . But the wolf is not only the most bloodthirsty, he is also the swiftest and lustiest of our larger quadrupeds. This hardiness, his fierce boldness, his cruel lust for fight and blood, together with his hunger for the flesh of corpses which makes him a night visitor of battlefields, make the wolf the companion of the God of Battles.')

The most prominent attributes which we may expect to have been used for the purposes of symbolism are thus swiftness of movement, insatiable lust for blood, cruelty, a way of attacking characterized by a combination of boldness and cunning craftiness, and further the associations with the ideas of night, death and corpse. As is easy to see, the savage and uncanny features characteristic of the wolf have made him specially suited to represent the dangerous and immoral side of nature in general and of human nature in particular. These features explain why the wolf has played a considerable part in different theologies. In Egypt the wolf was a sacred animal, and Osiris himself appeared in a wolf's shape when he returned from the dead to urge and help Horus take revenge on Set.[1] Two towns were named after the wolf, one in upper Egypt and one in lower Egypt. The wolf-god, Ap-uat, acted as a psychopomp, thus again illustrating the connection between the ideas of wolf and death, and opened the way to the gates of bliss,[2] a belief which psycho-analysts would associate with the infantile sadistic conception of coitus. In early times there were cannibalistic sacrifices to Ap-uat,[3] and in the Twelfth Dynasty he appears to have been regarded as the son of Osiris who defended him and walked in front of him at the ceremonial processions.[4]

In Teutonic mythology the two wolves, Freki and

[1] Diodor. Sic. *Biblioth.* i. 88.
[2] E. A. Wallis Budge, *Osiris and the Egyptian Resurrection*, 1911, vol. ii. pp. 159, 316.
[3] Wallis Budge, *op. cit.* vol. i. p. 197.
[4] *Idem, op. cit.* vol. ii. p. 5.

Geri, were the companions of Odin,[1] although Grimm's view that they could represent the god himself appears to be doubtful.[2] The wolf Fenrir, the offspring of Loki and brother of Hel, the goddess of death, plays a central part in numerous myths.[3] Still better known is the story of Sigmund's and Sinfjötli's lives as werewolves, as narrated in the Völsunga Saga,[4] where also the mother of King Siggeir masquerades as a She-wolf.[5] St. Patrick is said to have changed Vereticus, King of Wales, into a wolf.[6] In America also the wolf is a sacred animal, as is shown by the religious wolf-dances of the Tonkanays in Texas;[7] the Ahts believe that men who go into the mountains to seek their manitou are after a time changed into wolves. The Nez Perces tribe in America believe that the whole human race is descended from a wolf.[8]

In Greece the wolf was sacred to the Sun God, who appeared in the form of a wolf as he slew the Telchines of Rhodes.[9] It has been keenly debated whether the title of the Lycaean Zeus was derived from λύκος (= wolf) or from λύκη (= light). Although many of the highest authorities have held the former view, the latest opinion would appear to favour the latter.[10] Nevertheless there is no question but that the wolf cult was closely associated, through sacrifices, lycanthropic beliefs, etc., with the Lycaean Zeus, and Sir James Frazer[11] pertinently says: 'The connexion of Lycaean Zeus with wolves is too firmly established to allow us seriously to doubt that he is the wolf-god.'

To the same confusion of words mentioned above has been ascribed also the oldest Werewolf legend that has

[1] A. Wuttke, *Der deutsche Volksaberglaube der Gegenwart*, Dritte Ausgabe, 1900, S. 279.
[2] W. Mannhardt, *Roggenwolf und Roggenhund*, 1865, S. 50.
[3] B. Thorpe, *Northern Mythology*, 1851, vol. i. pp. 49-52.
[4] *Völsunga Saga*, translated by E. Magnússon and W. Morris, 1870 edition, p. 20.
[5] *Ibid.* p. 14.
[6] S. Baring-Gould, *The Book of Were-Wolves*, 1865, p. 58.
[7] H. R. Schoolcraft, cited by Clodd, *op. cit.* p. 92.
[8] M. D. Conway, *Demonology and Devil-Lore*, 1879, vol. i. p. 141.
[9] Hertz, *op. cit.* pp. 31-33.
[10] A. B. Cook, *Zeus*, 1914, vol. i. pp. 63, 64.
[11] J. G. Frazer, *Pausanias*, vol. iv. p. 386.

come down to us, namely, the well-known one of Lycaon, of which different versions have been related by Apollodor, Eratosthenes, Hyginus, Lycophron, Ovid and Pausanias; in this connection it is of interest to note that the Werewolf belief has persisted in Greece into modern times.[1] Some writers have even derived the whole subsequent Werewolf superstition to this. Fiske[2] mildly comments on this view: 'To suppose that Jean Grenier imagined himself to be a wolf, because the Greek word for wolf sounded like the word for light, and thus gave rise to the story of a light-deity who became a wolf, seems to me quite inadmissible.' One may add that it is typical of the conclusions reached when psychology is neglected in mythological studies. As elsewhere with mental processes, a superficial association here probably covers an inner connection of ideas. Two such connections between the ideas of wolf and light or sun may be briefly mentioned; they both belong to the strong forces operative in creation. Swiftness of movement—a prominent attribute of the wolf—is in mythology often brought into connection with fruitfulness on the one hand and wind and sun on the other. The idea of the ceaseless movement of the sun is one of the reasons for its frequent association with the horse in Indian, Greek and Teutonic mythology, a topic which is dealt with at length in Part III of this book. The association of fertility with the swift wind is similarly widespread;[3] we need merely point to the Greek and Roman beliefs that the west wind can impregnate horses[4] and women, a belief which survived until recently in Portugal,[5] and further to the German custom of sowing when the west wind blows.[6] This is perhaps the reason why it was over the

---

[1] J. C. Lawson, *Modern Greek Folklore and Ancient Greek Religion*, 1910, p. 240.
[2] J. Fiske, *Myths and Myth-Makers*, 1872, p. 88.
[3] [The reader is referred to a study of this association in the author's *Essays in Applied Psycho-Analysis*, 1923, pp. 275-282.]
[4] E. S. Hartland, *Primitive Paternity*, 1909, vol. i. pp. 22, 35, 149, 150. M. Jähns, *Ross und Reiter in Leben und Sprache, Glauben und Geschichte der Deutschen*, 1872, Bd. i. S. 265.
[5] Th. de Cauzons, *La Magie et la sorcellerie en France*, 1911, t. i. p. 161.
[6] E. H. Meyer, *Germanische Mythologie*, 1891, S. 256.

west door of Gladheim, the Teutonic world of bliss, that a wolf hung.[1] The second connection springs from the contrast association between begetting and destruction, between the fertilizing and the destructive power of the sun,[2] further between its effective warmth by day and in the summer—hence its phallic symbolism[3]—on the one hand, and its powerlessness and its descent at night and in the winter on the other. It is doubtless significant that Apollo, the Sun-God who was identified both with Zeus and with the wolf, before he became identified with the former was above all the God of Death, and in this connection we may recall that in Etruscan tomb-paintings Hades himself is coifed in a wolf-skin.[4] His association with the wolf is still older, since before she bore him his mother, Leto, turned into a wolf to hide herself from Hera's wrath.

The wolf played a still more important part in Rome, as indeed the Romulus-Remus story itself indicates. There is reason to infer that in the original belief the founders of Rome were not only suckled by a wolf, but actually born of one: in other words, that the saga arose from a totemistic conception.[5] The priests of Soranus, the Sabine Death-God, who later became identified with Apollo, were called Hirpi (=wolves), and a kind of robbery formed a part of their cult. In Rome the wolf was the sacred animal of Mars, who was also originally a Death-God. The God Lupercus probably represented a group of attributes split off from the personality of Mars and united to constitute a new Godhead. His wife Luperca stood for the wolf that suckled Romulus and Remus. Their priests were called Crepi, an older form of Capri (=goats). Lupercus was only a subsidiary name of the God Faunus, Februus or Innus (from *inire*, to have intercourse). According to Schwegler,[6] the title

¹ Mogk, *op. cit.* S. 48.
² See Karl Abraham, *Traum und Mythus*, 1909, S. 53.
³ W. Schwartz, 'Der rothe Sonnenphallos der Urzeit', *Zeitschrift für Ethnologie*, 1874, S. 167, 409.
⁴ Cook, *op. cit.* p. 99.
⁵ See Otto Rank, *Der Mythus von der Geburt des Helden*, 1909, S. 40-44.
⁶ F. C. A. Schwegler, *Römische Geschichte*, 1853–58, Bd. i. S. 361.

Lupercus is derived from *lupus* and *hircus*, thus signifying wolf-goat: 'Eine Bezeichnung, welche die beiden Seiten der in Faunus sich darstellenden chthonischen Macht, die zerstörende lebenvernichtende und die hervorbringende, lebenerzeugende als wesentliche Konnexe zumal ausspricht.' ('A designation which expresses at the same time both sides of the chthonic power represented by Faunus, the life-destroying and the life-giving.') The festival of the Lupercalia (February 15) seems to have represented purification through marriage. From the word *februare* (= *inire*), after which the month is named, comes Februata or Februaris, a subsidiary title of Juno the patron goddess of marriage. Werewolves were believed to exercise their baneful activities in February,[1] and, according to Andrée,[2] most epidemics of Lycanthropy have in fact raged in this month. In reference to the sexual significance of the subject we may add a passage from Herman[3]: 'Auch im Italienischen bedeutete lupa sowohl Wölfin als auch Buhlerin (vulva) und aus den Tempeln der Luperca wurden die späteren Bordelle oder Lupanare.' ('In Italian lupa signifies both wolf and also wanton (or vulva) and the lupercal temples became the later brothels or Lupanars.')

The etymology of the term Werewolf has given rise to many curious attempts;[4] it was first properly solved in the year 1211 by Gervasius of Tilbury. 'Wer' signifies man (Latin *vir*, Sanskrit *viras*: compare *Wergeld*). 'Wolf' originally meant robber (Sanskrit Vricas);[5] in the Rig-Veda the wolf is called the robber,[6] and there was once the custom of hanging a wolf by the side of every thief on the gallows.[7] The Romans used the generic term *versipellis* (= skin-changer). The French word *loup-garou* (spelt by Bodin[8] *loup-varou* and by older writers *loup-*

[1] Donat de Hautemer, quoted by Guolart, *Thrésor des histoires admirables et mémorables de nostre temps*, 1600, t. i. p. 336.
[2] R. Andrée, *Revue de l'Orient*, 1888.
[3] G. Herman, 'Genesis', Bd. iii., *Bakchanalien und Eleusinien*, Zweite Auflage, S. 67.
[4] See Hertz, *op. cit.* S. 3, 4. [5] Hertz, *op. cit.* S. 56.
[6] Conway, *op. cit.* p. 140.
[7] Hertz, *op. cit.* S. 57. [8] J. Bodin, *Démonomanie*, 1593, p. 195.

warou[1]) probably comes from the Norman *garwolf*[2] (Werewolf), and hence is tautological. In later French it got written *waroul*, from which comes the Scottish *wroul* and *worlin*.[3]

The Werewolf superstition is exceedingly widespread; Hertz[4] has collected examples of it from the most diverse countries. The person concerned was generally believed to have been seized by an irresistible impulse, a ravenous craving, to have changed their appearance and roamed through the fields devouring sheep and other animals or even human beings, especially children. As a rule the state was a temporary one, recurring at night, and there could be long lucid intervals. Spontaneous transformation into a wolf was as a rule achieved by the person either donning a wolf's skin[5] or by his merely turning his own skin inside out.[6] For he was supposed to wear a wolf's skin under his own, a belief which gave rise to horrible tortures in the Middle Ages, when suspected persons were hacked to pieces in the endeavour to find the hairy growth.[7] Hair and Werewolf were closely associated ideas, as is illustrated by the Russian name for Werewolf, 'volkodlak' from *volk* = wolf, and *dlak* = hair. Werewolves could be recognized when in human form by having heavy eyebrows that met together,[8] or by having hair on the palms of their hands. The sexual association of hair is of course well known. It was believed that the wolf's skin could be discarded, and if it was burnt the particular subject lost the power of transforming himself into a wolf;[9] on the other hand, if one took away his human garment while he was in the wolf condition, he had to stay a wolf for ever.[10] This last point is a familiar *motif* in mythology, for example,

---

[1] See J. Grimm, *Deutsche Mythologie*, Vierte Ausgabe, 1876, S. 916.
[2] Hertz, *op. cit.* S. 91.
[3] G. W. Dasent, *Popular Tales from the Norse*, second edition, 1903, p. cxli.
[4] See also J. Hansen, *Zauberwahn, Inquisition und Hexenprozess im Mittelalter*, 1900, S. 19; and H. R. Schoolcraft, *The Myth of Hiawatha*, 1856, pp. 136, 339.
[5] Meyer, *op. cit.* S. 69.   [6] Fiske, *op. cit.* p. 89.
[7] Clodd, *op. cit.* p. 84.   [8] Grimm, *op. cit.* S. 918.
[9] Marian Roalfe Cox, *op. cit.* p. 124. Grimm, *op. cit.* S. 917.
[10] Grimm, *loc cit.*

in the fairy tales of swan-maidens. The wolf's skin could be donned only when the person was naked,[1] a feature that was worked up into an interesting incident in the celebrated old English tale of William and the Werewolf.[2] The transformation was complete except for the eyes; the explanation Hertz[3] gives for this is: 'Da die Seele unverändert bleibt, so erfährt auch das Auge, der Seele Spiegel, keine Veränderung; am Auge werden die Verwandelten erkannt.' ('Since the soul remains unchanged, so also does the eye, the mirror of the soul, undergo no change; one recognizes the transformed person by his eye.') In mythology, however, the eye may symbolize an important part of the body as well as the soul, an interpretation which fits better to the following variant related by Grimm[4]: 'Ein Mann wurde durch eine Hexe verwandelt, er heulte vor ihrer Tür, um erlöst zu werden, und nach drei Jahren gab sie nach und schenkte ihm eine menschliche Haut, um ihn damit zu befreien; er zog sie über sich, aber sie bedeckte seinen Schweif nicht, so dass er zwar wieder Menschengestalt erlangte, aber den Wolfsschwanz behielt.' ('A man had been transformed by a witch. He howled outside her door for deliverance, and after three years she relented and gave him a human skin with which to release himself. He drew this over himself, but it did not cover his tail, so that when he regained human form the wolf's tail remained.') The idea is the same as in the story of the Devil, who is to be recognized by his cloven hoof which he cannot conceal. In both cases the phallic symbol of the animal nature remains an unalterable constituent of their being.

The popular idea about the reasons why anyone became a Werewolf bears a remarkable resemblance to those concerning other mythological creatures, e.g. swan-maidens, etc., and it would lead us too far from our theme to enter on a full explanation of them here. The

[1] Grimm, loc. cit.
[2] The Ancient English Romance of William and the Werewolf, edited with an introduction and glossary by Sir Frederick Madden, 1832.
[3] Hertz, op. cit. S. 49.　　　　　　　[4] Grimm, loc. cit.

ecognize him;[4] a peculiarly
appropriate measure, which must remind us of the
method of 'releasing' a Vampire by eating his flesh, was
to make three sharp stabs at his forehead.[5]

When the mediæval scholastic theologians got to work
on the problem they accepted the facts, but, whereas
some were of opinion that the animal transformation
really happened, others maintained that it was merely a
deception of the devil's.[6] All agreed, however, that the
proper treatment of the condition was to destroy, pre-
ferably to burn, the unfortunate object. Bodin[7] defends
the correctness of this procedure as follows: 'Plusieurs
medecins voyant une chose si estrange, et ne sçachant
point la raison, pour ne sembler rien ignorer, ont dict et
laissé par escript, que la Lycanthropie est une maladie
d'hommes malades qui pensent estre loups, et vont

A. von Haxthausen, *Transkaukasia*, 1856, Bd. i. S. 322. B. Stern, *Medizin,
Aberglaube und Geschlechtsleben in der Türkei*, 1903, Bd. ii. S. 359.
[2] Grimm, *loc. cit.* Hertz, *op. cit.* S. 84.
[3] Grimm, *op. cit.* S. 918. Thorpe, *op. cit.* vol. ii. p. 169.
[4] Fiske, *op. cit.* p. 92. Hertz, *op. cit.* S. 85.
[5] Baring-Gould, *op. cit.* p. 107.
[6] Hertz, *op. cit.* S. 7, 8.   [7] Bodin, *op. cit.* pp. 201, 202.

courans parmy les bois: Et de cet advis est Paul Aeginet:
mais il faudroit beaucoup de raisons, et de tesmoings,
pour dementir tous les peuples de la terre, et toutes
les histoires, et mesmement l'histoire sacrée, que Theo-
phraste Paracelse, et Pomponace, et mesmement Fernel
les premiers Medecins et Philosophes qui ont esté de leur
aage, et de plusieurs siecles, ont tenu la Lycanthropie
pour chose tres-certaine, veritable et indubitable. Aussi
est ce chose bien fort ridicule de mesurer les choses
naturelles aux choses supernaturelles, et les actions des
animaux, aux actions des esprits et Dæmons. Encores
est plus absurde d'alleguer la maladie, qui ne seroit sinon
en la personne du Lycanthrope, et non pas de ceux qui
voyent l'homme changer en beste, et puis retourner en sa
figure.' The most important changes that the Church
brought about in this superstitious idea related to the
cause of the supposed events. Innocent Werewolves had
been laid under a spell by the Devil or else by witches
under his orders. The guilty ones had been affected on
account of their sins, which usually consisted of heresy
or of standing in relation with the Devil. A special
variant of Werewolf was the Büxenwolf (*Büxen* is Low
German for trousers), who possessed this privilege in
return for making a pact with the Devil.[1] The heathen
idea that the transformation could be brought about by
decree of fate was not reinforced by the Church; but
there is one example of Christian influence in this direction, namely, the belief that a child born on Christmas
Day was destined to become a Werewolf: the reason
proffered for this was that its mother had dared to conceive on the same day as the Virgin Mary.[2]

It is comprehensible that the belief in Werewolves
played a great part during the era of witch persecutions.
Hertz[3] writes: 'In der christlichen Zeit, wo man die
Existenz der heidnischen Götter zugab, um sie für Teufel
erklären zu können . . . entstand mit dem Hexenglauben
die Vorstellung von Menschen, die sich mit Hilfe des

---

[1] Hertz, *op. cit.* S. 87.   [2] Stern, *op. cit.* S. 363.
[3] Hertz, *op. cit.* S. 134.

Satans aus reiner Mordlust zu Wölfen verwandeln. ᴖ
wurde der Werwolf in düster poetischer Symbolik das
Bild des tierisch Dämonischen in der Menschennatur, der
unersättlichen gesamtfeindlichen Selbstsucht,[1] welche
alten und modernen Pessimisten den harten Spruch in
den Mund legte: Homo homini lupus.' ('In the Christian
era, when one admitted the existence of heathen gods so
as to explain them away as devils . . . there arose with
the belief in witches the idea of men who from pure lust
of murder used Satan's help to turn themselves into
wolves. The Werewolf thus became in sinister poetical
symbolism the image of the animal and demoniacal in
human nature, of the insatiable egotism that is the
enemy of the whole world,[1] which inspired old and
modern pessimists to the hard saying: Homo homini
lupus.') It was believed that Werewolves gathered together just as witches did, that they travelled through
the air, held a Sabbath, showed reverence to their Master
who impressed his sign on them (stigma), and indulged
in sexual orgies among themselves.[2] Many of these details were made public at the trials, such as that of
Verdun and Burgot in the year 1521, of which many
reports have come down to us;[3] both were burned in
Besançon. According to de Lancre[4] these victims admitted 'qu'ils prenoyent autant de plaisir lors qu'ils
s'accouploient brutalement auec les louues, que lors
qu'ils s'acointoyent humainement euec des femmes'.
They further described how the Devil had transformed
them into wolves by rubbing them with an ointment;
those accused in a trial at Salzburg in the year 1717 made
the same confession. The anointing evidently refers to
the well-known witch's ointment.

Werewolves, just as witches, had a special relation to

[1] [This expression must remind one of Freud's recent conception of a
'Todestrieb'.]
[2] H. Freimark, *Okkultismus und Sexualität*, S. 319.
[3] H. Boguet, *Discours des sorciers*, 1603, p. 370. L. F. Calmiel, *De la folie*,
1845, t. i. p. 234. Remigius, *Daemonolatria*, 1698, vol. ii. p. 183. J. F. Wolfes-
husius, *De lycanthropia*, 1591, p. 31.
[4] Pierre de Lancre, *Tableau de l'inconstance des mauvais anges et démons*,
1612, p. 321.

cats, and in many respects form a counterpart to them. The wolf was sacred to Odin, the cat to his wife Freya.[1] Male magicians transform themselves into wolves, female ones into cats[2]; further, the details of the procedure are in both cases the same.[3] The two *motifs* are combined in an old Tartar heroic saga[4]: 'Bürüh-Chan, ein Herrscher über sechshundert Wölfe, lebte bald als ein goldglänzender Wolf, bald als Mensch. Der Knabe Altenkök fängt ihn in einer Schlinge und fordert von ihm auf den Rat eines Greises die Katze, welche er in seinem Zelte hege. Als sie der Knabe nach Hause gebracht, verwandelt sie sich in ein schönes Weib; denn sie ist die Tochter des Wolfsfürsten, der nun seinem Eidam reiche Mitgift schenkt.' ('Bürüh-Khan, a ruler over six hundred wolves, passed part of his time as a wolf gleaming like gold,[5] part of it as a human being. The boy Altenkök caught him in a trap, and on the advice of an old man demanded of him the cat which he kept in his tent. When the boy brought her home she turned into a beautiful maiden, for she was the daughter of the wolf-chieftain, who now bestowed a rich dowry on his son-in-law.') Finally, according to Majolus,[6] the Werewolves in Courland actually hate witches and destroy them whenever they can; this is evidently connected with the legend in which the ghostly legion indulges in a wild pursuit of pixies.

In consequence of the attention devoted to the subject by the Church, Werewolf trials became pretty frequent towards the end of the sixteenth century; in some districts, for instance in the Jura,[7] the cases assumed an epidemic form. Most of the accused admitted their guilt, and described in detail their transmogrification, together with their nocturnal deeds of devouring animals and human beings. The most celebrated trials were those of

---

[1] Grimm, *op. cit.* S. 873. [2] Grimm, *op. cit.* S. 915.
[3] Hertz, *op. cit.* S. 71-74.
[4] M. A. Castren, *Ethnologische Vorlesungen über die altaischen Völker*, 1857, S. 233.
[5] Compare the above reference to wolf and brightness or light.
[6] De Lancre, *op. cit.* p. 307. [7] Clodd, *op. cit.* p. 83.

four persons, Jaques Bocquet, Clauda Jamprost, Clauda Janguillaume and Thievenne Paget, in 1538,[1] Gilles Gernier in 1573,[2] of four members of the Gandillon family in 1598[3] and of Jean Grenier in 1603[4]; three of the Gandillons were hanged and burned, the fourth was torn to pieces by the people. A Werewolf was executed in Salzburg as recently as 1720.[5] In France the belief was given its death-blow early in the eighteenth century by an anonymous satire, the author of which was the Abbé Bourdelot: 'Les aventures de Monsieur Oufle' (anagram for le fou). The belief in the real existence of Werewolves has by no means died out: Krauss[6] relates a fully developed Werewolf story from the Balkans in the year 1888. I have myself spoken to people in France who firmly believed in their existence, and the belief is also still held in French-Canada.[7]

The relationship between the beliefs *in Werewolves and in Incubi* is a somewhat indirect one, as will be presently shown, but it is remarkable what a close connection exists between the former and the popular equivalent of the latter, namely, the belief in the male and female Nightmare bogies (German *Alp* and *Mahre* respectively) from which the Incubus concept was derived. The seventh son, for instance, is destined to become a Werewolf,[8] the seventh daughter a Night-hag.[9] According to a Danish tradition, if a woman stretches a foal's caul over four sticks and creeps through it naked at midnight, she will bear her future children without pain, but every boy will be a Werewolf and every girl a Nighthag.[10] This may be compared with the following Scandinavian superstition: 'When a woman procures an easy labour for herself by creeping through a horse's collar,

[1] Boguet, *op. cit.* p. 363.   [2] Bodin, *op. cit.* p. 192.
[3] Boguet, *loc. cit.*   [4] P. de Lancre. *op. cit.* p. 313.
[5] Sigm. Riezler, *Geschichte der Hexenprozesse in Bayern*, 1896, S. 293.
[6] F. S. Krauss, *Slavische Volksforschungen*, 1908, S. 139.
[7] Beaugrand, *La Chasse galerie. Légendes canadiennes*, 1900, pp. 36-54.
[8] L. Strackerjan, *Aberglaube und Sagen aus dem Herzogt. Oldenburg*, 1867, Bd. i. S. 377.
[9] F. F. A. Kuhn und F. L. W. Schwarz, *Norddeutsche Sagen, Märchen und Gebräuche*, 1848, S. 420.
[10] Meyer, *op. cit.* S. 67. Thorpe, *loc. cit.*

the child becomes a night-bogey (an *Alp*).'[1] According to Meyer[2]: 'Die Katzen, die unter einen Sarg und von da unter das Bett eines Neugeborenen springen, können dasselbe in einen Werwolf oder eine Mahr verwandeln.' ('A cat that has climbed under a coffin and then under the bed of an infant can transform the latter into a Werewolf or a Night-hag according to its sex.') Witches possess the same power, and children that have not been protected against them by baptism are called heathen wolves.[3] The Werewolf gets into a house through the water vent, as a Night-hag enters through the key-hole.[4] One can recognize a Werewolf by his eyebrows meeting in the middle, just as one does a male[5] or a female[6] night-bogey (*Alp* or hag) that oppress people during sleep, as well as Indian magicians.[7] The wolf-shirt is as important to a Werewolf as her swan-shirt to a swan-maiden. The children of the rye-fiend (*Roggenfrau*), whose function it is to oppress rye-workers during their siesta, become rye-wolves (*Roggenwölfe*), who operate under the same conditions.[8] Finally, the release of the Werewolf from his spell proceeds along almost identical lines as that of the Night-hag, the swan-maiden, etc.

Perhaps the most convincing proof of the connection is to be found in the fact that on the Danish island of Bornholm the name for a male night-fiend (*Alp*) is 'marul', a word compounded of 'mara' and 'varul' = werewolf.[9]

Like the Incubi, or rather their popular equivalent of night-bogey (*Alp*), Werewolves were regarded as connected with the souls of the deceased, *i.e. revenant* ancestors.[10]

The connections *between the Werewolf and Vampire* superstitions are even closer. To begin with, we have the

[1] I. and O. von Düringsfeld, cited by Freimark, *op. cit.* S. 409.
[2] Meyer, *op. cit.* S. 68.　　　　　[3] Meyer, *loc. cit.*
[4] Meyer, *op. cit.* S. 69.　　　　　[5] Wuttke, *op. cit.* S. 275.
[6] J. W. Wolf, *Zeitschrift für deutsche Mythologie*, 1853, Jahrgang. i. S. 198.
[7] Somadeva.　　　　　[8] Mannhardt, *op. cit.* S. 31.
[9] Wolf von Unwerth, 'Eine isländische Mahrensage', *Wörter und Sachen, Kulturhistorische Zeitschrift für Sprach- und Sachforschung*, 1910, Bd. ii. S. 182.
[10] Fiske, *op. cit.* pp. 76, 77.

belief prevailing in the south-east of Europe that Werewolves become Vampires after their death. A modern
refinement of this belief, prevailing in Elis, is that even
those who eat the flesh of a sheep that had been killed
by a wolf may become Vampires after their death.[1]
Naturally it is in this part of the world, where the belief
in Vampires was most firmly rooted, that the two ideas
are most closely associated,[2] although two of the best
authorities, Andrée[3] and Krauss,[4] maintain that they
can always be distinguished. But the mere fact that the
Slav word *vukodlac* (the Servian variant), which originally meant Werewolf, is generally used in Bulgaria and
Servia to designate a Vampire,[5] undoubtedly means that
the people saw a close connection between the two ideas.
In Russian the word was *volkodlak*, in Czech *vilkodlak*.
In Greece the same word, there spelt *vrykolakas*, is also
the general term for a Vampire, though it is of interest
to note that it is still occasionally used in its original
sense of Werewolf,[6] and that on the outlying islands,
where the Slavonic influence penetrated less, the older
Greek terms for Vampire still persist.[7] Under the Greek
Church it was believed that a child born on Christmas
Day was destined to become a Vampire, under the
Roman that it would become a Werewolf.

The Werewolf, although not so regularly as the Vampire, has many associations with the idea of *Death*. The
close connection between the wolf and the Death Gods
of antiquity was indicated above. The ghost wolf in his
rôle as psychopomp plays as important a part as the
ghostly wild dog[8]; even in later times the howling of a
wolf or of a dog has been regarded as a death omen. He
is connected with the ideas of travel by night and night-
riding in general. The terrible night fiends of Northern
folklore, who are among the ancestors of the mediæval

[1] Curtius Wachsmutt, *Das alte Griechenland im Neuen*, 1864, S. 117.
[2] Hertz, *op. cit.* S. 113. Wuttke, *op. cit.* S. 278.
[3] R. Andrée, *Ethnologische Parallelen und Vergleiche*, 1878.
[4] Krauss, *op. cit.* S. 137.   [5] Grimm, *op. cit.* S. 880-881.
[6] C. Robert, *Les Slaves de Turquie*, 1844, t. i. p. 69.
[7] Lawson, *op. cit.* p. 384.
[8] W. W. Sikes. *British Goblins*, 1880, pp. 233-236.

witches, rode on wolves.[1] Many legends of Werewolves evidently spring from the related idea of the ghostly furious host and the wild hunt. Peucer's[2] description of the night march of thousands of Werewolves led by a huge man armed with a whip made of chains—evidently the Devil—is strikingly reminiscent of the numerous stories of this theme.[3] According to Mannhardt,[4] even the rye-wolf, like the hound of the wild hunt, was thought to be a psychopomp, *i.e.* to convey souls.

In this connection it is important to note that a Werewolf may be not only a transmogrified living man, but also a corpse which has arisen from the grave in the form of a wolf, a variety known as a ghost Werewolf. Hertz[5] relates the following case: 'Ein merkwürdiges Beispiel ist der gefährliche und grausame Wolf von Ansbach im Jahre 1685, welcher für das Gespenst des verstorbenen Bürgermeisters gehalten wurde.' ('A curious example was the dangerous and cruel wolf of Ansbach in the year 1685 which was taken to be the ghost of the deceased Mayor.') The wolf was finally killed. 'Darauf zog man ihm die Haut ab für die fürstliche Kunstkammer, machte ihm von Pappe ein Menschengesicht mit einem Schönbart lang und weissgraulich, ein Kleid von gewichster fleischfarbrötlicher Leinwand und eine kastanienbraune Perrücke; so wurde er auf dem "Nürnberger Berg vor Onolzbach" an einem eigens dazu errichteten Schnellgalgen aufgehängt.' ('Whereupon his skin was removed and preserved in the Royal Museum, while the body was decked with a human mask wearing a long grey beard, a garment of shining flesh-coloured linen and a chestnut wig. In this fashion he was hanged on a specially erected gallows on the Nuremberg "Berg vor Onolzbach."') As a rule the transformed corpse was believed to be that of a damned soul who could find no rest in his grave,[6] this being again a point of contact with the Vampire belief. An historic example of this is

---

[1] Grimm, *loc. cit.*
[2] C. Peucer, *Les Devins*, 1584, p. 198.
[3] Grimm, *op. cit.* ch. xxxi.
[4] Mannhardt, *op. cit.* S. 31.
[5] Hertz, *op. cit.* S. 88.
[6] Hertz, *op. cit.* S. 109.

the case of King John 'Lackland' of England, whose dead body was believed to have been changed into a Werewolf as the result of the papal excommunication. Bosquet[1] writes concerning this: 'Ainsi se trouva complètement réalisé le funestre présage attaché à son surnom Sans-Terre, puisqu'il perdit de son vivant presque tous les domaines soumis à sa suzeraineté, et que, même après sa mort, il ne put conserver la paisible possession de son tombeau.'

Over and over again the behaviour of the Werewolf closely resembles that of the Vampire. In Armenia sinful women are punished by having to pass seven years as female Werewolves; when the horrible wolfish lusts seize them they first devour their own children, then those of their relatives, and then strange children, in the same order as Vampires follow.[2] Another Armenian monster, the Dachnavar, that stands between the Werewolf and Vampire, sucks the blood from the soles of a passer-by.[3] According to Hertz[4]: 'Am auffallendsten die Vermischung der Vorstellungen von Werwolf und Vampir in Danziger Sagen, wo es heisst, man müsse den Werwolf verbrennen, nicht begraben; denn er habe in der Erde keine Ruhe und erwache wenige Tage nach der Bestattung; im Heisshunger fresse er sich dann das Fleisch von den eigenen Händen und Füssen ab, und wenn er nichts mehr an seinem Körper zu verzehren habe, wühle er sich um Mitternacht aus dem Grabe hervor, falle in die Herden und raube das Vieh oder steige gar in die Häuser, um sich zu den Schlafenden zu legen und ihnen das warme Herzblut auszusaugen; nachdem er sich daran gesättigt habe, kehre er wieder in sein Grab zurück. Die Leichen der Getöteten findet man aber des anderen Tages in den Betten und nur eine kleine Bisswunde auf der linken Seite der Brust zeigt die Ursache ihres Todes an.' ('The most striking admixture of the conceptions of Werewolf and Vampire occurs in the Dantsic legend,

---

[1] A. Bosquet, *La Normandie romanesque et merveilleuse*, 1845, p. 238.
[2] Hertz, *op. cit.* S. 28.
[3] Stern, *op. cit.* Bd. i. S. 359.   [4] Hertz, *op. cit.* S. 89.

which runs as follows. A Werewolf must be burnt not buried, for he has no rest in the earth and will awaken a few days after the burial. In his ravenous hunger he then devours the flesh of his own hands and feet, and when he can find nothing more in his own body to eat he burrows out of the grave at midnight, attacks the sheep and cattle, or even climbs into houses so as to lie on those asleep and suck the warm heart's blood out of them; after he has sated himself he returns to his grave. The bodies of the murdered people are found in their beds the next day with only a small bite on the left side of the breast to show the cause of their death.') Werewolves have even been confounded with ghouls: in France a special kind of Werewolves, called Loubins, visited the churchyards in hordes in order to devour the corpses.[1]

We see, therefore, that the *revenant motif* is common to the Vampire and Werewolf superstitions, while from the blood-sucking of the former to the devouring lust of the latter is only a small step, corresponding as it evidently does to the development from the first to the second oral stage of infantile sexuality. The two conceptions are thus throughout interwoven with each other.

We have now to consider the psychological meaning of the superstitious belief in Werewolves. The three essential constituents of the belief are, as we have seen, the ideas of animal transformation, of ravenous cannibalism and of nocturnal wandering. I shall argue that the most important contributions to these three elements were furnished by the experiences of anxiety dreams of a kind that represent only a slight elaboration of the typical Nightmare. In this connection Wundt[2] cautiously remarks: 'Ebenso enthält der Werwolfmythus möglicherweise in der Umschnürung des Leibes mit dem Gürtel aus Wolfshaut, die die Umwandlung eines Menschen in den Wolf bewirken soll, sowie in den die Überwältigung

---

[1] Donat de Hautemer, *loc. cit.* F. Pluquet, *Contes populaires*, 1834, p. 14.
[2] W. Wundt, *Völkerpsychologie*, Zweiter Band. *Mythus und Religion*, Zweiter Teil, 1906, S. 120.

des Opfers durch den Werwolf begleitenden Angstge-
fühlen, Wirkungen der Alp—und verwandten Angst-
träume, wie sich denn auch die Vampyr—und die Wer-
wolfsage an manchen Orten gemischt haben. Auch spielen
hierbei ausserdem die teils im Traum, teils in der geisti-
gen Störung vorkommenden Vorstellungen der Tierver-
wandlung ihre Rolle.' ('It is possible that the Werewolf
myth similarly contains effects of Nightmares and allied
anxiety dreams, notably in the idea that the transformation of a human being into a wolf was supposed
to have been brought about by encircling the body with
a girdle of wolf-skin, as also in the feelings of terror
experienced by the victim who was overpowered by the
Werewolf; it is to be noted further how the Werewolf
and Vampire legends have intermingled in many parts
of the world. The ideas of animal transformation, which
occur both in dreams and in mental disturbances, also
play their part here.')

In the first place, the very fact that the phenomena
in question were supposed to occur at night, and during
the sleep of the victims, should lead one to suspect an
origin in dream experiences. In the second place, the
extraordinary intermingling and interchangeability of
the Werewolf with the Incubus and Vampire beliefs,
both of which we have shown to have probably been
derived in the main from dream experiences, would
strongly suggest a similar origin here also. In the third
place, the three elements enumerated above bear specially close relations to the *motifs* of anxiety dreams.

It is interesting that any two of these three elements
can occur together without the third: (1) Nocturnal
wandering and animal transformation we are already
familiar with in the case of the Vampire. (2) Animal
transformation and cannibalistic lust are found together
with the rye-wolf (*Roggenwolf*). He does not wander by
night, it is true, but it is to be noted that his depreda-
tions take place during the (mid-day) sleep of the victims.
(3) Nocturnal wandering and cannibalistic lust often
occur together apart from the idea of animal transforma-

tion. Thus the Thessalians, Epirotes and Wallachians believe in somnambulists who wander about by night and tear human beings with their teeth.[1] From this idea of behaving like a wolf it is only a step to actual transformation into a wolf.

We have previously traced the belief in *animal transformation* largely to dream experiences.

The belief in *night wandering, i.e.* the belief that a given person can be in two places at the same time, certainly originates, as does actual somnambulism, also from dream experiences, for its development can still be observed among savages. It was believed that the real body of the Werewolf lay asleep in bed while his spirit roved the woods in the form of a wolf[2]; further, when the wolf was wounded, corresponding wounds were to be found on the human body that remained at home.[3] The similarity with the ideas of savages on dreams, such as were pointed out in the first chapter, is plain enough. There are various sources for these travelling dreams, since they can symbolize a considerable number of repressed wishes: the wish for freedom from compulsion, one which the idea of a wolf very well represents,[4] and especially for independence from the father; the wish for heightened potency, symbolized by swift movement, etc. The ultimate source of interest in movement is to be sought in the sexual component of agreeable sensations of this kind experienced by the infant.[5]

The third element would in psycho-analytical terminology be described as an oral-sadistic or cannibalistic impulse. That the lust for tearing and devouring flesh is oral-sadistic in nature is evident to anyone acquainted with sexual pathology, and has, indeed, been pointed out

[1] Stern, *op. cit.* Bd. i. S. 360. See also B. Schmidt, *Volksleben der Neugriechen,* 1871, Bd. i. S. 166.
[2] A good example of this is described by A. Lercheimer, *Ein christliches Bedenken und Erinnerung von Zauberei,* Dritte Auflage, 1597, Kap. xii.
[3] J. W. Wolf, *Niederländische Sagen,* Nr. 242, 243, 501.
[4] Conway, *op. cit.* p. 141.
[5] Sigm. Freud, *Drei Abhandlungen zur Sexualtheorie,* Zweite Auflage, 1910, S. 53, 54. [*Gesammelte Schriften,* Bd. v. S. 76.]

by various other writers.[1] The wolf symbolism is specially well suited to represent this, and the effect is
heightened by the fact that Werewolves were supposed
to be even more savage than other wolves. Sadistic
tendencies prove in analysis to be derived from two
sources. On the one hand we have the primary sadistic
erotism of the young child, beginning with the oral-
sadistic attitude towards the mother's breast—in which
connection we recall the essentially dental nature of
the wolf sadism—and revealing itself most typically in
the classical belief in the sadistic conception of parental
coitus. On the other hand there is the jealous hostility—
later sexualized—against the parent of the same sex, so
that both sources of sadism are rooted in the Oedipus
complex. It is perhaps not a matter of chance that hatred
of the father was a striking characteristic in the actual
cases of Lycanthropy,[2] *i.e.* where people really imagined
that they wandered about at night in the guise of wolves.
The cannibalistic idea of devouring human flesh, so
characteristic of the Werewolf superstition, is derived
from both the sources just mentioned, *i.e.* the erotic and
the hostile; in the unconscious, as we know well from
psycho-analysis, there is for these different motives the
wish to devour both the loved and the hated object.[3]

These sadistic tendencies have, of course, many manifestations in waking life, but the majority of them, *e.g.*,
those that lie behind certain neurotic symptoms, are
veiled, and very seldom reach elsewhere the fierce
intensity which is so frequently met with in certain
types of anxiety dreams. This consideration would lead
one to ascribe to such dreams a considerable part in
generating beliefs founded on the sadistic tendency,
though not such a predominant one as with the two
other elements discussed above.

[1] See, for example, Clodd, *op. cit.* p. 84. Dankmar, 'Curiosa aus der Teufels-
periode des Mittelalters', *Psychische Studien*, 1899, Jahrg. xxvi. S. 27, 80, and,
best of all, Baring-Gould, *op. cit.* ch. ix.

[2] De Lancre, *op. cit.* p. 317.

[3] [In his book on *Totem und Tabu*, 1913, Freud has, in connection with
the totemistic banquet, shown the importance of cannibalism for the development of religious ideas.]

From this point of view it is not surprising to hear that the group of unconscious ideas that lies behind the belief in, and fear of, Werewolves occasionally bursts through into consciousness in a positive form, with the result that the person afflicted with the delusion of being a wolf indulges in corresponding behaviour. As early as in the second century a medical work, by Marcellus Sidetes,[1] pointed out that Lycanthropy was a form of insanity. He says that men are most attacked with this madness in February, that they skulk in cemeteries and live alone like ravening wolves. Clinically they would be classified as cases of sadism, frequently combined with cannibalism and necrophilia; they may or may not be associated with an actual lycanthropic delusion, there being many authentic examples of both.

In this connection it is interesting to note that the ideas associated with that of wolves reveal how profoundly the people apprehend the essence of anti-social behaviour to be sadistic in nature.[2] For instance, the Norse word *vargr* meant both wolf and a godless man. It is cognate with the Anglo-Saxon *wearg*, a scoundrel, Gothic *vargs*, a fiend. The Ancient Norman laws said of criminals condemned to outlawry, *Wargus esto*: be an outlaw (or wolf); in the Lex Ripuaria the expression was 'Wargus sit, hoc est expulsus'. In the laws of Canute an outlaw was actually designated a *verevulf*. Among the Anglo-Saxons an outlaw was said to have the head of a wolf, and the legal form of sentence ran: 'He shall be driven away as a wolf, and chased so far as men chase wolves farthest.'[3] This is doubtless also the meaning of the following passage in the first chapter of the Völsunga Saga: 'Thus it is well seen that Sigi has slain the thrall and murdered him; so he is given forth to be a wolf in holy places, and may no more abide in the land *with his father*.'[4]

---

[1] See W. H. Roscher, 'Das von der "Kynanthropie" handelnde Fragment des Marcellus von Side' in the *Abhandlungen der sächsichen Gesellschaft der Wissenschaften*, Phil.-hist. Classe, 1897, Bd. xvii. Teil 3, S. 1-92.
[2] [Cp. Freud's *Das Unbehagen in der Kultur*, 1930.]
[3] These data are all taken from Baring-Gould, *op. cit.* pp. 48, 49.
[4] Italics not in original.

The psychological relationship between the Vampire and Werewolf superstitions may be shortly expressed. The former is much more closely connected with the *revenant* idea, though, as we have seen, the difference between the two in this respect is one of degree only. Further, whereas the Vampire belief is more concerned with sucking tendencies, both oral and vaginal, the Werewolf one is throughout sadistic in nature. The Incubus and Werewolf superstitions may be thus contrasted: in the former belief the attention is more concentrated on the emotions of the person who has been attacked in sleep by a monster, in the latter on the attitude of the attacking monster himself. It may be said that the masochistic component of the sexual instinct comes to expression in the Incubus belief, the sadistic in the Werewolf one; but it must be added that the former belief is constituted rather from the genital phase of libidinal development, the latter from a pregenital one, and this is the reason why the Incubus belief is more connected with the pure Nightmare experience and the Werewolf one with other, allied forms of anxiety dream.

CHAPTER VI

THE DEVIL

INTO the construction of the idea of the Devil, the representative of the evil in man, there has entered an almost countless number of different factors. Analytic study of similar constructions of the human phantasy shows, however, that most of these factors are merely contributory, each phantasy being grouped around a central nucleus. It is not my purpose here, even if I had the capacity, to attempt to deal with these contributory factors in detail, and I propose to select out of the many problems contained in the subject the following three for discussion: (1) What is the central psychological meaning of the belief? (2) How did it come to be so prominent and sharply defined at a particular epoch? (3) In what relation does it stand to the experiences of the Nightmare?

In a psychological study we must start from the assumption that the Devil is a creation not of heaven, as the theologians still teach, but of the human mind. As Graf[1] says: 'Er wurde nicht vom Himmel herabgestürzt, sondern erhob sich aus den Abgründen der menschlichen Seele.' ('He was not cast down from heaven, but arose out of the depths of the human soul.') And that these depths, when fully explored, will be found to be definitely susceptible of comprehension there can be as little doubt. Freud[2] writes: 'Der Teufel ist doch gewiss nichts anderes als die Personifikation des verdrängten unbewussten Trieblebens' ('For the Devil is certainly nothing else than the personification of the repressed, unconscious instinctual life'), and Silberer[3] adds: 'Der

[1] A. Graf, *Geschichte des Teufelsglaubens*, Zweite Auflage, übersetzt von R. Teuscher, 1893, S. 2.
[2] Sigm. Freud, 'Charakter und Analerotik', *Sammlung kleiner Schriften zur Neurosenlehre*, Zweite Folge, 1909, S. 136. [*Gesammelte Schriften*, Bd. v. S. 265, *Collected Papers*, vol. ii. p. 49.]
[3] H. Silberer, 'Phantasie und Mythos', *Psychoanalytisches Jahrbuch*, 1910, Bd. ii. S. 592.

Teufel und die finsteren dämonischen Gestalten der Mythen sind, psychologisch genommen, funktionale Symbole, Personifikationen des unterdrückten, nicht sublimierten elementaren Trieblebens.' ('The Devil and the sombre dæmonic figures of the myths are—psychologically regarded—functional symbols, personifications of the suppressed and unsublimated elements of the instinctual life.') Our first problem, therefore, is to ascertain *which* components of the instinctual life constitute the source of the belief in the Devil.

This question evidently belongs to the series of those that have to do with anxiety emotions. The whole history of the Devil is one of constant dread, and indeed so strongly was it impregnated with this emotion that the very presence of a Devil in disguise could be detected by the intense dread and terror he left behind, one which had the effect of making the bystanders paralysed, mute and ice-cold.[1] As a starting-point for our investigation may be taken a remark of Pfister's,[2] in which the belief in the Devil is traced back to 'infantile experiences of fear' in the life of the individual. Since the origin of infantile terror is now known,[3] it naturally suggests itself to one to investigate the descriptions of the belief in the Devil in the light of this new knowledge. This procedure has led me to formulate the following conclusions, the evidence for which will presently be brought forward: *The belief in the Devil represents in the main an exteriorization of two sets of repressed wishes, both of which are ultimately derived from the infantile Oedipus situation:* (a) *The wish to imitate certain attributes of the father, and* (b) *the wish to defy the father; in other words, an alternating emulation of and hostility against the father.* Both sources contain repressed material: the latter obviously does, and even the former differs from the early piety which later expresses itself in the belief in God through being more

[1] Graf, *op. cit.* S. 67-68.
[2] O. Pfister, *Die Frömmigkeit des Grafen Ludwig von Zinzendorf,* 1910, S. 94.
[3] See Sigm. Freud, 'Analyse der Phobie eines fünfjährigen Knaben', *Psychoanalytisches Jahrbuch,* 1909, Bd. i. S. 1. [*Gesammelte Schriften,* Bd. viii. S. 127. *Collected Papers,* vol. iii. p. 147.]

directly concerned with admiration for the darker, 'evil' side of the father's nature and activities. In this respect the Devil personifies the Father, while in the other he personifies the Son; he thus represents unconscious aspects of the Son-Father complex, sometimes the one side being the more prominent, sometimes the other. The corresponding female Oedipus situation also contributes material of no less importance. For the reasons that this forms the subject of the next chapter and that it is largely the obverse of the male contribution, it will be simpler to confine ourselves for the present to the latter.

*   *   *   *   *

Before developing this theme further I shall pass next to consideration of the second problem mentioned above. We shall have at once to renounce a presentation of the purely historical aspects of the subject; for these the reader is referred to such books as those by Conway, Grimm, Roskoff and Gener, particularly to the last-named, which is perhaps the fullest and most objectively philosophical work on the subject. A brief abstract of the more important historical data, however, is essential for our general orientation. The first point to be insisted on here is that the Devil, in the strict sense of the word, is a purely Christian conception, the earlier data being merely material out of which the conception proper was formed. To attack our problem, therefore, we shall have briefly to consider the nature of this earlier material.

The idea of evil supernatural powers, although perhaps not absolutely universal, is exceedingly widely spread among ruder peoples,[1] and was so with the civilized peoples of antiquity. On investigating specific instances more closely, however, it is striking to note how very rarely these powers were *purely* evil in nature. With almost the sole exception of the Persian Ahriman, described in the Vedida section of the Zend-Avesta, one may say that before the advent of Christianity there was no definite conception of a supernatural being pro-

---

[1] See a review of this in G. Roskoff, *Geschichte des Teufels*, 1869, Bd. i. S. 17-23.

fessionally devoted to evil. The Brahmanic Vritra, the Hindoo Siva, the Egyptian Set (or Typhon), the Greek Pan, the Teutonic Loki, were all decidedly Gods, to be not merely propitiated but worshipped, and they fundamentally differed from the mediæval Devil. Greece, as might have been expected from her other illustrious attributes, was distinguished for the subordinate part played in her theology by anxiety feelings. At first sight Judaism appears to resemble Hellenism in the slight development of evil beings in its theology, but the reasons were quite different in the two systems and the comparison redounds to the credit of Hellenism. There is this significant fact to be noted: that, coincidently with the growth of the Satan idea in the later history of the Jews—an idea that followed the Babylonian exile and which was derived from either the Persian Ahriman or, as Robertson[1] thinks more probable, from the Babylonian Goat-God—the character of the Yahweh belief changed and approximated much more nearly to the modern one in a benevolent God. In the earlier history of the Jews Yahweh combined the attributes of both God and Devil; evil as well as good proceeded directly from him, so that, as Graf[2] truly says, 'man braucht nur einigermassen auf das Wesen Jehovas zu achten, um sogleich gewahr zu werden, dass neben einem solchen Gotte für einen Teufel wenig Platz übrig ist' ('It needs little reflection on the nature of Jehovah to realize that by the side of such a God there was not much room left over for a Devil'). As Conway[3] remarks in the same sense: 'The Jews originally had no Devil, as indeed had no races at first; and this for the obvious reason that their so-called gods were quite equal to any moral evils that were to be accounted for,' and Gener[4] says of the Jewish God: 'Il est dieu et diable à la fois; mais plus fréquemment il est diable.'

The Jewish example is especially interesting as con-

[1] J. M. Robertson, *Pagan Christs*, 1903, p. 84.   [2] Graf, *op. cit.* S. 18.
[3] M. D. Conway, *Demonology and Devil-Lore*, 1879, vol. ii. p. 56.
[4] P. Gener, *La Mort et le Diable*, 1880, p. 372.

tributing to the solution of the problem whether the Devil conception is of independent origin, as maintained by the theologians, or the result of that mythological process known as 'decomposition' in which different attributes of an originally unitary personality become invested with independent existence so that several different personalities come into being. The fact that the distinction between the ideas of God and Devil represents a late stage in cultural development, succeeding to the primitive idea of supernatural beings that are at the same time good and evil, speaks strongly in favour of the view taken here, namely that God and Devil were originally one,[1] and this is definitely confirmed by the Jewish example. After giving a detailed study of the matter, Gener[2] discusses whether Satan represents (1) one of the degraded gods of neighbouring tribes conquered by Yahweh, or (2) the Hazazel of Leviticus, or (3) simply a differentiated emanation of Yahweh himself, a 'dédoublement'—to use Gener's own term. He definitely decides in favour of the last view, which evidently is the true one, not only from the whole history of the evolution of Yahweh, but also from Satan's own behaviour; in the book of Job, for instance, he appears as a loyal servant of Yahweh, as a sort of intelligent detective who tests people and finds out their weaknesses. Conway[3] is also of the same opinion, even in respect of the very differently constituted Devil of the New Testament: 'The descriptions of the Devil in the Bible are mainly borrowed from the early descriptions of the Elohim, and of Jehovah in his Elohistic character.'

This conclusion of the original identity of God and Devil receives an interesting confirmation through etymological study of the word 'Devil'. Like the cognate French *diable*, German *Teufel*, Old High German *Tuivel*, as well as the Greek *diabolos*, it is ultimately derived

---

[1] [This conclusion was accepted by Reik, *Der eigene und der fremde Gott*, 1923, S. 139, and Freud, 'Eine Teufelsneurose im siebzehnten Jahrhundert', *Imago*, Bd. ix. S. 14 (*Gesammelte Schriften*, Bd. x. S. 409, and *Collected Papers*, vol. iv. p. 450).]

[2] Gener, *op. cit.* S. 389-391.   [3] Conway, *loc. cit.*

from a primeval root DV, which in Sanscrit is found in two forms, *div* and *dyu*, the original meaning of which was 'to kindle'. From the former come, in addition to our Devil, the Teutonic *Tius* (the god of Tuesday), *Tiwas* or *Zio*, the Greek *theos*, Latin *deus* or *divus*, French *dieu*, Welsh *diw*, Lithuanian *diewas*, Gipsy *dewel*, all of which signify 'God'; further, the word *deva* or *daeva*, which to the Brahmin means God, but to the Persian and Parsee means Devil. From the second form come the Indian *Djaus* (the Brahman sky-god), the Greek *Zeus* (Z = Dj), and the Latin *Jupiter* (old Latin *Diovis*). The same remarkable polarity is shown by the non-personal words derived from the same root. On the one hand there is the Latin *dies* = day, the Keltic *dis* = day-star or day-god, Sanscrit *dyaus* = day, and on the other hand the Aryan *dhvan* (whence the Greek *thanatos*) = death, Teutonic *devan* = to die, Aryan *dvi* = to fear, and the Greek *deos* = dread. Still more remarkable is the fact that the polarity words *par excellence* are of similar origin. The Sanscrit *dva*, Latin *duo*, English *two*, Welsh *deu*, all mean 'two' (compare the English 'double' with the Old High German for devil, *Deudel*), while the Greek *dys* signifies both 'to separate into two' and 'evil'.[1] The primary identity of the ideas of God and Devil can thus be demonstrated quite independently of psychological considerations, though these would in themselves be decisive.

The growth of Christianity brought an increasing definition of the Devil conception as the only possible explanation of the evil raging in the world. This was indeed inevitable from its extreme renunciation of the

[1] Of especial psychological interest is the following fact. The common English euphemism for devil is 'deuce' (Old English *dewes*), which one might at first sight expect to find derived from the sources just mentioned (cp. Zeus and St. Augustin's Dusius-Incubus). According to Skeat, however, it originated as follows: Its first meaning, still commonly used, was to denote the two in dice and card games, having been introduced for this purpose in Plantagenet times from the French *deux*. The 'losing two' in these games naturally signified ill-luck and hence got associated with the devil, first through the explanation 'Oh, the deuce'. As a result of this circuitous connection the word has now two meanings that are almost identical with those of the Greek *dys*, which it resembles in sound and with which it is etymologically cognate.

world as something essentially sinful. Such renunciation was carried by certain sects to even greater lengths than by the mother church. Many of the early Gnostics had believed in a Being with mixed good and evil attributes, Demiurgos, the creator of the world and foe of Christ, and when influenced by the degenerate form of Zoroastrianism taught by the Persian Mani in the third century this idea was developed by the Manichæans into a formal system. In it *all* nature, all animals, and all worldly desires were the Devil's domain. About the eleventh century this sect and others merged into the conglomerate body known as the Cathari from the tom-cat in whose shape Lucifer was represented. The Albigenses and other heretics also laid great stress on the sinfulness of nature. The influence exerted on the Catholic Church by these happenings was a two-fold one. In the first place, these teachings penetrated into her very bosom and enormously strengthened the early beliefs in the essential wickedness of worldly desires, with the result that the conception of sin was developed to an extent never heard of before or since. In the second place, she deliberately exploited the Devil idea as a powerful weapon to fight all heresies, declaring that heresy came only from the Devil and, later on, that it was synonymous with Witchcraft. It took some time before the value of the Devil for this purpose was perceived. In earlier times he had been to a great extent neglected. The Council of Braza, for instance, in 563, had proclaimed: 'If anyone alleges, with Priscillian, that the Devil makes certain creations, and that by his own virtue he creates thunder and lightning, tempests and drought, let him be anathema.' Later, however, the heretics, by their insistence on the powers of evil, had unwittingly put into the hands of the Church a weapon that proved their undoing.

The use of this weapon was already to some extent familiar to the Church in her fight against non-Christian religions. St. Paul himself (1 Corinthians, x. 20) had expressly declared heathen gods to be merely demons, and the Church applied this doctrine in conscientious detail

to one god after another of the classical and other
heathen theologies. It was soon found, however, impossible to carry the matter through in this simple way,
and it was decided—for the first time officially by Pope
Gregory I. in 601—to institute, on the basis of the
famous Accommodation Theory, a thorough-going amal-
gamation and absorption of other religions into Christianity. The festivals, cults, and personal attributes of
the foreign deities were pooled and redistributed among
Christian ones, some falling to the lot of Christ, God the
Father, Mary and the numerous saints, and others to the
Devil and his subordinates.[1]

As a result of this syncretizing procedure we find that
a great number of the physical and mental characteristics of the mediæval Devil are individually derived
from a great variety of extra-Christian sources. Thus,
to mention only a few examples[2]: Like Pan, the personification of nature, the Devil combined human and animal
attributes, particularly in his physical appearance, lived
in caverns and lonely places, and suddenly startled
people (Panic); his goat-like body, cloven hoofs and tail,
he inherited from Pan and the other satyrs, from the
German forest-sprites and from the he-goat that was
sacred to Thor. From Thor also came his red beard, his
habit of building bridges, and his evil odour; the last-
named attribute is connected both with the goat and
with the sulphurous odour left after a thunderstorm,
and in fact one of his by-names was Hammer,[3] taken from
Thor's thunder-hammer. Like Zeus and Odin he had
special power over the weather, and to the latter he
owed his horse's foot and the raven as his sacred animal.
Like Odin he travelled by night and bore away people

[1] It is, of course, impossible to describe here any of this interesting process.
In relation to the Teutonic religions it has been most fully investigated by
J. Grimm in his *Deutsche Mythologie*, 1876.
[2] See Grimm, *op. cit.* 4e Ausgabe, 1876, Kap. xxxiii.; Roskoff, *op. cit.*
Zweiter Abschnitt, Kap. 1 and 2, etc.; A. Wuttke, *Der deutsche Aberglaube der
Gegenwart*, 1900, S. 35-37.
[3] The phallic significance of this has been pointed out by G. W. Cox, *Mytho-
logy of the Aryan Nations*, 1870, vol. ii. p. 115, and E. H. Meyer, *Germanische
Mythologie*, 1891, S. 212.

as the Wild Hunter; on such occasions he wore Odin's dress of either a grey mantle with a broad hat pressed down on the head or a green coat with a feather in his hat. Both the Devil and Odin discovered the game of dice, which was later replaced by cards, and to this day cards are known in puritanical circles in England as 'the devil's game'. Like Odin, too, he was a master-smith and builder, and his old German name was that of Smith Wieland or Voland (English Weyland, our modern St. Valentine), who was a descendant of Odin's. The Devil is often portrayed as limping, a characteristic curiously related to the one just mentioned. Not only did the German smith Wieland (Wotan) limp, but also the Greek one, Hephaestos (Vulcan) who was cast from Heaven by Zeus, just like the Persian devil Aeshma (the Biblical Asmodeus); one of the two he-goats that bore Thor's waggon also limped, as did the horse that carried Baldur.[1] Like Loki, the fire-god, the Devil was bound by the gods and had to await his day of deliverance when all hell would be let loose. His black colour was borrowed from Saturn, who, according to Simrock,[2] was identified with Loki, and from the Indian Vritra, the god of darkness. The torch under his tail came from the Roman Bacchanalia.[3] In early times the Devil used actually to appear to Christians in the guise of the classical gods; thus, in the fourth century he appeared to St. Martin sometimes in the form of Jupiter, sometimes in that of Venus or Minerva; he took such shapes even as late as the twelfth century.

If we now inquire why the belief in the Devil assumed the proportions it did in the Middle Ages, although it is obvious that the answer must be found in the peculiar social and moral conditions of that period, yet the factors leading up to these were so complex and involved that only the most generally acting ones can be mentioned here. As an example of this complexity we may cite the

---

[1] Limping is a familiar unconscious symbol of castration.
[2] K. Simrock, *Handbuch der deutschen Mythologie*, 1878, S. 346.
[3] F. Hedelin, *Des satyres, brutes, monstres et démons*, 1627 (1888 ed.), p. 129.

modern demonstration that matters so apparently remote
as the recent introduction of the banking system[1] and
the improvement of town architecture[2] were indirectly
factors of considerable importance. Still there can be no
doubt that the main driving force came from the Church
itself. The Church has always had three sets of dangers
to cope with: unbelievers or pagans without; dissensions
and scandals within; and, part within and part without,
heresy. At the beginning of the Middle Ages the Church
had in all of these three connections strong reasons for
fortifying the belief in the Devil. The first of the three
might be called a positive reason, the other two negative. The conquering of paganism in Europe took much
longer than is commonly supposed, but nevertheless by
the twelfth century the main battles had been won, and
there remained only detailed guerilla fighting. The
Church could therefore afford to discard the more positive
aspects of syncretism and to revert to the uncompromising
attitude of the early Church, where there was no question
of enriching Christian worship with Pagan borrowings
and all non-Christian beliefs and rituals were appropria-
ted only as fodder for the underworld. The military and
political successes of the Church over Paganism ended
in the growth and elaboration of the Devil idea because
there was no longer the need to find any use for the
remains of Paganism except to feed this idea with it in
the ways we illustrated above. The other two reasons
were of quite another kind, signs not of strength but
of weakness. Discredited by the failure of its prophecies
(the end of the world at 1000 A.D. and numerous other
dates) and by moral and ecclesiastical scandals,[3] torn
by internal political and religious dissensions, its very
existence threatened by powerful heretical sects,[4] the
condition of the Church in the twelfth century was such
as called for the most desperate measures. To attribute

[1] Gener, op. cit. p. 582.
[2] J. Hansen, Zauberwahn, Inquisition und Hexenprozess im Mittelalter, 1900,
S. 329.
[3] See Roskoff, op. cit. Zweiter Abschnitt, Kap. vi.
[4] Gener, op. cit. p. 566. Hansen, op. cit. p. 214.

all its difficulties to the activity of the Devil, and in this way to distract the people from contemplating its weaknesses by terrifying them with an external danger, one moreover with which the Church knew itself competent to deal, was a device at which it eagerly clutched; it is one to which Governments in embarrassment have seldom failed to have recourse. The people, in abject misery at their social condition, devastated with pestilence[1] and war,[2] and in consequence of their misfortunes saturated with the sense of sinfulness, fell an easy prey to the Church's teachings. Indeed, these teachings at moments overreached themselves, for the people, in despair at the obvious failure of God and the Church to relieve their misery, greedily absorbed the doctrine of the wonderful powers of the Devil, so that not a few took refuge with him; probably the definite nature of the bargain driven in the well-known pacts appealed to them more than the unending and often inefficacious prayers to the saints. The extent of the belief in the Devil's influence on even the most trivial everyday happenings was so colossal that one cannot read the records of the time without thinking that Europe was being visited by a mass psychoneurosis of an unusually malign type. His activities were so manifold that, according to Wier, they had to be divided among 44,435,556 subordinates,[3] while a single woman, Joanna Seiler, was said to have been exorcised of no fewer than a hundred million.[4]

Most important of all, however, was the powerful suppressing influence exerted by the Church on all worldly desires, with the consequent outbreak of these in other directions. A good example of this is furnished by its attitude towards the desire for knowledge, which, as is well known, it condemned root and branch almost as

---

[1] Roskoff, *op. cit.* Bd. ii. S. 113-117, makes an appalling list of these.
[2] Of these the Mongolian irruption, the Crusades, and, later on, the Hundred Years' War between England and France seem to have exerted the greatest influence.
[3] C. L. Louandre, *Sorcellerie*, p. 37. J. A. S. Collin de Plancy, *Dictionnaire infernal*, 1818, t. i. p. 166.
[4] J. Jühling, *Die Inquisition*, 1903, S. 11.

being the source of all evil—a reversion to the first
chapters of Genesis. The suppressed instinct for knowledge, however, never took such bizarre forms as during
the Middle Ages, with its passionate search for the philo-
sopher's stone, the elixir of life, and the universal solvent,
with its devotion to astrology and alchemy, and with
its interest in all manner of magical procedures. This
craving for knowledge became closely associated with the
idea of the Devil, as indeed was formally taught by the
Church, and the beginning of the witchcraft epidemic
was the persecution of magicians. Unusual knowledge
was at once ascribed to a pact with the Devil; it was, for
instance, the reason why Pope Sylvester II, in the tenth
century, was suspected of having concluded such a pact.

This suppressing influence of the Church naturally
bore above all on sexual impulses, the source of all sin.
Sexual repression has assumed different forms in different ages, a matter of considerable importance in the
history of culture. In the nineteenth century, for instance, it seems to have been predominantly directed
against exhibitionism, with a marked extension to excremental functions; so that sexuality in the Victorian
era tended to be called 'shameful' or 'disgusting' rather
than 'sinful'. In the early Middle Ages repression was
directed against sexual activities in general as being inherently sinful, and particularly with all its force against
incest;[1] this is very comprehensible, inasmuch as Christian
theology is principally concerned with the sublimation
and glorification of an incest myth.[2] At the same time,
owing perhaps to the difficulty of marriage engendered
by the peculiar social and economic conditions,[3] and the
extent to which religious celibacy was practised, incest
seems to have been unusually common during this
period.[4] If, therefore, as is here maintained, the Devil

---

[1] E. Westermarck, *The History of Human Marriage*, 1891, p. 155, expresses
the interesting view that all sexual repression originated in the reaction against
incest, one which psycho-analytic investigation fully confirms.

[2] See, in this connection, Otto Rank, *Der Mythus von der Geburt des Helden*,
1909, S. 46-51.   [3] Gener, *op. cit.* p. 617.

[4] J. Michelet, *La Sorcière*, 3e ed., 1863, pp. 156-159.

idea essentially represented the guilty aspects of an incest symbolism, it must have been singularly well
adapted to the needs of the time, and the fact that Devil
worship constituted a detailed caricature of Christian
worship receives a deeper significance. It is especially
worthy of note that the principal crime committed at
the Witches' Sabbath was incest: Michelet,[1] for instance,
writes: 'Selon ces auteurs (De Lancre, etc.) . . . le but
principal du sabbat, la leçon, la doctrine expresse de
Satan, c'est l'inceste.'

* * * * *

After this very condensed discussion of the second of
our initial problems we may now return to the first. The
evidence in favour of the solution of it offered above may
most conveniently be presented under four headings.
Since the Devil may personify the 'evil' aspects of either
son or father, and as the son's attitude towards the
father may be either imitation or hostility, we find that
he is portrayed in four different aspects, though these
are never sharply separated from one another. He may
thus personify:

(1) The Father towards whom is felt admiration.
(2) The Father against whom is felt hostility.
(3) The Son who imitates the father.
(4) The Son who defies the father.

These aspects will now be illustrated in this order; as will
be seen, a given attribute may represent more than one
of the primary tendencies.

(1) *The Father towards whom is felt admiration*

This aspect provides the largest component in the
conception of the Devil. The reason for this is probably
its double source, on the one hand in the son's admiration, and on the other in the daughter's repressed (libidinal) love. We see here the Devil as a rival to God, the
love for whom is drawn from the same two sources.

[1] Michelet, *op. cit.* p. 155.

In the first place may be noted the Devil's wonderful *powers*, which far exceeded those of ordinary beings. According to the Manichaean belief, which strongly influenced Christianity, he was actually the Creator of the mundane world and united in himself the most extraordinary capacities. He controlled the thunder and lightning, the wind and rain, powers previously ascribed to various gods. The infantile sexual symbolism of these beliefs need only be mentioned here. Abraham[1] has dealt fully with a part of it (lightning), and the mythological significance of rain (urine and semen) is well known, as is the flatus symbolism of thunder;[2] we have seen above that the Devil's evil odour was largely associated with his capacity of making thunder. It is important to note that the Devil's power especially related to *secret* and *magical* affairs. He was the master of all forbidden arts, the so-called 'black arts'. This was why he was the chief resort of magicians and other people who wanted either knowledge they were forbidden to have, or power to perform deeds beyond ordinary human capacity.

These powers would be put at the service of human beings in despair, usually on certain conditions, such as that they would henceforth belong to the Devil and do his bidding: just like the parents who do something for a child on condition that he is 'good', *i.e.* do what they want. In many legends he appears as a friendly helper of mankind who protects those in distress—particularly widows and orphans!—and aids them over their difficulties; Conway[3] and Wünsche[4] narrate a large number

---

[1] K. Abraham, *Traum und Mythus*, 1909, S. 29, 30 u.s.w.

[2] 'Le Tonnerre ce n'est qu'un pet; c'est Aristophane qui le dit' (*Bibliotheca Scatologica*, Art. 'Oratio pro Guano Humano'). J. Harington (*The Metamorphosis of Ajax*, 1596, p. 94) recalls the adventure of Socrates who, when Xantippe crowned him with a chamber-pot, carried it on his head and shoulders, saying to the laughing bystanders:

> 'It never yet was deem'd a wonder,
> To see that rain should follow thunder.'

[3] Conway, *op. cit.* ch. xxvii. 'Le bon diable'.

[4] A. Wünsche, *Der Sagenkreis vom geprellten Teufel*, 1905, Cap. vii. 'Der geprellte Teufel als Helfer der Menschen in allerlei Notlagen und Anliegen.'

of such stories. We here see the Devil playing the part
of the friendly father, and the correspondence between
the two conceptions is at times extraordinarily close in
detail.[1]

Very striking is the circumstance that the mediæval
Devil absorbed all the legends previously told of *giants*,
that mythological transformation of the child's conception of its parents.[2] The three main ideas combined here
are those of age, strength and size. One of the Devil's
attributes was his extreme age;[3] and many of his by-
names, *e.g.*, *Old* Nick (Hnikar), *Old* Davy, etc., seem to
hint at this. All the special interests and characteristics
of the giants of old were transferred *en bloc* to the Devil;
a number of them are fully related by Grimm,[4] so that
the details need not be given here. Chief among them was
his interest in building,[5] one that we would trace onto-
genetically to one of the infantile conceptions of parental
child-making; according to this babies—and therefore
other interesting objects—are constructed out of in-
testinal contents, an interest which later becomes transferred to the idea of formations out of sand, mortar, etc.[6]
Wünsche[7] writes: 'Bei näherer Betrachtung erweisen
sich ferner alle die Sagen, nach denen der Teufel mäch-
tige Dämme, die quer durch den See gehen, Mauern nach
Art der Zyklopen und Brücken, die hoch in den Himmel
hineinragen und über Abgründe, Schluchten und Täler
führen, errichtet, als christianisierte örtliche Riesen-
sagen. Auch Hünen- und Brunhildebetten berühren sich
mit Teufelsbetten.' ('On closer examination all the sagas
in which the Devil erects mighty dams that run straight
across lakes, cyclopean walls, and bridges that range
high into the sky and lead over abysses, ravines and

---

[1] [Compare in this connection Freud, 'Eine Teufelsneurose im siebzehnten
Jahrhundert', *op. cit.*]
[2] See Meyer, *op. cit.* S. 143, for a detailed account of the attributes of
mythological giants.
[3] Grimm, *op. cit.* S. 826.
[4] Grimm, *op. cit.* S. 852-856, and *Nachtrag*, S. 301.
[5] See Wünsche, *op. cit.* Cap. ii., 'Der geprellte Teufel als Baumeister'.
[6] The primitive passion of children for building has been extensively studied
by R. A. Acher, *American Journal of Psychology*, Jan. 1910, p. 116 *et seq.*
[7] Wünsche, *op. cit.* S. 14.

valleys prove to be Christianized giant sagas of various localities. Cairns, barrows and "Brunhilda beds" also get connected with "Devil beds" '.) Nor did the Devil content himself with copying the deeds of the giants, for on various occasions he used to appear in their actual shape; thus St. Anthony saw him as 'a monstrous giant whose head reached to the clouds', as did also St. Brigitta, and Dante depicted Lucifer as of giant size.

The theme of the 'returning dead' has been discussed above in the chapters on the Incubus and Vampire, and its connection with ancestor worship and incest pointed out. It is therefore of interest to note that it was a favourite practice on the part of the Devil to appear at night in the guise of some person who had died,[1] particularly to appear to a woman in the form of her father. The explanation of this was hinted at more than three hundred years ago by Thomas Nashe,[2] who writes: 'It will bee demaunded why in the likenes of ones father or mother,,or kinsfolks, he (the devil) oftentimes presents himselfe unto us? No other reason can bee guiven of it but this, that in those shapes which hee supposeth most familliar unto us, and that wee are inclined to with a naturall kind of love, we will sooner hearken to him than otherwise.'

Psycho-analysis has shown that the primary source of the boy's envy of the father relates to his sexual potency. As will presently be illustrated, the visits and temptations of the Devil were predominantly of a libidinous nature. In further accord with this link with the father idea is the close relation between the Devil and the *Snake*, for—as was pointed out in a previous chapter—the phallic significance of the snake is specifically connected with the father's member; this creature, with its mysterious and insinuating behaviour is admirably adapted to symbolize the secret activity of the father so envied by the boy. The tempter of the Old Testament

[1] Graf, *op. cit.* S. 57, 58, 65-67. P. L. Jacob, *Curiosités infernales*, pp. 35-37.
[2] *The Works of Thomas Nashe*, 1904 edition, vol. i., 'The Terrors of the Night' (1594), p. 348.

was styled Leviathan (=insinuating serpent) in the Kabbalah, and his equivalent in other countries, such as Ahriman in Persia, Apep in Egypt, Midgard in Norway, Set in Egypt and Vritra in India, were also commonly portrayed in the form of a snake; we might also mention the evil snake or dragon crushed by Apollo, Bellerophon, Heracles, Krishna, Odin, St. George and other heroes. Indeed, in this respect the Devil was in excellent company, for—as was expounded earlier in connection with the practice of Incubation—not only has the Snake-God been one of the most general objects of worship all over the world, but the gods of more civilized communities often assumed this guise, usually when engaged on love adventures. The circumstances of these disguises provide in themselves a clue to the meaning of the snake beliefs, and the early fathers of the Jewish and Christian Churches held that the serpent of the Garden of Eden symbolized evil lust.[1] The Christian Devil frequently appeared in the form of a snake or fiery dragon;[2] St. Anthony testified to the former from his own experience, as did St. Coleta.[3] With the Devil the sexual nature of the symbolism is shown in a much grosser manner than with the classical gods, for not only was his tail composed of a snake, or else carried a snake's head at its tip, but his very arms were similarly constituted. As for his penis, this also was built to imitate the shape and movements of a snake;[4] probably that is why we read of such descriptions as the following:[5] 'il a une virilité gigantesque, couverte d'écailles, hérissée de piquants.'

The directly libidinous character of the Devil and his temptations is emphasized by every writer on the subject and is incorporated in innumerable stories.[6] It will suffice to select a single passage from Freimark,[7] of a kind that could be indefinitely multiplied: 'Den ersten

[1] Roskoff, op. cit. Bd. i. S. 195.   [2] Grimm, op. cit. S. 833, 851.
[3] Le Loyer, Discours et histoires des spectres, visions et apparitions, 1605, p. 353.
[4] Graf, op. cit. S. 50, 51.
[5] R. Brévannes, L'Orgie satanique à travers les siècles, 1904, p. 115.
[6] See, for instance, Jacob, op. cit. pp. 85-96.
[7] H. Freimark, Okkultismus und Sexualität, S. 297.

Anstoss zum Teufelsbund geben fast ausschliesslich
sexuelle Motive. . . . In allen Berichten über die Verführung zur Hexerei und zum Teufelsbund nimmt unverhüllt die sexuelle Verführung die erste Stelle ein.'
('The first impulse to the Devil's pact proceeded from
almost exclusively sexual motives. . . . In all reports on
the seduction to witchcraft and the pact sexual seduction openly takes the first place.') This was the sin above
all else that the Church most warned against. Sinistrari,[1]
for instance, says: 'ratione tantae enormitatis contra
Religionem, quae praesuppositur coitu cum Diabolo,
profecto Daemonialitas maximum est criminum car-
nalium.' A favourite device for accomplishing his design
was for the Devil to deceive a woman by impersonating
her lover or husband,[2] just as the Incubus did. Bodin[3]
relates cases where the Devil even solicited and seduced
girls of six, 'qui est l'aage de cognoissance aux filles'!
The sexual temptations to which Buddha, Zoroaster and
other divine Beings had been subjected were in Christian
times transferred to various saints, most of whom, such
as St. Anthony, St. Benedict, St. Elizabeth and St.
Martin withstood them, whilst others, such as St. Vic-
torinus, succumbed.

As is well known, the Devil's favourite metamorphosis
was into a he-goat, the classical symbol of lasciviousness;
it was its almost invariable guise at the Witches' Sabbath.
Being ignorant of mythology, many Christian writers
were much puzzled at this; Scaliger,[4] for instance, considers it simply a marvel. Bodin,[5] on the other hand,
suspected the meaning of it, and writes: 'Mais c'est bien
chose estrange, que Satan . . . prend la figure d'un Bouc,
si ce n'est pour estre une beste puante et salace. . . . Or la
proprieté des Daemons est d'avoir puissance sur la
cupidité lascive et brutale.' Incidentally, one more proof

---

[1] P. Sinistrari, *Demoniality* (seventeenth century), 1879 edition, p. 218.
[2] J. G. Dalyell, *The Darker Superstitions of Scotland*, 1835, p. 554. Hinkmar, quoted by J. Hansen, *op. cit.* S. 73.
[3] J. Bodin, *De la demonomanie des sorciers*, 1593, p. 212.
[4] Smith, *Scaligerana*, 1669, Part ii. Article 'Azazael'.
[5] Bodin, *op. cit.* p. 190.

of the original identity of the Devil and God conceptions
is the fact that not merely was the goat the symbol of
numerous deities of antiquity, but also that Pan, the
goat-god *par excellence*—from whom the Devil derived
so many of his attributes—has been identified with the
highest God of the Babylonians, Mithra,[1] with the
Egyptian God Min[2] (the representative of the male
principle) and even with Zeus himself.[3]

The minutest attention was devoted in the Middle
Ages to the sexual attributes of the Devil, and particularly to the organ concerned.[4] This was generally sinuous,
pointed and snake-like, made sometimes of half-iron and
half-flesh, at other times wholly of horn, and was commonly forked like a serpent's tongue; he customarily
performed both coitus and pederastia at once, while
sometimes a third prong reached to his leman's mouth.[5]

The mediæval Devil was far from being the first one
to be renowned for his lasciviousness. Not to speak of
the deities of classical antiquity, we find the same trait
recorded of most evil precursors of the Christian Devil.
The reputation of Pan himself was such that he was
known to the theologians of the Middle Ages as the
Prince of Incubi.[6] In the Koran the Devil is known only
as a seducer.[7] The worship of the Brahman Shiva, the
evil creator and destroyer of the world, is a purely
phallic one.[8] The Bedouin ghoul, the Buddhist Mara,
the Persian Aêshma-Daêva (the ancestor of the Jewish
Asmodai), the Syrian djinn—all have the same lascivious reputation; even in far-off Australia the Iruntari-

---

[1] J. M. Robertson, *Pagan Christs*, 1903, p. 315.

[2] W. M. Flinders Petrie, *The Religion of Ancient Egypt*, 1908, p. 59.

[3] R. P. Knight, *The Symbolical Language of Ancient Art and Mythology*, 1876
edition, p. 137.

[4] See, for instance, Pierre de Lancre, *Tableau de l'inconstance des mauvais
anges et démons*, 1612, pp. 224, 225.

[5] [Miss M. A. Murray, in her book *The Witch Cult in Western Europe*, 1921,
p. 178, makes the interesting suggestion that these descriptions are to be
explained by the custom of the leader of the witch covens, the representative
of the Devil, being compelled by the exigencies of his devotees to have recourse
to the aid of artificial phalli, probably of leather.]

[6] Collin de Plancy, *op. cit.* t. ii. p. 135.

[7] Eickmann, *Die Angelologie und Dämonologie des Korans*, 1908, S. 44.

[8] E. Sellon, *Annotations on the Sacred Writings of the Hindus*, 1902, p. 9.

via, or evil spirits, are addicted to the practice of cai.̣
ing off women in the dark.[1] But the Devil's reputation
surpassed all these to such an extent that Milton[2] could
call one of his shapes:

> Belial, the dissolutest spirit that fell,
> The sensualest, and, after Asmodai,
> The fleshliest Incubus.

In connection with the same Father aspect of the Devil
is to be mentioned his close association with Nature,
the personification of the Mother, and particularly with
the hidden parts of Nature; it is characteristic of the
incestuous significance of the Devil idea that, through
this association, Nature herself—just as women did in
the early days of Christianity—becomes conceived of as
the evil side of the universe. The Devil dwells in remote
places, being especially fond of dark forests and of
treasure spots, such as gold mines.[3] He penetrates into
caverns and into the very interior of Mother Earth, *i.e.*
into places quite inaccessible to ordinary beings (=
children). Other association between the ideas of Devil
and Mother will be mentioned in due course.

2. *The Father against whom is felt hostility*

Here the Devil presents himself not as a tempter and
seducer, but as a pursuer, as the enemy of mankind. All
the paternal arbitrariness, savage cruelty, unjustness,
petty tyranny and general unreasonableness that dis-
figures the Yahweh of the Old Testament[4] were inherited
to the full by the Christian Devil. The resemblance of
this picture to the one that many a child conceives of as
accurately describing his father is only too striking. The
Devil mocks at the endeavours and strivings of men,
derides their ambitions and makes sport of their failures.
He teases, annoys and harms them out of pure enjoy-

[1] B. Spencer and F. J. Gillen, *The Native Tribes of Central Australia*, 1899,
p. 517.
[2] Milton, *Paradise Regained*, Book ii. line 150.
[3] Le Loyer, *op. cit.* p. 340.
[4] See Gener, *op. cit.* pp. 368-377, for an exposition of this.

ment at doing so, undoes their labour and baffles all their efforts. Mankind lives in one constant fight with him, in either the resisting of attractive temptations or the thwarting of his mischievous assaults. The Oedipus situation, both male and female, is thus reconstructed in its entirety.

The Devil's hostility to man is, characteristically enough, especially prominent in the legends he inherited from the giants (=grown-ups). In these he performs all manner of deeds to hinder and injure;[1] he heaves huge blocks of stone at churches and nunneries, dams rivers so as to cause floodings, builds walls to keep out human beings from his domains, and so on. Men have to fight against him in his giant form, just as the young gods fought against the Titans of old.

In this fight human beings were by no means always defeated. Many are the tales in which the Devil is circumvented and cheated, and it is noteworthy that these tales also are mostly taken from heathen ones in which the giants were the antagonists.[2] For instance, according to Wünsche,[3] 'Hinter dem Schmiede von Bielefeld, Apolda u.s.w. in den bekannten Märchen, der den Teufel im Sacke auf dem Amboss ganz windelweich hämmert, so dass er ein Zetergeschrei erhebt und um seine Freilassung bittet, verbirgt sich, wie wir unten zeigen werden, sicherlich der seinen Hammer auf das Haupt des Riesen schwingende Thor. Ist doch "Meister Hammerlein" auch ein gebräuchlicher Beiname des Teufels.' ('Behind the Smith of Bielefeld, Apolda, etc., in the well-known folk-tales, who hammers the Devil in a sack on an anvil till he is limp as a rag, so that he shriekingly implores to be set free, is certainly concealed —as we shall presently show—Thor swinging his hammer on the head of the giant. After all, 'Master Hammerkin' is also a common nickname for the Devil.') Incidentally, the fact that the Devil can thus be identified both with

[1] See Grimm, op. cit. S. 852-855, and Nachtrag, S. 301. Wünsche, loc. cit.
[2] See especially Wünsche's book, in comparison with the chapter 46 on 'Der geblendete Riese' in L. Laistner's Das Rätsel der Sphinx, 1889, Bd. ii. S. 109-151.
[3] Wünsche, op. cit. S. 13, 14.

Thor and his hammer on the one hand, and on the other hand with the giant Thor overcomes is a good illustration of our thesis that the Devil can represent both elements in the Father-Son equation. A favourite device was to bargain with the Devil for the sale of a soul on condition that he carried out some work before cock-crow, and then at the last moment to make a cock-crow by pinching it or to imitate the sound so that wakened cocks in the neighbourhood really crowed. Even a horse could hoodwink the poor Devil.[1] It is significant for the present argument that in all these stories the Devil was circumvented by guile, never by force; slyness and guile are notoriously the only weapons of the weak child against a parent's opposition.

A powerful person who is easily cheated by a weaker one is naturally conceived of as stupid, or at least as naïve. This contemptuous view is one that children often entertain of their parents, partly for the reason just stated, and partly as an over-compensatory reaction to the other occasions when they feel their ignorance in contrast with the parents' knowledge. The tales in which the Devil, presenting at times an incredible naïveté, is easily hoodwinked form an extensive chapter in the history of demonolatry,[2] and have furnished an important source for the later conception of clowns, buffoons and stage-fools.[3] Psycho-analysis of the individual stories, which we must renounce here, shows clearly the infantile sources of the motives and definitely confirms the conclusions here represented in brief.

The child-like contempt for the Devil also shows itself in many other ways, especially in denial of his potency. None of the buildings he erects can he complete, his plans and schemes are almost always thwarted at the last moment, and on one point in particular all writers

[1] M. Jähns, *Ross und Reiter*, 1872, Bd. i. S. 87.
[2] See Wünsche, *op. cit.* cap. viii. 'Der dumme, geprellte Teufel', and the section on 'Der dumme Teufel' in Roskoff, *op. cit.* Bd. i. S. 394-399.
[3] See the section on 'Der Teufel als Lustigmacher' in Roskoff, *op. cit.* Bd. i. S. 399-404. [Reference may also be made to the analysis of Punch in my essay on 'Symbolism', *Papers on Psycho-Analysis*, 3rd ed. 1923, pp. 162-164, 166-167.]

are unanimous—his lack of semen and consequent sterility; as we shall see later, this last belief has a deeper
source than mere contempt. To the same set of beliefs
may also be ascribed the Devil's supposed detestation
of salt, for this can be shown to be an ancient mythological symbol for semen;[1] Bodin[2] was therefore in a
sense right when he accounted for the Devil's aversion
for it on the ground that it is a 'symbol of eternity'.

Even many of the devices employed to ward off the
Devil's assaults originate in infantile and sexual symbolism. A renowned one, often effective when all else
failed, was to expose one's buttocks and expel flatus at
him; no less a person than Martin Luther had recourse
to it.[3] Psycho-analysis has shown that the deepest
source of the child's defiance of his parents is his refusal
to control his sphincters at their bidding, and in consequence the acts just mentioned have been used the world
over as a sign of defiance or contempt. Another more
general device for opposing the Devil's might consisted
in waving in front of him the Holy Cross, or in simply
making the sign of the cross. The unconscious phallic
significance of this symbol has long been known,[4] so that
to expose the cross of Christ (the Son) before the Devil
would unconsciously be equivalent to the child's exhibi-
tionistic defiance of paternal authority.

The most powerful refuge of the threatened human
being, however, was to call on the Virgin Mary for help.
Indeed, so universal was this that the whole matter
largely resolved itself into a standing fight between the
Devil and the Holy Mother. Roskoff,[5] who gives many
examples of this, says: 'Die Thätigkeit des Teufels wird
überdies vornehmlich entwickelt und hervorgerufen

---

[1] See Ernest Jones, 'Die symbolische Bedeutung des Salzes in Folklore und
Aberglaube', *Imago*, 1912, Bd. i. S. 361 and 454. [Reprinted as ch. iv. of *Essays
in Applied Psycho-Analysis*, 1923.]
[2] Bodin, *op. cit.* p. 278.
[3] Freimark, *op. cit.* S. 84. The original references are given by J. G. Bourke,
Scatologic Rites of all Nations, 1891, pp. 163, 444.
[4] C. Howard, *Sex Worship*, 1902, cap. viii. 'The Serpent and the Cross'.
T. Inman, *Ancient Pagan and Modern Christian Symbolism*, 1874. S. Rocco,
Sex Mythology, including an Account of the Masculine Cross, 1898.
[5] Roskoff, *op. cit.* Bd. ii. S. 198-205.

durch dessen Hass gegen die heilige Jungfrau, der um so mehr gesteigert wird, als diese, nach Frauenart, sich in alle Angelegenheiten hineinmengt und ihr, wie im gewöhnlichen Leben, in allem willfahren wird, so dass sie ihrenWillen immer durchsetzt und ihre Schützlinge, die nun einmal ihre Gunst durch eifrigen Marienkultus erlangt haben, auch nie fallen lässt, wenn sie übrigens auch die ärgsten Lumpen sein sollten.' ('Moreover, the activity of the Devil was especially developed and evoked by his hatred for the Holy Virgin. This hatred was all the more increased by her habit of meddling in all affairs, in the manner of women, and of always getting her own way, so that she never leaves her protégées in the lurch once they have won her favour by zealous worship at the Mary cult, even though they be the most scoundrelly rascals.') It is surely impossible to overlook the analogy between this situation and that of the child running to his mother for protection against an ill-tempered father, with the consequent marital bickering.[1]

(3) *The Son who imitates the Father*

The Devil was not altogether the enemy of God; in certain respects he might almost be called His representative, or at least His agent. Not only did he mock and torture the people he had succeeded in tempting to sin,[2] but he apparently went out of his way to punish the wicked.[3] He was specially severe in respect of sexual indulgence; one of his persecutions was, to quote Graf,[4] 'einen Mann und ein Weib bei fleischlicher Sünde in flagranti zu ertappen und beide unauflöslich aneinander zu fesseln, more canino' ('to surprise *in flagranti* a man and woman in carnal sin and to bind them together inseparably, *more canino*'). It is noteworthy that in the Old Testament, at the time when the conceptions of God and

---

[1] [I have suggested that the same mechanism accounts for the present form assumed by the game of chess; see *International Journal of Psycho-Analysis*, vol. xii. 1931, p. 4.]

[2] Roskoff, *op. cit.* Bd. i. S. 270.

[3] Jacob, *op. cit.* pp. 22-33.   [4] Graf, *op. cit.* S. 136.

Devil were only beginning to get disengaged from each other, the association between the two was much closer than later, and the Devil appears really as the obedient servant of God the Father, differing from the good angels only in respect of the unpleasant nature of the tasks allotted him.

This 'identification' with God is at times very close indeed, and it is interesting to note that it was deliberately striven for by the Devil, who copied God to a truly remarkable extent. As until the past half-century the worship of Christ has been on the whole more prominent than that of God the Father, it is not astonishing that the Devil's resemblance to the Son has been greater than that to the Father. His physical appearance was at first depicted as beautiful and majestic,[1] often closely resembling Christ's; indeed he sometimes actually appeared in the exact form of Christ.[2] It was only in the Middle Ages that he became invested with ugly and grotesque traits.[3] Like Jesus, the Devil had twelve disciples,[4] descended into hell and was born again,[5] had his home in special churches, was worshipped at regularly recurring festivals, and had his followers baptized, while the details of the Devil's Sabbath caricatured the Holy Mass so closely that the resemblance greatly angered the theologians, who had of course no notion of the psychological identity of the two. The Devil even had a special Bible of his own; it was written in Bohemia and is now in the Royal library in Stockholm.[6] Further, he copied the Trinitarian conception itself.[7] It is little wonder that this habit of caricaturing earned him the title of 'God's ape'.

[1] Graf, op. cit. S. 52-54.
[2] Graf, op. cit. S. 64. Roskoff, op. cit. Bd. ii. S. 194.
[3] In the remarkable paintings by Wiertz we have a return to the earlier conception which Giotto was previously the last to depict.
[4] Grimm, op. cit. Nachtrag, S. 292, 302.
[5] A. Lehmann, Aberglaube und Zauberei, Deutsche Übersetzung, zweite Auflage, 1908, S. 114.
[6] A. Nyström, Christentum und freies Denken, 1909, S. 161.
[7] Didron (in his Manuel d'iconographie chrétienn., Iconograph H. p. 23) shows the French idea of the devil trinity in the fifteenth century. Dante's Satan was three-faced. Eusebius called the Devil 'Three-headed Beelzebub'.

Like Jesus also the Devil was provided with an earthly
mother and no father, and characteristically enough she
was a giantess, even larger than her son;[1] in some versions she appears as his grandmother. The mother seems
to have been composed of at least three figures. Both the
death-goddess Hel[2] and the mother of the giant Grendel[3]
contributed to the idea; one of the Devil's later by-names
was Grendel, perhaps the same as the English fire-demon
'Grant' of whom Gervasius of Tilbury speaks. Then
Wünsche[4] points out that 'wahrscheinlich bildet auch
die Sage von der Ellermutter, der neunhundertköpfigen
Mutter Hymirs, die die beiden Götter Thor und Tyr
beim Besuch in ihrer Wohnung durch Verstecken vor
ihrem grimmigen Sohn rettet, die Grundlage zu der
volkstümlichen Figur von des Teufels Grossmutter. Im
Märchen vom Glückskinde bei Grimm Nr. 29 heisst des
Teufels Grossmutter geradezu noch Ellermutter' ('the
basis for the popular figure of the Devil's Grandmother
is probably laid also by the saga of Ellermutter, the
nine-hundred-headed mother of Hymir, who saved the
two gods Thor and Tyr from her ferocious son by hiding
them when they visited her dwelling'). In most of these
legends, as in the last one mentioned, the Devil really is
again a mythological presentation of the hated father;
hence the replacement of the mother by the grandmother.
The same remark applies to the old saying that thunder
or rain during sunshine comes from the Devil beating his
mother.[5]

The conception of the Devil as the Son is another, very
natural ground for the belief that he has no semen, and
the bisexual nature of the whole belief is shown in the
idea that he can impregnate a woman only after having
first obtained some semen by acting as a Succubus to a
man,[6] which was the reason why it was always cold.[7]
This curious procedure gave rise to the most hair-

[1] Grimm, op. cit. S. 841.   [2] Wuttke, op. cit. S. 37.
[3] Roskoff, op. cit. Bd. i. S. 164.   [4] Wünsche, op. cit. S. 15.
[5] Grimm, op. cit. S. 842.
[6] W. G. Soldan, Geschichte der Hexenprozesse, 1880 edition, Bd. i. S. 181.
[7] Jacob, op. cit. p. 86.

splitting controversies to decide whether the offspring in such circumstances legally belonged to the original owner of the semen or to the Devil,[1] and whether the same rule was to apply here as in the case when the Devil acquired the semen from a man's nocturnal pollution.[2] To this idea of the sexual incapacity of the child I would also relate the belief in the limping God or Devil, which as Tylor[3] has pointed out, is to be found in the most varied stages of cultural development; incapacity to walk is among neurotics a frequent symbol for sexual impotence. The belief is of course highly over-determined, and has to do with all sorts of ideas connected with the castration complex. Castration wishes against the Father (God) are contained in it, while on the other hand the fact that the limp is so often the result of being hurled from heaven points to the castration fears of the son, his dread that the father will punish him in this appropriate manner.

Finally, we may mention in connection with the aspect of the Devil here under discussion his extraordinary capacity for gratitude; on the rare occasions when he is honestly treated he shows the highest appreciation of the treatment.[4]

(4) *The Son who defies the Father*

This is the prime aspect of the Devil, the Arch-rebel; his insubordinate disobedience and final insurrection against the authority of God the Father is the very paradigma of revolution. According to Origenes,[5] it was his arrogance and presumptuousness that constituted the reason for his being cast out of heaven, while, according to Irenäus, Tertullian and others,[6] the chief reason was his envy of God. The latter seems to be the earlier of the

---

[1] J. Sprenger und H. Institoris, *Der Hexenhammer*, 1588. Deutsche Übersetzung, 1906, Erster Teil, S. 51.
[2] Sprenger und Institoris, *op. cit.* Zweiter Teil, S. 64.
[3] E. B. Tylor, *Researches into the Early History of Mankind*, 3rd ed., 1878, pp. 365-371.
[4] Conway, *op. cit.* vol. ii. pp. 389, 395.
[5] Cited by Roskoff, *op. cit.* Bd. i. S. 231.   [6] Roskoff, *loc. cit.*

two; Roskoff[1] says: 'Das Motiv zur Feindschaft des Bösen gegen die Gottheit, der Ursprung des Bösen in der Welt ist sowohl nach der hebräischen Vorstellung vom nachexilischen Satan als auch in den Mythen anderer Völker, namentlich der Parsen, auf den Neid zurückgeführt, der in der Ich- und Selbstsucht wurzelt.' ('In the Hebrew idea of Satan as conceived after the exile as well as in the myths of other peoples, notably the Parsees, the reason for the enmity of the Evil One against the Godhead, and therefore the source of evil in the world, is to be traced to *envy*, which originates in selfishness.') What Nietzsche called the slave-morality of Christianity has always regarded pride as one of the deadly sins.

As is well known, a boy's insubordination against his father is not simply a matter of hostility; it is always accompanied by envy, which means admiration and desire to emulate. In his revolt, therefore, as a rule he in no sense frees himself from his father's influence. Whether he copies him directly or proceeds to the opposite extreme of trying to be as unlike him as possible is psychologically irrelevant; both reactions are equally imitation. This mixed reaction precisely applies to the Devil. He either tries to imitate God exactly or else, as we shall presently see in some detail, he does everything in just the opposite way from God's. His behaviour is thus ultimately derived altogether from God's, whether positively or negatively—another proof of the original identity of the two Beings. Further, the precise correspondence of the Devil's behaviour in this respect with that of earthly sons supports the thesis here sustained of the origin of the Devil idea in the relations between son and father.

The bond that unites him—against his will—to God also displays itself in his jealousy of anyone to whom God shows special favour, another trait typical of childhood. In the legend of St. Coleta it runs:[2] 'Der alte Feind habe die Eigentümlichkeit, je mehr er sehe, dass sich jemand Gott nähere, desto mehr suche er ihn zu ver-

[1] Roskoff, *op. cit.* Bd. i. S. 194.　　[2] Roskoff, *op. cit.* Bd. ii. S. 160.

folgen, zu beunruhigen und abzuhalten, grössere Übel
über ihn zu verhängen und sie zu vermehren.' ('The old
Enemy has this peculiarity, that the more he observes
anyone approaching God the more he seeks to persecute
him, to annoy him and thwart him, to hang misfortunes
over him and to multiply them.')

The same motive of jealousy is probably also the explanation of his attitude towards Jesus, although of
course this was partly determined also by the identification of God the Son with God the Father. Through God's
action in sending Christ to redeem mankind, the struggle
for the ownership of its members became primarily one
between Christ and the Devil. The doctrine of Salvation
was constructed out of it,[1] and, as Graf[2] ironically remarks, 'Seltsam genug! Unter den Menschen war niemals
die Rede soviel von Satanas, niemals wurde er so sehr
gefürchtet wie nach dem Siege Christi, nach dem Voll-
zug der Erlösung.' ('How curious! There was never so
much talk about Satan, never was he so much dreaded,
until after the victory of Christ, after Salvation had
been achieved.') The Devil, again imitating God, made
desperate efforts to capture the world by providing a
son of his own who would conquer Christ. Merlin and
Robert the Devil represented two such attempts,[3] but
the former was saved to God through his mother's re-
pentance and the latter through his own. Nero, Moham-
med and Luther, no less than several of the Popes, were
similarly reputed to be sons of the Devil, begotten for
this purpose. In the Middle Ages the fear of the threatened Antichrist was terrific, and the tension of anxious
expectation of his birth was heightened to indescribable
terror by recurrent rumours and prophecies of the
event.[4]

Finally, the Devil's passionate hatred of injustice and
his custom of defending the innocent, particularly the
poor and weak, against their persecutors accords with

[1] Roskoff, *op. cit.* Bd. i. S. 224-229, 273.
[2] Graf, *op. cit.* S. 22.
[3] Graf, *op. cit.* S. 198-203.   [4] Conway, *op. cit.* pp. 389, 390.

the aspect of the Devil idea as a representation of the feelings of the rebellious Son.

*   *   *   *   *

We may now turn to our *third problem*, namely the relation of the belief in the Devil to the experiences of the Nightmare. The considerations adduced in the first chapter would lead one to expect that in the creation of such an 'anxiety-idea' *par excellence* as the belief in the Devil, a considerable part must have been played by the most intense anxiety experience known to man, namely the Nightmare. This inference has been drawn by several previous writers. We have, for instance, already cited the opinions of Clodd and Höfler on this matter.[1] It is in full accord with this conclusion that the Devil is pre-eminently a demon of the night, for it is by night that he mostly appears, and it is at night that his powers are believed to reach their zenith.[2]

It would be quite intelligible if this belief had in part originated in the manifest content of the Nightmare, with its terrifying visions, and this is evidently the view of previous writers, notably Laistner, but a careful comparison of the belief with the latent content of the Nightmare shows such an extraordinary resemblance between the two as definitely to demonstrate an inherent relationship between them.

It was pointed out above that the two chief characteristics of the latent content of the Nightmare are that it is essentially sexual and predominantly incestuous. Of the sexual activities of the Devil no more need be said; it is sufficiently illustrated by the Abyssinian proverb: 'When a woman sleeps alone, the Devil sleeps with her.' It is especially noteworthy that the predecessors of the mediæval Devil were all formal Incubi. Pan, from whom the Devil took over so many attributes, was the equivalent of Ephialtes,[3] the spirit who provided us with what was till recently the scientific name for the Night-

[1] See Part II. p. 73 and Part II. p. 85 respectively.   [2] Graf, *op. cit.* S. 108.
[3] W. H. Roscher, *Ephialtes, Eine pathologisch-mythologische Abhandlung über die Alpträume und Alpdämonen des klassischen Altertums*, 1900, S. 57-62.

mare; the fauns of Greece were also active Incubi.[1] Casting further back we find that the storm demons of Babylonia and of India, the alu[2] or marut[3] respectively, the precursors of Ares and Ephialtes, were called 'the crushers' from their habit of lying on the breast of sleepers; the Teutonic giant Grendel, of whom mention has also been made above, had the same custom.[4]

The facts just cited indicate that the belief in the Devil is closely connected with ancestor worship; more than three hundred years ago Burton[5] expressed the view that devils were merely the souls of the departed, *i.e.* of ancestors. If the thesis here maintained is correct, namely that the Devil idea is the projection of repressed wishes connected with the father, it follows that intercourse with him symbolizes incest with the father. The fact that the snake, the symbol of the father's phallus, plays an equally prominent part in the Devil idea as in the rest of the Nightmare mythology illustrates the origin of both in incestuous thoughts.

In the various stories of the Devil we find many details strongly suggestive of the mental processes characteristic of dreams, and two of them may be briefly mentioned here. One of the most typical of these is the power of transformation. We have mentioned above the capacity of the Devil for assuming any human form he wished,[6] and also have called attention to the frequency with which he appeared in the shape of a serpent or he-goat. But there was no possible kind of animal whose form he did not assume at times,[7] and he even had the power of changing human beings into animals.[8] Another example is the psychological process known as 'reversal', the putting or doing things backwards or upside down, which Freud[9] has shown to be exceedingly character-

---

[1] Roskoff, *op. cit.* S. 146.
[2] T. G. Pinches, *The Religion of Babylonia and Assyria*, 1906, p. 108.
[3] G. W. Cox, *The Mythology of the Aryan Nations*, 1870, vol. ii. pp. 222, 253.
[4] Grimm, *op. cit.* S. 849.
[5] R. Burton, *The Anatomy of Melancholy*, 1826 ed., vol. i. p. 5.
[6] See Jacob, *op. cit.* pp. 33-43.
[7] Graf, *op. cit.* S. 59, 138.   [8] Roskoff, *op. cit.* S. 305.
[9] Sigm. Freud, *Die Traumdeutung*, Dritte Auflage, 1911, S. 257.

istic of dream productions—perhaps even more so than
of other unconscious processes. Most of the writers on
the Devil have noted this feature, especially in regard
to the Sabbath. Thus those present at this festival dance
backwards[1] in a ring, in the *reverse* direction to the sun
(widdershins) with their faces *turned away* from the
centre,[2] they dip their *left* hand in the holy water[3] (the
Devil's urine[4]), make the sign of the cross in the *reverse*
direction,[5] partake of *black* bread at the Mass[6] and while
this is being performed make use of *black* candles.[7]
The Devil himself had a *second face* on the buttocks,
and this was often the face of a beautiful *woman*,[8]
his penis was often situate *behind* instead of in *front*,[9]
his person emitted a hellish stink that contrasted with
the heavenly fragrance of the Saviour,[10] and so on.

To the dream origin may also be largely attributed
the circumstance that coitus with the Devil was as a
rule extremely painful and disagreeable,[11] for this is
often so in anxiety dreams in which coitus takes
place.

A few words may now be said on the resemblances
between the belief in the Devil and those discussed in
the three preceding chapters. The first of these, the
belief in the Incubus, was an essential constituent of the
Devil idea, since according to the orthodox view the
Incubi themselves were simply devils. Even with the
immediate equivalent of the classical Incubi, the
German Alp, the idea of the Devil stood in the closest
association,[12] one, however, we cannot pursue further
here, for the theme is purely a mythological one.

[1] Grimm, *op. cit.* S. 895.
[2] Lehmann, *op. cit.* S. 114.
[3] Brévannes, *op. cit.* p. 123.
[4] B. Picart, *Coutumes et cérémonies religieuses*, 1729, vol. viii. p. 69.
[5] Brévannes, *loc. cit.*
[6] De Lancre, *op. cit.* p. 460.
[7] Th. de Cauzons, *La Magie et la sorcellerie en France*, t. i. p. 240.
[8] Brévannes, *op. cit.* p. 115.
[9] De Lancre, *op. cit.* p. 217.
[10] Roskoff, *op. cit.* Bd. ii. S. 156.
[11] Delrio, *Les Controverses et recherches magiques*, 1611, p. 187. O. Henne am
Rhyn, *Der Teufels- und Hexenglaube*, 1892, S. 68.
[12] See Grimm, *op. cit.* S. 847, and *Nachtrag*, S. 298.

The relation between the belief in the Devil and that in the *Werewolf* and Vampire lies more in the latent content common to them than in external similarities, but even in the latter respect many points of interest may be observed. Thus the Devil was commonly named 'the soul-robbing wolf' by the Fathers of the Church,[1] and in the laws of Canute he is termed 'vôdfreca verewulf'.[2] In the Middle Ages the Devil was known as the arch-wolf, Archilupus, and he often appeared in the guise of a wolf.[3] Grimm[4] traces the Slavonic names for the Devil (Polish *wrog*, Servian *vrag*, etc.) to the Old High German *warg* (=wolf), and the Slavonic evil spirit Czernobog usually appeared in the form of a wolf.[5] The mediæval Devil's descent from a wolf seems to have been mainly Teutonic, notably from Odin's two wolves. Wünsche[6] writes: 'Neben Loki wird aber auch dem Fenrirwolf nach mehreren missglückten Versuchen mit einem von den Zwergen verfertigten unzerreissbaren Bande von den Göttern eine Fessel angelegt. In der Redensart: "Der Teufel ist los", haben wir sicher noch eine Erinnerung an Fenrirs wiederholtes Sichfreimachen von den starken Banden und Stricken, die ihm von den Göttern um den Hals geschlungen wurden.' ('The Gods after several unsuccessful attempts managed to bind the Fenrir wolf, as well as Loki, with an unbreakable girdle manufactured by the dwarves. In the saying "the Devil is loose" we certainly have a memory of the numerous occasions on which Fenrir broke loose from the strong chains and cords that the Gods had fastened round his neck.') In the Middle Ages the Devil was also called 'the wolf of hell', and Grimm[7] remarks: 'der Teufel hat seinen ungeheuren Rachen mit Wolf und Hölle gemein' ('the Devil has a monstrous gorge in common with the wolf and with hell'). Of historical interest is the case of Angela de

---

[1] The association between Satan and a wolf is still current, as may be seen from Browning's poem, 'Ivan Ivanovitch'.
[2] Grimm, *op. cit.* S. 32.
[3] J. Ennemoser, *Geschichte der Magie*, zweite Auflage, 1844, S. 791. W. Hertz, *Der Werwolf*, 1862, S. 17.
[4] Grimm, *loc. cit.*   [5] Roskoff, *op. cit.* Bd. i. S. 174.
[6] Wünsche, *op. cit.* S. 13.   [7] Grimm, *loc. cit.*

Labarethe, who is remembered as the first woman to be burned for having sexual relations with the Devil—in 1275 in Toulouse; the result of the intercourse was that she bore a monster with a wolf's head and a tail like a snake.[1]

Of the two cardinal features of the *Vampire*, namely the belief that he is a *revenant* and his habit of sucking blood from a sleeper, the former is the more prominent in the Devil belief and was discussed above. The nearest indication I have found to the second feature concerns the old German devil Grendel, mentioned earlier: Grimm[2] writes of him 'er trinkt das Blut aus den Adern und gleicht Vampyren, deren Lippen von frischem Blut benetzt sind. In einer altnordischen Saga findet sich ein ähnlicher Dämon, Grûnr aegir genannt . . . er trinkt das Blut aus Menschen und Thieren' ('he drinks the blood out of the veins and thus resembles vampires, whose lips are sprinkled with fresh blood. In an Old Norse saga there is to be found a similar demon, by the name of Grûnr aegir, . . . he drinks the blood of human beings and of animals'). The reason I should give for the absence of the blood-sucking feature is that with the Devil there is no question of a corpse, and in our discussion of the psychology of Vampirism we saw how closely connected the idea of blood-sucking is with the problem of decomposition and re-vivification.

We may now conclude this chapter with a few general remarks on the belief in the Devil. We have seen that the infantile conflicts relating to the parents found one of its earliest expressions in peopling the universe with a number of powerful supernatural beings who were sometimes friendly, often ill-disposed, but always in need of propitiation. In the development of this set of beliefs dream experiences have probably played a predominant part. Mainly as the result of a pronounced tribal or national spirit, some peoples, notably the Jews, gradually fused these beings and thus developed a kind

---

[1] E. L. de Lamothe-Langon, *Histoire de l'Inquisition en France*, 1829, t. 2, p. 614.   [2] Grimm, *op. cit.* S. 849, 850.

188 NIGHTMARE AND MEDIÆVAL SUPERSTITIONS PT. II

of practical monotheism. This process, however, brought with it the necessity of allotting the good and evil attributes of the superior powers to two distinct Persons, and the more was good ascribed to the one the more did evil concentrate in the other. The exaggerated notion of sin characteristic of Christianity, and the sharper contrast between good and evil inculcated by its doctrine of salvation, resulted, it is true, in a loftier conception of God, but also in the creation of a Devil beside the horror of whom all earlier conceptions pale. In the past century or so, and especially during the last fifty years, the intensity of the Devil belief has largely faded, the belief in a benevolent Deity having proved the more tenacious of the two; the psychological explanation of this different fate with the two beliefs is in itself a matter of considerable interest, the discussion of which, however, would lead us too far from the present theme. The change did not come about without considerable theological struggle, since it obviously increased the difficulty of reconciling the existence of evil with the omnipotence of a benevolent Deity. The problem of evil, which has always proved baffling to theologians because inherently insoluble on theological premises, has been mainly circumvented by recourse to the view, developed in the fifth century, 'dass die Übel der Welt als Strafe oder als unbegreifliches Besserungsmittel zum heilsamen Fortschreiten in der Erkenntnis, zur Übung in der Geduld im Hinblick auf eine bessere Zukunft zu betrachten seien'[1] ('that the evil in the world is to be regarded as a punishment or as an incomprehensible means of improvement towards wholesome progress in knowledge and as an exercise in patience with a view to a better future'). How long humanity will rest content with such sophisms it is hard to say; the continued success of Mrs. Eddy's teaching that evil does not exist objectively, but only subjectively, would seem to point to a growing dissatisfaction with the orthodox explanations, though this consideration might have been a source of more encouragement

[1] Roskoff, *op. cit.* S. 267.

had that lady herself found it possible to dispense with her elaborate system of demonic influences.

Still the Devil dies hard. As Freimark[1] puts it, 'Werwolf und Vampir hatten für den Kulturmenschen längst ihre Schrecken verloren, nicht einmal mehr die Kinder mochten sie fürchten und auch das Alpdrücken des Hexenwahns hatte Europa von sich abgeschüttelt, nur Satan wich nicht.' ('Werewolf and Vampire have long since lost their terrors for educated people, they do not even frighten children any longer, and Europe has even shaken off the nightmare of the witchcraft delusion; only Satan does not yield.') We still occasionally read in the newspapers of a clerical exorcism of an hysteric possessed by the Devil,[2] and the belief in an actual Devil is still officially held by the Catholic Church and by most clergy of other Churches. One of the scenes of the closing years of the enlightened nineteenth century that deserves to live in history was the famous Miss Vaughan swindle,[3] in which Pope Leo XIII and several bishops officially blessed a lady who, though born of a union between her mother and the Devil, had been triumphantly saved to the Church; in the next year, 1897, Taxil confessed that not only the whole story, but even the lady herself, was a product of his imagination.

[1] Freimark, *op. cit.* S. 334.
[2] It will hardly be believed, but when practising in Canada (in 1911) I had considerable difficulty in dealing with a physician (!) who wanted to treat a case of dementia praecox by reading to her passages from the Bible so as to drive out the devil which he was convinced was inside her.

[To bring the matter still more up to date, I may quote from the *Sunday Times* of March 30, 1930, the case of a Ruthenian who so fully accepted his fellow-villagers' belief that he was possessed by the Devil that, after failing to get relief from the local priest's endeavours at exorcism, he hanged himself. His family and neighbours refused to touch the body, and it had to be buried by the authorities.]
[3] M. Kemmerich, *Kultur Kuriosa*, S. 229-234.

CHAPTER VII

WITCHES

THE problems relating to Witches, although intimately allied to those of the belief in the Devil, are still more complicated than these: for on the one hand there entered into the construction of the belief in Witchcraft even more factors than into the idea of the Devil, and on the other hand it concerned not imaginary beings, as the Incubus, Vampire, Werewolf and Devil beliefs did, but actual living and suffering human beings. It will never be known how many of these actually believed in the reality of the supposed occurrences. It is certain that many did not, for after confessing them under the most gruesome torture they admitted their innocence to their father-confessor, on the strict condition that he was to keep silent and thus allow them to be executed without being subjected to fresh and unendurable torture. Often, however, the mental state of the victims was such as to make them convinced that they had truly committed the 'crimes' of which they had been accused.

As in the previous chapter, we may distinguish several problems here, particularly:

(1) The fundamental psychological explanation of the belief in the idea of Witches;

(2) The reason why the epidemic belief broke out at a given period; and

(3) The relations between it and the experiences of Nightmare.

The thesis that will be maintained here in regard to the first of these problems is that *the Witch belief represents in the main an exteriorization of the repressed sexual conflicts of women, especially those relating to the feminine counterpart of the infantile Oedipus situation.* Just as the child's conception of the father becomes dissociated into

its beneficent and its malevolent aspects, giving rise to
the beliefs in a God and a Devil respectively, so does
that of the mother divide into the corresponding two,
which give rise to the beliefs in Goddesses (Mater Dei,
etc.) and female fiends respectively. Riklin[1] has incidentally suggested that the conception of giantesses,
witches and the like, represents the girl's attitude towards the mother as a sexual rival, and this view agrees
with the one here put forward. But, just as both sexes
contributed to the conception of the Devil, so we shall
find that both contributed to that of the Witch.

Before considering the historical aspects of the Witch
belief it will be well to discuss the essential features of
it in its fully developed stage. These may broadly be
divided into three groups, which were originally independent of one another and became fused only in the
course of the thirteenth century. They are:

1. Those concerning the relation of the Witch to her
   fellow creatures;
2. Those concerning her relation to the Devil; and
3. Those concerning her relation to God.

* * * * *

These three features may be briefly designated by the
words Maleficium, Pact and Heresy respectively. In the
Witch epidemic proper the Maleficium was the least
characteristic, so that we may dismiss it first. Although
it was the element that least sharply distinguished the
Witch proper from the ancient magician and soothsayer,
being indeed a direct continuation of the attributes of
these, it was nevertheless of cardinal importance in the
persecution of Witches. The reason for this was as follows. The initiative for the persecution came, as is well
known, mainly from the Church, which was greatly concerned to uproot heresy and to counteract the power of
the Devil. The laity, however, was not primarily interested in these theological undertakings, so the Church
had to stimulate their zeal by combining the objects of
its persecution with the primæval notion of harmful

[1] F. Riklin, *Wunscherfüllung und Symbolik im Märchen*, 1906, S. 74.

192 NIGHTMARE AND MEDIÆVAL SUPERSTITIONS PT. II

magic (Maleficium). Roused by the dread of this they
joined forces with the Church to destroy, for different
reasons, the hated sources of Maleficium, which the
Church declared to be one with heresy and pacts with
the Devil. Without this combination the antagonism to
Witches could never have achieved the universal intensity it did, one which can only be described as constituting an epidemic panic. We have therefore to inquire
carefully into the nature of the dread in question.

The harmful activities of Witches extended from
trivial annoyances to the gravest injuries, including
even death itself. Careful consideration of them reveals,
in my opinion, that the dread behind the belief in this
Maleficium was the fundamental fear of mankind concerning incapacity or failure of the sexual functions. The
reasons for this conclusion are that nearly all examples
of bewitching relate either directly to the production of
sexual impotence (including sterility) or to symbolic re-
presentations of this.

In the first place, it is to be observed that the most
frequent manifestation of Witchcraft was the direct interference with sexual functions, and particularly the
bringing about of impotence. Hansen[1] remarks: 'Die
Behexung trifft weitaus am häufigsten die geschlecht-
lichen Beziehungen zwischen Mann und Weib.' ('The
act of bewitching affected the sexual relations between
man and woman far more often than anything else.') In
the celebrated Bull on Witchcraft[2] the subject of Maleficium is treated under seven headings, of which six are
concerned directly with the sexual functions and one
with the transformation into animals. The well-known
Malleus Malificarum[3] devotes four chapters to a de-

---

[1] J. Hansen, *Zauberwahn, Inquisition und Hexenprozess im Mittelalter*,
1900, S. 479.
[2] Quoted in *Der Hexenhammer*, Deutsche Übersetzung von Schmidt, 1906,
Erster Teil, S. 107. [An English translation of this has recently been published
for the first time.]
[3] *Der Hexenhammer, op. cit.* Erster Teil, ch. 8, 9 and Zweiter Teil, ch. 6, 7.
See S. 131, 143-145 for the differential diagnosis between impotence from
coldness of nature and impotence from witchcraft, and J. Hansen, *op. cit.*
S. 88-92, 166, on the significance of this difference for divorce.

tailed consideration of the question of the means whereby this impotence is brought about, and lays special
stress on the fact that, in contrast with it, Witchcraft
cannot interfere with any other natural human function,
such as eating, walking, etc.[1] It fully discusses also the
different ways in which the penis can be 'bewitched
away', either in reality or through illusion. One favourite
measure was by the use of the *ligature de l'aiguillette*,
of which Brévannes[2] states that no less than fifty different procedures for its employment have been described. In the fifteenth and sixteenth centuries this was
in such frequent vogue, and was so generally feared, that
it became customary to carry out marriages in secret so
as to avoid the evil spell. The *Maleficium* extended its
influence further in the same direction. Through it the
love between a given man and woman could be annihi-
lated, barrenness of women and sterility of men induced,
the intra-uterine embryo destroyed and miscarriages
effected.[3] Even when all these perils were passed the resulting offspring was not safe, since Witches had a
passion for devouring new-born children, unbaptized
ones being especially exposed to this danger.

Most of the other instances of *Maleficium* symbolize
the same fear. The next most frequent was the destruction of crops, through rain or hailstones, or the render-
ing infertile of the land belonging to a particular person;
in all ages the association between the fertility of mankind and that of nature has been conceived to be very
intimate, as is shown by the fact, among a thousand
others, that the same Goddesses presided over both.
Even the minor instances of Witchcraft allow of the
same interpretation. Common ones of these, for example, were turning the milk sour (*i.e.* damaging the
semen), hindering butter-making (the symbolic meaning
of which has been elucidated by Abraham[4]), and inter-

[1] *Der Hexenhammer, op. cit.* Erster Teil, S. 127.
[2] R. Brévannes, *L'Orgie satanique à travers les siècles*, 1904, p. 71.
[3] These and many other details mentioned in the present chapter are taken from Hansen, *op. cit.*
[4] K. Abraham, *Traum und Mythus*, 1909, S. 66.

fering with the action of the spindle, *i.e.* with the work-
ings of the machine.[1] The only bodily function that
Witches could harm apart from the sexual one was that
of urinating, a function more closely allied to the sexual
than is generally realized;[2] in France to inflict this injury
was called *cheviller*.[3]

The belief that Witchcraft could bring about illness
and death[4] is connected with the same complex, for
psycho-analysis has shown that an undue fear of these
is conditioned by a deeper dread of impotence, with
which the other ideas easily become associated. A further
source for this belief is the association between it and
the idea of a sadistic assault; folk thought mostly regards illness and death as the consequence of an attack
on the part of an evil demon who violently overpowers
one—ultimately the antagonistic father. The action of
Witchcraft in this respect was performed by means of
poison, either material or incorporeal, and poison—*i.e.* a
fluid that produces serious effects on being taken into
the body—is a common unconscious symbol for semen,
as we know from the delusions of depressed and anxious
patients.

It is noteworthy that the charms by which *Maleficium*
was warded off were, appropriately enough for the talion
law, for the most part sexual symbols, as indeed have
been most magical charms, amulets, etc., of all ages.
The two most widely believed in as efficacious against
Witchcraft seem to have been salt[5] and horseshoes. As
was pointed out in the preceding chapter, *salt* is in folklore one of the most widely spread symbols for semen,
and therefore fertility; salt and water is a common folklore equivalent of urine,[6] *i.e.* the infantile semen.[7] Salt

[1] See Freud, *Die Traumdeutung*, Dritte Auflage, 1911, S. 211.
[2] See J. Sadger, 'Über Urethralerotik', *Psychoanalytisches Jahrbuch*, 1910,
Bd. ii. S. 409.
[3] J. A. S. Collin de Plancy, *Dictionnaire infernal*, 1818, t. i. p. 7.
[4] J. Grimm, *Deutsche Mythologie*, Vierte Ausgabe, 1876, S. 965.
[5] S. Seligmann, *Der böse Blick und Verwandtes*, 1910, Bd. ii. S. 34. A. Wuttke,
Der deutsche Volksaberglaube der Gegenwart, 1900, S. 95, 258, 283.
[6] J. G. Bourke, *Scatologic Rites of all Nations*, 1891.
[7] See Sadger, *op. cit.*

and bread (symbol of fæces, another infantile sexual material[1]) were also widely used against Witchcraft. The mixture of the two emphasized the idea of fertility;[2] the same mixture, by the way, was also used for bringing to a girl the picture of her future lover in a dream.[3] *Horseshoes*, that universal talisman of good luck, were also extensively used to guard against Witches;[4] Lawrence,[5] who has discussed at length the folklore of the horseshoe, calls it the 'anti-witch charm *par excellence*'. The vulval symbolism of this is pretty generally recognized by students of folklore and others. Other objects of allied shape and meaning have also been employed for the same purpose: thus stones with a hole bored through them, called from this connection 'hag-stones' or 'holy stones'.[6] Several of these objects are mentioned together in Butler's *Hudibras* (ii. 3. 291), where it is said that the conjuror could

> Chase evil spirits away by dint
> Of sickle, horseshoe, hollow flint.

Other anti-witch charms that may be just mentioned are: an upright knife,[7] a broomstick,[8] a horse's skull,[9] and the figure of a goblin's foot (a pentagram)[10]; the first two are masculine symbols, the other two bisexual ones.

The explanation of this mass belief in the *Maleficium* of Witches is not simple. It must have a very general basis, since something akin to it may be traced in varying measure at all epochs. In general one may remark that there exists the closest connection between magic and sexuality, as Bloch,[11] Hansen[12] and others have demonstrated, so that one is justified in suspecting the

---

[1] See Sigm. Freud, *Sammlung kleiner Schriften zur Neurosenlehre*, Zweite Folge, 1909, S. 168. [*Gesammelte Schriften*, Bd. v. S. 178; *Collected Papers*, vol. ii. p. 68.]

[2] Aigremont, *Fuss- und Schuhsymbolik und Erotik*, 1909, S. 55.

[3] Wuttke, *op. cit.* S. 244.

[4] J. Brand, *Popular Antiquities of Great Britain*, 1849, vol. iii. pp. 16, 17.

[5] R. M. Lawrence, *The Magic of the Horseshoe*, 1899, p. 88.

[6] J. G. Dalyell, *The Darker Superstitions of Scotland*, 1835, p. 140. E. H. Meyer, *Germanische Mythologie*, 1891, S. 119, 137.

[7] Wuttke, *op. cit.* S. 259.   [8] Wuttke, *op. cit.* S. 130.

[9] Lawrence, *op. cit.* p. 87.   [10] Grimm, *op. cit. Nachtrag*, S. 456, 459.

[11] I. Bloch, *Das Sexualleben unserer Zeit*, Zweite Auflage, 1907, S. 128.

[12] Hansen, *op. cit.* S. 12.

source of the *Maleficium* of Witches, which so largely
turned on the question of impotence, to be similarly of
a sexual nature.

The problem can be divided into the motives, real or
supposed, activating the Witches' behaviour or inten-
tions and, on the other side, the causes of the obviously
exaggerated fear on the part of their victims. In respect
of the former question Hansen[1] has suggested the following explanation. He traces it back to the Orient and
says: 'Sie dürfte in der Vielweiberei, und zwar gleich-
mässig in der natürlichen Eifersucht der Frauen eines
Mannes und der physischen Entnervung dieses Mannes
ihren Ursprung haben. Diese Art von *Maleficium* hat
einen ausgesprochen weiblichen Charakter; sie hat viel
dazu beigetragen, ältere, auf die Liebeserfolge der jün-
geren, eifersüchtige Frauen in den Verdacht der Hexerei
zu bringen.' ('It probably takes its origin in polygamy,
both in the natural jealousy of women in these circumstances and in the physical exhaustion of the men. This
kind of *Maleficium* has a pronouncedly feminine character; it greatly contributed to bringing older women,
jealous of the success of their younger sisters, under the
suspicion of Witchcraft.') This suggestion of Hansen's
may be supported by the consideration that in the
Middle Ages the loss of men in the numerous wars was
so great as to make the social conditions approximate to
those of the Orient; indeed polygamy was on this account allowed in Germany by special laws passed for the
purpose. The importance of the Crusades also in this
respect has been pointed out by Buckle.[2] This would probably account for a good deal of the inimical attitude of
unsatisfied women towards more fortunate people, and
not only towards other women, for on account of their
tendency to blame their facultative partners for their
lack of gratification, such women often vent their hostility on men as well.

---

[1] J. Hansen, *op. cit.* S. 12.
[2] H. T. Buckle, *History of Civilisation in England*, 1857, World's Classics
Edition, vol. i. p. 129.

More important, however, is the question of why the imaginary victims of this hostility should have been so terrified. The fears on the part of women, which appear to have related principally to conception and child-birth, one can understand as a continuation of the childhood fears of the same order which arise from the child's sense of guilt. To such women 'Witches' must have been personifications of the hated and feared mother who is felt to be inimical to the private wishes of the girl. It has to be remembered that the human heart is always ready to fear harm, ill-luck, etc., as a punishment for its own buried hostile or criminal wishes, the idea of punishment being naturally projected on to the other person concerned, in this case the mother.

The corresponding problem in regard to men is more obscure, i.e. the question how it came that they developed such a terror of certain women. We know, of course, that there is a deep-seated propensity on the part of men, as of women, to dread interference with their sexual functions and that this is always connected with the idea of punishment for their own guilt wishes ; and we may suppose that the inability of women to obtain sufficient gratification at this epoch for the reason advanced above would make the matter of masculine potency of unusual importance at such a time. But we are more accustomed in psycho-analysis to finding this idea of retaliatory punishment associated with the thought of other men, primarily with the father, rather than with that of women. Perhaps we get a clue from the well-known fact that Witches on the whole tended to belong to one of two groups, either ugly, hateful old women, or beautiful and charming young ones. I would suggest that in the former case we have to do with a displacement mechanism, the fear belonging to the father being transferred to women. We should not forget that the essential source not only of the Witches' power, but also of their conduct, was derived from the Devil, under whose orders they acted: the Devil, however, as was shown in the previous chapter, is a personification of the wicked father. Further, up to the thirteenth century, before the association with the Devil and with the idea of heresy was artificially forged, Maleficium was mostly exercised by men, by sorcerers; it was only after this date that the Church, to serve its own purposes, bodily transferred the primary attributes of the older male sorcerers to the new race of Witches. This was, after all, only a continuation of the Church's characteristic attitude towards women, a matter that will be commented on presently. Attractive women, just for the reason of their attractiveness, were the principal source of 'evil', *i.e.* of guilt and danger, and thus had drawn on to them the hostility of all who were concerned with the problem of 'sin', most of all the celibate Church. With the other class of women another factor entered, namely their own masculinity; the homosexual attributes of a certain class of older women, notably those of a misanthropic nature, naturally made it easy to identify them with the idea of the hostile father.

The view that Witches (and sorcerers) were invested with attributes derived from the child's conception of its parents, principally of disliked and dreaded parents, is supported by the interesting fact that there were many traces of the other, more friendly aspects of parents to be observed in them. Their actions were by no means invariably inimical to their fellow creatures. By means of various propitiatory approaches they could be persuaded, just like both God and the Devil, to exert their superhuman powers on behalf of those in need of their help. Thus their ability to foretell future events and to see things that were happening at a distance was frequently called into requisition. Of most assistance, however, was their power of invoking love, by love-philtres, love-charms, etc., or of destroying it where a hated rival was concerned: Witches have been known to go so far on occasion as to carry a lover to his mistress through the air on their goat.[1] They could even be induced to cure

[1] Robert Burton, *The Anatomy of Melancholy*, 1826 edition, vol. i. p. 79 and vol. ii. p. 289.

the impotence caused by sorcery; in reference to this Seligmann[1] says: 'Eine Hexe heilte die Männer, indem sie mit ihnen während einer Nacht im Ehebett schlief.' ('A Witch healed men by sleeping for a night in the marriage bed.')

We have next to consider the second group of characteristics, those to do with the Witch's relations to the Devil, which was the distinctive feature of the witch-craft epidemic. The pact with the Devil was the chief accusation at Witch trials, perhaps because from the nature of the circumstances it could more easily be 'proved' than either Maleficium or heresy, possibly because the Courts found it a more fascinating theme than these. Wuttke[2] states: 'Hauptgegenstände der Anklage waren der, meist auch geschlechtliche, Verkehr mit dem Teufel, die Hexenfahrt durch die Luft und der dort mit Tanz, Schmaus und oft auch mit Unzucht gefeierte Hexensabbat, wo dem Teufel gehuldigt und manchmal geopfert wurde; die Schädigung von Menschen und Vieh erscheint dagegen als Nebensache.' ('The main counts in the charges were the—usually sexual—intercourse with the Devil, the flight through the air, and the Witches' Sabbath, celebrated with dances, carousals and often also with obscenities, at which adoration of the Devil and often sacrifices to him took place: besides these the injuring of men and cattle appeared as almost trivial.') Soldan[3] similarly designates the pact with the Devil as the 'kernel' of the Witch trials. Ennemoser[4] writes: 'Dem späteren Begriff der Hexen ist unzüchtige Buhlschaft wesentlich, sie besiegelt das geschlossene Bündnis und verleiht dem Teufel freie Macht über die Zauberinnen, ohne diesen Greuel kommt überhaupt keine Hexe vor.' ('Lecherous amours were essential to the later conception of Witches. They sealed the pact and conferred on the Devil complete power over the sorceress. No Witch

[1] Seligmann, *op. cit.* Bd. i. S. 335.
[2] Wuttke, *op. cit.* S. 153.
[3] W. G. Soldan, *Geschichte der Hexenprozesse*, bearbeitet von H. Heppe, 1880, Bd. ii. S. 397.
[4] J. Ennemoser, *Geschichte der Magie*, Zweite Auflage, 1844, S. 844.

exists who has not passed through this horrible scene.')
Roskoff[1] says: 'Das spezifische Hexenwesen der eigentlichen Periode der Hexenprozesse beruht nicht mehr
bloss auf der Abweichung von Glaubens- und Lehrsätzen
der Kirche, sondern, wie aus der Bulle Innozenz VIII
und dem *Hexenhammer* ersichtlich ist, lautet die Anklage vornehmlich auf: "Bündnis mit dem Teufel und
vertrautesten Umgang mit demselben." ' ('The specific
nature of Witches in the real period of the Witch trials
no longer consisted of a mere departure from the doctrines of the Church, but, as is evident from Innocent
VIII.'s Bull and the *Malleus Maleficarum*, the principal
charge was "Pact with the Devil and the most intimate
relations with him".')

There cannot be any doubt that the central feature of
this bond with the Devil was the sexual relationship.
Both the older authorities, such as Bodin,[2] De Lancre,[3]
the authors of the *Malleus*,[4] and the more recent ones,
are quite unanimous on this point. Thus, to quote only
a few passages of a kind that could be multiplied almost
indefinitely, we may cite Freimark[5]: 'Den ersten Anstoss
zum Teufelsbund gaben fast ausschliesslich sexuelle
Motive. . . . In allen Berichten über die Verführung zur
Hexerei und zum Teufelsbund nimmt unverhüllt die
sexuelle Verführung die erste Stelle an.' ('The first
motive leading to the pact with the Devil was almost exclusively sexual in nature. . . . In all reports on the
attraction to witchcraft and compounding with the
Devil sexual temptation frankly takes the first place.')
Hansen[6]: 'Jede Hexe steht in geschlechtlichem Verkehr
mit dem Teufel. . . . Gerade durch diesen Verkehr wird
das dauernde Verhältnis zwischen Hexe und Teufel un-
terhalten.' ('Every Witch stood in a sexual relationship
to the Devil. . . . It was precisely through this relation-

---

[1] G. Roskoff, *Geschichte des Teufels*, 1869, Bd. ii. S. 213.
[2] J. Bodin, *De la démonomanie des sorciers*, 1593, p. 208, etc.
[3] P. de Lancre, *Tableau de l'inconstance des mauvais anges et démons*, 1612,
livre iii. disc. v.
[4] *Der Hexenhammer*, op. cit. Erster Teil, S. 108, etc.
[5] H. Freimark, *Okkultismus und Sexualität*, S. 297.
[6] Hansen, op. cit. S. 481.

ship that the lasting association between the Witch and the Devil was maintained.') Bloch[1]: 'Der Begriff des Weibes als Hexe drehte sich fast nur um das Geschlechtliche, das meist als "Teufelsbuhlschaft" vorgestellt wurde.' ('The conception of woman as Witch revolved almost exclusively around the sexual theme, pictured mostly as licentiousness with the Devil himself.') Quanter[2]: 'Die sexuellen Exzesse mit dem Teufel waren das einzige, was mit breitem Behagen den Hexen nachgesagt wurde.' ('Sexual excesses with the Devil was the sole thing that with general complacency was rumoured of Witches.') Nyström[3]: 'Das Spezifische der Hexenprozesse in ihrer eigentlichen Periode bestand in der Beschuldigung der Teufelsbündelei und des Geschlechtsverkehrs mit dem Teufel.' ('The specific feature of the Witch trials in their proper epoch consisted in the accusation of pacts and sexual intercourse with the Devil.') It was indeed believed that only after sexual intercourse with the Devil did the Witch obtain her magical powers.[4]

The notion of unlimited lechery with the Devil is evidently based on that of unsatisfied lasciviousness, an attribute that seems to have been commonly ascribed to women in the Middle Ages. As the Devil is the symbolic personification of the father, the source of the whole idea is plainly derived from unconscious incestuous longings, a subject that, as has been already pointed out, appears to have acquired special significance in the Middle Ages; further evidence in support of this view of the matter will presently be adduced. Just as many women, the mystics and saints, gratified their desires by attaching them to the idea of God, so did others, in a grosser way, by attaching them to the equivalent ideas of Incubus, Demon or Devil. The difference between the two processes is perhaps from this point of view,

[1] Bloch, *op. cit.* S. 129.
[2] R. Quanter, 'Der Hexenglaube des Mittelalters', *Geschlecht und Gesellschaft*, 1910, Bd. v. S. 367.
[3] A. Nyström, *Christentum und freies Denken*, 1909, S. 244.
[4] J. J. Ritter von Alpenburg, *Mythen und Sagen Tirols*, 1857, S. 256.

as Maury[1] has well pointed out, less than might appear.

Considering now the relation of Witch to Devil in a little more detail, we may conveniently divide the subject into a study of Witches:

1. At the Sabbath.
2. On the way to the Sabbath.
3. At home.

1. The *Sabbath* itself has been so vividly described by many writers that little need be said about it here. It is enough for our present purpose to emphasize the two cardinal features: its essentially sexual nature, and the parody it constitutes of religious ceremonies. The Sabbath was far from being a disorderly gathering: it consisted in a series of ceremonies more or less regularly carried out.[2] These were, in order: the entrance and procession, the acts of homage to Satan, the banquet, the Black Mass, the *danse du sabbat*, and finally the sexual orgy in which incestuous acts were performed between the nearest possible relatives.[3] The incestuous element is thus brought to the foreground both in the last-mentioned fact and through the symbolism of union with the Devil. The parody of the Christian rites was complete to the last detail and is indignantly commented on by most of the older writers.[4] Grimm[5] traces it to the envious desire on the part of the Devil to ape God, but a fuller explanation of it is that the underlying psychological significance of the two sets of ceremonies is in many respects identical, though the unconscious complexes at work are more directly indicated in the case of union with the Devil.

---

[1] L. F. A. Maury, *La Magie et l'astrologie*, 1860, 2e partie, ch. iii., 'Les mystiques rapprochés des sorciers'. See especially pp. 405, 406, 410, 411. See also F. Steingiesser, *Das Geschlechtsleben der Heiligen*, 1908.

[2] J. Michelet, *La Sorcière*, 3e édition, 1863, pp. 147-167.

[3] P. de Lancre, *op. cit.* p. 223. C. Kiesewetter, *Geschichte des Okkultismus*, Bd. ii. S. 461.

[4] For instance, de Lancre, *op. cit.* p. 460.

[5] Grimm, *op. cit.* S. 895.

The central ceremony of the Black Mass[1] may be taken as in the highest degree symbolic of this union, and therefore of the Sabbath itself. In it the youngest and most beautiful of the Witches, the Queen of the Sabbath, served as an altar,[2] after she had been baptized in the Devil's urine and the sign of the cross made *backwards* with the *left* hand. As she lay prone the sacred host was prepared by kneading on her buttocks a mixture of the most repulsive material, fæces, menstrual blood, urine, and offal of various kinds; this represented the famous modern *confarreatio*, the food of infamous love. We need not here go into the detailed symbolism of the proceeding, which would render necessary a discussion of the meaning of theophagy, necrophilia and other matters that do not directly concern the present theme; suffice it to say that this symbolism, as Pfister[3] has pointed out in his analytic study of two mystics, is throughout a sexual one.

2. The mode of *travel to the Sabbath* (*Hexenfahrt*) was a problem that greatly exercised the mediæval theologians. It was generally accepted that it was a flight through the air, but opinions were divided whether the body itself was transported or only the soul. It was ultimately decided that the former was the true view and that the sleeping body left behind was a counterfeit of the Devil's, arranged to deceive the husband or relative of the absent Witch. The sources of the belief in such travels by night are manifold, but they all stand in the closest relation to dreams and to sexuality. Even in the tenth century Regius von Prüm,[4] and in the twelfth century John of Salisbury,[5] maintained that the belief was an illusion originating in dream experiences, and

[1] Brévannes, *op. cit.* pp. 120-135. E. Laurent und P. Nagour, *Okkultismus und Liebe*, Deutsche Ausgabe, 1903, S. 134, 135, 246.
[2] G. W. Cox (*The Mythology of the Aryan Nations*, 1870, vol. ii. pp. 113-121), T. Inman (*Pagan and Modern Christian Symbolism*, 2nd ed., 1874, p. 74), and others have pointed out the female symbolism of the altar. The female body has at various times been used as an altar, even, it is stated, by the early Christians (Brévannes, *op. cit.* p. 38).
[3] O. Pfister, *Die Frömmigkeit des Grafen Ludwig von Zinzendorf*, 1910, S. 76, 77, 113.
[4] Quoted by Hansen, *op. cit.* S. 80.   [5] *Id. op. cit.* S. 134.

204 NIGHTMARE AND MEDIÆVAL SUPERSTITIONS PT. II

this view was held later by Weier and many other writers; it is indeed suggested by the very fact that the travel by night almost always took place when the woman was in a deep sleep.[1] The correspondence between the numerous descriptions of the Witches' flight and certain types of dreams is so absolute as to leave no doubt at all that this is the correct explanation.[2] It is just as certain that the meaning of such dreams is a sexual one, as will presently be shown.

In the belief in question three fairly distinct ideas are concerned, those of travelling, flying and riding respectively. Psycho-analysis has shown that dreams of *travelling* are almost constantly associated with sexual motives, such as exploration of inaccessible places, death wishes about hated rivals, escaping with the loved parent away from the competing one,[3] and so on; the subject has been already dealt with to some extent in previous chapters. *Flying* dreams similarly are individually determined and symbolize various wishes, but the ultimate source of these is always the same, namely, the sexual excitation of various movements (dandling, chasing, etc.) in early childhood;[4] the phenomenon of erection is in both sexes the kernel of the whole conception of flying. In his experimental studies on dreams the Norwegian psychologist Mourly Vold came to the conclusion that dreams in which the dreamer sees either himself or another flying or floating in the air are produced by gentle sexual excitation. The most obviously sexual idea, however, is that contained in the symbolism of *riding*,

---

[1] Bodin, *op. cit.* pp. 184, 185.
[2] See Brand, *op. cit.* vol. iii. p. 9. Freimark, *op. cit.* S. 310. The resemblance was clearly pointed out in the seventeenth century by Oldham (*Works*, 6th ed., p. 254):

> As men in sleep, though motionless they lie
> Fledg'd by a dream, believe they mount and flye;
> So witches some enchanted wand bestride,
> And think they through the airy regions ride.

[3] This has been well illustrated by J. Sadger. *Heinrich von Kleist, Eine pathographisch-psychologische Studie*, 1910, S. 60.
[4] Sigm. Freud, *Die Traumdeutung*, Dritte Auflage, 1911, S. 201-203.

which in dreams typically represents the act of coitus itself.[1] Sometimes this interpretation comes quite openly to expression; thus Delassus[2] quotes the following instance: 'Martin d'Arles raconte, dans son livre des superstitions, qu'une dame très pieuse se voyait souvent, en songe, chevauchant à travers la campagne avec un homme, qui abusait d'elle, ce qui lui causait une très grande volupté.' Similarly Jähns[3] says: 'So kam es vor, dass ehrbare Matronen ihren Beichtvätern vertrauten: "sie fühlten, dass sie unwillkürlich Nachts über Feld und Aue ritten; ja, wenn sie mit dem Ross über ein Wasser setzten, so wohne irgend jemand ihnen mit dem vollen Lustgefühl des Aktes bei". Da war denn der offenbare Hexenritt und die offenbare Vermischung mit dem Satan eingestanden.' ('It thus happened that respectable matrons admitted to their father confessors that "they felt as though they had involuntarily ridden by night over field and meadow, and that when their steed leaped over any water it was like someone having intercourse with them in the most voluptuous way". We have before us, therefore, a direct admission of the Witch-ride and union with Satan.')

Sometimes Witches turned men into horses for the purpose of riding on them to the Sabbath[4] (a typical dream inversion), sometimes in company with the Devil, who rode in front on a staff while the Witch sat behind.[5] More often the Devil himself was the steed, in the form of either a horse[6] or a he-goat. The latter animal was the usual mode of riding, and its well-known lubricity (see the passage on goat-symbolism in the preceding chapter) made it admirably adapted to express the sexual idea

[1] Compare the expression for night emissions, 'The Witches are riding him'. The resemblance between witch-riding and Nightmare was pointed out by Burton (*op. cit.* p. 134) over three hundred years ago: 'and in such as are troubled with incubus, or witch-ridden (as we call it); if they lie on their backs, they suppose an old woman rides and sits so hard upon them, that they are almost stifled for want of breath.'
[2] J. Delassus, *Les Incubes et les Succubes*, 1897, p. 35.
[3] M. Jähns, *Ross und Reiter*, 1872, Bd. i. S. 412.
[4] F. S. Krauss, *Slavische Volksforschungen*, 1906, S. 49.
[5] Grimm, *op. cit.* S. 895.
[6] *Der Hexenhammer*, *op. cit.* Zweiter Teil, S. 44.

thus represented.[1] On some occasions the Witch would stick a pole into the goat's back parts on which could be carried either her companions[2] or the children[3] she had to bring to the Sabbath. Frequently the pole alone, usually in the shape of a broomstick, would suffice as a steed. Jähns[4] has shown that this was a representative of a horse or other carrier (compare the hobby-horse series of ideas); the phallic significance is as evident here as with the numerous other forms of magic staffs. The Polish night-fiend, the Upierzyca, a winged or feathered creature, is thus named from the lightness with which she can rise in the air like a bird. The idea of human beings, or the Devil himself, being transformed into animals is, as has several times been remarked, eminently characteristic of dreams, and in 1230 Guillaume of Paris in discussing the Witch question expressly declared that it has this origin.[5]

A minor feature in connection with the flight through the air that is of some interest was the well-known Witch's salve that was necessary for the performance. This has to be rubbed well into the body, particularly over the abdomen, upper part of the thighs and the feet until a warm glow was experienced.[6] It had also to be rubbed into the broomstick[7] that conveyed the Witch to the Sabbath, and Grimm[8] relates an instance where it was rubbed into a calf used for this purpose. The favourite materials used in the composition of the ointment seem to have been the guts and fat of little babies,[9] murdered for the purpose, the blood of a bat, but many other sub-

---

[1] The goat is the national animal emblem of Wales; in one of the Welsh legends a king chases his favourite she-goat over a precipice, and as she falls she turns into a beautiful maiden. W. Sikes, *British Goblins*, 1880, p. 54.

[2] Jähns, *op. cit.* S. 415.

[3] G. C. Horst, *Zauber-Bibliothek*, 1821, Erster Teil, S. 216.

[4] Jähns, *op. cit.* S. 415, 416.

[5] Quoted by Hansen, *op. cit.* S. 138.

[6] Grimm, *loc. cit.* Laurent und Nagour, *op. cit.* S. 122. J. Wier, *Histoires, disputes et discours des illusions et impostures des diables*, traduction française, 1577, p. 165.

[7] Hansen, *op. cit.* S. 449. Wier, *loc. cit.*

[8] Grimm, *loc. cit.*

[9] De Lancre, *op. cit.* pp. 112, 119. Reginald Scot, *The Discoverie of Witchcraft*, 1584, Book iii. p. 40. Wier, *loc. cit.*

stances were also used, particularly such drugs as acon-
ite, hyosyamus, belladonna and opium. The explanation of this curious device is by no means obvious. De
Lancre[1] says: 'Le Diable use d'ongaens graisses et
onctions, pour imiter nostre Seigneur, qui nous a donné
le sainct sacrement de Babtesme et celuy de la Saincte
onction.' This, however, leaves unexplained, among
other things, the special connection between the ideas of
anointing and flight through the air.

The act of anointing has in all ages had a peculiar significance, and has generally been connected with the idea
of conferring special powers on the person—king or
priest—anointed; in various religious ceremonies it plays
a similarly important rôle. A comparative study of the
circumstances in which anointing is performed makes it
highly probable that the act has some sexual symbolism,
and the intimate relation of it to the Witches' flight and
the Sabbath strongly confirms this view. Freimark[2] adduces evidence to show that actual ointments were used
at various times for the purpose of producing voluptuous
dreams, and mentions a number of substances with
aphrodisiac, intoxicating and anæsthetizing properties
that have been thus employed. Kiesewetter[3] instituted
experiments on himself to investigate the matter, and
says he experienced as a result various travelling and
flying dreams. It is known nowadays that no drugs can
do this directly, so that the belief in their potency must
have been an important factor in the effect. It is noteworthy that there has always existed a connection between the ideas of ointment and easy movement, one no
doubt fostered by its physical qualities. The very word
'grease' itself comes from the Latin *Gratiae* (=Greek
Charites who used to wash Aphrodite with oil) and the
Vedic equivalent of the Charities were the shining steeds
who drew the chariot of Indra, the sun (=phallos)[4]; to
descend from the sublime to the comical, one is reminded

---

[1] De Lancre, *op. cit.* p. 212.   [2] Freimark, *op. cit.* S. 306-316.
[3] Kiesewetter, *op. cit.* Bd. ii. S. 579.
[4] Cox, *op. cit.* vol. i. p. 426; vol. ii. pp. 2, 35.

of the modern American expression for rapid movement, 'greased lightning'. The idea of rapid movement was very naturally associated with cutaneous sensations, and it used to be believed that the magic salve could actually change the person's skin into that of an animal famous for swiftness. There is the classical story of Pamphile, in Apuleius' *Golden Ass*, using a salve to grow feathers over her body until she could fly away as a bird, and in the Middle Ages it was similarly used to procure the transformation into Werewolves and thus endow the person with the powers of rapid flight.[1] While all this is so it cannot provide the full explanation, for it does not account for the deeper sexual symbolism. The evident relation of mucus and semen to the movements of coitus is probably the source of this symbolism, and I have shown elsewhere[2] that in early childhood the same association is formed between the ideas of movement and the excretory acts (considered as sexual performances). It is therefore intelligible that the phallic broomstick on which the Witch 'rode' had to be rubbed with ointment, and it is likely enough that the same accessory was at times employed in the actual gathering of Witches' covens where the leader who represented the Devil had a full night's work in front of him.

This view is confirmed by the fact that there existed a close connection between the acts of anointing and of drinking magical liquids. The Witch, after rubbing in the ointment, partook of some magical fluid to enable her to travel.[3] Now, as Abraham[4] has shown in detail, magical drinks that confer wonderful powers regularly symbolize semen: thus the Vedic soma, the Greek ambrosia and nectar, the Teutonic odrerir, etc. In the *Iliad* (xiv. 170) Homer relates how the Goddess Hera anoints her whole body with ambrosia the scent of which fills heaven and earth.

[1] S. Baring-Gould, *The Book of Were-Wolves*, 1865, pp. 71, 79, 92.
[2] *Zentralblatt für Psychoanalyse*, 1911, Jahrgang i. *Jahrbuch für psychoanalytische und psychopathologische Forschungen*, 1912, Bd. iv.
[3] Freimark, *op. cit.* S. 306, 308. Laurent und Nagour, *loc. cit.*
[4] See Abraham, *op. cit.* S. 63.

3. Apart from the Sabbath and the Travel by Night the Witch when at home maintained her relations with the Devil in several ways. In the first place he, or one of his subordinate demons, constantly accompanied her as her 'familiar', an idea resembling the totemistic beliefs so general in, for instance, Norwegian folklore.[1] The familiar was usually a tom-cat: at the meeting of the Catharist sect of heretics in the thirteenth century the Devil used to appear as a tom-cat, and the sect has been supposed to have received its name from this.[2] Cats have played an extensive part in the mythology of female supernatural beings. The old German sorceresses used on occasion to change themselves into cats.[3] Cats are particularly associated with the idea of riding, and indeed served at times for this purpose in the Witches' flight.[4] This belief seems to have been mainly derived from Teutonic mythology. Roskoff[5] writes: 'Freyja fährt auf einem mit zwei Katzen bespannten Wagen, den Symbolen des starken Zeugungstriebes. . . . Die der Freyja geheiligte Katze macht das Mittelalter zum Tiere der Hexen und Nachtfrauen.' ('Freya travels in a chariot spanned with two cats, symbols of a powerful procreative instinct. . . . The Middle Ages converted Freya's sacred cats into the animals of the Witches and Women of the Night.') So did the companions of Holda,[6] a prototype of the night demon aspects of the Witches. In Southern countries cats were replaced for this purpose by their relatives, lions; for instance, the chariot of Heracles was drawn by two lions, and so on. Besides this symbolic way of accompanying Witches the Devil, as will be pointed out later, used at times to appear to them in the form of an Incubus.

The subject, however, that attracted most attention in this context was that of possession by the Devil. Graf[7]

[1] B. Thorpe, *Northern Mythology*, 1851, vol. i. p. 115.
[2] Grimm, *op. cit.* S. 891. Hansen, *op. cit.* S. 229.
[3] Grimm, *op. cit.* S. 915.
[4] Jähns, *op. cit.* S. 415.   [5] Roskoff, *op. cit.* Bd. i. S. 159.
[6] Jähns, *op. cit.* S. 384.
[7] A. Graf, *Geschichte des Teufelsglaubens*, Deutsche Ausgabe, 1893, S. 137.

defines this as follows: 'Der Teufel konnte sich damit begnügen, den Menschen nur äusserlich zu quälen, indem er die Angriffe und Bedrängungen vervielfachte, oder auch innerlich peinigen, indem er in ihn einfuhr. Im ersten Fall hatte man die eigentliche sogenannte Obsessio, im zweiten die Possessio.' ('The Devil could content himself with torturing from without, by multiplying assaults and afflictions, or he could also torment from within, by entering into the person. In the former case there is the properly called "obsession", in the latter "possession".) In modern language the difference between the two would be indicated by the terms obsessional neurosis and hysteria respectively. As might have been expected, the latter predominantly affected women. The characteristics of demoniacal possession, and the epidemics it has given rise to, are too well known to need relating here.[1] As the occurrence is still far from rare there has been opportunity of investigating it from a clinical point of view, and it has been shown that it may constitute a symptom of various mental affections.[2] Müller[3] writes: 'Was sich in den Hexenprozessen durchgängig wiederholt, sind Entwicklungskrankheiten der Jugend oder des Alters bei Weibern, die über die klimakterischen Jahre hinaus sind, halb irre Zustände, Nervenkrankheiten, die so oft Gegenstand einer abergläubigen, dem Zeitalter angemessenen Auslegung waren, und endlich wirklich Buhlerei, und zwar, wie es scheint, oft mit verkappten Personen oder mit bekannten Personen, in deren Gestalt gerade jetzt einmal der Teufel erscheint.' ('What repeatedly took place throughout the Witch trials was the occurrence of developmental diseases of youth or else climacteric disturbances among women, half states of nervous or mental disorder, which were often presented in terms of the superstitions of the

---

[1] See Maury, *op. cit.* Seconde Partie, ch. ii. 'Origine démoniaque attribuée aux maladies nerveuses et mentales', pp. 256-338, and E. Murisier, *Les maladies du sentiment religieux*, 1903, pp. 148-ʳ51.

[2] A. J. C. Kerner, *Geschichten Besessener neuerer Zeit*, 1835. J. L. Nevius, *Demon Possession and Allied Themes*, 1894. Ch. Pezet, *Contribution à l'étude de la Démonomanie*, 1909.

[3] Johannes Müller, *Über die phantastischen Gesichtserscheinungen*, 1826, S. 67.

age, and on the other side actual licentiousness, often
apparently with persons, disguised or known, in whose
form the Devil was supposed to appear.') Of the various
disorders the one in which the condition occurs with
special frequency is hysteria, and in view of our modern
knowledge concerning the sexual ætiology of hysteria,[1]
including the hysterical attacks which symbolize coitus,[2]
it may be well briefly to quote the evidence of hysteria
in the demoniacal possession of the Witches. Among the
hysterical symptoms then observed[3] were: Bulimia, pica,
anorexia nervosa, vomiting (frequently of foreign bodies,
such as needles), globus hystericus, pseudocyesis, general
tremblings and rapid tremors, coitus-like movements,
mediumistic phenomena, narcolepsy, fainting spells,
somnambulism, catalepsy, amnesia, 'lying', tedium
vitae, negativism, double or multiple personality—in
short, all the symptoms that have recently (by Babinski,
etc.) been declared never to occur except when artificially
created through the *dressage* of physicians brought up in
the Salpêtrière traditions. The description of the convulsive seizures, with all the accompaniments of these,
shown by the possessed nuns of Louviers[4] tallies in every
detail with the accounts of hysterical seizures given in
modern medical text-books; even the term *arc en cercle*
is employed. Of especial interest in the light of modern
knowledge is the fact that exorcism of the patients was
followed by an outpouring flood of 'disgusting and obscene' talk, that in other words the treatment consisted
in a form of abreacting.

Not only were the symptoms of hysteria present in
Witches, but also the stigmata. Indeed so constant were
these that they were relied upon as the most convenient

[1] Sigm. Freud, 'Allgemeines über den hysterischen Anfall', *Sammlung kleiner Schriften zur Neurosenlehre*, Zweite Folge, 1909, Kap. vi. S. 146. [*Gesammelte Schriften*, Bd. v. S. 225; *Collected Papers*, vol. ii. p. 100.]

[2] Sigm. Freud, *op. cit.* S. 150. [*Gesammelte Schriften*, Bd. v. S. 259; *Collected Papers*, vol. ii. p. 104.]

[3] Graf, *op. cit.*, S. 153-160. P. L. Jacob, *Curiosités infernales*, pp. 43-65, 90. Bodin, de Lancre, Laurent und Nagour, *op. cit.* S. 116. Wier, etc.

[4] Jean le Breton, *De la défense de la vérité touchante la possession des religieuses de Louviers*, 1643. Ese, *Traicté des marques des possédés et la preuve de la véritable possession des religieuses de Louviers*, 1644.

212   NIGHTMARE AND MEDIÆVAL SUPERSTITIONS   PT. II

and certain method of ascertaining whether a given woman was or was not a Witch. Reginald Scot[1] writes: 'If she have any privy mark under her armpit, under her hair, under her lip, or in the private parts, it is presumption sufficient for the judge to proceed and give sentence of *Death* upon her.' The main test employed by the professional 'Witch-finders' was the so-called *épreuve du stylet* for the discovery of anæsthetic areas. Sinistrari[2] tells us about the distribution and nature of these areas: 'It is imprinted on the most hidden parts of the body: with women, it is usually on the breasts or the privy parts. Now, the stamp which imprints these marks is none other but the Devil's claw.' As is commonly observed with hysterical stigmata, the anæsthetic areas did not bleed when pricked.[3] Freimark[4] has pointed out that such marks were also supposed to be characteristic of various heretical sects that preceded the full development of the Witch concept.

The psychological explanation of the phenomena of possession is not difficult to psycho-analysts. I will merely quote a passage from a non-analytical writer, Freimark,[5] who gives the outline of it in the following words: 'Tragen die Phänomene des Somnambulismus und Mediumismus in der Regel nur ihren Entstehungsursachen nach sexuellen Charakter, so sind diejenigen der Besessenheit durch und durch sexueller Natur. . . . Das urteilende Ich, das alle nach der bestehenden Gesellschaftsordnung, nach Religion, Moral und dem Milieu, in dem es sich entwickelt, als ungehörig betrachteten Gefühle und Vorstellungen unterdrückte, in das Unterbewusstsein zurückschob, wo sie sozusagen ein eigenes Leben führten, wird von dem dort im Laufe der Zeit sich ausbildenden Gefühls- und Vorstellungskomplex überrumpelt und die Bewusstseinsspaltung ist vollzogen.

---

[1] Reginald Scot, *op. cit.* p. 15.
[2] P. Sinistrari, *Demoniality* (*17th Century*), English Translation, 1879, p. 27.
[3] Santerre, *Histoire des diables de Loudun*, 1694, p. 318.
[4] Freimark, *op. cit.* S. 280.
[5] Freimark, *op. cit.* S. 54, 57. See also S. 62-69, 353, and Maury, *op. cit.* p. 258.

... Einen ähnlichen Vorgang können wir im Traumleben beobachten; und der Somnambulismus und auch der Mediumismus zeigen das, was uns der Traum lehrt, in verstärktem Masse.' ('Whereas the phenomena of somnambulism and mediumism generally betray their sexual character only in their causative factors, those of possession are through and through of a sexual nature. ... The controlling Ego, which suppressed all feelings and ideas regarded as unseemly by the prevailing social order —according to religion, morality, and the environment in which this has been developed, and which has driven them into the subconscious where they so to speak lead their own life, was overpowered by the complex of feelings and ideas that got built up there in the course of time, and the splitting of consciousness is then complete. ... We may observe a similar process in dream life; and somnambulism and mediumism show in an intensified fashion what dreams teach us.')

*   *   *   *   *

We have now to take up the *second problem,* namely the question of why the Witch epidemic took place just when it did. The researches made on this problem in the middle of the last century by Ennemoser,[1] Michelet,[2] Roskoff,[3] Soldan[4] and Wächter[5] have of late years been extended and corrected by Hansen,[6] von Hoensbroech,[7] Längin,[8] Lea,[9] Lempens,[10] Riezler[11] and others, and most of the points have now been pretty fully elucidated. The three most important conclusions that emerge from these investigations are:

1. That the conception of Witchcraft in its strict sense

---

[1] Ennemoser, *op. cit.* Vierte Abschnitt, Zweite Abteilung.
[2] Michelet, *op. cit.*
[3] Roskoff, *op. cit.* Bd. ii. Dritter Abschnitt.   [4] Soldan, *op. cit.*
[5] Wächter, *Die Hexenprozesse, ein kulturhistorischer Versuch,* 1865.
[6] Hansen, *op. cit.* and *Quellen und Untersuchungen zur Geschichte des Hexenwahns und der Hexenverfolgung im Mittelalter,* 1901.
[7] von Hoensbroech, *Das Papsttum in seiner sozialkulturellen Wirksamkeit,* dritte Auflage, 1901, Bd. i. S. 380-600.
[8] G. Längin, *Religion und Hexenprozess,* 1888.
[9] H. C. Lea, *History of the Inquisition in the Middle Ages,* 1887. *History of the Inquisition in Spain,* 1907.
[10] Lempens, *Geschichte der Hexen und Hexenprozesse,* 1880.
[11] S. Riezler, *Geschichte der Hexenprozesse in Bayern,* 1896.

was a totally new one in the Middle Ages, and that the Witch epidemic proper dates from the middle of the fifteenth century;

2. That the factors cooperative in the production of it were extraordinarily involved; and

3. That the essential responsibility for it unquestionably rests on the Roman Catholic Church.

The Church, for various motives, deliberately constructed the belief in Witches, like that in the Devil, out of disparate material already present in folklore. Hansen[1] puts the matter clearly when he says: 'Der Begriff vom Hexenwesen . . . ist keineswegs aus dem Spiel der Volksphantasie frei erwachsen, sondern wissenschaftlich, wenn auch in teilweiser Anlehnung an Volksvorstellungen, konstruiert und fest umschrieben worden; er ist in seinen Elementen durch die systematische Theologie der mittelalterlichen Kirche entwickelt, strafrechtlich in der Gesetzgebung von Kirche und Staat fixiert, schliesslich auf dem Wege des kirchlichen und weltlichen Strafprozesses, und zwar zuerst durch die Ketzerinquisition, zusammengefasst worden.' ('The conception of Witches . . . is in no way a free growth out of the play of popular phantasy, but was scientifically constructed and defined, although with the help of popular ideas. It was developed in its elements by the systematic theology of the Mediæval Church, legally established in the laws of Church and State, and finally built up into a whole by means of ecclesiastical and lay criminal trials, first of all by the Inquisition of Heretics.') Most of the folk elements of the conception were for centuries denied by the Church, who only gradually accepted them one by one. As she did so, she fused them more and more closely together, until early in the fifteenth century a totally new conception was formed and officially proclaimed. Hansen[2] says: 'Wie bereits angedeutet wurde, erweisen sich die Verfasser der literarischen Quellen des 15. Jahrhunderts, welche uns jenen Kollektivbegriff der Hexe definieren, sämtlich als von der Überzeugung durchdrungen, dass es sich bei

[1] Hansen, *op. cit.* Vorwort, S. 6.　　　[2] *Id., op. cit.* S. 145.

der von ihnen geschilderten Art des Hexenwesens um eine *neue* Erscheinung . . . handelt. Die beteiligten Inquisitoren zeigen sich geradezu überrascht von der Existenz dieser neuen Sekte.' ('As has already been indicated, the authors of the literary sources of the fifteenth century who have defined for us the collective idea of Witch show themselves to be one and all permeated by the conviction that the kind of Witch being they describe was a *new* phenomenon. The Inquisitors concerned were absolutely surprised at the existence of this new sect.') Jühling[1] just as emphatically observes: 'Es gab freilich schon im Altertum den Begriff der Zauberinnen, aber die Hexe an und für sich ist eine Ausgeburt spezifisch christlichen Aberglaubens.' ('The concept of sorceresses had, it is true, existed in olden times, but the Witch herself is a spawn of specifically Christian superstition.')

It is impossible here to attempt to unravel what Roskoff[2] calls the 'complicated network of multifarious threads' that constitutes the Witch belief, but a few words may be said about the history of its main features. The ideas concerning heresy, relations with the Devil, and the Sabbath are mainly, though not exclusively, of a religious nature; on the other hand the beliefs in *Maleficium*, in animal transformation and in the travels through the air of night-fiends, which will now be discussed, took their source from folk mythology. *Maleficium* had always been a punishable offence among both the ancient Romans and Germans, but not the acts involved in the Striga or Incubus beliefs. The history of the origin of Witchcraft is the story of how the Church skilfully and gradually, during the course of two centuries, developed a new concept and forced it on to a whole civilization. The attitude of the early Church was entirely opposed to the rudimentary forms of this concept previously in existence. Lehmann[3] points out: 'Auf

---

[1] J. Jühling, *Die Inquisition*, 1903, S. 299. See also Ennemoser, *op. cit.* S. 780, 781, and Roskoff, *op. cit.* Bd. ii. S. 214-225.
[2] Roskoff, *op. cit.* Bd. ii. S. 315.
[3] A. Lehmann, *Aberglaube und Zauberei*, Zweite deutsche Ausg., 1908, S. 105. See also J. N. Sepp, *Orient und Occident*, 1903, S. 140, 150.

der Synode zu Paderborn 785 stellte man folgenden Satz auf: *"Derjenige, welcher, durch den Teufel verblendet, nach Art der Heiden glaubt, dass jemand eine Hexe sein kann und deshalb dieselbe verbrennt, wird mit dem Tode bestraft."* Zu dieser Zeit wird also nicht die Hexe, sondern der Glaube an dieselbe verfolgt und bestraft. Diese Bestimmung wurde von Karl dem Grossen bestätigt und war in den folgenden Jahrhunderten die Richtschnur für die Stellung der Kirche gegenüber allen Anklagen wegen Hexerei. Noch deutlicher tritt die Auffassung der Kirche von Hexerei im sogenannten *Ancyranischen Kanon Episcopi* hervor, welche um das Jahr 900 entstand. Hier wird den Bischöfen befohlen, "in ihren Gemeinden den Glauben an die Möglichkeit dämonischer Zauberei und nächtlicher Fahrten zu und mit Dämonen als reine Illusion energisch zu bekämpfen und alle diejenigen, welche einem solchen Glauben huldigen, aus der kirchlichen Gemeinschaft auszustossen." ' ('The following thesis was put forward at the Synod of Paderborn in 785: *Whoever, deceived by the Devil, believes in the fashion of the heathen that anyone can be a Witch and burns her on this account is to undergo punishment by death.* At this time, therefore, it was not the Witch, but the belief in Witches, that was persecuted and punished. This ordinance was confirmed by Charlemagne, and was for several centuries the principle that guided the Church in respect of accusations of Witchcraft. The views of the Church on Witchcraft were still more plainly expressed in the so-called *Canon Episcopi of Ancyra* which was composed in the ninth century. Here the Bishops were commanded "energetically to combat in their dioceses the belief in the possibility of demoniacal magic and night journeys to or with demons as being pure illusion, and to expel from community with the Church all those who cherish such beliefs." ') This enlightened Canon (which, incidentally, was not composed at the Council of Ancyra, its actual date being uncertain) goes on to explain how dreams can deceive people and give rise to such beliefs; it maintains, in fact, the thesis of the present book. Even

before this the Council of Ireland in 466 had anathema-
tized Christians who believed they were sorcerers and
forbade them to be received in the Church until they had
done penance.

By the thirteenth century, however, the alarming increase and power of the heretical sects[1] against the
Mother Church led the latter, as was pointed out in the
preceding chapter, to undertake the fiercest measures
for the suppression of them, and she cleverly enlisted
the lay arm by fusing the ideas of Witchcraft and heresy.
The Papal Bull issued by Gregory IX in 1227 became
the nucleus of the future Inquisition, and later in the
same century Alexander IV formally declared Witchcraft to be one with heresy. The great influence of
Thomas Aquinas at this time was also thrown in the
scale and was an important factor in developing the concept of Witchcraft.[2] Relatively little advance was made
in this direction after this until the fifteenth century.

At this point we may pause to consider historically the
individual elements of the Witch belief in more detail
and note how one by one they became fused with the
idea of heresy. The first one to undergo this fate was that
of *Maleficium*,[3] and this was the principal one to win
over the people to the support of the Church in·its fight
against heresy. The popular belief in *Maleficium*, which
the Church had always been interested in from the point
of view of idolatry, became linked with the Devil idea,[4]
and therefore to that of heresy.[5] It was this first element
that also proved the most lasting one in the whole constituent series. Hansen[6] says: 'Das *Maleficium*, mit Aus-
nahme des Wettermachens, ist ohne alle Unterbrechung
von der kirchlichen und bis in das 17. Jahrhundert auch
von der staatlichen Autorität als Realität angenommen,
seine Kraft ist nie ernstlich in Abrede gestellt worden;
es zieht sich wie ein roter Faden auch durch die Ge-

---

[1] See Hansen, *op. cit.* S. 212-216, 232.
[2] Soldan, *op. cit.* Bd. i. S. 160.   [3] See Hansen, *op. cit.* S. 9-14.
[4] Hansen, *op. cit.* S. 451. W. Wundt, *Völkerpsychologie*, Zweiter Band,
'Mythus und Religion', Zweiter Teil, 1906, S. 400.
[5] Hansen, *op. cit.* S. 23, 39, 239.   [6] *Id.*, *op. cit.* S. 13.

schichte der strafrechtlichen Verfolgung.' ('*Maleficium*, with the exception of the element in it concerning the belief in control over the weather, was continuously accepted as reality by the ecclesiastical authorities, and up to the seventeenth century also by state authorities. Its power was never seriously denied. The theme runs like a red thread through the history of criminal persecution.')

It is impossible to trace here the numerous legends relating to *women who fly by night*[1] since that would take us into the realms of mythology, although much confirmatory evidence for our main thesis could be gained by so doing; for such beliefs are closely related to Nightmare experiences and to the belief in Succubi. It must suffice to remark that they evidently played a considerable part in the elaboration of the Witch concept. Contributions came from the Greek Persephone (=strangler),[2] the Roman *Striga* (Italian *Strighe*, Swiss *Strãggeli*),[3] the Teutonic elves,[4] the German *Waldfrauen* and *Weisse Frauen* (Bertha, Holda[5])—the descendants of the Northern Frigg. It was believed, for instance, that a Witch became a *Drude* when she attained the age of forty,[6] while on the other hand a young *Drude* was likely to become an old Witch;[7] according to Grimm,[8] 'Drute ist eins mit Mahre' ('a *Drude* is identical with the night-fiend of the Nightmare'). The Church was for many centuries strongly opposed to believing in the possibility of night flights. The idea was denied by the celebrated *Canon Episcopi*;[9] it was again denied in 906 by Regino of Prüm, in 1020 by Burkard of Worms, in the twelfth century by John of Salisbury, and in 1230 by Guillaume of Paris.[10] The subject was fiercely contested in great detail throughout the thirteenth century[11]

[1] See Grimm, *op. cit.* S. 907. Hansen, *op. cit.* S. 15-18.
[2] Roskoff, *op. cit.* Bd. i. S. 136.
[3] Hansen, *op. cit.* S. 14. Sepp, *op. cit.* S. 120, 231.
[4] Meyer, *op. cit.* S. 135.
[5] Graf, *op. cit.* S. 266, 277. Grimm, *op. cit.* S. 803-810. Roskoff, *op. cit.* Bd. i. S. 157-159. Wuttke, *op. cit.* S. 29-31, 47.
[6] Sepp, *op. cit.* S. 122.
[7] J. V. Grohmann, *Aberglaube und Gebräuche aus Böhmen*, 1864, Bd. i. S. 23.
[8] Grimm, *op. cit.* S. 1042.   [9] Roskoff, *op. cit.* Bd. i. S. 271.
[10] Hansen, *op. cit.* S. 80, 83-85, 134, 136.   [11] *Id.*, *op. cit.* S. 191-209.

and the definite belief was not generally accepted by the
Church authorities until 1450.[1] It then proved to be of
decisive importance in firmly establishing the Witch
delusion, principally through the connection between it
and the Sabbath; it was indeed the stories of flights
through the air ascertained by the Inquisition that
settled the question for the Church and appeared to
prove finally the identity of heretical meetings and Witch
Sabbaths.[2]

The allied theme of *transformation* of human beings
into animals, similarly a primordial folk phantasy, experienced a course parallel to that of the night flight
idea. Energetically denied at first by the Church,[3] who
punished believers in it as severely as they did those in
the flight idea, it was for a time hotly contested[4] and
finally accepted, though the acceptance was not general
until 1525.[5]

The idea of the *Sabbath* was elaborated by the Church
in connection with the naturally secret meetings of
heretics, who were accused of carrying out at them all
sorts of orgies and misdeeds just as the early Church
itself had been in Roman times.[6] The first full account
of it appears in a Witch-heresy trial at Toulouse in 1335.[7]
It was probably strengthened by the Teutonic legends
of the wild hunt and wild army. The memory of the
Roman Bacchanalia[8] and Athenian Cotyttia[9] also no
doubt played a part: indeed the very word 'Sabbath' in
relation to Witches has been supposed to be a form,
altered by Jewish Manichaeans, of the Sabos where
Bacchus was worshipped, a name derived from σαβάζειν
=to dance.[10] This memory was sustained in the Middle

[1] Hansen, *op. cit.* S. 303-306, 409, 455-458.
[2] *Id., op. cit.* S. 235, 238.
[3] *Id., op. cit.* S. 18, 83-87.   [4] *Id., op. cit.* S. 189, 190.
[5] *Id., op. cit.* S. 455.
[6] *Id., op. cit.* S. 21, 226, 227. O. Henne am Rhyn, *Der Teufels- und
Hexenglaube*, 1892, S. 68.
[7] E. L. de Lamothe-Langon, *Histoire de l'inquisition en France*, 1829, t. iii.
p. 233.   [8] Freimark, *op. cit.* S. 279.
[9] F. Hedelin, *Des Satyres, brutes, monstres et démons* (1627), 1888 ed., p. 124.
[10] *Id., op. cit.* p. 131. G. Herman, *Genesis*, Bd. iii. 'Bakchanalien und
Eleusinien', Zweite Auflage, S. 103.

Ages by the well-known Feast of Fools,[1] though the true origin of this was pre-Christian.[2]

The *Black Mass*, the central point of the Sabbath, is of very ancient origin. Sexual union in public has, in both ancient[3] and modern[4] semi-religious cults, in both civilised[5] and savage[6] nations, been performed as a sacred ceremony. We need not trace the history of this, nor occupy ourselves here with unravelling the psychological meaning of the well-recognized sexual perversion that characterizes it. What is noteworthy in the present context is that as either an open perversion or a superstition the Black Mass has survived long after the Witch epidemic was at an end,[7] *i.e.* after the delusion of Witchcraft had again been resolved into its constituent elements, and that it persists even to the present day.[8]

The belief in *lustful indulgence* between Witch and Devil is again a relatively late constituent of the Witch delusion. The idea of such intercourse between human and supernatural beings was of course always present among the people, as has been amply illustrated in earlier chapters of this book, but it was for long strenuously denied by the Church, *e.g.* in 900 by Burkard.[9] Until the twelfth century it was quite distinct from sorcery,[10] and became connected with it only through the linking of the Sabbath idea with heresy, about 1250.[11] It was accepted by Gervasius of Tilbury in the year 1214,[12] and by Thomas Aquinas in the same century.[13] The first instance of it being the accusation at a Witch trial was in 1275, when Angela de Labarethe was burned

[1] Roskoff, *op. cit.* Bd. i. S. 363.   [2] Bourke, *op. cit.* ch. iii. pp. 11-23.
[3] S. Rocco, *Sex Mythology*, 1898, p. 46.
[4] W. H. Dixon, *Seelenbräute*, Deutsche Übersetz. 1868, Bd. i. S. 273-278.
[5] E. Sellon, *Annotations on the Sacred Writings of the Hindus*, 1902 ed., pp. 26, 27.
[6] J. Cook, *An Account of a Voyage round the World*, 1821, vol. ii. p. 127.
[7] Brévannes, *op. cit.* pp. 180-233. Laurent und Nagour, *op. cit.* S. 137-142. G. Legué, *Médecins et empoissonneurs*, p. 185.
[8] J. Bois, *Le Satanisme et la magie.* Cp. the novels by J. K. Huysmans, *Là-bas*, and R. Schwalbé, *Chez Satan.*
[9] Hansen, *op. cit.* S. 83.   [10] *Id., op. cit.* S. 19.
[11] Ennemoser, *op. cit.* S. 791, 845. Roskoff, *op. cit.* Bd. ii. S. 216.
[12] Hansen, *op. cit.* S. 142.
[13] Soldan, *op. cit.* Bd. ii. S. 181.

for having sexual intercourse with the Devil.[1] Before this
time the act was not treated as a sin, perhaps because
of its being thought to occur, if at all, only against the
will of the victim.[2] It was, however, hard to maintain
this view in the face of the evident attachment of the
victims to the Devil, as shown even by nuns.[3] After the
second half of the thirteenth century the belief belonged,
as Hansen[4] puts it, to the 'permanent store of theological
science'.

Although the various elements of the Witch concept
were for the greater part developed by the middle of the
thirteenth century and were gradually becoming con-
solidated into a definite system of beliefs, Witch trials
proceeded rather languidly during the following two
hundred years. It was, however, only a lull before the
storm, and this broke out as a true epidemic towards
the end of the fifteenth century. There were reasons for
both the delay and for the occasion of the subsequent
outbreak. In the interval theologians were busily occupied in discussing and elaborating the general conception, which, as was remarked above, was not fused into
a harmonious whole until the middle of the fifteenth
century. The method of legal procedure had also to be
perfected, and the attempt to transfer the necessary
powers from the lay to the clerical arm met with considerable opposition. The Civil courts were concerned
only with *Maleficium*, and it was not until 1400 that
they were prepared to recognize fornication with the
Devil as a criminal charge.[5] Soldan[6] is of opinion that the
experiences gained in the Crusades exerted a considerable influence in this respect by making the laity familiar
with Oriental ideas of intercourse between human and
supernatural beings.

A factor that cannot easily be over-estimated was the
sex problem within religion itself, for it was only the
concentration of the whole Witchcraft idea on women

[1] Lamothe-Langon, *op. cit.* t. ii. p. 614.   [2] Hansen, *op. cit.* S. 180.
[3] Steingiesser, *op. cit.* S. 44.   [4] Hansen, *op. cit.* S. 187.
[5] *Id.*, *op. cit.* S. 396.   [6] Soldan, *op. cit.* Bd. i. S. 179.

...t made it possible for the phobia to be generalized among the population at large. Probably all religions, and notably the Christian religion, represent solutions of the masculine Oedipus complex and are worked out by men with this unconscious end in view, the problems of women being a secondary matter. We have seen that the conflict between son and father is dealt with by dividing the figure of the latter into two, God the good father and the Devil the bad father. To diminish this conflict as far as possible it was important to diminish the significance of feminine charms and desires. The one thing that would be more intolerable than anything else would be indications of sexual desires on the part of women, and, as we have repeatedly pointed out, this is what fornication with the Devil really represented. It is only considerations such as these that render at all comprehensible the inhuman and barbaric attitude of the Christian Church towards women. What this attitude, often commented on by modern writers,[1] was in earlier days is hard to realize without reading the original discussions about women, particularly those that culminated in the Witchcraft period as represented by De Lancre,[2] Bodin,[3] and above all the *Malleus Maleficarum*.[4] The behaviour of the Church in ascribing all manner of unworthy traits to women, and even debating whether she had a soul at all or was merely a beast, was without question due to its degrading attitude towards sexuality in general, and was a manifestation of a morbid misogynous revulsion produced by extreme repression. It is likely that this was intensified during the Middle Ages by the social conditions then prevailing, the depletion of the male population through wars leading to a state of widespread jealousy and dissatisfaction among the women. The upshot was the turning of fear and hate against a certain class of women, against those who were either strongly sexual or else filled with hate themselves

---

[1] See, for instance, Jühling, *op. cit.* S. 319, 320.
[2] De Lancre, *op. cit.* pp. 57, 58.
[3] Bodin, *loc. cit.*   [4] *Der Hexenhammer, op. cit.* Erster Teil, S. 92-106.

from dissatisfaction. The unusual or hysterical women of earlier times were magicians, soothsayers, prophetesses: in the Middle Ages they became Witches. As Michelet[1] epigrammatically puts it, 'La Sibylle prédisait le sort et la Sorcière le fait. C'est la grande, la vraie différence'.

Towards the end of the fifteenth century two events took place that had the result of definitely inaugurating the Witch epidemic proper. They were the issuing of the famous Papal Bull by Innocent VIII in 1484, and the publishing of the *Malleus Maleficarum* by Sprenger and Institoris in 1487. In Innocent's Bull, a document that has been stigmatized as a 'product of hell', special stress is laid on the two ideas of fornication with the Devil and the production of impotence through *Maleficium*,[2] *i.e.* the two ideas that, for the reasons expounded above, were absolutely intolerable and, if taken seriously, must infallibly result in an outbreak of savagery. In the *Malleus* these matters, as well as those of flight through the air and the Sabbath, are argued to the finest point of sophistry, and the rules laid down are of such a nature as to prevent the escape from horrible torture or death of any woman that might be accused by a spiteful neighbour. Without quoting the denunciatory language of such writers as Ennemoser,[3] Henne am Rhyn,[4] Mannhardt[5] and Nyström,[6] one may fairly describe this book as unique in the annals of bigotry and cruelty; we note it in passing as constituting a landmark of decisive importance for the subsequent epidemic. It was followed in the next hundred and fifty years by a number of books in a similar strain, of which the chief were those by Bodin,[7] Carpzov,[8] Delrio,[9] Glanvil,[10] King James I,[11]

---

[1] Michelet, *op. cit.* Introduction, p. ix.
[2] The full text of the Bull is given by Roskoff, *op. cit.* Bd. ii. S. 222-225.
[3] Ennemoser, *op. cit.* S. 812.
[4] Henne am Rhyn, *op. cit.* S. 87.
[5] W. Mannhardt, *Zauberglaube und Geheimwissen*, Vierte Auflage, 1909, S. 240.
[6] Nyström, *op. cit.* S. 251.
[7] Bodin, *op. cit.*
[8] Benedict Carpzov, *Practica nova rerum criminalium*, 1635.
[9] Delrio, *Inquisitiones magicae*, 1599.
[10] J. Glanvil, *Sadducismus triumphatus*, 1681.
[11] King James I, *Daemonologia*, 1615.

Remigius,[1] and Torreblanca,[2] and even by a newspaper, the notorious *Hexen-* or *Druden-Zeitung* (in 1627).

The epidemic was now unloosed that raged irregularly over Europe for well-nigh three centuries. The total number of victims will never now be known. Voigt's well-known estimate of nine and a half millions is certainly an over-statement, although Soldan[3] thinks that the number ran well into the millions. Nyström[4] calculates that it is greater than that of those killed in all the European wars since the beginning of our era [till, of course, the recent Great War]. Largely because of the activity of the Inquisition—directed in this case, it is true, more against heretics than against Witches—the population of Spain fell within two centuries from twenty millions to six; one man alone, Torquemada, is said to have burned 10,220 in eighteen years and to have condemned 97,371 to the galleys.[5] Nearly every country in Europe suffered. Those that came off best were the countries under the Greek Church, the Netherlands, and —with the exception of the frightful Mora explosion in 1670[6]—Sweden. Even distant America had its minor epidemic.[7] And although the actual extent of the epidemic may have been exaggerated by some writers nothing can exaggerate the horror of the detailed cruelty, which it would be hard to parallel at any age in any other part of the world. Sepp[8] truly says: 'Nie haben die Menschen blinder gegen einander gewütet, nie hat die Christenheit sich angesichts aller Welt mehr blamiert als in den Hexenprozessen.' ('Never have human beings raged more blindly against one another, never has Christianity brought more discredit on itself in the face of all the world as in the Witch trials.')

---

[1] Remigius, *Daemonolatria*, 1595.   [2] Torreblanca, *Daemonologia*, 1615.
[3] Soldan, *op. cit.* Bd. i. S. 452, 453.   [4] Nyström, *op. cit.* S. 273.
[5] Nyström, *op. cit.* S. 230, 232.
[6] Ennemoser, *op. cit.* S. 814. Nyström, *op. cit.* S. 279-281.
[7] See M. D. Conway, *Demonology and Devil-Lore*, 1879, vol. ii. pp. 314-317, and Howard Williams, *The Superstitions of Witchcraft*, 1865, p. 264.
[8] Sepp, *op. cit.* S. 130. See also E. Clodd, *Myths and Dreams*, 1891, p. 59. Hansen, *op. cit.* S. 3, 5. O. Stoll, *Suggestion und Hypnotismus in der Völkerpsychologie*, Zweite Auflage, 1904, S. 397, 398.

In seeking an explanation for this extraordinary state of affairs the chief point to bear in mind is that it was not due to a sudden and incomprehensible aberration of the human spirit, as might at first sight appear, but that it was entirely congruous with the prevailing views of the period. The Witch delusion was 'rationalized' to such an extent that it quite harmonized with the conceptions of the universe then current.[1] Indeed it might well be maintained that the most striking feature of such works as the *Malleus* and Glanvil's *Sadducism* is not the cruelty and stupidity so much as the remarkable intellectual subtlety with which they defend the most irrational theses. The factors entering into the mental state that paved the way for the delusion are extraordinarily involved,[2] but the most important were the abnormal attitude of the Church towards sexual matters and the social condition of the times. The critical period of all in the formation of the delusion was the fourteenth century. Of this Gener[3] well says: 'Ce n'est pas un siècle normal, c'est un siècle malade. . . . Son histoire est tout entière contenue dans celle de la pathologie. Il semble qu'il subisse les approches de l'agonie du monde féodal et l'aurore d'une ère nouvelle. Dans ses souffrances il y a quelque chose du râle de la mort et des douleurs de l'enfantement. L'égarement de sa raison est celui de la sibylle avant la prophétie.' Some of the features were mentioned in the preceding chapter, and here we may confine our attention to summarizing the cardinal factors in the development of the Witch epidemic. Of these unquestionably the most important was the deliberate machination of the Catholic Church. The three fundamental components of the Witch concept were *Maleficium*, pact with the Devil, and Heresy, which may be described as the Witch's relation to Man, to the Devil and to God respectively. The Church's activity consisted

---

[1] For an excellent presentation of this see Sir Walter Scott, *Letters on Demonology and Witchcraft* (1829), fourth edition, 1898, p. 153.

[2] See on this matter Hansen, *op. cit.* S. 328-331. Roskoff, *op. cit.* Bd. ii. S. 315-359.

[3] P. Gener, *La Mort et le Diable*, 1880, p. 595.

in exploiting the first of these so as to get the second punished with the aim of destroying the third. The already present belief in *Maleficium* was employed to inflame the persecution, the evidences of the Devil pact obtained through hysteria and torture were the readiest means of securing the victim, while the prime motive was the endeavour to stamp out heresy. Once the process was well under way there can be little doubt that it served also to excite and gratify certain human tendencies in their rudest and crudest forms. The two most obvious of these were sadism and sexual curiosity. Concerning the theoretical discussions on Witchcraft, Bloch[1] says: 'Es gibt keine sexuelle Frage, die nicht von den theologischen Kasuisten in subtilster Weise erörtet worden ist, so dass ihre Schriften uns zugleich ein lehrreiches Bild der Phantasietätigkeit auf geschlechtlichem Gebiete geben.' ('There is no sexual question that was not discussed in the most subtle way by the theological casuists, so that their writings provide us with an instructive picture of the functioning of phantasy in the sexual sphere.') Jühling[2] brings out this point even more sharply in connection with the lust of the celibate Inquisitors in stripping, examining and questioning their victims; children of seven[3] and women of eighty-five[4] were made to confess to fornication with the Devil, with all its accompanying details. Further, the whole procedure was, as Roskoff[5] has plainly shown, extensively used by individuals to wreak their malignity, hatred and envy in falsely accusing their rivals or enemies.

The end of the Witch epidemic needs almost as much explanation as its origin, though this has occupied students to a far less extent. The history of the wane is most fully detailed by Soldan.[6] Holland had the honour of being the first country to abolish legal Witch persecu-

[1] Bloch, *op. cit.* S. 132.
[2] Jühling, *op. cit.* S. 321. See also Henne am Rhyn, *op. cit.* S. 97, and Williams, *op. cit.* p. 215.
[3] Nyström, *op. cit.* S. 245. [4] Jühling, *op. cit.* S. 323.
[5] Roskoff, *op. cit.* Bd. ii. S. 331-343.
[6] Soldan, *op. cit.* Bd. ii. S. 263-339. See also Henne am Rhyn, *op. cit.* S. 115-156.

tion, in 1610, Geneva followed in 1632, Sweden in 1649 and England in 1682. In other countries it lasted much longer. The last official execution in England took place in 1682, in Scotland in 1697, in France in 1726, in Saxony in 1746, in the rest of Germany in 1749, in Bavaria in 1775, in Spain in 1781, in Switzerland in 1782 and in Poland in 1793. The Inquisition itself lasted in Spain until 1834, in Italy until 1859, but the last time it had put anyone to death was in 1826. Witches were lynched in England in 1751 and in 1863(!), in Germany in 1836 and in France in 1850; one was mobbed nearly to death in Italy, at Milan, in 1891. In Russia various Witch trials, persecutions and mobbings were by no means rare at the end of the last century, and the Witch belief is still current there.[1] In South America there was a regular epidemic between the years 1860 and 1877, a considerable number of Witches being officially burned; one was officially burned in Peru as recently as 1888. At the beginning of the present century two Irish peasants tried to roast a Witch on her own fire. [In 1926 two cases called public attention to the survival of belief in Witchcraft in Western Europe. One was in Tipton, in Staffordshire, where two men were summoned for threatening a supposed Witch, and a number of witnesses testified that they were afraid to go near the woman on account of her evil spells. The other was at Bordeaux, near which place a certain Abbé Desnoyers, who was believed to be none other than Satan himself, was flogged for bewitching a Madame Mesmin and other people; he had despatched birds whose droppings gave rise to fungi of obscene shapes which emitted such appalling odours that those who breathed them were smitten with horrible diseases.[2] We note here again the characteristic combination of anal and sadistic motives to which attention was called in the previous chapter. Finally, to bring the matter up to date, mention may be made of a case

[1] B. Stern, *Geschichte der öffentlichen Sittlichkeit in Russland*, 1908, Bd. i. S. 56, 81-92, Bd. ii. S. 288-290.
[2] [R. Lowe Thompson, *The History of the Devil*, 1929, p. 154.]

reported in the *Times* in the present year of grace, 1930, where a Witch and her family were boycotted and threatened by their neighbours in Mecklenburg.]

It is very instructive to note that towards the end of the Witch epidemic the delusion once more dissolved into its constituent elements and did not fade as a whole. The first to disappear was the belief in fornication with the Devil and the orgies of the Sabbath, of which relatively little is heard after 1650. The belief in flight by night was the last part of this group to go, and it is indeed still held by some people.[1] The Inquisition persecuted heresy long after it had ceased to do so *via* Witchcraft. The most refractory element was its oldest one, namely *Maleficium*, and for more than a century little has been heard of any other aspect of Witchcraft.[2] Officially, however, the Roman Catholic Church still holds to every element in the whole conception, from the influencing of weather by sorcery to pact with the Devil.[3]

The disappearance of the Witch epidemic is customarily explained by invoking the change in the view of the universe brought about by the rise in science, but several considerations made it unlikely that this factor, important as it may have been, could have been the only one. In the first place, it cannot account for the rapid diminution in the Witch belief that took place in the second half of the seventeenth century,[4] for the new scientific discoveries had by this time penetrated into only a small circle. Then these discoveries in physics, *e.g.* by Kepler, Harvey, Newton, etc., concerned matters only very indirectly connected with the subject of Witchcraft, while it cannot be maintained that a scientific way of thinking was at that time, or indeed is even

---

[1] See, for example, W. W. Sikes, *British Goblins*, 1880, pp. 163, 164.

[2] Wuttke, *op. cit.* S. 155.

[3] F. A. Göpfert, *Moraltheologie*, 1897, Bd. i. S. 470. Hagen, *Der Teufel im Lichte der Glaubensquellen*, 1899, S. 8. A. Lehmkuhl, *Theologia moralis*, 1890, Bd. i. Nr. 335, 879. Marc, *Institutiones morales Alphonsianae*, 1893, Bd. 1, S. 543, J. E. Pruner, *Lehrbuch der katholischen Moraltheologie*, 1875, S. 263. Henne am Rhyn, *op. cit.* S. 153-157. Soldan, *op. cit.* S. 340-346.

[4] In England, where I have studied the current opinions in most detail, most of the change took place within twenty years.

now, at all generally diffused. The explanation strikes
me as being altogether too intellectualistic, since both
the origin and the disappearance of such beliefs as that
in Witches are predominantly matters of emotion. [This
scepticism was similarly expressed by an anonymous
writer in the *New Statesman*, April 3, 1915: 'Men did not
cease to believe in witchcraft because the evidence was
against it, but because they gradually got a vague idea
that such things did not happen. It is by faith rather
than by reason that we have come to disbelieve in a
world of witches. As Lecky has said, "if we considered
witchcraft probable, a hundredth part of the evidence
we possess would have placed it beyond the region of
doubt."']

An important clue is perhaps furnished by the fact
that the Witch delusion crumbled through its most important element being eliminated, namely the belief in
fornication with the Devil, and I would suggest the
following explanation for this. In the seventeenth century, particularly about the middle of it, there was a
notable increase in Puritanism, the political manifestations of which in all European countries are well known,
and partly as a development of this and partly as a
reaction against it the general attitude towards both sex
and sexuality underwent a very extensive change.[1] Instead of its being loudly declaimed and stamped as a
dangerous sin it became more and more suppressed as a
topic of public discussion. A hypocritical compromise
was reached, still maintained,[2] by which it was allowed
to exist on condition that people were discreet about it.
Now this change of attitude was quite inconsistent with
a continuance of the Witch epidemic, for the Witch
trials consisted largely of ventilating in great detail the
most repellent aspects of sexuality. In short, the feeling

---

[1] The change in the attitude towards sexuality which occurred in the seventeenth and eighteenth centuries has been carefully studied by E. Fuchs in his
valuable works: *Illustrierte Sittengeschichte vom Mittelalter bis zur Gegenwart*;
Renaissance (mit Ergänzungsband), 1909; and *Die Galante Zeit* (mit Ergänzungsband), 1910.

[2] [No longer true since the War.]

gradually increased that the performances of Witches were too improper a theme to be dwelt on: such things were simply not done. With this elimination of the sexual aspects, and its necessary concomitants, the pact with the Devil, the Sabbath and the Travel by Night, Witch trials became more and more impossible. The Witch conception therefore dissolved into its original elements.

Let us consider the fate of these in order. Intercourse with supernatural beings reverted first to folklore, as has been expounded in earlier chapters of this book, and finally to the sphere of erotic dreams. Heresy continued and does so still, but the power of the Church to persecute it diminished for two reasons. It could no longer be combined with the dread of Witchcraft, and then the political power of the Catholic Church was so broken by the wars of the seventeenth century that in exhaustion the nations had to accept an attitude of greater religious tolerance, one which the State has gradually forced on the Church in all countries. There remained *Maleficium*, the original form of sorcery. The sting had been taken out of this, however, by the waning of the idea of feminine incest which had accounted for the greater part of the morbid dread. Left to itself *Maleficium* was inadequate to maintain official prosecutions, in spite of numerous agitated attempts[1] in this direction, and the belief was restored from the field of jurisprudence to that of folklore, where it has lingered on in an increasingly attenuated guise into our own days.

The very factor, therefore, namely excessive sexual repression, that had made the Witchcraft epidemic possible in the first place was, when developed to a more intense degree, an important one in destroying its own fruit. We are familiar with clinical parallels to this process: many neurotic manifestations of a given stage of repression become incompatible with a more intense one, the erotic source of them being intolerable, and so dis-

[1] Soldan (*op. cit.* Bd. ii. S. 263) has remarked that in the period from 1690 to 1718, so critical in regard to the Witch belief, no fewer than twenty-six books were published in its defence, lamenting its decline and the insufficiently energetic measures taken against Witches.

appear. It is possible that an external observer might have foretold in the fourteenth century that the Witch-craft delusion then being formulated must for intrinsic reasons be as self-limited as a fever, carrying with it, just as this does, the seeds of its own cure.

* * * * *

We come now to the *third problem*, namely the relation of the Witch concept to the experiences of Nightmare. There is no direct connection between these experiences and the driving force behind the Witch persecutions— the endeavour to uproot heresy, or between it and the folk belief that the Church exploited for its purpose— the *Maleficium* of sorcery, although the topics of both heresy and sorcery are indirectly related to the ideas underlying the Nightmare experiences, *i.e.* the ideas belonging to the incest conflict. It is quite otherwise with the third constituent of Witchcraft, the belief in the pact with the Devil, which welded them all into a single entity and without which the Witch epidemic would have been impossible: for this constituent is inherently connected at every point with the Nightmare. This con-clusion has never been more clearly demonstrated than in the remarkable *Roman de la Rose*—published anony-mously in 1280, the author being the ecclesiastical Jehan de Meung—and it is nowadays no longer possible to deny. The essentially dream origin of the ideas centering around the Night flight has been expounded above in detail, and the idea of fornication with the Devil is evidently a form of Incubus belief which must have been largely determined by the Nightmare experiences so common in hysteria;[1] the prevailing theological views of the time lent them an appearance of reality, as they so often have with other hallucinatory experiences (visions, etc.). Müller[2] says: 'Ihren sinnlichen Versuchun-gen und ihrer Furcht vor dem Versucher, vor dem sinn-lichen Teufel kann sie nicht entgehen. In den phan-

---

[1] On the Nightmare experiences of Witches see Ennemoser, *op. cit.* S. 869, and Wuttke, *op. cit.* S. 151.
[2] Johannes Müller, *op. cit.*

tasiereichen Zuständen des Halbwachens und Traums unterliegt sie der sinnlichen Erscheinung dessen, was ihre Sinne wünschen und was die religiöse Vorstellung fürchtet. Das Phantasiebild hat für sie Objektivität, sie kann die Anklage des Teufelsumganges nicht von sich ablehnen.' ('The "Witch" could not escape the temptations of her senses and her fear of the seducer, of the sensual Devil. In dreams and when half-awake, mental states so rich in phantasy, she was overcome by the plastic vision of what her senses craved and what the religious teaching dreaded. The phantasy picture was for her objective and she could not deny the accusation of intercourse with the Devil.')

The Witch idea is an exteriorization of a woman's unconscious thoughts about herself and her mother, and this is one of the reasons why Witches were for the most part either very old and ugly or very young and beautiful. As was pointed out in connection with the Sabbath, fornication with the Devil represents an unconscious incestuous phantasy.

The resemblances between the beliefs relating to *Devil, Witch, Incubus* and Night-bogey (*Alp*) are so intimate that they may be said to present merely different aspects of the same theme. Even in fine details the correspondence is very striking. Thus Witches, just like the Devil, the Night-bogey (*Alp*) and Night-hag (*Mahre*) had a cloven hoof (*Drudenfuss*)[1] and a hollow back.[2] Exactly the same amulets—knife, horse-shoe, salt, etc.— were used as protection against Witches, the Devil, and the Nightmare. Coitus in all these cases was mostly disagreeable and devoid of pleasure.[3] The Night-bogey (*Alp*), just like the Witch, rode on horses and flew like a bird,[4] and so on. The Southern Slavs have many beliefs connecting the Mara and Witch.[5] Some hold that a Mara is a Witch who has rued her evil deeds and decides to

---

[1] Wuttke, *op. cit.* S. 155.
[2] Grimm, *op. cit.* S. 903. Henne am Rhyn, *op. cit.* S. 38, 68.
[3] Gener, *op. cit.* p. 524. Henne am Rhyn, *op. cit.* S. 68.
[4] L. Laistner, *Das Rätsel der Sphinx*, 1889, Bd. ii. S. 82, 275.
[5] Krauss, *op. cit.* S. 147, 148.

confine herself to plaguing men during sleep. Others that a Mara is a maiden ripe for marriage who will become a Witch after it; in Herzogovina such a Mara is herself the daughter of a Witch.

The connections between the Witch belief and that in *Vampires* and *Werewolves* are less striking, but many indications of them are nevertheless present. The typical blood-sucking of the Vampire is rarely met with among Witches, but closely allied themes occur. Witches were passionately fond of at least drinking blood, particularly that of young people;[1] no doubt the main idea underlying this is that of sunamitism,[2] *i.e.* rejuvenation through contact with the young, an idea not far removed from that of the Vampire renewing his life through drinking the blood of the living. Milton refers to this belief in *Paradise Lost* (ii. 662):

> Nor uglier follow the Night-hag, when call'd
> In secret riding through the air she comes,
> Lured with the smell of infant blood, to dance
> With Lapland witches. . . .

Five Witches were burned in Lausanne in 1604 for having in the guise of wolves set upon a child. They took the child to the Devil, who sucked all its blood out through the big toe and then boiled the body down to obtain materials for the necessary ointment.[3] Witches were also addicted to the more harmless habit of milking cows, and they could even extract milk from a spindle, a hand-towel or the haft of a hatchet;[4] the meaning of this will appear when one recollects the unconscious equivalency of milk and semen. The German *Alp* used to suck milk as well as blood[5] and, according to Stoll,[6] the superstition still prevails in Germany that snakes suck the milk from cows by night; in Wales it was

[1] J. J. von Goerres, *Christliche Mystik*, 1842, Bd. iv. S. 2, 216. Krauss, *op. cit.* S. 79. E. H. Meyer, *Indogermanische Mythen*, 1883, Bd. ii. S. 528.
[2] Laurent und Nagour, *op. cit.* S. 208-227.
[3] Nynauld, *De la Lycanthropie*, 1615, pp. 50, 52.
[4] Grimm, *op. cit.* S. 896, 897.
[5] Laistner, *op. cit.* Bd. i. S. 61, and Bd. ii. S. 82.
[6] Stoll, *op. cit.* S. 215.

234 NIGHTMARE AND MEDIÆVAL SUPERSTITIONS PT. II

believed that snakes would suck milk from the human breast.[1] In Scotland and Wales Witches were even until recently believed to transform themselves into hares for the purpose of obtaining milk by sucking cows' udders;[2] in Denmark and Sweden they get it by simply despatching hares to the cattle.[3] In mythology hares are synonymous with cats, and the word 'puss' is still used for both in the country districts of England; it is therefore intelligible that hares sometimes function, *e.g.* in Wales, as the 'familiars' of Witches[4] in place of the more usual cats. Even the *revenant* nature of the Vampire is indicated in the Danish belief that dead people in certain circumstances change into hares.[5] Further curious associations are the Russian belief that future Vampires may be recognized during their life by their having a hare-lip, and the East European one that a dead person becomes a Vampire if a cat runs over his grave.[6] Still another Vampire trait is to be found in the Ghoul stories related at many trials in which the Witches exhumed and devoured the corpses of sorcerers.[7] Just like a Witch, the Dalmatian Koslak, who is actually a Vampire, can predict the weather and can travel faster than anyone else.[8] We thus see that the Witch belief has endless points of contact with the phenomena discussed in earlier chapters.

The same is true of the connection between *Witches* and *Werewolves*. The persecution and execution of Werewolves in the sixteenth and seventeenth centuries were mainly possible through the prevailing belief in the power of Witches to transform themselves into animals. They could turn either themselves or others into Werewolves.[9] Of special interest in regard to the association already discussed between the ideas of Witch ointment,

[1] J. Rhys, *Celtic Folklore*, 1901, p. 690.
[2] W. Hertz, *Der Werwolf*, 1862, S. 113 (several references).
[3] Thorpe, *op. cit.* vol. ii. p. 192.
[4] C. I. Elton, *Origins of English History*, 1890, p. 297.
[5] Thorpe, *loc. cit.*
[6] W. Mannhardt, *Zeitschrift für deutsche Mythologie*, 1856, Jahrg. iv. S. 260.
[7] De Lancre, *op. cit.* pp. 199, 402.
[8] Krauss, *op. cit.* S. 125.
[9] *Der Hexenhammer, op. cit.* Erster Teil, S. 155-157. Nynauld, *loc. cit.*

night flights and animal-transformation, is the fact that this change into a Werewolf was believed to be brought about by means of a magic ointment. Thus in 1521 a man called Michel Verdun (or Verdung) was burned at Besancon for turning himself and a companion into Werewolves,[1] and in a Witch trial as late as 1717 the victims were accused of turning themselves into Werewolves in the same way.[2] The close association between Witches and cats was mentioned above, and Grimm[3] refers to the ancient sorcery belief that men can be transformed into wolves and women into cats, a wolf and cat evidently meaning Devil and Witch respectively. A similar association existed between the *Mahre*, the German precursor of Witches, and Werewolves: a seventh child became, if a boy, a Werewolf, if a girl, a *Mahre*.[4]

We may conclude this chapter with the following quotation from Hansen,[5] one of the first authorities on the subject: 'Die Hexenverfolgung ist ein kulturgeschichtliches Problem, das, wenn es auch als tatsächlich abgeschlossen gelten darf, doch mit unserer Zeit noch enger zusammenhängt, als man auf den ersten Blick zuzugeben geneigt sein dürfte. Die Elemente des Wahns, auf denen sie sich aufgebaut hat, werden noch heute fast ausnahmslos in den Lehren der geltenden religiösen Systeme weitergeführt. . . . Von der Verantwortung für seine Entstehung wird die Menschheit sich aber doch erst dann ganz entlastet fühlen können, wenn sie auch den kläglichen, noch nicht überwundenen Rest der ihm zu Grunde liegenden Wahnvorstellungen ausgeschieden haben wird, der trotz aller inneren Haltlosigkeit in den herrschenden religiösen Systemen noch heute sein Dasein fristet.' ('The persecution of Witches is a problem in the history of civilization which, even though it may count as being closed in fact, nevertheless has closer connections with our own time than might at first glance

[1] H. Boguet, *Discours des sorciers*, 1608, p. 370. S. Leubuscher, *Der Wahnsinn*, 1848, S. 68.
[2] Riezler, *op. cit.* S. 293.   [3] Grimm, *op. cit.* S. 915.
[4] Laistner, *op. cit.* Bd. ii. S. 354.
[5] J. Hansen, *op. cit.* Vorwort vii. and S. 538.

appear. The elements of the delusion on which it was founded still to-day continue almost without exception in the teachings of the prevailing religious systems. . . . Mankind will not be able to feel relieved from the responsibility for its occurrence until it has extruded as well the miserable relics, still not overcome, of the delusional ideas at the basis of it, which in spite of their being intrinsically untenable still live on in the ruling religious systems.')

SUMMARY

IT would seem worth while now to review the characteristic features common to the five groups of phenomena considered above. In the first place—and this is one of the main theses of this book—they all represent constructions built out of numerous elements which not only had an independent existence previously among the beliefs of European peoples, but which are still to be found to-day in widely separated parts of the world. For the fusing of the constituents into a composite belief the Christian Church bears in every case the prime responsibility, in four cases the Roman Catholic and in one the Orthodox Greek Church. It is worthy of note that leading authorities of the Church had repeatedly, previous to the twelfth century, denied the truth of the popular beliefs in these constituents, particularly sorcery, lewd intercourse with Incubi, transformation of human beings into animals, night journeys with demons and witchcraft, and they insisted on the dream origin of these beliefs: it was reserved for the Middle Ages to plunge into an obscurantism that the so-called Dark Ages had rejected. The composite beliefs in question endured approximately three hundred years; after their course was run they did not vanish, but dissolved once more into their original elements. Even the fully developed beliefs have lasted on among the uneducated portions of society, and that this is far from rare may be illustrated by the fact that the present writer has personally met with people who were as convinced of the truth of these beliefs as the general population was in the Middle Ages: belief in the constituent elements themselves is far more widely spread and may at times be encountered even among the educated. During the Middle Ages and later belief in these five superstitions tended to assume epidemic proportions and then gave rise to frightful suffering and an outbreak of persecutory mania almost without parallel.

The five superstitions were closely interwoven together, and in many respects even passed over into one another. The psychological meaning of them is even more closely connected than their outward appearance. All the elements out of which the five superstitious beliefs were built were projections of unconscious and repressed sexual material. In this material two features are above all noteworthy, the prominence of incestuous wishes and of infantile forms of sexuality.

The actual formulation of the superstitions after they had been fully developed was influenced by a variety of factors, principally of a social and religious nature; the analysis of them is thus an historical problem. The most important were two features in the attitude of the Christian Church: the fear and hate it displayed towards unorthodox worship, which to it was equivalent to disobedience against God; and the abnormally exaggerated effort it expended in the service of sexual repression, particularly in its horror of incest. It cannot be chance that these two features, which evoked as savage emotions and conduct as human beings are capable of, represent the two sides of the fundamental Oedipus complex, revolt against the father and sexual love towards the mother.

The relations the five superstitions bear to the Nightmare are especially close. The superstitions themselves may psychologically be designated as phobias the latent content of which represents repressed incestuous wishes. In the intensity of the dread accompanying them they are surpassed by no other experience than that of the Nightmare and allied anxiety dreams. In many of their features they contain a symbolism highly characteristic of anxiety dreams. Other features common to both are: the sudden transformation of one person into another or into some animal; the occurrence of phantastic and impossible animal forms; the alternation of the imagined object between extreme attractiveness and the most intense disgust; the apparently simultaneous existence of the same person in two different places; the idea of flying or riding through the air; and the apprehension of sexual acts as torturing assaults. The central point of the latent content both of the Nightmare and the five superstitions here examined is composed of repressed incestuous wishes relating to coitus. In four out of the five there are also present other sexual wishes, various perversions of infantile origin, just as there are with the anxiety dreams that do not belong to the classical Nightmare type. Nightmares have even shown at times the tendency, so prominent with the superstitions, to assume epidemic form.[1] The extensive accord obtaining between the Nightmare and these superstitions, not only in their essential psychological signification but also in many points in their manifest structure, makes it probable that actual dream experiences were of very considerable importance in making the elaboration of them possible.

[1] See, for instance, Laurent, cited by Parent, *Grand Dictionnaire de Médecine*, t. xxxiv. Art. 'Incubi'.

PART III

THE MARE AND THE MARA: A PSYCHO-ANALYTICAL CONTRIBUTION TO ETYMOLOGY

CHAPTER I

INTRODUCTION

THE word 'Nightmare' originally meant a 'night-fiend'. These night-fiends were held responsible for the experiences of terrifying dreams, and the word was then used to denote the dreams themselves, so that its original meaning is becoming forgotten. Chatterton could still write:

> Hark! the death-owl loud doth sing
> To the nightmares as they go.

The word was more particularly used to denote a female night-fiend, night-hag, or, as she was also called, a 'nighte-wytche'.

The word Nightmare itself comes from the Anglo-Saxon *neaht* or *nicht* (=night) and *mara* (=incubus or succubus). The Anglo-Saxon suffix *a* denotes an agent, so that *mara* from the verb *merran*, literally means 'a crusher', and the connotation of a crushing weight on the breast is common to the corresponding words in allied languages (Icelandic *mara*, Danish *mare*, Low German *moore*, Polish *mora*, Bohemian *mûra*, Swedish *mara*, Old High German *mara*). They are ultimately derived from an Indo-Germanic root of great interest, *MR*, to which we shall later devote our attention. From the earliest times the oppressing agency experienced during sleep was personified, more often in a female guise; it was depicted as being either extremely attractive or else extremely hideous. The earliest member of the spirit world of which we have any record is this 'oppression fiend' (*Druckgeist*), the generic name for which is *mara*. Krauss[1] rightly remarks that 'Wenn irgend ein Glaube allen Völkern der Erde zu allen Zeiten und unter allen Zonen gemeinsam

---

[1] F. S. Krauss, *Slavische Volkforschungen*, 1908, S. 146.

war und ist, so ist es der Marglaube'. ('If ever a belief
was and is common to all peoples of the earth at all ages
and in every zone, it is the belief in the Mara.')

Three hundred years ago the word *mare* alone was
commonly used to designate the nightly visitor to whose
agency was ascribed the terrifying nightmare dreams.[1]
The Teutonic word from which it comes, *mara*, is, however, quite distinct from the word *mare*, a female horse.[2]
The latter dates from the Anglo-Saxon *mere*, the female
form of *mearh*, a horse. The same assimilation between
the two words occurs in Dutch as well as in English, for
the second half of the Dutch word for Nightmare, *i.e.*
Nachtmerrie, also means a mare.[3] Let us pursue a little
further the history of the word *mare* = a female horse.
Jähns[4] cites twelve allied words with a corresponding
number of feminine forms. Instances are: masculine, Icelandic and Old High German *mar*, Middle High German
march, Modern High German *Mahr*; feminine, Old
Norse *merr*, Finnish *märä*, Middle High German
meriche and *mare*, Modern High German *Märhe*.
The last-named word is nowadays written incorrectly
Mähre. It may be mentioned that Vignoli[5] went so far
as to derive the word *mara* of our Nightmare from an
Old High German word *mar* = horse, thus making the
idea of horse the primary one in the whole group of
Nightmare sagas to a quite unjustifiable extent. The
root from which the word *mare* is derived is thought to
be of Keltic origin, being recorded as such by Pausanias,
and the word is cognate with the Irish *marc* and Welsh
march = horse.

In both German and English these words very early

[1] See Reginald Scot, *The Discoverie of Witchcraft*, ed. 1665, p. 85.
[2] It is true that Grimm, in his *Deutsche Mythologie* (4e Ausg. S. 1041), though
not in his later *Wörterbuch*, expresses the opinion that the latter word is derived
directly from the former, which if true would at once clinch the argument of
Part III. of this book, but the generally received opinion is as I have stated it
in the text.
[3] W. W. Skeat, *An Etymological Dictionary of the English Language*, 1910,
p. 401.
[4] M. Jähns, *Ross und Reiter in Leben und Sprache, Glauben und Geschichte
der Deutschen*, 1872, Bd. 1, S. 12, 13.
[5] T. Vignoli, *Myth and Science*, 1882, p. 77.

obtained a predominantly feminine signification, very likely because of its similarity to the other word *mara* = night-hag, and in both, more completely so in English, the corresponding masculine form has now fallen into disuse. In fact, this feminine signification is so strong that in various countries the word has been used to denote several other female creatures; for instance, in Breton *march* means a cow. Jähns[1] gives this fact as the explanation of the flavour of contempt[2] that the word has acquired in German, for till late in the Middle Ages only the male horse was considered to be noble, the female passing as common. There is an old folk riddle in German that relates to this: 'Welcher Kaiser hat die schlechtesten Pferde? Der von Österreich, denn er hat Mähren!' ('Which Emperor has the worst horses? The Emperor of Austria, for he has Moravia—*i.e.* mares!') The masculine word of the same root actually came to signify in German a bad or decayed horse ('ein schlechtes, heruntergekommenes Pferd'), and it is still used in this sense in the Upper Adige district of South Tirol in the form *march*. Since the ninth century the word *Mähre* (= mare) has been used in German to designate a harlot, a lecherous woman or—occasionally—an ugly old woman; current examples of this are the Bavarian *morch*, the Carinthian *merche*, and the Low German *mär*.

The present point of interest is this. It might readily be supposed that the assimilation of the second half of the word Nightmare to the English word for a female horse, a mare, is a matter of no special significance. But psycho-analysis has with right become suspicious of manifestations of the human spirit that are easily discarded as meaningless, and in the present case our suspicions are strengthened when we learn that in other countries the ideas of night-hag and female horse are closely associated, although there is not the linguistic

[1] Jähns, *op. cit.* S. 13, 14.
[2] Compare the stress laid by Alfred Adler on the importance that contempt for feminine traits has in the development of the psychoneuroses, *Zentralblatt für Psychoanalyse*, 1911, Jahrg. i. S. 20 and elsewhere.

justification for it that exists in English. Forestalling the discussion that will presently follow, I would maintain the thesis that there are in the human mind deep reasons why the two ideas in question naturally become associated, and that the linguistic assimilation in English of the two words is a simple consequence of this psychological fact. The matter seems to me worth pursuing for two reasons. If we find, as we shall, that various folk beliefs about the mare are closely parallel to those about the Nightmare, and further that the former have the same underlying meaning as we have attributed to the latter, then we shall have obtained a corroboration of no small value of the truth of our general conclusions regarding the significance of the Nightmare and the part it has played in affecting human beliefs. In the second place, the evolution of the words denoting these two ideas should prove an interesting study in semantics in general and perhaps yield some conclusions of interest to the science of etymology.

Our present theme, therefore, is the association between human beings and animals in the imagination. The general psychological implications of this theme I have discussed elsewhere[1] at some length and need only repeat at this point the conclusions there reached. The most important for our present purposes are that the ideas unconsciously represented by the presence of an animal in a dream, neurotic symptom, myth or other product of the imagination are always derived from thoughts about a human being, so that the animal simply stands for this human being; that the human being in question is in most cases specifically a parent; and that the ideas thus represented belong to the group of repressed wishes and fears that centre around infantile sexuality. In a word, therefore, the presence of an animal in such contexts always denotes the action of an incest complex. We shall now choose a particular example of this interchangeability, namely that of human beings into horses, and note the threads that connect such an

[1] Part II. pp. 63, 64.

idea with those we have already studied when considering the part played by Nightmares in folklore and
superstition.

I had originally intended to divide into two groups
the material now to be presented, which should illustrate
respectively the associations on the one hand between
the ideas of mare and female fiend and those between
horse and male fiend. This proved to be impossible for a
reason which is in itself instructive. The sexes simply refused to be separated so neatly as this classification
would pretend. Exactly as in anxiety dreams, the sex
and the sexual attitude both of the dreamer and of the
supposed nightly visitor are extraordinarily interchangeable, so to separate the material in the logical manner
I had proposed would have been to do violence to the
facts themselves. One cannot lay too much emphasis on
the fact that sex inversion plays a highly characteristic
and most important part, not only in anxiety dreams,
but in all the products of the imagination derived from
them or influenced by them.

CHAPTER II

THE HORSE AND THE NIGHT-FIEND

IN the human imagination of all ages horses have been extensively connected with ideas of the supernatural. Not only evil demons and lecherous visitors of the night, but Divine beings themselves have frequently assumed an equine guise, and, as elsewhere, the ideas relating to good and evil supernatural beings pass insensibly into one another. In Hindu mythology it is taught that the first horse was created as a by-product when the gods and demons were jointly churning the Ocean of Milk to extract nectar from it.

There is also no sharp difference of sex in these various associations, but a study of extensive material inclines me to the conclusion that the female connotations are more often associated with the terrifying and the erotic, while the noble and divine connotations have more often male associations; it should be observed that these two statements are not counterparts.

Though we shall have to range somewhat beyond it, our particular concern is with the identification of *mara* with *mare*, and we may therefore begin with some remarks on the frequency with which the ideas of woman and mare have been brought together in the imagination. Jähns,[1] in giving many examples of this, writes: 'Ganz eigentümlich und beispiellos ist die innige *Zusammenstellung von Pferd und Frau* in Dichtung, Spruchweisheit und Redensart. . . . Diese Zusammenstellung von Frau und Pferd ist uralt.' ('Quite peculiar and without example is the intimate *juxtaposition of horse and woman* in poetry, proverbial wisdom and sayings. . . . This juxtaposition is primeval.') Among the proverbs he quotes to illustrate this are the following:

---

[1] M. Jähns, *Ross und Reiter in Leben und Sprache, Glauben und Geschichte der Deutschen*, Bd. i. 1872, S. 77.

'Dein Weib, dein Pferd, dein Schwert leih nicht her!'
('Lend not thy wife, thy horse, thy sword.') 'Seinem Gaule
und seinem Weibe soll man nie den Zügel schieszen
lassen!' ('One should never give a free rein to one's steed
or one's wife.') 'Freien ist wie Pferdekauf; Freier tu' die
Augen auf!' ('Courting is like buying a horse; suitor, keep
your eyes open.') He calls attention to the specially frequent analogy between horse and rider on the one hand
and a married couple on the other. In many countries
the ideas of bride and horse are brought together.[1] 'In
Preussen sagt man: "Kommt der Bräutigam zur Hoch-
zeit geritten, so löse man ihm gleich nach dem Absteigen
den Sattelgurt,[2] das sichert seiner künftigen Frau eine
leichte Entbindung". Bei den hannöverschen Wenden
werden vor der Wohnung des jungen Paares die Rosse
vom Hochzeitswagen abgespannt und die Braut muss
den Wagen in vollem Laufen vor dem Hause vorbei
ziehen. Tut sie das recht geschickt und ohne anzu-
stossen, so wird's auch wenig Anstoss in der Ehe geben.'
('They say in Prussia: "If the bridegroom comes on
horseback to the wedding one should loosen the saddle-
girth[2] as soon as he dismounts, for this ensures his future

---

[1] Jähns, *op. cit.* S. 377.

[2] This symbolic equating of the horse's saddle-girth and harness with the
human vulva is commonly met with in folklore. Von Düringsfeld (quoted by
H. Freimark, *Okkultismus und Sexualität*, S. 409) relates: 'In einigen Gegenden
Skandinaviens nimmt die Braut dem Pferde, auf dem sie zur Trauung reitet,
vor der Kirche den Zaum ab und löst ihm die Sattelgurte, um ein leichtes
Kindbett zu haben. Sie erreicht diesen Zweck auch, wenn sie durch ein Pferde-
geschirr kriecht, aber dann wird nach dem Volksglauben das Kind ein Alp.'
('In some districts of Scandinavia the bride takes the reins off the horse on
which she has ridden to the wedding in front of the church and loosens his
saddle-girth so as to have an easy childbirth. She achieves this purpose also
if she creeps through a horse's collar, but then, according to popular belief,
the child will be a night-bogey.') An allied symbolism has given rise to a large
number of practices of creeping through holes to avoid witchcraft, bad luck
or illness. Some of these are quoted by S. Seligmann (*Der Böse Blick und
Verwandtes*, 1910, Bd. i. S. 327-328): *e.g.*, 'in Ostfriesland lässt man ein Kind,
das unaufhörlich schreit, durch ein Pferdehalfter kriechen'. ('In East Frisia
one makes a child that continually cries creep through a horse's halter'), a
custom still in force also in the south of England. To cure impotence a man
drinks wine that has been poured through his wedding-ring, and so on. An
almost equally large number of beliefs maintain the exact contrary of this,
asserting that to creep through a hole, *e.g.*, to walk under a ladder, brings bad
luck. Common to both sets, of course, is the conviction that the act in question
is of magical significance. (For details concerning the symbolic significance of the
girdle see O. Stoll, *Das Geschlechtsleben in der Völkerpsychologie*, 1908, S. 475-483.)

wife an easy childbirth". Among the Wends of Hanover
the horses of the wedding carriage are taken out of the
traces in front of the young couple's house and the bride
has to pull the carriage past the house. If she does this
skilfully and without running into anything[1] there will
be little friction in the marriage.') An old Devon legend,
an account of which was published in 1683, tells of a
female ghost who appears as a mare,[2] whence Tom
Pearce's grey mare of the popular ballad. In one of
Boccaccio's stories (Ninth day, Tenth story) a woman is
by magic turned into a mare. In the Middle Ages in
France it was believed that the souls of priests' concubines were after their death changed into black mares
(les juments au diable) and had carnal intercourse with
the Devil.[3]

The interchangeability of woman and mare is thus to
be found in the most diverse fields, in literature, folklore, superstition, and so on. The following examples
from the higher mythology will illustrate also the interchangeability of the sexes here, a feature on which we
often have occasion to remark. The god Loki, in order to
cheat the giant out of Freija, turned himself into a mare
and by neighing beguiled away the giant's chief stand-
by, his stallion Svadilfari, by whom he conceived Odin's
famous horse Sleipnir. Among the Ancient Kelts the
worship was prevalent of Epona, a goddess in the form
of a mare, the patroness of horses.[4] In the Icelandic Song
of Hildebrand a brown horse saves an unhappy lady
from her husband on the condition that she is not to
speak while he carries her, and then turns into a handsome prince.[5]

If, now, one studies the various associations to the
idea of 'horse' in mythology and folklore it becomes
plain that the two attributes of the horse that have

[1] There is here a play on the word *Anstoss*, to run into, to take offence at.
[2] S. Baring-Gould, *Devonshire Characters and Strange Events*, 1906, p. 171.
[3] P. Sébillot, *Le Folk-lore de France*, 1906, t. iii. ' La faune et la flore', p. 149.
[4] E. Anwyl, *Celtic Religion*, 1906, pp. 30, 31.
[5] See a rather similar story in L. Laistner, *Das Rätsel der Sphinx*, 1889,
Bd. ii. S. 101.

especially caught the imagination are (1) his strong, *swift movement*, and (2) his magnificent *shining appearance*. In a subsequent chapter I shall consider the psychological significance of these attributes and the underlying connection between them. In many spheres, *e.g.*, in sun worship, it is hardly possible to distinguish between them.

The high significance that the idea of *movement* has in this connection is brought out in the following quotation from Jähns[1]: 'Es sind in der vorliegenden Liste *dreiundsechzig verschiedene, selbstständige deutsche Namen des Pferdes* aufgeführt worden, ganz abgesehn von der Fülle lokaler oder historischer Varianten. Dreiundzwanzig diser Benennungen, und unter ihnen die allerhervorragendsten, sind von der *Bewegung* abstrahirt, einundzwanzig sind Geschlechtsbezeichnungen, zehn beziehn sich auf *Jugend* oder *Kleinheit* des Pferdes, zwei knüpfen an sein *Gewiher* an und sieben endlich an andere *besondere Eigenschaften*.' ('In the preceding list *sixty-three different and independent German names for a horse* are given, quite apart from the mass of local or historical variants. Twenty-three of these designations, and among them the most prominent, relate to movement, twenty-one denote the sex of the animal, ten refer to the youth or smallness of the horse, two have to do with neighing, and finally seven refer to special attributes.') In other words, fifteen times as many expressions for a horse (in German) are derived from the idea of movement as from any other single attribute except its sexedness. Examples of the names derived from the idea of movement are *Pferd* (cognate with the English *palfrey*), *Ross* (English *horse*), *Hengst* and *Mähre* (English *mare*) itself; this last is distantly cognate with the French *marcher*, to walk, the Scottish *merk*, to ride, the Wallachian *merg*, to go (from which the Wallachian *murghe* = horse), and the English to *march*.

Consideration of movement in connection with a horse brings us at once to the idea of *riding*. The very word

[1] Jähns, *op. cit.* S. 39.

'ride' originally meant simply movement in general,[1] a trace of which movement is retained in such expressions as 'to ride in a train, carriage, etc.' Now in every language riding is one of the commonest euphemisms for coitus, the analogy—in position and movement—between rider and horse and man and woman being sufficiently evident. Nocturnal emissions are known as 'witch-riding', and in German are indicated by the expression 'es reiten ihn Hexen' ('witches are riding him'), a substitute for the older expression 'dich hat geriten der Mar'[2] ('the night-fiend has ridden you') from which we get the corresponding English phrase of 'mare-riding'. In German a man lacking in virility is called a 'Sonntagsreiter' ('Sunday rider') or a 'Bauerreiter' ('peasant rider'),[3] and a name for the honeymoon is 'Stutenwoche' ('mare week'). In his section on 'Reiten als Bezeichnung der Begattung' ('Riding as a designation for coitus') Jähns[4] writes: 'Das Mittelalter liebte der Art Vergleiche ganz auszerordentlich und konnte sich nicht satt hören an hiehergehörigen Anecdoten und Zötchen. Unmöglich können wir dise Anknüpfungen hier näher verfolgen wollen; einige Andeutungen mögen genügen, namentlich unter Hinzufügung der Versicherung, dasz dis Feld reichlich bebaut ist. . . . Doch genug! Auf disem Gebiete taugt keine Theorie; da sehe jeder selbst zu.' ('The Middle Ages was quite extraordinarily fond of this particular comparison and was never tired of listening to anecdotes and bawdy jokes on it. It is impossible for us to pursue this association indefinitely; a few illustrations must suffice, especially if we assure the reader that this ground is richly sown. . . . But enough! In this field no theory is of use. Everyone can see for himself.') A classical example of the same symbolism is to be found in Voltaire's *La Pucelle* (Chant XIII) in the scene where the English soldier attempts to rape Joan, a passage which some critics have thought to be borrowed from a

---

[1] Jähns, *op. cit.* S. 150.
[2] J. Grimm, *Deutsche Mythologie*, 4e Ausg., 1877, Bd. iii. S. 372.
[3] Jähns, *op. cit.* S. 156-157.   [4] *Id., op. cit.* S. 229-230.

similar one in Ariosto's *Orlando Furioso*, where the prince discovers the dwarf in bed with his wife. Then there is the well-known passage from Chaucer:[1]

> . . . In principio,
> Mulier est hominis confusio.
> (Madame, the sentence of this Latyn is,
> Womman is mannes joy and mannes blis.)
> For when I fiele a-night your softe syde,
> Al be it that I may not on you ride,
> For that your perche is made so narrow, allas!
> I am so ful of joy and of solás,
> That I defye both vision and dreme.

When such an analogy is so striking as to force itself into literature and conversation one may be sure that its widespread use in the unconscious is even more firmly established, as is well known to every psycho-analyst. We may therefore expect to find many indications in mythology of the nightly visitor being associated with riding. Already in the Ynglingasaga we are told of King Vanlandi in Upsala being trodden to death by a mara.[2] The idea of treading or trampling is akin to that of riding, and indeed the French word for nightmare, *cauchemar*,[3] is derived from the Latin *calcar* (= a spur, from *calx*,[4] a heel) and *mar*;[5] the equivalents in Italian (*pesaruole*) and Spanish (*pesadilla*) come from *pesar* = press, weigh on.[6] In the Völsunga saga Swanhild is trampled to death by horses as a punishment, an appropriate 'talion' one, for having sexual intercourse with her bridegroom's son.[7]

[1] *Canterbury Tales*, 'Nonne Prestes Tale'.
[2] B. Thorpe, *Northern Mythology*, 1851, vol. ii. p. 19.
[3] Collin de Plancy (*Dictionnaire infernal*, 1818, t. i. p. 105) relates the discussion in the Middle Ages as to the nature of this. Delrio decided that it was an imp of Beelzebub, called 'le démon dépuceleur'.
[4] It is perhaps not chance that this word was chosen, for there are many connections between the ideas of stone (*calx*) and horse. From *calx* comes the Scottish *calk* = horse's spur, and also *calculate*, a mythical attribute of horses. The close relation of horse, stone and mountain will be noted below, and Keltologists have explained the first syllable of the frequently met with 'Pferdeberge' as coming from the Gaelic *per* (Latin *petra*, French *pierre*); the Christian representative of the Pferdegott (Horse-God) Psychopomp Odin is called Peter (*petrus*).
[5] L. F. A. Maury, *La Magie et l'astrologie*, 1860, p. 254.
[6] Grimm, *op. cit.* Bd. i. S. 384.
[7] G. W. Cox, *The Mythology of the Aryan Nations*, 1870, vol. i. p. 284.

After what has been said earlier about the significance of animals in the unconscious it is not surprising to learn that in legends in which the theme of riding occurs we often meet also with that of metamorphosis. The visitor appears, now as a human being, now as a horse, and one may change directly into the other. This interchange is all the more easily effected in that horse and rider are often identified as one in the imagination. Jähns[1] lays emphasis on this point in a special section devoted to it, where he states categorically 'Ross und Reiter sind ein Doppelwesen' ('Steed and rider constitute a double being'). The matter is, however, still further complicated by the fact that either the visitor or the visited may be conceived of as the rider and that this rôle may be interchanged. Moreover, the belief is widely held that when a horse is attacked by sweating and shivering, resembling an anxiety attack, it is because it has had a nightly visitor in the form of a mara,[2] so that the night-fiend may visit a horse in the form of a human being, or a human being in the form of a horse; it is plain that these 'anxiety attacks' of the horse are equated to nocturnal emissions accompanied by fear, for the same explanation is given of both. I shall quote two tales that illustrate several points in this group of beliefs: the first is from Denmark, the second from North Germany. 'There was once in Jutland a queen who was a great lover of horses; she had one in particular to which she was most attached, and which occupied her thoughts both waking and dreaming. It frequently happened, when the groom entered the stable at night, that he found this horse out of order, and thence concluded that it had been ridden by the Mara. Taking, therefore, a bucket of cold water, he cast it over the horse, and at the same moment saw that the queen was sitting on its back.'[3] 'In Usedom there once lived a man, who had a horse that had always

---

[1] Jähns, op. cit. S. 162.
[2] W. Golther, Handbuch der germanischen Mythologie, 1895, S. 117. Grimm, op. cit. Bd. ii. S. 880. Krainz, cited by Laistner, op. cit. Bd. i. S. 172. Laistner, op. cit. Bd. ii. S. 82.
[3] Thorpe, op. cit. vol. ii. p. 170.

been vigorous and in good condition, but at once became meagre and lost strength; and notwithstanding that it was well fed, never could recover. This appeared very singular to the owner, and he thought the matter over and over, but could not satisfy himself. At length he sent for a cunning man, who, on seeing the horse, said that he would soon find a remedy. He remained there that night, and at midnight went to the stable, stopt a knot-hole in the door, then fetched the owner of the horse, and they both entered the stable. To his great astonishment he there saw a woman of his acquaintance sitting on the horse, and, although she strove with all her might, unable to descend from it. It was the Horse-mare that was so caught. She besought them most earnestly to set her free, which they did, but only after she had promised never to repeat her visits.'[1] This latter story is repeated in a Brandenburg saga from Mellentin,[2] with the interesting addition that the woman found on the horse the next morning was the prettiest girl in the village: it is one more example of the extraordinary way in which ugly old women and beautiful damsels constantly change places in all Night-mare themes.

We have repeatedly seen that the terror of the nightly visitor, *i.e.* of the Nightmare, is literally a deadly fear, *i.e.* it is amongst other things a fear of being done to death, castration and death being, as we know, closely allied ideas. This is as much as to say that night-fiends and death fiends are beings that cannot be sharply distinguished. The same conclusion is true in connection with horses. Horses can be 'ridden' to death by a death fiend just as they can be exhausted by a mara. The deathly ride may take place in the stable or the horse may be carried away to participate in the 'wild hunt' we shall presently have to discuss.[3] Sometimes this simple idea has become displaced, or rather replaced, on to human beings. Thus in the Frickthal it is believed that

[1] Thorpe, *op. cit.* vol. iii. pp. 75-76.
[2] Jähns, *op. cit.* Bd. i. S. 413.   [3] Laistner, *loc. cit.*

the sweating of a horse in its stable betokens an early death in the neighbourhood.[1]

Many Teutonic legends date from the old belief that the goddess Hel used to throw herself upon sleeping men in the form of a horse.[2] Hel was later identified with Death. In times of pestilence she rides on a three-legged horse and strangles people; when a sickness rages it was said that 'Hel is going about', or when in the night the dogs howled, 'Hel is among the dogs'. In Denmark in former days a living horse was interred in every church-yard before any human corpse was buried in it. 'This horse re-appears and is known by the name of the "Hel-horse".' It has only three legs, and if anyone meets it, it forebodes death. Hence is derived the saying when any-one has survived a dangerous illness: 'He gave death a peck of oats' (as an offering or bribe).[3]

Returning now to the idea of the Nightmare visitor to a human being assuming the guise of a horse or mare we may consider the following evidence. Jahn[4] says: 'als Schimmel hockt die Mahrte auf in Pommern' ('in Pom-erania the Mara plays high cockalorum in a horse's guise), and Montanus[5] gives us a vivid picture of the performance: 'an der untern Wupper dringt die Mahrte in Rossgestalt durch die Schlüssellöcher in Schlafkam-mern, legt die Vorderhufe auf des Schläfers Brust und starrt ihn mit glühenden Augen auf beängstigende Weise an' ('in the lower Wuppenau (in Switzerland) the mara penetrates through the key-hole into the bed-chamber in the guise of a steed, lays her fore-hoofs on the sleeper's breast, and with glowing eyes stares at him in the most alarming fashion'), a description which might well have been written in reference to one of the versions of the frontispiece by Fuseli in the present volume. There are many versions related of the following story with the typical metamorphosis theme. 'Eine Müllerin bei Bam-

[1] B. Stern, *Medizin, Aberglaube und Geschlechtsleben in der Türkei*, 1903, Bd. i. S. 420.

[2] Jähns, *op. cit.* S. 411.   [3] Thorpe, *op. cit.* vol. ii. p. 209.

[4] U. Jahn, cited by Laistner, *op. cit.* Bd. i. S. 172.

[5] Montanus, *Vorzeit*, 2e Ausg. Bd. i. S. 128, cited by Laistner, *loc. cit.*

berg trachtete ihren Knecht zu verführen; da es ihr nicht gelang, wollte sie ihn mürbe machen. Nachts kam sie als Ross zur Kammer herein, warf sich auf ihn und nahm ihm alle Kraft. Auf den Rat eines Mönches warf er der Mahr, als sie wieder in Rossgestalt kam, einen bereitgehaltenen Zaum über und liess das Ross beim Schmied beschlagen, am andern Morgen stand die Müllerin blutend an Händen und Füssen im Stalle.[1] In Oldenburg; ein Grossknecht wacht eines Nachts auf, und wie er einen grossen Schimmel vor seinem Bette sieht, springt er ihm auf den Rücken, reitet ihn nach der Schmiede und lässt ihn beschlagen. Des andern Morgens liegt die Frau krank; sie hat über Nacht etwas an die Füsse gekriegt.'[2] ('A miller's wife at Bamberg wanted to seduce her servant. Not succeeding in this, however, she determined to break his spirit. She came by night to his room in the form of a horse, threw herself on to him and robbed him of all his strength. On a monk's advice he got ready a bridle and threw it over the Mara on her next visit. Having thus caught the horse he got the smith to shoe her, and on the next morning there stood the miller's wife in the stable with her hands and feet all bleeding. In Oldenburg a foreman woke up one night and, seeing a large horse by his bed, sprang on its back, rode it to the smith and got it shod. The next morning the mistress was laid up, having injured her feet in the night.') Krauss[3] tells of a man who was frightfully plagued by a Mara until one night, during her visit, a friend saw a white hair moving up and down over the man's body. He cut it off and in this way cured the patient, but next morning the patient's horse was found dead in the stable: the Mara was no other than the horse. This last story is evidently an inversion of the other; both contain themes, such as shoeing, hair, bridle, the rich mythological implications of which we cannot pursue here. Another variant of the story is that in which two grooms slept together,

[1] A. Schöppner, *Sagenbuch der Bayerischen Lande*, 1853, Bd. iii. S. 293.
[2] L. Strackerjan, cited by Laistner, *op. cit.* Bd. i. S. 172.
[3] F. S. Krauss, *Slavische Volkforschungen*, 1908, S. 152.

one of whom was troubled by a Walriderske: she used to put a halter on him, thus turning him into a horse, and then ride on him the whole night in the most exhausting way. The companion watched, and one night as she came he seized the halter, threw it over her, turning her into a mare, and galloped on her to the smith to have her shod. Next morning the lady of the house lay ill in bed and had horseshoes on her feet.[1] This story is paralleled by one related by Erasmus Franzisci,[2] where, however, the nightly ride was to a witches' sabbath, and in which it was the sufferer himself who carried out the ruse.

Riding naturally leads to another aspect of the 'movement' theme, namely the innumerable beliefs to do with *travel or flight by night*. This connects also with the last subject of metamorphosis, since it is highly probable that both take their origin in dream experiences. It is generally agreed that the various beliefs about flight by night are derived from the familiar 'flying dream' experiences. Jähns[3] writes: 'Die nachtfarenden Weiber treten also in zwei verschiedenen Hauptformen auf: entweder als Nachtmare, die als rossegestaltete Dämonen zum drückenden Alb oder noch häufiger zum Träger des Träumenden werden, oder als Nachtreiterinen, welche dann selbst, als Aufsizende, schlafende Menschen oder schlummernde Rosse reiten.' ('Women who fly by night[4] appear in two distinct main forms: either as night maras who as demons in the guise of horses become an oppressive bogey or, still oftener, carry the sleeper, or else as nightriders who then themselves ride on sleeping people or sleeping horses.') We note again here the feature with which we became familiar above of the interchangeability of the ideas of 'riding on' and 'being ridden by'. Even in the sixteenth century the notorious 'witches' flight' was recognized (*e.g.*, by Wierus in his *De Praestigiis*

[1] Strackerjan, quoted by Laistner, *loc. cit.* A very similar story may be found in a Slavonic witch legend, Krauss, *op. cit.* S. 52-53.
[2] Quoted by Jähns, *op. cit.* S. 413.
[3] Jähns, *op. cit.* S. 411.
[4] Incidentally, a Cockney euphemism for prostitutes.

Daemonorum) as arising in a dream illusion, an opinion poetically handled by Oldham.[1]

We have seen that in mythology it is impossible sharply to separate the stories of riding from those of being ridden on. With the corresponding dreams, although the two themes are often interwoven, one may say that on the whole the former, typified in the familiar flying dream, is apt to be pleasurable, while the latter, more characteristic of the Nightmare itself, is nearly always unpleasant. But when one studies the latent content and dream sources of the two one finds a close similarity. Both of these kinds of dream represent a sexual act, usually conceived of in infantile and often sadistic-masochistic terms. It is thus comprehensible that the myths derived from them should be intimately related to each other, and also that the theme should be regularly connected with that of animal metamorphosis.

Night-fiends ride not only on horses, but also on any abbreviated representative of a horse. According to Grimm,[2] the oldest account of this is given by Guilielmus Alvernus, who describes them riding on reeds and rushes which turned into a live horse. He mentions also the Irish saga where rushes and blades of grass become horses as soon as the mara mounts them, and gives a number of similar examples. The Roman Strigas themselves rode on broomsticks.[3] As is well known, the later witches' ride could be performed on a great variety of objects, notably pitchforks, cart-shafts and broomsticks, as well as on living objects such as horses, cats, goats, etc. When more than one witch had to be carried the companion, less refined than our modern pillion riders, rode on a pole stuck into the goat's hindquarters.[4] The name of the Hörselberg itself, the favourite rendezvous of witches, and doubtless earlier for their predecessors the night-hags, is said to be derived from 'Horsa', a horse.[5] The modern ride on a broomstick is our chil-

[1] See Part II. p. 204.   [2] Grimm, *op. cit.* Bd. ii. S. 907.
[3] J. N. Sepp, *Orient und Occident*, 1903, S. 231.
[4] Jähns, *op. cit.* S. 415.   [5] *Id., op. cit.* S. 417.

dren's 'hobby-horse', which we shall meet again later, and when one remembers the psychological significance of collecting manias the metaphor 'to ride his hobby to death' is seen to be not such a distant relative of the old Night-flight on a magic staff as might at first sight appear.

That animal-worship in general is a part of phallic religion has often been pointed out,[1] and that the male horse is mythologically to be regarded as a phallic animal is also widely recognized.[2] Our psycho-analyses[3] fully explain this by disclosing how significant for the imagination of children is this big aggressive animal, with his habit of biting and trampling; the earliest impression of sexual acts may date from witnessing the copulation of stallion and mare.[4] It is evident, therefore, that the magic staff, broomstick, etc., must be symbols of the most essential attribute of this phallic animal.

I propose now to mention one special example of this phallic significance because of the light it throws on the theme under consideration, namely, the significance of movement.

We have insensibly glided from the theme mara = mare to that of the horse as a phallic animal, but this illustrates the remarkable interchangeability of the sexes in this whole group of myths. Female night-fiends ride on horses, become horses, acquire masculine attributes, and so on. The same is equally true of their descendants, the mediæval witches. The explanation of this state of affairs is that the forbidden wishes that furnish the driving force behind all these beliefs and myths are the repressed sexual desires of incest, and one of the most characteristic defences against the becoming con-

[1] See, for instance, C. Howard, *Sex Worship*, 1897. J. Wier, *Religion and Lust*.
[2] See Aigremont, *Fuss- und Schuh-Symbolik und -Erotik*, 1900 S. 17. R. P. Knight, *The Symbolical Language of Ancient Art*, 1876, pp. 76-78.
[3] See, for instance, Freud, 'Die Analyse der Phobie eines fünfjährigen Knaben'. *Psychoanalytisches Jahrbuch*, Bd. i. S. 1. [*Gesammelte Schriften*, Bd. viii. S. 127; *Collected Papers*, vol. iii. p. 149.]
[4] A. A. Brill, *Journal of Abnormal Psychology*, vol. v. p. 62, relates a striking instance of the part played by this observation in the development of a later neurosis.

scious of such desires is to repudiate them and conceal them through the mechanism of identification with the opposite sex. Hitherto we have been specially concerned with the female aspect of the relation between horses and human beings, but in order to understand the full meaning of it, and particularly to unravel the significance of the idea of movement in this connection, it will be necessary to consider other aspects as well.

The subject of Night Travel naturally leads us to those of the Night Hunt, the Wild Hunt, and the Furious Host. We have here to do with a large group of folk beliefs which group round the idea of a storm at night, and which mythologists have often explained as being simply the product of this experience. Although it is true, however, that stormy nights are associated with fear, it is not hard to show that the reason for this is that the conception of a storm is in the unconscious identified with other ideas which are the real source of the fears. We have, in fact, to do with much grimmer ideas even than that of a storm, with ideas that more nearly concern human interests, namely, ideas of death and castration. The connection between this group of beliefs and the experience of the Nightmare is most simply revealed by the considerations that the Babylonian demon of the storm, the *âlû*, had the custom of spreading himself over a man, overpowering him upon his bed and attacking his breast;[1] that the Hindu demons of the Nightmare, the *alii* and *maruts*, were gods of the storm;[2] and that the Greek name for the Nightmare, the term used by physicians until a century ago, was *Ephialtes*, which also meant 'hurricane'.[3]

The association between storm and danger at night is thus widely spread, but the most extensive data we have in connection with it are to be obtained from Northern

---

[1] T. G. Pinches, *The Religion of Babylonia and Assyria*, 1906, p. 108.
[2] Max Müller, *Physical Religion*, 1891, p. 311. Eickmann, *Die Angelologie des Korans*, 1908, S. 48.
[3] Cox, *op. cit.* vol. ii. p. 254. W. H. Roscher, *Ephialtes, eine pathologisch-mythologische Abhandlung über die Alpträume und Alpdämonen des klassischen Altertums*, 1900.

Europe. Here its highest development took place as a part of the cult of Odin, so that it will be desirable first to interpolate a few words on those aspects of Odin that concern us here; further information can be obtained from the writings of Grimm, Meyer and others. The belief in Wotan (Odin) is itself probably secondary to that in the Furious Host,[1] with which it is throughout intimately connected. The very name is related to: (A) the Old High German *wuot*, wildness, bacchantic pleasure,[2] and has thus come to signify 'the all-penetrating Being'.[3] 'Das althochdeutsche: *wuoti* bezeichnete nämlich nicht wie unser heutiges Wort *Wut* eine onmächtige Leidenschaft, sondern jedes unwiderstehliche Vorwärtsdringen, zunächst in der Welt der Körper, dann aber auch in der des Geistes.'[4] ('The Old High German *wuoti* denoted, not as with the modern German word *Wut* an irresistible passion, but every kind of irresistible pressing forwards, in the first place in the world of material objects, then in that of the spirit.') (B) The still more ancient Old High German *watan*, meaning to go, to gush out, from which *wuot* itself is derived as well as *wind*,[5] *weather*,[6] the German *Wade* (calf of the leg), and the Bavarian *Wueteln*[7] (to move, to swarm). From the same source come the old words for horse, *Watte* and *Wos*, and Jähns maintains that originally Wotan himself must have been conceived of in horse's form.[8] However this may be, he seems to have been almost inseparable from his famous white steed Sleipnir, and he may well be called the Horse-God *par excellence*; horses were sacred in his cult, a feature that generally means original identification, and were sacrificed to him.[9] His relations to death, to war, to wind, and to love were also very close. Many of his attributes were very evidently taken from the primitive conception of a stern and powerful father. Thus, his

[1] Laistner, *op. cit.* Bd. ii. S. 413.
[2] *Id., op. cit.* Bd. ii. S. 411.
[3] Grimm, *op. cit.* Bd. i. S. 109.
[4] Jähns, *op. cit.* S. 292.
[5] Grimm, *op. cit.* Bd. iii. S. 49.
[6] *Id., loc. cit.*
[7] Jähns, *loc. cit.*
[8] *Id., op. cit.* S 292, 347-348.
[9] A. Wuttke, *Der deutsche Volksaberglaube der Gegenwart*, 1900, S. 17.

capacity for outbursts of anger,[1] his custom of being seated in heaven from which he can look down on earth and see everything that happens there,[2] his all-embracing knowledge, his powers of magic.[3] He is 'Alprunen-kundig'[4] (versed in the magic formulas to ward off the Nightmare), and indeed this title is supposed to spring from an original identification of Wotan with the Alp.[5] He was the ancestor of many distinguished families, and the genealogical tree of the Anglo-Saxon kings and the Norse regents begin with Wotan,[6] an ancestry claimed even by Henry II of England.[7] His cult was especially developed in England, under the name of Odin, he being the Father of the English race. Kent was said to have been founded by Hengist and Horsa (*i.e.* Stallion and Horse), descendants of Odin;[8] Margate, one of its chief towns and supposedly the place of entry, derives its name from Märhe, from *mar* =horse, and the county itself still bears on its coat-of-arms the emblem of a stallion rampant.

The close association between Odin and the ideas of horse and father, both of which indicate virility, would lead one to expect other sexual attributes in him, and in fact we find many, both manifest and symbolic. Meyer[9] writes naïvely: 'Die Werbungen Odins um eine Jung-frau, die er in allerlei Umgestaltung und mit Trug auszu-führen pflegt, entsprechen dem gestaltwechselnden und lüsternen Wesen der Winde. Der Riesin Rindr stellt er in verschiedenen Gestalten nach. . . . Zweimal wird er von ihr, die einer abweisenden Riesin des Wirbelwinds oder der Wetterwolke gleicht, ins Gesicht geschlagen, zum dritten Mal sogar zu Boden gestossen, bis er sie durch Berührung mit den Runenstab wahnsinnig macht, d.h. den Wirbelwind zum tollsten Treiben bringt, dann aber fesseln lässt und als heilkundige Dienerin Vecha

---

[1] Grimm, *op. cit.* Bd. i. S. 114, 120.   [2] *Id., op. cit.* Bd. i. S. 113.
[3] E. Mogk, *Germanische Mythologie*, 1906, S. 45.
[4] E. H. Meyer, *Germanische Mythologie*, 1891, S. 233.
[5] Th. Puschmann, *Handbuch der Geschichte der Medizin*, 1902, Bd. i. S. 460, 464.
[6] Mogk, *op. cit.* S. 52.   [7] Meyer, *op. cit.* S. 234.
[8] Jähns, *op. cit.* S. 424.   [9] Meyer, *op. cit.* S. 248.

bewältigt. Beider Sohn ist Bous genannt.' ('Odin's courtships of a virgin, which he used to perform with guile and in all sorts of disguises, correspond to the changeful and wanton nature of the winds. He pursued the giantess Rindr in various guises. . . . Twice she slapped him in the face, as would an unrelenting giantess of the cyclone or of the storm-cloud. On the third occasion she even struck him to the ground, until he maddened her by touching her with his magic staff (!), *i.e.* brought the cyclone to the highest pitch of furious excitement; he then bound her and overpowered her. She became a priestess, called Vecha, with magic power in matters of health. Their son was named Bous.') Since this passage was written, however, it has been recognized that the human imagination is more concerned with other loves than with those of the winds. As we have repeatedly seen, the capacity for transformation is predominantly an erotic *motif*. It was highly developed with Odin, as indeed is indicated by his by-names of Fjolnir, the many-guised one, and Svipall, the seducer in disguise.[1] There is a characteristic story telling how he obtained the famous drink Odrerir, the mead of life; incidentally, Abraham[2] has clearly demonstrated the seminal symbolism of the various divine drinks, Odrerir, Soma, Ambrosia, Nectar, etc. This life-sap belonged to a giant and was kept in a mountain (!) by his daughter Gunnlod. Odin, in the suitable form of a snake, slipped into the mountain through a hole, won Gunnlod's love, and ever after enjoyed the mead of life.[3] He was in general the god of fertility, and many agricultural customs of the present day date from his cult.[4] They usually relate to his aspects as a wind-god, which we shall have occasion to comment on from this point of view in a subsequent chapter.

The best-remembered attribute of Odin's is that of his leading the nightly procession of riding souls. This is

[1] Mogk, *op. cit.* S. 44.
[2] Karl Abraham, *Traum und Mythus. (Schriften zur angewandten Seelenkunde*, Viertes Heft, 1909, Cap. xi.)   [3] Mogk, *op. cit.* S. 46, 47.
[4] Meyer, *op. cit.* S. 254-256. Wuttke, *op. cit.* S. 17.

represented sometimes as an army, sometimes as a hunt;
the former was more prominent in South Germany, the
latter in North Germany. The underlying idea is doubtless that of death, Odin being the Psychopomp who
bears away the soul. The original fear, as was pointed
out earlier,[1] must have been that of being killed, *i.e.*
castrated, by the dreaded nightly visitor, and every
effort was made to convert this into less unacceptable
terms. The conception of the deadly visitor as an enemy
was softened in various ways. Either he was a chieftain
whose army one joined, in which conception Teutonic
races used to go to war under the leadership of Wotan
and carrying a serpent-like pennon. Or the idea of death
was sexualized, usually on rather sadistic lines; if the
fearing person was a man this would be tantamount to
the well-known homosexual solution of enmity. Perhaps
one ought to call this a re-sexualizing of the situation,
for the original sexual wish that led to the fear of retaliatory castration or death reappears in a perverse
form. Death has always been pictured as being due to a
spirit who violently and against one's will robs one of
life.[2] Cognate to our present theme is the fact that he is
usually personified as riding on a horse.[3] Even the old
Charon appears on horseback in modern Greek songs;[4]
and among the people in Hungary the common name
for the funeral stretcher is 'Michael lova', Michael's
horse, while it is said of someone lying near to death:
'St. Michael's horse has already trodden on him'.[5]

In this function Odin's method of obtaining his victims was by thrusting a spear into them[6] or by throwing

[1] Part III. p. 255.
[2] I abstain here from opening up the vast subject of night-fiends who predict
or bring about death, unless they are directly connected with the present theme
of horse = fiend. In this country perhaps the best known would be the Gaelic
fershee (feminine *banshee*): see P. W. Joyce, *A Social History of Ancient
Ireland*, 1903, p. 265.
[3] Jähns (*op. cit.* S. 407) narrates some interesting legends of death being
connected with a horse's skull, *e.g.*, by a snake crawling out from it, that we
have no space here to detail.
[4] G. Roskoff, *Geschichte des Teufels*, 1869, Bd. i. S. 163.
[5] Ipolyi, *Zeitschrift für Mythologie*, Bd. ii. S. 274.
[6] Mogk, *op. cit.* S. 50.

a horse's leg at them;[1] we may safely regard these weapons as phallic symbols, especially as we still meet with them in this sense in the interpretation of dreams. Odin's spear Gungnir was in later myths replaced by a bow and arrow,[2] just like that of Eros-Cupid, and it is interesting to note, as Laistner[3] pointed out, that originally the conception of Eros was closely allied to that of Hermes, of whom, as we shall presently see, Wotan was the Northern equivalent. The chief English legendary descendant of Odin, Robin Hood, the 'King of the May',[4] whose name 'Hood' is derived from that of Wotan,[5] is also famous for his bow and arrow and rides round the (phallic) May-pole. Finally in this connection it may be pointed out that the idea of Wunsch (cognate with *Wonne*), the Teutonic god of love, who personified the outpouring, creative power, was derived from that of Odin, of whom he represented one aspect.[6]

Both as psychopomp and as wind-god Wotan is evidently related to Mercury and Hermes,[7] with whom Latin and other writers constantly identified him;[8] indeed the identification is preserved to the present day, for the English name for Wotan's day, *i.e.* Wednesday, is in French *mercredi*, i.e. *jour de Mercure*. From a close study of its detailed characteristics Laistner[9] has been able to trace the idea of the psychopompic bearing away of souls to the 'angstvolle Traumfahrt' (the dreadful dream travel or flight), and there can be little doubt that this experience is the chief source of all the various 'night travels', of which this is only one example. In accord with this conclusion is the fact that Hermes was the God of Dreams[10] and, according to Homer, slips

---

[1] Jähns, *op. cit.* S. 326. The phallic symbolism of the thigh has been pointed out by, among others, Aigremont, *op. cit.* S. 23.
[2] Meyer, *op. cit.* S. 251. [3] Laistner, *op. cit.* Bd. ii. S. 210.
[4] J. Brand, *Observations on the Popular Antiquities of Great Britain*, 1849, vol. i. p. 261.
[5] Meyer, *op. cit.* S. 230, 231.
[6] Grimm, *op. cit.* Bd. i. S. 114-118, Bd. iii. S. 50-55.
[7] It is interesting that the title Hermes should be cognate with the Hindu Saranyu (=horse). G. W. Cox, *op. cit.* vol. i. p. 423.
[8] Grimm, *op. cit.* Bd. i. S. 99, 111, 124. Meyer, *op. cit.* S. 229.
[9] Laistner, *op. cit.* Bd. ii. S. 225. [10] *Id.*, *op. cit.* Bd. ii. S. 210.

through a keyhole in the characteristic Mara fashion. Laistner[1] indeed calls the closely allied Eros the Greek 'Nachtalp' ('night bogey'), as Pan was their 'Tagalp' ('day bogey').

The most usual way in which this procession of scurrying souls was conceived of was as a *Wild Hunt*. This hunt was most often a pursuit after either an animal or a woman,[2] less often after a man; in some of them the woman when caught turned into a horse and was ridden on.[3] The chase after a mythical woman has been preserved in a great number of legends and sagas. Grimm[4] points out here the mythological connection between the ideas of huntsman and giant, *i.e.* father, and Laistner[5] has traced the pursued woman of the sagas to the mara herself, thus showing again how interchangeable are the rôles of pursuing and pursued. Odin's wild hunt gave rise to a whole series of legendary huntsmen,[6] some real, some fictitious, of which perhaps the best known are Hackelberg (or, better, Hackelberend), Ruprecht, Dietrich von Bern and 'der alte Fritz' in Germany, Hellequin, King Hugo, and Charlemagne—or simply Le Grand Veneur de Fontainebleau in France, King Waldemar in Denmark, Asgard in Norway, King Arthur (Arthur's chase), and Herne the Hunter of Windsor—not to mention the late lamented John Peel—in England, Ap Nudd[7] in Wales; the Wandering Jew legend itself is said to be related to it.[8] In Christian times various saints,[9] notably St. Hubert, St. Martin, St. Michael and St. Nicholas, have been endowed with certain attributes of Odin, above all with his function of leading the nightly procession, and many customs dating from this are still kept up in several European countries; to some extent this

[1] Laistner, *loc. cit.*   [2] Meyer, *op. cit.* S. 244-248.
[3] *Id.*, *op. cit.* S. 247.   [4] Grimm, *op. cit.* Bd. ii. S. 791.
[5] Laistner, *op. cit.* Bd. ii. S. 240.
[6] Grimm, *op. cit.* Bd. ii. S. 767-789. Meyer, *op. cit.* S. 237. Thorpe, *op. cit.* vol. ii. pp. 195-201.
[7] It has been thought that the name of London is derived from this King of the Fairies (C. Squire, *The Mythology of the British Islands*, 1905, pp. 255, 376, 392).
[8] Jähns, *op. cit.* S. 327. Meyer, *op. cit.* S. 237.
[9] Jähns, *op. cit.* S. 299-332. Meyer, *op. cit.* S. 256-257.

even applies to the persons of Christ and John the Baptist.[1] The tenacity with which the people have clung to these beliefs, so that the Church was compelled to compromise in regard to them, proves the significance that the underlying motives concerned must possess for the imagination.

An interesting heathen form of the procession in England was the 'hobby-horse' which was paraded at the time of Odin's festivals, *i.e.* at Christmas and on the first of May.[2] The root *hob* (Middle English and Old French *hobin* = horse) is a variant of Rob, from the French Robin.[3] In proper names in English an initial R is often replaced by H, cp. Hodge for Roger: similarly R is often replaced by D, as in Dick for Richard, hence the name Dobbin, the favourite modern name for a horse. The *hob*goblin Puck (Welsh *Pwca*) was also called Robin Goodfellow, as in Shakespeare. Robin in turn is an abbreviation of Robert, a Frankish name from the Old High German Ruodperht[4] (Modern High German -*berht*, English *bright*). We shall presently see that this epithet was frequently applied to steeds, and indeed Jähns[5] connects the allied words *hobble* and *hop* (German *hüpfen*) with the old German word for horse, *Hoppe*, which is cognate with the Greek ἵππος and has the connotation of movement. In the root *hobby*, therefore, are contained indications of the two fundamental attributes of horses that have been significant for the myth-making imagination, their appearance and their movement. At the time of Odin's festivals, Christmas and the first of May, the hobby-horse used to be ridden by Odin's lineal descendant, Robin Hood, whose very name signifies 'Odin's swift, shining steed'. It seems a far cry from the Father of Heaven to a hobby-horse; a quaint recrudescence of the original meaning appears in the modern French word for hobby-horse, first used

---

[1] Jähns, *op. cit.* S. 299, 317.   [2] Brand, *op. cit.* vol. i. pp. 473, 492.
[3] Sir J. A. H. Murray, *A New English Dictionary*, 1901, vol. v. pp. 314, 316.
W. W. Skeat, *An Etymological Dictionary of the English Language*, 1910, p. 522.
[4] Murray, *op. cit.* p. 735. Skeat, *op. cit.* p. 522.
[5] Jähns, *op. cit.* S. 38, 39.

towards the end of the eighteenth century, namely, *dada*.[1]

A final confirmation of the phallic symbolism of the horse is afforded by consideration of the various '*magic horses*' of mythology and folklore.[2] The two outstanding features of the series are the necessity of possessing this creature for the winning of wife and treasure and the theme of theft with which it is closely associated. This latter 'castration' theme is one that will occupy us more extensively in a subsequent chapter.

A typical example was the horse called 'Splendid Mane'[3] who belonged to the Gaelic 'God of Headlands' Manannân, who gave his name to the Isle of Man. Being the son of the Gaelic Neptune, Lêr, a point the significance of which will appear later, he was the patron of sailors, and constantly travelled to and fro between Ireland and the Western Isles of the Blest. His horse was swifter than the spring wind, and travelled equally fast on land or over the waves of the sea. Ultimately Manannân lent him to the sun-god Lugh, who at a critical moment refused to return him. In one of the Vedic hymns[4] we read that Indra, the predecessor of Brahma, owed his powers to his two steeds: when he was separated from them he became like a weak mortal. The simplest form of the complete story is perhaps the Hindu one in which the thief makes a hole in the wall and steals both the daughter and the treasure of the king.[5] It is evidently one form of the large group of legends of the Brunhilda type in which the hero overcomes various difficulties and finally wins the beautiful princess.[6] He is usually aided by either some magical instrument, sword, etc., or some living agency, often an animal, like Sigurd's horse Gram, that advises and guides him, and in the form that interests us here it is a magic horse with exceptional powers of speed. A pretty example of this is the Moorish

---

[1] Society for Pure English, Tract No. vii. p. 31.
[2] Jähns, *op. cit.* S. 354-360.   [3] Squire, *op. cit.* pp. 60, 98.
[4] *Rigveda*, Book x. Hymn 105, Strophe 3.
[5] Cox, *op. cit.* vol. i. p. 115.
[6] *Id.*, *op. cit.* vol. i. pp. 149-156 gives a list of these.

tale of Prince Ahmed, whom a dove tells how to find a wonderful Arabian steed in an almost inaccessible cavern: after overcoming a number of obstacles with the help of the steed he finally carries away the princess.[1] In myths proper the fairy-tale *motif* of overcoming obstacles is replaced by the idea of releasing a damsel from the spell cast upon her; the knight has to prove his courage by spending a night with her, or his virility by performing the sexual act with her three times within an hour, and so on.[2]

It is easy to see that the underlying theme with which these stories deal is the Oedipus one of overcoming the father and winning the forbidden mother. In many of them the magic weapon is torn from the father-imago before being put to its erotic use. In the Rigveda[3] the wonderful horse of the twin Acrins actually slays the serpent-monster himself, and among the seven adventures of Firdusi's hero Rustem is one in which the magic horse fights the monster and drives it away while his master sleeps. The phallic significance is shown by the fact that the horse's head or tail alone—common phallic symbols—can perform the same feats. Thus Indra annihilates his enemies, the ninety-nine monsters, with the head of a horse Dadhyanc,[4] just as Samson uses the jaw-bone of an ass for the same purpose. Another hymn praising him after his victories says: 'The tail of a horse wert Thou then, O Indra.'[5]

In most of the German versions the magic horse is first won by a deed of valour and then used to win the maiden. A common type of this kind is the Glass Mountain fairy-tale in which the stupid youngest son is carried away to a cavern by a giant; when the giant is asleep the youth cuts his head off and finds in the stall three (!) steeds of wondrous beauty with whose help he wins the princess.[6] Another example is the 'Dummhans' tale[7]: 'In

[1] Cox, *op. cit.* vol. i. pp. 151-154.   [2] Laistner, *op. cit.* Bd. i. S. 144.
[3] *Rigveda*, Book i. Hymn 117, Strophe 9.
[4] *Id.*, Book i. Hymn 84, Strophe 13, 14; Hymn 117, Strophe 22.
[5] *Id.*, Book i. Hymn 32, Strophe 12.
[6] Laistner, *op. cit.* Bd. ii. S. 117.   [7] *Id., op. cit.* Bd. ii. S. 51.

der Nacht kommt ein einäugiger Riese und will sich
Korn stehlen, da springt ihm Dummhans auf die Schul-
ter und reisst ihm das Auge aus. Der Riese verspricht
ihm seinen Beistand, wenn er das Auge wieder erhalte.
Hans gibt es ihm, erhält Ross und Rüstung, reitet den
Glasberg hinauf und gewinnt die Princessin zur Frau.'
('A one-eyed giant comes in the night to steal corn, but
stupid Hans springs on his shoulder and tears his eye
out. The giant promises to help him if he will restore his
eye. Hans gives it him back, receives a horse and armour,
rides up the glass mountain and wins the princess.') In
a Russian fairy-tale a pious son, Ivan Durak, keeps
watch for three nights on his father's grave. The grateful
father, or rather his spirit, promises him that whenever
he shall sound a whistle in time of need a magic grey
horse with flaming eyes would make its appearance for
his assistance. By means of this horse Ivan is able to
perform the feat of leaping three times to the height of
the wall of the palace where there hangs a picture of the
Czar's daughter, and thus wins the beautiful princess
for his wife.[1] In another version the horse enables him to
kiss the princess through twelve mirrors—evidently a
form of the glass mountain theme—and thus to win her.[2]
In the German counterpart the theme is presented in an
even more Hamlet-like fashion. There it is a fiend who
tears out the eye of an old man; the hero replaces it and
the grateful old man rewards him with the gift of the
necessary magic horse.[3]

In other stories the Oedipus *motif* is quite unveiled.
A young prince in a dream sees himself on the throne,
and on hearing of this presumption his father promptly
throws him out of the house. Later on the prince replaces
the stolen eye of an old man, who in his gratitude gives
him a chamber-key with which he can open all doors but
the ninth. He opens them all, however, and in the ninth
room finds a golden steed. After he wins the princess he

[1] A. de Gubernatis, *Die Thiere in der indogermanischen Mythologie*, Deutsche
Übersetzung, 1874, S. 229.
[2] Gubernatis, *loc. cit.*   [3] Laistner, *op. cit.* Bd. ii. S. 143-145.

discovers to his horror that he cannot marry her because she turns out to be his sister, the king being his own father. In one version he is consoled by finding in the forbidden chamber a 'maiden of gold' who becomes his wife.[1] An allied fairy-tale tells how 'der verstossene Jüngling kommt zu zwei blinden Alten und verschafft ihnen die Augen wieder; der dankbare Alte schenkt ihm die Gabe der Verwandlung, vermöge welcher er in unscheinbarer Gestalt auszieht und zwei Fürstentöchter gewinnt'.[2] ('The cast-out youth comes to two blind old men and restores their sight. The grateful men make him the gift of being able to transform himself, whereupon he assumes an invisible guise and wins two princesses.')

One theme in mythology leads to many others, and it is time to call a halt. In the next chapter I shall consider the infantile sources of these various beliefs and hope to throw light there on the inner meaning of the horse symbolism.

---

[1] Laistner, *op. cit.* Bd. ii. S. 144.   [2] *Id., op. cit.* Bd. ii. S. 146-147.

CHAPTER III

THE HORSE AND INFANTILE SEXUALITY

THE attempts mythologists have at various times made to unravel the part that sexual themes have played in the elaboration of myths and folklore beliefs have not met with much success. Three considerations baulked them. In the first place, many undeniably sexual themes seemed in themselves to be so unintelligible or repellent that it seemed easier to regard them as being simply metaphors for other, non-sexual, themes. A striking example of this was the habit of castrating the father that was apparently an established custom in the Uranos-Chronos-Zeus dynasty. This seemed to be so meaningless—or even unthinkable, if taken literally—that there was nothing for it but to assume that the castration was a plastic circumscription of some astronomical phenomenon—the waning of the moon, the seasonal diminution of the sun's strength, and so on; although it was never made clear why such simple phenomena had to be depicted in such an extraordinary disguise, or indeed in any disguise at all. In the second place, many of the interpretations of sexual symbolism gave the impression of being far-fetched and unconvincing, especially as no reason could be adduced why such symbolism should be employed at all. And in the third place a sexual theme would often culminate in some obscurity that was impenetrable, since the connection of it with the preceding sexual theme could not be fathomed. For all these reasons, not to mention the imperfect acquaintance that most mythologists displayed about the complexities of the sexual life, the progress made in this research, useful though the detailed work contained in it has often been, has not led to any valuable generalizations being established.

Freud's[1] work on infantile sexuality has completely changed this state of affairs. By unravelling the details of sexual development in the young child he has shown its complexity, and by discovering the unconscious conflicts between it and fear or guilt he has been able to explain why its manifestations are so often veiled in symbolic and other guises. Further, he and Abraham[2] have applied this clinical knowledge to the subject of mythology itself, and have made it probable that the creative impulse of myth-formation was in the main the endeavour to allay the disturbing emotions that take their ultimate origin in the only partly resolved conflicts of childhood, conflicts the effects of which persist into adult life to a far greater extent than has ever hitherto been even suspected. It is not too much to say that the key to mythology is the knowledge we have gained through psychoanalysis of infantile sexual conflicts.

In the present context the evidence of such factors playing a central part in creating the various mythical beliefs about the horse is so extensive that one is embarrassed to know how best to group and present them. Horses have evidently, for various reasons, been greatly admired and feared, and even deified. These exaggerated attitudes, and the corresponding beliefs, were derived only in small part from interest in the horse as such, far more from the opportunity its various attributes gave to presenting ideas of a purely human provenance. One has to imagine THE HORSE in a mythological sense, often a Horse-God, and to investigate its supposed attributes individually. One could, for instance, consider the relations of this mythical Horse to water, fire and wind in turn, each of which would provide a considerable chapter; we should have the river or sea horse-gods, the sun horse-gods, and the nocturnal or death horse-gods respectively. I find it more expedient, however, to divide the material into two màin parts according as it relates

[1] See particularly his *Drei Abhandlungen zur Sexualtheorie*, Zweite Ausgabe, 1910. [*Gesammelte Schriften*, Bd. v. S. 3.]
[2] Karl Abraham, *Traum und Mythus* (*Schriften zur angewandten Seelenkunde*, Viertes Heft, 1909).

to one or the other of the two most prominent features that distinguish infantile from adult sexuality.

A. Castration

Around this single word there centres in psychoanalytical work a complex series of ideas. It signifies there not so much castration in its biological sense as the simple idea of the penis being cut off. Such an idea is remote from the ordinary consciousness of adult life, as also from the facts of everyday reality, but it nevertheless plays an exceedingly important part in the unconscious mind, especially in childhood. Around it are clustered all the emotions related to the fear, guilt and punishment that are responses to the Oedipus wishes as expressed in masturbation. The dread of castration is essentially the fear of retaliation for the corresponding impulse directed against the rival parent, and it is the central starting-point of the sense of guilt that is later developed into conscience.

The whole matter is greatly complicated by the simple circumstance of the anatomical difference between the two sexes, for this is always interpreted in both sexes in terms of the castration fears. Both sexes tend at first to regard the female genital as merely a castrated genital, and this has fateful consequences for each in respect of their attitude towards the other. On the boy's side there is an attitude of contempt and a reinforcement of his fears, the justification for which he sees apparently confirmed. On the girl's side there is an attitude of envy and injustice, with a reinforcement of her sense of guilt at what she interprets as a punishment. [Freud has well named this phase in development the phallic stage, in which both sexes agree that the only positive expression of genitality is a phallus, so that all turns on the question of possessing or not possessing one. Traces of this stage are only too commonly preserved in adult life.]

A still further complication is added by more dynamic factors. It has been found that identification with the opposite sex is with both sexes one of the most powerful defences against the difficulties and dangers of the Oedipus situation. This is for certain reasons usually more manifest with the female than the male, though it is doubtful whether there is much difference between the two in the deeper layers of the mind.

With this knowledge in mind it becomes more possible to understand a number of facts in the folklore of the horse. Indicative of the phallic stage of development is, for instance, the alternation between attitudes of over-adulation and contempt for the creature according as it is used to symbolize the male or the female genital. We noted in the first chapter of this book[1] that the original Teutonic word for horse = masculine 'mar', feminine 'mare', came to be used almost entirely in its feminine form, and that the same word was used to designate a whore or contemptible woman. A female horse was in the Middle Ages a despised horse.

On the other hand, we have noted the wonderful powers attributed to the magic horse of legend and have seen how indispensable various heroes have found the possession of him to be. Even Indra himself became like a feeble mortal when deprived of his steeds.[2] Among the stories of the hero who can perform great deeds once he achieves possession of this magic creature, the explanation of which I gave in the preceding chapter, special interest attaches to those where the creature is at first a cripple or worthless and becomes valuable, noble or wonderful only after a further process. It is indeed rather the rule that the steed in question is born ugly, misshapen and deformed and only later becomes noble and handsome. Gubernatis[3] gives numerous examples of this from Indian, Russian and Teutonic legends. Thus the Hungarian magic horse Tatos was born with an ugly appearance, crippled and thin, as was the Indian Avuna, the chariot-horse of the sun. The horse of the sun-hero

---

[1] See Part III. p. 245.   [2] Part III. p. 269.
[3] A. de Gubernatis, *Die Thiere in der indogermanische Mythologie*, Deutsche Übersetzung, 1874, S. 222, 224, 229, 232, 233.

is sometimes a worthless mare who later changes into a gallant steed. The change seems to be a mysterious one. In most cases it is a simple evolution, but sometimes one replaces the other; for instance, the Acrins, the Hindoo counterparts of the Greek Dioscuri, make a gift of a perfect steed to the hero who had only a weak horse. Occasionally the magic steed retains a trace of his previous condition, such as in the *Mahâbhârata*, where the King of Horses, Uććaihcrava, Indra's steed, who is as swift as thought, is shining white save for a black tail, a relic of black magic attempted on him by evil serpents. There can be little doubt that this whole theme relates to the attaining of virility, or the overcoming of the fear of castration, two equally valid descriptions of the successful emancipation from childhood, a feat completely accomplished only by heroes.

I may incidentally remark that this group of legends once more exemplifies a point on which stress was laid in an earlier chapter, namely the extraordinary identification or interchangeability of horse with rider. To cite one example only: The Acrins, the famous riders of Hindoo mythology, derive their name from *acra* = a horse, the word originally signifying 'swift'.[1] At the same time they are identical with the steeds that draw the sun's chariot, with Indra's steeds, with the rays of the sun, and with the sun-god Indra himself. In some accounts, by lending him a magic horse, they enable the hero or the sun-god to capture the princess, in other versions it is they who perform this feat themselves; sometimes it is the hero who captures his master's horse and elopes, sometimes the hero, helped by his master's daughter, changes into a horse and escapes with her.[2] In prefacing a number of examples that prove his statement, Gubernatis[3] writes: 'Die Sonne ist zu gleicher Zeit ein Held und ein Pferd; sie ist "der Schnelle", *acva*, ein Wort, das die beiden hervorragenden Eigenschaften ebensowohl des Helden wie des Sonnenrosses umfasst;

---

[1] Gubernatis, *op. cit.* S. 220.   [2] *Id., op. cit.* S. 234.
[3] *Id., op. cit.* S. 256.

der Held stirbt, der Held wird verbrannt: das Pferd wird
ebenfalls geopfert; der Held tritt aus dem Stall heraus;
ebenso das Pferd; der Held entführt das Pferd. Der Held
entschlüpft dem Dämon: das Pferd rettet den fliehenden
Helden; der Held stürmt im Kampfe vor: das Pferd ist
es, das ihn andringen lässt.' ('The sun is at the same
time a hero and a horse. He is "the swift one", *acra*, a
word that comprises the two most prominent attributes
of both the hero and the sun-steed. The hero dies, the
hero is burned; the horse also is sacrificed; the hero
emerges from a stable; likewise the horse; the hero
elopes with the horse. The hero evades the demon; the
horse rescues the escaping hero; the hero throws himself into the fight; it is by means of the horse that he can
charge forwards.')

This last quotation beings us to one of the most
interesting features of the horse in mythology, his association with the sun. The most important links connecting
the two ideas are probably the notions of irresistible
movement, luxuriant fertility and shining splendour,
and we shall presently see that the roots of these are
very far-reaching. At this point, however, we are concerned only with the ideas to do with the horse-sun
theme that originate in the phallic stage of infantile
development. The close association of fire- and sun-
worship with phallicism has long been recognized,[1] the
sun—with its heat, its creative power, its daily erection
and decline, and its diurnal plunge into water and night
—being one of the most widely spread phallic symbols
of religious mythology.

Almost everywhere in religious mythology one finds
the horse and the sun intimately connected. In the Rig-
Veda of Ancient India, from which some examples were
quoted above, the two were formally identified,[2] so that

[1] See Abraham, *op. cit.* S. 30, 31, 41, 44, 52, etc., for a clear description of
the symbolism, also G. W. Cox, *The Mythology of the Aryan Nations*, 1870,
vol. ii. pp. 112-115, and W. Schwartz, 'Der rothe Sonnenphallos der Urzeit;
eine mythologisch-anthropologische Untersuchung', *Zeitschrift für Ethnologie*,
1874, S. 167, 409.
[2] Gubernatis, *op. cit.* S. 220-276, etc. M. Jähns, *Ross und Reiter in Leben
und Sprache, Glauben und Geschichte der Deutschen*, 1872, Bd. i, S. 249. Max

it is sometimes hardly possible to draw a distinction between them or tell to which of the two a given passage refers. The Acrins themselves, the Hindoo twin horse-gods of whom mention has already been made, were the sons of a mare, Tvashtrîs, who was the spouse of Savitar (the sun, doubtless also pictured here in equine form).[1] Agni, Indra, Savitar, Krishna, the Dioscuri, Mithra, Zeus, Poseidon ἵππιος, Mars, Apollo, Pluto and the Teutonic Odin hardly ever appear except mounted, are often identified with horses, and owe much of their vic-torious career to their steeds. Among goddesses of whom the same is true may be mentioned the Vedic Aurora, Athene ἵππεια and Aphrodite ἱπποδάμεια. Throughout Oriental countries, in Babylonia,[2] Persia,[3] Syria,[4] etc., we find horses sacred to the sun-god, to whom they are regularly sacrificed and with whom they must have been originally identified.

That the conceptions of sun-god and goat-god should so often occur together in Babylonian, Persian and Greek mythology, as Robertson[5] has shown that they do, is from this point of view quite intelligible, the lecherous attributes of the goat being well known; as is also the fact that the Hindoo sun-god Arusha (from *arushi* = mare) can in detail be identified with the Greek love-god Eros, the son of the god Ares whom we shall presently have to consider further. The streaming, shining rays of the sun have always been specially identified with the horse's *mane*, and Jähns interestingly points out how in Sanskrit, Greek and German the terms for 'mane' and 'shining' are closely allied;[6] we have al-ready[7] referred to the magic horse of the Gaelic god

---

Müller, *Chips from a German Workshop*, 1867, vol. ii. p. 132, etc. *Lectures on Language*, Second Series, p. 482. E. C. M. Senart, *Essai sur la légende de Buddha*, 1882, 2ᵉ éd. p. 66.

[1] *Mahâbhârata*, i. 2599.
[2] W. St. C. Boscawen in *Religious Systems of the World*, 1904, cap. 'The Religion of Babylonia', p. 20.
[3] J. M. Robertson in *Religious Systems of the World*, 1904. Cap. 'Mithraism', p. 196.   [4] 2 Kings xxiii. 11.
[5] J. M. Robertson, *Christianity and Mythology*, 1910, pp. 343-356.
[6] Jähns, *op. cit.* S. 250.   [7] Part III. p. 269.

Manannân, whose name was actually 'Splendid Mane', and we may also mention in this connection the wonderful golden mane ascribed by the Egyptian Tryphiodoros to the famous horse of Troy.[1] The same analogy has also brought together the ideas of sun and lion,[2] and later astrologers replaced the picture of the horse in the old Indian zodiac by that of the lion. The horse becomes identified not only with the streaming rays of the sun, but with the updarting flames of fire, so that in the Veda we have the *Robits* of Agni, the fire-god, as well as the *Harits* (= glisteners) of Indra, the Sun-god.[3] It is thus suitable that the Teutonic Sleipnir, who has all the attributes of a sun-steed, should be the offspring of the fire-god Loki.[4] The sexual significance of mane as of hair in general is familiar enough, whether from biological considerations or from the numerous legends of the Samson type.

Odin, the horse and wind god, has been in many respects identified with the Greek Ares and the Latin Mars;[5] his sun-god character, incidentally, is plain enough from the date of his festivals, Twelfth Night and the First of May. Now both these classical names are said to be derived from the Mar root in question,[6] from which also is derived the name of the Maruts, the storm winds of the Vedas.[7] These, as their name denotes, are called the crushers or grinders, and they were worshipped as destroyers and reproducers—two closely allied ideas; it is interesting that Ares has also been called the crusher or grinder, the name being in fact cognate with the Greek Moliones, the mill-men or crushers. In the earlier chapters of this volume we saw how central in the whole Nightmare conception is the idea of pressing, crushing, grinding. To grind, from classical myths to

[1] Gubernatis, *op. cit.* S. 224.
[2] See Abraham (*op. cit.* S. 53) on the symbolism of the lion.
[3] Cox, *op. cit.* vol. i. p. 426, vol. ii. p. 2.
[4] Jähns, *op. cit.* S. 346, 348.
[5] F. Y. Powell in *Religious Systems of the World*, 1904. Cap. 'Teutonic Heathendom', p. 285.
[6] Cox, *op. cit.* vol. i. p. 32. Jähns, *op. cit.* S. 328.
[7] Cox, *op. cit.* vol. ii. p. 222.

modern slang, has always been a symbol for sexual intercourse, as may be illustrated from the following passages by Nork.[1] 'In der symbolischen Sprache bedeutet aber Mühle das weibliche Glied (μυλλός, wovon *mulier*), und der Mann ist der Müller, daher der Satyriker Petronius *molere mulierem* für: Beischlaf gebraucht. Der durch die Buhlin der Kraft beraubte Samson muss in der Mühle mahlen (Richter xvi. 21), welche Stelle der Talmud (Sota fol. 10), wie folgt, commentirt: Unter dem Mahlen ist immer die Sünde des Beischlafs zu verstehen. Darum standen am Feste der keuschen Vesta in Rom alle Mühlen still. . . . Wie Apollo war auch Zeus ein Müller (μυλεύς, Lykophron, 435), aber schwerlich ein Müller von Profession, sondern insofern er als schaffendes, Leben gebendes Prinzip der Fortpflanzung der Geschöpfe vorsteht. . . . Ist nun erwiesen, dass jeder Mann ein Müller, und jede Frau eine Mühle, woraus allein sich begreifen liesse, dass jede Vermählung eine Vermehlung.' ('In symbolic language a mill signifies the female genital (μυλλός, from which comes *mulier*) and the husband is the miller, hence Petronius' use of *molere mulierem* (to grind a woman) to describe the sexual act. Samson when robbed of his strength by Delilah has to grind in the mill[2] (Judges, xvi. 21), on which passage the Talmud comments as follows: by the phrase "grinding corn" one has always to understand the sin of carnal intercourse. This is why all the mills had to stand still in Rome at the festival of the chaste Vesta. . . . Like Apollo, Zeus was also a miller (μυλεύς, Lykophron 435), though scarcely one by profession— only in so far as he represents the creative, life-giving principle of propagation. . . . It is now clear that every husband is a miller and every wife a mill, from which it is intelligible that every marriage (*Vermählung*) is a making of meal (*Vermehlung*).') In this connection one thinks also of the Roman *confarreatio*, where the

[1] F. Nork, *Mythologie der Volkssagen und Volksmärchen*, 1848, S. 301, 302.
[2] A typical talion punishment.

espousal was signalized by the couple partaking of the same cake, and of our own wedding-cake customs.

Like Mars, Ares was originally a purely chthonic god[1] and only later acquired his evil significance of a storm god[2]. The ideas of reproduction and rapid travel are once more found in connection with 'Alp' beings, and we shall see that the horse-sun theme is equally well represented in the group. The Latin Mars was originally, as is well known, an agricultural deity, *i.e.* of reproduction. Cox adds:[3] 'In his own character, as fostering the wealth of corn and cattle, he was worshipped at Praeneste, as Herodotus would have us believe that Scythian tribes worshipped Ares, with the symbol of a sword, one of the many forms assumed by the Hindu Linga. As such, he was pre-eminently the father of all living things, Marspiter, the parent of the twin-born Romulus and Remus.' In this latter connection it is perhaps not irrelevant to say that the word *mar* in Persian signifies snake, and in Chaldean Lord or Master. As a title of a god the term Mar probably originates in the Scythian. In reference to this Wake writes:[4] 'The primitive meaning of *Ar* was "fire", from which the lion, or the symbol of the Sun-god, was called *ari*, the Sun-god himself having a name Ra. Strictly, therefore, Mar would denote "fire-worshippers", a title which, as is well known, was especially applicable to the ancient Medes. The *Aryans* generally appear to have been Sun- or Fire-worshippers, and probably they have received their name from this fact; this would seem to be much more probable than the ordinary derivation of the name Aryan from the root *ar*, "to plough".' Layard has made it highly probable that the rapid spread of Mithraism in Rome was due to its being connected with the worship of Mars, and indeed some figures of Mithra-Mars consist of a human body encircled

---

[1] H. O. Müller, *Ares*, 1848. O. Stoll, *Die ursprüngliche Bedeutung des Ares*, 1835.
[2] L. Preller, *Griechische Mythologie*, 1854, Bd. i. S. 226. Sauer, in A. Pauly's *Real-Encyclopädie der klassischen Altertumwissenschaft*, 1905, Bd. v. S. 657.
[3] Cox, *op. cit.* vol. ii. p. 311.
[4] G. Staniland Wake, *Serpent Worship*, 1888, p. 112.

by a serpent and having the head of a lion. The Persian name for the sun-god Mithra was Mihr, which may well be related to Mar (gleam); Mihr literally means both the sun and love, being, as Robertson remarks, the Persian equivalent of Eros.[1]

A cognomen of Ares was Hippios,[2] and in the early period of the worship of Mars this god was called Mars Gradivas on account of the fruitfulness (vegetation and springs) that followed his steps.[3] It is of interest that, just as we have seen throughout in the mythology of the horse, Mithra himself was a hermaphrodite, being often represented as a divine couple.[4]

An interesting side-issue of the 'brilliant horse-sun' theme is suggested by Jähns:[5] 'Die Eigenschaft blendender Unnahbarkeit muste übrigens das Bild des Rosses ganz besonders zum Gränz- und Feldzeichen geeignet erscheinen lassen. Es war ja sehr natürlich dass man grade an der Landesgränze die Neidstange errichtete, und möglicherweise stammt vom Aufrichten eines Gränzbildes in Gestalt einer Märhe (March, Marke) überhaupt das Wort Marke im Sinne von "Gränze" und damit zugleich das Zeitwort *markiren* oder merken. Leztere Bedeutung führt dann zum Begriffe *Mark* als Gewichtseinheit. Und nun dürften sich auch leicht Worte wie *markten, marché* und *marchand* anschliessen.' ('The attribute of dazzling unapproachability must have made the image of a horse specially suited as a sign to mark off borders. It was very natural for people to erect a "pole of covetousness" at the very frontier of a country, and very possibly it is from erecting a frontier sign in the form of a mare (old German *march, marke*) that the word *Marke* in the sense of "border" is derived, and from that the time expression *markiren* (to mark time) or *merken* (to attend, to mark). This signification then leads to the idea of *mark* as a unit of weight. And we

---

[1] J. M. Robertson, *Pagan Christs, Studies in Comparative Hierology*, 1903, p. 303.
[2] Jähns, *op. cit.* S. 328.
[3] J. M. Robertson in *Religious Systems of the World*, 1904, *op. cit.* p. 199.
[4] *Ibid.*   [5] Jähns, *op. cit.* S. 256.

can easily add such words as *markten* (to deal), *marché* (market) and *marchand* (tradesman).') Jähns' semantics is certainly a little wild here, but I believe his etymological conclusions themselves to be ultimately correct. In this connection I might mention that the borders between England and Wales are still called the marches (*march* incidentally is the Welsh for 'horse'). Perhaps also the Greek *Moira*, the apportioner, belongs to this circle, and also the Middle English *mere* = boundary.

The phallic significance of the sun explains, amongst others, the two following matters. The sunset, with the plunge of the sun into the western sea, would be regarded as symbolizing an act of coitus, and actually in the religion of India, where the sun and Linga are equally prominent, the male principle (Siva) is symbolized as fire, and the female (Vishnu) as water. Of the sun-steed god Surya it is written: 'I have beheld the permanent orb of the sun, your dwelling-place, concealed by water where (the hymns of the pious) liberate his steeds.'[1] Probably this is one reason for the association of fruitfulness with the West, *e.g.* the West Wind, an association furthered by the fact that this is in Europe the rainy wind. The conception is further developed in Greek mythology, where the sun-god Heracles fights savagely with the centaurs. Such creatures, as we shall presently see, are specially closely connected with water and seem to haunt places having a female symbolism. A fight with them thus represents ultimately the infantile sadistic conception of coitus, together with the assault on the father's penis that is so closely associated with the maternal genitalia. Many legends are based on this sunset theme: one, in the story of Perceval, 'relates how to that knight, when he was in the middle of a forest much distressed for the want of a horse, a lady brought a fine steed as black as a blackberry. He mounted and he found this beast marvellously swift, but on his making straight for a vast river the knight made the sign of the

[1] Cox, *op. cit.* vol. i. p. 385.

cross, whereupon he was left on the ground, and his
horse plunged into the water, which his touch seemed to
set ablaze.'[1] This is evidently a variant of the Arthurian
legend, in which the Lady of the Lake brought the famous sword Excalibur to the king; he wielded it loyally
till the time of his death when he flung it back to the
lake whence it came; this is a play on the motives of procreative power and impotence.

The themes of impotence and castration just hinted at
play a most important part in sun mythology, and indeed
probably furnish the main reason for the rôle of the sun
in early religions. The identification of the waxing and
waning sun with the phallus, and particularly with the
father's phallus, brought with it the projection of repressed wishes and fears relating to this organ. All
nations have taken a remarkable interest in the phenomenon of the annual increase and decrease of the sun's
activity. The vital interest that these phenomena often
have for hunting and agricultural pursuits evidently
stirred even more intimate emotional responses. Complicated rituals and festivals[2] have been instituted with the
aim of establishing some stable relationship between
man and these disturbing phenomena, of affording
some reassurance that the threatened catastrophe would
not befall them.

The decrease of the sun's power after midsummer was
felt as a symbolic or portending castration, and indeed
still is so in the unconscious. The sun's rays, *i.e.* the
horse's mane, the hero's locks, visibly diminished, and
the observation, as always, was given this symbolic
meaning. Ancient Asiatic ideas actually depicted the
change in the notion of the sun-hero, *e.g.* Heracles, becoming a female, and believed that when he was robbed
of the golden hair in which his strength resided he would,
like Samson, be delivered helpless into the hands of his
enemies.

---

[1] J. Rhys, *Celtic Folklore*, 1901, vol. ii. p. 438.
[2] Cox, *op. cit.* vol. ii. p. 113, clearly points out the phallic significance of
these festivals.

The early Teutons expressed the same idea in an even more forcible and plastic way. According to them the sun-hero lost after midsummer not only his locks, but his very head. This is why a headless rider, or at most a rider who carries his head under his arm, appears in such a countless number of superstitious beliefs, legends and fairy-tales, especially those clustering around Midsummer Night, St. John's Eve.[1] The centre of this Teutonic folklore is plainly Odin himself; it is he who is the beheaded (*i.e.* castrated) sun-rider. And just as Heracles in his passage through the zodiac becomes feminine on reaching the sign of Cancer, so, according to the Teutons, did the sun travel backwards like a crab after passing midsummer. So the horse on which the headless rider journeys usually has his shoes nailed on backwards, as have the male nixes (water horses) whom we shall meet later.[2]

The Christian religion adopted here its usual syncretic attitude towards the older mythology. The famous story of John the Baptist's beheading, together with his name and the fact of his birth being six months earlier than that of Jesus, *i.e.* in midsummer, naturally destined him to be the carrier of the old beliefs. Even in the New Testament a suitable passage was found: 'He must increase, but I must decrease' (St. John iii. 30). Like Heracles and Samson, he was betrayed and castrated (beheaded) by the woman who loved him. In the numerous German stories connecting him with Odin[3] there is one interesting one that reveals the identification with the old Storm-god. It relates how when Herodias kissed the head on the charger a stormy wind from his mouth blew at her so violently that she is still floating about in the air.

Something might here be said about the old 'need-fire' customs of Midsummer Eve, but to keep to the present subject I will mention only one point, namely

---

[1] The *motif* has even lingered in modern American romances: cp. Mayne Reid's *The Headless Horseman*.
[2] Jähns, *op. cit.* S. 277.   [3] *Id., op. cit.* S. 317.

that in Russia, and probably also in Germany, horses played an important part in the ritual of this fire.[1]

In connection with the *motif* of *headlessness* the reader is referred to earlier passages[2] in which it was shown how the head alone can possess all the wonderful properties of the magic steed, being indeed the quintessence of this phallic creature. The same symbolism applies, as was there pointed out, to other parts of the body, *e.g.* the ears and particularly the tail; in the *Mahâbhârata*, for instance, the name of the first horse to be created, the king of horses and Indra's own steed, Uććaihcrava, really means 'the erect-eared one'. Jähns[3] thinks that the sun, with its rays, was probably first identified with the *head* of the horse, with its mane, and he quotes from the Rig-Veda a hymn addressed to the horse:

> Thee I recognized from afar,
> The winged one darting from heaven;
> On the beautiful dustless path
> I saw the winged head hasten.

A special significance has been attached to the horse's head in practically all countries, and it has been used for the most diverse objects, to guard against enemies, to keep away evil demons, to bring good luck, fruitfulness, etc., etc. Lawrence[4] has collected a number of examples of these, which need not be referred to in detail. Many of the related customs are still in force at the present day, *e.g.* among the South Slavs,[5] in Wales,[6] in many parts of Germany,[7] etc. In many places, *e.g.* the last-mentioned, the customs are derivatives of the old Odin's procession; I well remember the chief bogey of my childhood, the horse's head (Welsh 'pen-y-ceffyl')[8] carried

[1] Jähns, *op. cit.* S. 318.   [2] Part III. p. 270.
[3] Jähns, *op. cit.* S. 250.
[4] R. M. Lawrence, *The Magic of the Horseshoe*, 1899, ch. xii.
[5] F. S. Krauss, *Slavische Volkforschungen*, 1908, S. 50. /
[6] W. W. Sikes, *British Goblins*, 1880, p. 256. Thomas, *La Survivance du culte totémique des animaux dans le pays de Galles*, 1898, p. 40.
[7] S. Seligmann, *Der Böse Blick und Verwandtes*, 1910, Bd. ii. S. 129.
[8] To this creature Part III. of the present book owes its existence, the writing of it being inspired ultimately by the desire to understand the relationship between that particular bogey and night terrors in general. As a contribution to the psycho-analysis of the unconscious motives impelling to research,

round on a pole at Christmas time. Of especial interest is the belief that a horse's head will guard against the nocturnal visits of the Nightmare.[1] This contains the same symbolism as the belief that the Nightmare can be averted by a broom,[2] or by a sharp knife.[3]

The same significance has been extensively transferred to the idea of the *hat*, the phallic symbolism of which has long been recognized.[4] A special broad hat was one of Odin's invariable personal attributes. So much did it attract the imagination that the name of St. Hubert, the Christian heir of Odin's interest for the chase and for riding, signifies 'the hat-carrier'.[5] There is a whole series of legends in which the hat of a night-fiend (*Alp*) has been stolen or lost and he gratefully rewards with treasure whoever restores it.

The stolen hat here is evidently equivalent to the stolen eye, of which several examples were given in the last chapter,[6] the connection between the theme and the castration wishes of the Oedipus complex being plain enough. There is also an intrinsic connection between the hat and eye in this context. When the fiend's hat is stolen he is no longer invisible and then loses his power of tormenting sleepers, *i.e.* copulating with them; the same result follows when he loses his eye. Thus if the fiend can be seen or cannot see he is impotent.[7]

The theme of '*one-eyedness*' plays an extensive part in the Nightmare (*Alp*) legends and superstitions: Laistner[8] has made a specially full study of it. As was just remarked, the (sexual or tormenting) power of the night-

---

I may further mention that the psychological starting-point of the whole work was a childish dislike, on the grounds of supposedly effeminate associations, of my first name, Alfred. I discarded the name as soon as I could, but on discovering in later years that the meaning of it could be construed as 'learned in Nightmare' it occurred to me, at first unconsciously, that my childish dislike might be put to some practical use and the matter finally disposed of.

[1] A. Wuttke, *Der deutsche Volksaberglaube der Gegenwart*, 1900, S. 128.
[2] L. Laistner, *Das Rätsel der Sphinx*, 1889, Bd. ii. S. 321. Lawrence, *op. cit.* p. 39.
[3] Laistner, *op. cit.* Bd. i. S. 108. E. H. Meyer, *Germanische Mythologie*, 1891, S. 137.
[4] Hargrave Jennings, vol. ii. pp. 56-60.
[5] Jähns, *op. cit.* S. 323.   [6] Part III. p. 271.
[7] Laistner, *op. cit.* Bd. ii. S. 57.   [8] *Id., op. cit.* Bd. ii. Kap. 41, 46, etc.

fiend resides in his eye, and the dread of the 'evil eye' constitutes such an extensive chapter among human superstitions that I shall refrain from opening it up here.[1] We have repeatedly observed the bridge between these malignant fiends on the one hand and the highest gods on the other, and the two are connected in this symbolism also. The Eye of God is one of the best known symbols for his creative power and for his pursuing and retributive tendencies. Surya, the Vedic Helios, was called 'the eye of Mithra, Varuna and Agni'.[2] As is well known, Odin was one-eyed, and Wuttke explains this by the fact that the sun is the eye of heaven, of which Odin was the God.[3] Mogk[4] goes deeper than this, however, in pointing out that all 'menschenfressende Dämonen, die Polypheme, fast bei allen Völkern einäugig erscheinen, so geht auch die Einäugigkeit Wotans auf eine Zeit zurück, da die Menschen noch Angst vor seiner seelenraubenden Natur hatten.' ('All demons who devour human beings, the Polyphems, appear as one-eyed among almost all peoples, and Wotan's one-eyedness itself goes back to a time when man still dreaded its capacity to rob him of his soul.')

Here and there one catches glimpses of material older than that derived from either the phallic phase of sexual development or even the excrementitial one that will be described in the next section, namely from the primordial penis-womb phantasies of infancy. It is in the womb that the dreaded fight with the father's penis takes place, and so the idea of obtaining the magic weapon is often associated with places symbolizing the womb. The magic steed, for instance, is in many legends discovered in a cavern or valley. Odin obtained his magic sap of life from a cavern, and when he leads his Furious Host at night they emerge from a hole in a mountain. Great personages in whose death it is impossible to believe live on in the hollow of a mountain, like King Frederick

---

[1] See S. Seligmann, *Der Böse Blick und Verwandtes*, 1910.
[2] Cox, *op. cit.* vol. i. p. 384.   [3] Wuttke, *op. cit.* S. 17.
[4] E. Mogk, *Germanische Mythologie*, 1906, S. 50.

Barbarossa; for long the people of Bohemia refused to believe that the famous Taborites were exterminated in the battle of Lipany (1434) and maintained that they were merely hiding in a cave in the mountain Blanik.[1] We shall presently see that this theme of 'penis in a womb' is extensively connected with that of stealing, a matter that throws a fuller light on the infantile phantasies in question.

These selections from the vast material available should suffice to show how greatly the mythological beliefs about the Horse, and the corresponding Nightmare *motifs* about the night-fiend, have been influenced by the particular infantile phase of sexual development known as the phallic stage, with its accompanying castration wishes and fears.

B. EXCREMENTITIAL SEXUALITY

As startling as the psycho-analytical discovery of the extraordinary part played by castration thoughts in the course of the young child's development, and in the unconscious mind of the adult, was the further one of a still earlier phase, a pregenital one, in which the child's mind apprehends sexuality very largely in terms of excremental processes. Nevertheless it is on reflection intelligible that both the anatomical propinquity of the respective organs and their close physiological associations should render this inevitable in the dawn of sexual development before this function has yet become adequately differentiated. In fact the adult emancipation of sexual from excremental processes is but rarely complete, and traces of the old association—even apart from gross perversions—are common enough; the very use of the word 'dirty' in reprehension of sexual indulgence—the stock phrase of our school authorities—is in itself indicative of this. If, therefore, my main contention is correct, that Nightmare experiences and the mythological beliefs about horses that are associated

[1] F. Lützow, *Bohemia : an historical Sketch*, 1895, p. 170.

with this are the expression of infantile sexual conflicts that continue to operate in the adult unconscious because they were not adequately resolved in childhood, we may expect to find both direct and, still more, indirect signs of excremental activities among the constituents of these beliefs and of sexual potency being expressed in terms of them. It is even possible that our investigation of the topic may have more than this confirmatory aim and will yield conclusions of general value on the deepest symbolism of the horse in mythology.

We shall consider the three main excretory processes, those relating to urine, fæces and flatus, in this order. With the first of these, urine, the phantasies are for obvious reasons usually expressed in terms of water, that of impregnation with urine—the infantile equivalent of semen—being associated with the actual connection between water and fruitfulness in nature. On the whole it may be said that when the idea of water is being used symbolically in mythology one natural source of water—rain—signifies urine, the other—the gushing out of subterranean water springs—more often the uterine waters.

Let us return to our starting-point. The Celtic word *march*, from which the word *mare* itself is probably derived, is allied to the modern English words *marsh*, *mere* and *moor*, which signify damp places, and to the Gaelic *mara*, all of which are cognate with the numerous *MR* words for sea, French *mer*, Welsh *môr*, Russian *more*, etc. Now it is very remarkable that night-fiends who assume the shape of horses are, as we shall presently see, almost always connected with ideas of water. Laistner[1] remarks: 'Die Rossgestalt des Alps ist hauptsächlich an dem im Wasser hausenden Lur haften geblieben.' ('The horse guise of the night-fiend has been retained from the Lure who dwells in water.')

In general the ideas of horse and water have always been closely associated, suggesting that something about

[1] Laistner, *op. cit.* Bd. i. S. 172.

a horse instinctively brings to the mind the idea of water. Jähns[1] points out that even the names that denote horse spring from common roots for those that denote water: the Latin *aqua* and *equus* (Old High German *ach* and *ech* respectively) are derived from the old Indo-Germanic *akrâ* (=water) and *akva* (=steed), both of which come from the root *ak* = to hasten. The same may apply to *Ross* itself, 'denn *ur* und *or* sind uralte, jeden *Ur*sprung bezeichnende Wörter, welche vilen Sprachen zur *Quell*bezeichnung dienten.˙Das lateinische *orire* = "entstehen" gehört zu diser Wurzel, und es ist nicht unwahrscheinlich, dasz auch das altdeutsche *ors* hier anknüpft in ser vilen Lokalitätsbezeichnungen auf *Wasser* deutet und somit als eine *gemeinschaftliche Bezeichnung für Quelle und Ross* erscheint. . . . Dasz Wörter wie *Renner* und *rinnen* zusammenhängen, ligt auf der Hand. In der antiken Dichtung ist von merkwürdiger Durchsichtigkeit in diser Beziehung der Name einer Nebengestalt des Poseidon, nämlich des rosseberümten troischen *Rhesos*. Denn diser Name bedeutet gradezu den "Rinnenden" (von ῥέω), und darum füren auch zwei *Flüsse* disen Namen: einer in Troas, ein andrer in Bythinien.' ('For *ur* and *or* are primitive words which many languages use to denote the idea of "source". The Latin *orire* (= to arise) belongs to this root, and it is not improbable that the Old German *ors*, which in many names of places indicates water and thus seems to be a common designation for "horse" and "spring", is also connected with it. . . . That words like *Renner* (=race-horse) and *rinnen* (=to stream) are related is plain enough. A clear example in this connection from classical writings is a guise of Poseidon, that of the Trojan Rhesos so famous for his glistening steeds. For this title simply means "the streamer" (from ῥέω), and hence has given the name to two livers, one in Troad, another in Bithynia.') Further than this, the place names formed from horse names generally contain a reference to water as well. Jähns,[2] after giving a list of

---

[1] Jähns, *op. cit.* S. 279, 280.   [2] *Id., op. cit.* S. 215.

some six hundred and fifty such words, writes: 'Hier sei nur aufmerksam gemacht, wie sich überreich und fast ausnahmslos bei jeder der aufgefürten Benennungen die Verbindung zwischen den Rossenamen und der Bezeichnung des Wassers, der rinnenden Flut ergiebt. Überall begegnen wir den Pferdenamen in fester Verschwisterung mit Silben wie: ach, bach, bore, brunn, bronn, quell, see, u.s.w.' ('Here one need only call attention to the fact of how extraordinarily rich with every one of these place names is the connection between the word for horse and that for running water. Everywhere we come across names for horses in close conjunction with syllables like: ach, bach, bore, brunn, bronn, quell, see, etc.')

This is perhaps the place to say something about the occurrence of creatures, half man and half horse, which have played a considerable part in mythology. Not only are they of general interest to us in confirming the views expressed above concerning the identification of human and animal interests and the important relation in which they stand to dream life, to which I am inclined to refer the origin of most mythical monsters, but they are particularly closely connected with the present theme of Horse and Water, and thus form a counterpart to the interchangeability of Hero and Horse which we studied in the preceding chapter in connection with the Sun-God. Centaurs, to take the classical example of these creatures, have an essentially watery origin. Kronos, the Greek Saturn, begot one by Philyra, the daughter of the water, while the others were the offspring of Ixion and Nephele (cloud). From a careful study of various coins and engravings Knight[1] has proved the erotic significance of the Centaurs, who were indeed sometimes confounded with Satyrs; various legends discussed by Cox[2] confirm this conclusion, which Laistner[3] also independently reached. The word itself, which signifies biting, reminds one of the sadistic conception of the horse, so often found in dreams. Other Grecian monsters show a

---

[1] Knight, *op. cit.* pp. 77-78.   [2] Cox, *op. cit.* vol. ii. pp. 54, 67.
[3] Laistner, *op. cit.*, Bd. i. S. 309, 313.

similar fusion of two animals. Thus the Hippocampen were half horse and half fish (hermaphroditic). The Bucentaurs were half men and half ox or horse; Bucentoro is the name of the state-galley of the Doge of Venice, used at the annual ceremony of marrying the Adriatic by throwing a ring into it.[1]

Combined figures such as the centaurs rarely occur in Northern mythology, but allied ones are quite common. There are a number of water demons who appear either in equine form or as human beings who in some respects resemble horses (neighing, etc.). The generic name for them is Nixie.[2] In Bohemia the Nix is actually called *Hastrmann* (=horse-man).[3] Laistner traces analogies between Poseidon and the German Nix.[4] The belief in question has been extensively developed in Scotland, where it is still held in outlying parts; a great many legends and tales are related of the water-horses there, the colloquial name of which is 'kelpie'.[5] A female kelpie can be transferred into a woman, and *vice versa*. The main characteristic of the Nixies,[6] the Kelpie,[7] and the Manx Glashtyn[8] is that they attack people of the opposite sex and carry them off to their watery home. They even intermarry: a child was born in Shulista of such a union as recently as 1794, the father being a Sun God in exile. A Midas-like fusion of horse and man occurs in a Welsh legend, of King March ap Meirchion (*March* = Welsh for 'horse') who resembled a man in all except his ears, which were horse's.

One of the most prominent attributes for water is its *movement*, one we have seen also to be a central one of horse symbolism. The movement may be either flowing,

---

[1] Jennings, *op. cit.* vol. ii. p. 41. O. Stoll, *Das Geschlechtsleben in der Völkerpsychologie*, 1908, S. 435.
[2] Wuttke, *op. cit.* S. 48-51.   [3] Jähns, *op. cit.* S. 278.
[4] Laistner, *op. cit.* Bd. ii. S. 445, 449.
[5] J. F. Campbell, *Popular Tales of the West Highlands*, 1860, vol. ii. pp. 190-193. J. Jamieson, *Scottish Dictionary*, 1880, vol. iii. p. 15. C. Mackay, *A Dictionary of Lowland Scotch*, 1888, p. 105.
[6] Wuttke, *op. cit.* S. 49.
[7] J. G. Dalyell, *The Darker Superstitions of Scotland*, 1835, pp. 543-544. J. A. Macculloch, *The Misty Isle of Skye*, 1905, pp. 235, 239.
[8] J. Rhys, *Celtic Folklore, Welsh and Manx*, 1901, vol. i. p. 289.

as with most of the examples Jähns cites, or undulatory.
The latter has repeatedly led to 'sailing' and 'riding' being
identified.[1] We still say 'the ship rides on the waves',
and in English the white waves are commonly called sea
horses. The Greek word for helmsman meant literally
'the rein-holder', and Odin, the Teutonic Horse-God, at
times appears as a helmsman.[2] It is little wonder, therefore, that the sailor, who 'rides on' his ship, should regard her as feminine.

We have seen the Horse-God in the form of a Wind-
or Storm-God, and in that of a Sun-God: we have next
to meet him in the form of a Water-God, principally a
Sea-God or River-God. As illustrating this relation between Horse and Water it is instructive that Poseidon-
Neptunus, the creator of horses and discoverer of the
riding art, was the Sea God. Odin himself often appeared
as a Water God, under the name of Nikarr;[3] from this
comes the modern English name for the devil 'Old Nick',
and also the fact that St. Nicholas was the patron of
mariners.[4] It has been supposed that the extensive
horse-worship in Greece arose as the result of a pun.[5]
The deity Hippa, which signifies the Soul of Everything,
was derived from the Phœnician Hip, 'the Parent of
All'. According to Hesychius, *hippon* means the sexual
parts of a man or woman,[6] and the deity Hippa was
therefore represented by phallic symbols. Bryant[7] states
that Hippa was the same as the Phrygian Cybele, the
mother-goddess. The name Hippios was applied to
several gods, *e.g.* Poseidon and Ares, and the name
Hippia to several goddesses, *e.g.* Hera and Athena; in
fact, at Colonos Poseidon and Athene shared a common
altar. The confusion between the God Hippios and the
horse Hippos, however, depended on more than a play

[1] Jähns, *op. cit.* S. 222, 223; Bd. ii. S. 9.
[2] Grimm, *op. cit.* Bd. iii. S. 57.   [3] *Id., op. cit.* Bd. i. S. 123.
[4] J. Brand, *Observations on the Popular Antiquities of Great Britain*, 1849,
vol. ii. p. 520.
[5] A. Wilder, Editor of R. P. Knight, *The Symbolical Language of Ancient
Art and Mythology*, 1876, pp. 79, 80.
[6] It is very interesting that even here hermaphroditism, which is characteristic of the whole sexual mythology of the horse, is evident.
[7] J. Bryant, *Analysis of Ancient Mythology*, 1774–76, vol. iii.

of words, as did that between the Nightmare and the
Nightmara, there being many other associations between
the ideas of deity and horse.

Everything goes to show that, beyond this idea of
movement, the actual link between the ideas of Horse
and Water is the *reproductive powers* of both. This is
illustrated in a very large number of legends and beliefs,
of which a few examples must suffice.

Jähns[1] writes: 'Im Sanskrit heist das Pferd *Sri-
Bhratri*, d.i. Bruder der *Sri*, der Göttin der Frucht-
barkeit, weil es gleich ihr aus den Wellen des Meres
emporgestiegen sei. Im Zend-Avesta der Perser erscheint Anahita, die Göttin des überirdischen befruch-
tenden Wassers, mit vier weiszen Rossen.' ('In Sanscrit
the horse is called "Sri-Bhratri", *i.e.* brother of Sri the
Goddess of Fertility, because like her it was born of the
sea waves. In the *Zend-Avesta* of the Persians, Anahita,
the Goddess of the fructifying waters above, appears
with four white steeds.') In Greece and Rome the horse
was sacred to Neptune and the Rivers, to which it was
sacrificed. According to Knight,[2] who regards the horse
as a symbol of the reproductive powers, the reason why
the horse appeared on Carthaginian coins was because of
its association with water. As the figure on these coins
was surmounted by a winged disc we have here a condensed expression of the three main aspects of the Horse
God, *i.e.* the Water God, Sun God and Storm God (flight
through the air). It is probably a representation of Saturn
himself, the chief deity of the Carthaginians, who was
believed to have appeared in equine guise when he paid
his addresses to Philyra, the daughter of Oceanus.[3]

Both in India and Greece it was believed that the
horse's saliva had magic properties, particularly for the
generating and saving of life—two very similar ideas, as
Rank[4] has well shown. The saliva of the magic Sun-

[1] Jähns, *op. cit.* S. 272.   [2] Knight, *op. cit.* p. 76.
[3] Virgil, *Georgics*, iii. 92.
[4] O. Rank, 'Belege zur Rettungsphantasie', *Zentralblatt für Psychoanalyse*,
1911, Jahrg. i. S. 331; 'Die "Geburts-Rettungsphantasie" in Traum und
Dichtung', *Zeitschrift für Psychoanalyse*, Jahrg. ii. S. 43.

horse was equivalent to ambrosia and was even identified with it.[1] When he was robbed of this salivary
ambrosia he lost his strength and died. The Indian
Acvins were known not only as wonderful riders,[2] but
as exceptionally skilled physicians. The sons of Aesculapius, the Father of Medicine, are to be identified with
the twin Dioscures, the Greek equivalents of the Acrins.
Ovid, in the second book of the *Metamorphoses*, describes how Ocyrhoë was appropriately transformed into
a mare as a punishment for predicting that Aesculapius
would through medical science save mankind from death.
In short, the fluid issuing from the horse (saliva, urine,
semen) was regarded as having magical properties in
respect of life itself; it was the essence of life.

The fruitfulness of the horse itself is chiefly manifested
by means of contact of his hoof with the earth, a theme
that has many roots. In the first place, the leg and foot
themselves symbolize in folklore, as Aigremont has
amply shown,[3] the male generative organ; this is especially likely with the aggressive leg of the horse. Secondly,
the horse's hoof and shoe symbolize the female organ;
the curved shape lends itself especially to this identification, which is already common with foot and shoe in
general.[4] Aigremont traces this latter identification to a
telluric origin, *i.e.* to the contact of the foot with the
mother earth,[5] but there are probably anal-erotic
elements also at work here. The horse's hoof is therefore
especially well adapted to symbolize both the male and
the female reproductive powers. From it may spring
various forms of life, the two chief being vegetation and
springs. Borek, Mahomet's silver-grey mare, possessed
this quality in a high degree, for 'unter deren Füssen
empfing selbst der Wüstensand die Eigenschaft, Leben
zu erzeugen, und verwandelte sich in Gold.'[6] ('Beneath
its feet even the desert sand acquired the property of
creating life, and was changed into gold.') This quality

[1] Gubernatis, *op. cit.* S. 273, 274.   [2] V.s.p.
[3] Aigremont, *Fuss- und Schuh-Symbolik*, 1909, S. 23, 24.
[4] *Id., op. cit.* S. 8, 9, 12, etc.   [5] *Id., op. cit.* S. 21.
[6] Jähns, *op. cit.* S. 272. Evidently a cloacal motive.

belongs to human beings and to gods, as well as to horses. Aigremont[1] writes: 'Saaten, Blumen, Früchte entsprossen unter den Schritten des segnenden Fusses der Göttin. Dieser alte Mythenzug kehrt in Sagen und Märchen gar vieler Völker wieder, ist fast Allgemeingut der Menschheit geworden. Nach der altägyptischen wie indischen, nach der romanischen wie deutschen, nach der japanischen wie slavischen Volksanschauung spriessen Blumen unter den Tritten edler Frauen, Königinnen oder verkannter Aschenbrödels hervor.' ('Harvests, flowers, fruits sprout and ripen under the tread of the goddess's benign foot. This ancient mythological *motif* recurs in the legends and fairy tales of very many nations and has almost become the common property of mankind. In the popular view of the Old Egyptians as of the Indians, of the Romans as of the Germans, of the Japanese as of the Slavs, flowers spring forth under the tread of noble women, queens or misjudged Cinderellas.') Men, various legendary heroes and gods possess the quality equally with woman and goddesses, another proof of the hermaphroditic nature of foot symbolism. The horses of deities and heroes bring the same blessing as they ride over the land, and many legends and stories are still believed in which tell of the field mare that makes the corn grow.

Even more frequently than by the growth of vegetation is the trampling of horses followed by the issuing forth of springs. No better symbol of reproduction could be found, for this represents the pouring out of both the male principle (semen, urine) and the birth itself (uterine water). Both sources of water can be produced in this way, the one being on the whole a male process, the other a female. The mythical origin of the magical Hippocrene on Helicon is an instance of both forms. One source of it there was obtained by a stroke of the hoof given by the wonderful horse Pegasus (from $\pi\eta\gamma\dot\eta$ = spring[2]), the offspring of Poseidon and Medusa. The stroke let loose a heavy rainstorm, which gave rise to the spring;[3]

---

[1] Aigremont, *op. cit.* S. 17, 18.   [2] Jähns, *op. cit.* Bd. ii. S. 9.
[3] *Id., op. cit.* S. 274.

the analogy may well be drawn between heavy rain and the forcible micturition of the horse, an association maintained in many bawdy jokes. It is interesting that just like the magic wand, the wishing-rod and other similar symbols, the (male) tread of the hoof can disclose precious metals that are hidden in the earth,[1] once more a cloacal *motif*. At times ambrosia itself spurts out of the magic horse's hoof, and as we know ambrosia to be a symbol for semen this again shows how the leg and foot must have a phallic meaning. In the *Rigveda*[2] we read that the Agni, the magic horses, spurted out a divine fluid from their forefeet, and that the horse which the Acvins presented to the sun-hero filled a hundred beakers with intoxicating fluid from his hooves.[3] In this connection may also be mentioned the following facts: Mistletoe, which as a seminal symbol was sacred to the horse-worshipping Druids, is a valuable charm against the Nightmare.[4] Dew, which has the same significance,[5] dripped from the mane of the Teutonic Nightsteed (Sleipnir, etc.), and indeed Jähns connects the Latin word for this *ros* with the German *Ross*.[6] Hair itself has several sexual meanings, being indeed biologically a secondary sexual characteristic. One that I do not remember having been pointed out, but which I have several times found during psycho-analysis, is an association with fæces. Indeed, even in connection with horses it may be mentioned that the manes of the sacred Teutonic horses were plaited with threads of gold, and the horses themselves were frequently named after this characteristic;[7] it was a general superstition in the Middle Ages that horse's hair, laid in manure water turned into poisonous snakes (cp. Medusa's snake-hair). One finds this indicated by Shakespeare:[8]

> Much is breeding,
> Which, like the courser's hair, hath yet but life,
> And not a serpent's poison.

[1] Jähns, *op. cit.* S. 283.   [2] *Rigveda*, vi. 75, 7.   [3] *Ib.*, i. 116, 7.
[4] B. Thorpe, *Northern Mythology*, 1851, vol. ii. p. 30.
[5] Abraham, *op. cit.* S. 63.   [6] Jähns, *op. cit.* S. 280.
[7] *Id.*, *op. cit.* S. 421.   [8] *Antony and Cleopatra*, Act i, Sc. 2.

The second source of the Helicon Hippocrene was through a female process, an underground spring produced by Permessos, a River God. Hippocrene itself may be translated in German by the names Rossbach (Horsebrook), or better *Mar*bach,[1] two common place names. This more usual female process of producing springs is described in a number of Teutonic legends,[2] *e.g.* in regard to Baldur's steed, Charlemagne's (which gave rise to the famous sacred well at Aix), etc.

It is well known that the mysterious properties of the foot have repeatedly been transferred to the shoe,[3] so that it is to be expected that the *horseshoe* would acquire the significance of the water- and life-giving horse's hoof itself. This is so in fact. The wide-spreadness of the belief in horseshoes is as remarkable as the manifoldness of its virtues. Aigremont says:[4] 'Der Glaube an das Hufeisenglück ist über die ganze Welt verbreitet. Alle Rassen und Völker, die den Gebrauch der Hufeisen kennen, haben ihn.' ('The belief in the luck of horseshoes is widespread over the whole world. All races and peoples that know the use of horseshoes have it.') Horseshoes keep away evil spirits and witches, avert the Evil Eye, guard from illness, bring life, prosperity and happiness, in short are in every way lucky. It would be superfluous to relate any instances for this,[5] for it is still one of the most living of beliefs. The favourite places to nail a horseshoe are over doors, especially stable doors, and on the masts of ships; Lord Nelson had one nailed to the mast of the *Victory* at Trafalgar, and Lord Roberts carefully collected them on his South African campaign. The belief has been rationalized in the most curious ways, such as through its connection with the birth of Christ in a stable, etc., but it has many times been pointed out that it is the same symbol as

[1] Jähns, *op. cit.* S. 215.
[2] Aigremont, *op. cit.* S. 16. Jähns, *op. cit.* S. 274-276.
[3] Aigremont, *op. cit.* S. 45, etc.   [4] *Id., op. cit.* S. 70.
[5] See Brand, *op. cit.* vol. iii. pp. 16-18, 25. S. Seligmann, *Der Böse Blick,* Bd. ii. S. 11-13, 129. B. Stern, *Medizin, Aberglaube und Geschlechtsleben in der Türkei,* 1903, Bd. ii. S. 288, 339. Wuttke, *op. cit.* S. 130, and especially Lawrence, *op. cit.*

appears in the form of the Christian *vesica piscis*, the Cestos of Aphrodite, the magic necklace of Hermania, the Nibelung ring, the ship of Isis and Athene, the Achaian Argos, Noah's ark, the chest of Osiris, the Holy Grail, King Arthur's Round Table, the girdle of Hippolyte, the Order of the Garter (the highest Court honour in England), all kinds of magical cups and horns, the Egyptian mystical door of life, the religious altar, the Yoni of Vishnu, and a host of others;[1] the symbolism is quite simply revealed in the German expression for defloration, 'Sie hat ein Hufeisen verloren' ('She has lost a horseshoe'). It is therefore of especial interest that the horseshoe has always been one of the chief charms used against the Nightmare;[2] the mind of the people has seemed dimly to perceive that, in satisfactory circumstances, the Yoni will better than anything else prevent the distressing night visits of the Mara. Of similar significance is the plan of placing the shoes at the side of the bed with the toes pointing towards the door; this is evidently intended for women, and indeed is especially efficacious in guarding against the Alp fiend.[3] The association between horse and sea is still kept up in Italian customs, where the evil eye is averted partly by the *mano cornuta*,[4] and partly by the use of amulets representing a mermaid sitting on a centaur.[5] Another similar amulet is the hag stone or holy stone, the designation holy denoting both its sacred nature and the fact that it has been bored (holey); they avert labour pains,[6] various elves,[7] but especially the Nightmare.[8] Of interest in this connection are the lucky snake-stones of various countries (Pliny's *anguinum*), glass rings formed by the hissing together of the breath of several serpents, and

[1] See Cox, *op. cit.* T. Inman, *Ancient Faiths embodied in Ancient Names*, 1873. R. P. Knight, *A Discourse on the Worship of Priapus*, 1863.
[2] Lawrence, *op. cit.* pp. 90, 95.
[3] Grimm, *op. cit.* Bd. iii. S. 449.   [4] Lawrence, *op. cit.* p. 12.
[5] Seligmann, *op. cit.* Bd. ii. S. 310.   [6] Dalyell, *op. cit.* p. 140.
[7] Meyer, *op. cit.* S. 137.
[8] B. Henderson, *Folk-lore of the Northern Counties of England*, 1879, p. 166. Lawrence, *op. cit.* p. 75. *Northumberland*, Folk-Lore Series, 1903, p. 51.

finally passed like an egg.[1] Without any symbolism at all
the vulva of the mare itself is used in India to avert the
Evil Eye, as it was in ancient Rome to make both love
potions and poisons—thus illustrating the characteristic
ambivalence of the unconscious: it here formed the
main ingredient of the deadly poison Hippoman.[2] Lastly,
in this connection may be mentioned that the Irish word
for vulva is *maar*, an interesting fact in view of the
Celtic origin of *Mähre*.

From these considerations it will be plain that the
Horse's foot is singularly adapted to symbolize both the
male and female principle, in other words the whole reproductive side, or what later ages have chosen to call
the 'animal side' of our nature. It has therefore become
a demoniacal attribute in general, and has become attached to a great number of mythical beings. Even in
its naked form it has special significance attributed to it;
thus in the Netherlands a horse's foot is hung up in a
stable to prevent a Mara or witch from riding the horses.[3]
We find already in Greece that not only were the centaurs provided with a horse's foot, but also the priests
who served the oracle at Dodona, and who were called
Hippodes.[4] Odin himself had a horse's foot, as had
various other nightly visitors, such as the Pschezpolnica
of the Wends, the mythical he-goat, and the Alp himself.[5] The shape became influenced by that of the oriental pentagram;[6] in Croatia the Mora has feet in the form
of a pentagram.[7] Hence arose the pentagram ('Drudenfuss') of Teutonic sorceresses. The mediæval Devil never
appeared without his horse's foot,[8] and the witches became endowed with the same attribute. In modern times
the expression 'cloven hoof' has passed into common
usage in a metaphorical sense, the most usual connotation of it being animal or sexual. The fertility concept

---

[1] J. B. Deane, *The Worship of the Serpent*, 1833, pp. 260-264.
[2] C. F. von Schlichtegroll, *Liebesleben im klassischen Altertum*, S. 338.
[3] Seligmann, *op. cit.* Bd. ii. S. 129. Thorpe, *op. cit.* vol. ii. p. 328.
[4] Jähns, *op. cit.* S. 271.
[5] Laistner, *op. cit.* Bd. ii. S. 259.   [6] Meyer, *op. cit.* S. 58.
[7] Krauss, *op. cit.* S. 148.   [8] Brand, *op. cit.* vol. ii. p. 517.

of the horse's foot was ingeniously strengthened by the Greeks in the following fancy. In a later representation of the frightful Medusa (in Aristophanes) she appears, not with her usual ass's legs, but with one leg made of ore, the other of ass's dung.[1] This connection between the ass, the pre-eminently phallic animal, and dung, the fertilizing manure, represents a very condensed piece of symbolism.

So far we have been considering the urethral-erotic elements in the Horse-Nightmare mythology as expressed by the connection between the ideas of water and fertility. There are several links that enable us to pass from this theme to that of the anal-erotic elements, since a number of the mythological ideas in question receive contributions from both sources. Let us take, for example, the ideas investing the sun's rays. We saw in the preceding chapter what an important attribute they are of the Horse-Sun God, and how the diminution in them after the summer solstice was dreaded as a reminder of castration. Here the rays are regarded as a symbol of the phallus as well as of semen, and there is a considerable series of myths in which they play this part so openly as to lead to pregnancy in the virgin on whom they fall.[2] Similarly the sun's rays are regarded as a form of fire, and since Abraham's[3] work we are familiar with the seminal symbolism of this in mythological thought. On the other hand, there is ample evidence of pregenital factors being at work in the composition of this group of ideas. Freud[4] some time ago hinted that the infantile and unconscious equivalent of fire is urine, and the truth of this has since been fully established. The usual description of the sun's rays as streaming or pouring rather than as being ejected naturally accords better with the analogy with the infantile, preseminal fluid; it is a parallel to the 'flowing' mane of the

---

[1] Aigremont, *op. cit.* S. 25.
[2] See, for instance, E. S. Hartland, *Primitive Paternity*, 1909, vol. i. pp. 25, 26.
[3] Abraham, *Traum und Mythus*, 1909, Cap. 4.
[4] Freud, *Sammlung kleiner Schriften zur Neurosenlehre*, 1909, 2e Folge, S. 137. [*Gesammelte Schriften*, Bd. v. S. 267; *Collected Papers*, vol. ii. p. 50.]

Horse-God. Their colour and shining appearance are features that aid in this identification, but these features evidently have also another pregenital origin, the anal-erotic one. Much stress is laid in these myths on the like-ness of the sun's rays to gold, the most typical uncon-scious symbol of fæces, while many stories are related of the *golden* mane of the magic horse and of the night-fiend's long tresses being interwoven with gold. As I have elsewhere pointed out,[1] the idea of hair itself is very often associated in the unconscious with that of fæces, the notions of dirt and of perpetually shedding being com-mon to both.[2]

Another theme connecting the two pregenital ele-ments in question is that of *stealing*. Stealing in myth-ology, as in unconscious phantasy in general, signifies an injury, a deprivation or even mutilation, and is ulti-mately a symbol for castration. To steal money is to perform a pederastic assault—money = fæces—with a castrating motive, hence the neurotic dread of being cheated or having even small sums stolen. It is interest-ing in connection with the present topic that one of the titles of Hermes, whom we have seen earlier to have been one of the Greek equivalents of the Horse-God Odin, was the Master Thief. Abraham[3] has clearly demon-strated the sexual significance of the myth about the stealing of fire from heaven, and Hermes himself was one of the gods who was supposed to have first brought fire to mankind.[4] In mythology we meet the stealing *motif* mainly in the three following connections: (1) Theft of a symbol for the genital organ, the most direct of the cas-tration themes. The chief examples of this in the present circle of ideas are fire, the eye, the hat and the magic steed. Several instances of these were recounted in the preceding chapter. (2) Theft of a woman. To be deprived of the sexual object is often the equivalent of being de-

---

[1] 'Einige Fälle von Zwangsneurose', *Jahrbuch der Psychoanalyse*, 1912, Bd. iv. S. 580.
[2] See O, Stoll, *op. cit*. S. 120-240, for ethnological material amply confirming this conclusion.
[3] Abraham, *op. cit*. S. 31.   [4] Cox, *op. cit*. vol. i. p. 120.

prived of sexuality, *i.e.* of the genital organ itself. To be carried off oneself by the Psychopomp, *i.e.* parted from the loved one, is a variant of this that connects directly with the first *motif*; as I pointed out earlier,[1] the dread of the Nightmare is at the same time dread of castration and dread of death. (3) Theft of treasure. This is a much over-determined *motif*. It is often to be equated to theft of wife, she being the greatest treasure. As we have just seen, however, this does not contradict the meaning of theft of penis, particularly as in the unconscious fæces (= treasure) is often equated to the penis. And, because of the homosexual significance pointed out above, it is one of the worst forms of castration, and for this reason is an extremely frequent mythological theme. To the earlier instances we may add a couple more, which illustrate several of the features to which attention has been called. 'Im Elendstale ist eine grosse Klippe, darin wohnt eine Jungfer, die zeigt sich zwischen elf und zwölf mit einem silbernen Schlüssel; wem sie diesen hinhielt, der sollte ihn mit dem Stocke nehmen. Das tat ein Köhler, da öffneten sich durch den Schlüssel drei Türen, dann kam er in eine Höhle, da standen gesattelte Rosse, dahinter lag Pferdemist. Er musste sich davon mitnehmen, als er aber über eine Brücke ging, schüttelte er ihn ins Wasser, da klingelte er und war Gold.'[2] ('In Elendstal is a high cliff where there dwells a maiden. She shows herself between eleven and twelve[3] with a silver key, and whoever she offers this to should take it with his stick. A certain charcoal-burner once did this and the key opened three (!) doors through which he came into a cavern (!) where there stood saddled horses with dung behind them. He had to take away with him as much of this as he could, and as he crossed a bridge he showered it into the water where it jingled and turned into gold.') 'Vor der verbotenen Kammer fand der Knabe eine Pfütze voller Gold, tauchte den Finger darein und verband ihn mit einem Stückchen

---

[1] Part III. pp. 255, 265.
[2] Laistner, *op. cit.* Bd. i. S. 144.   [3] The regular night-fiend time.

Zeug. Als der Drakos aufwachte und den Verband sah, musste jener ihn abnehmen, da war der Finger vergoldet; der Drakos packte ihn nun und tauchte ihn ganz in die Pfütze, und davon ward er am ganzen Leibe golden.'[1] 'In einer mährischen Variante ist der Knabe zum Wärter des Rosses bestellt, aber er soll sich vor einem gewissen Brunnen hüten; als er dennoch den Finger eintaucht, entsteht plötzlich ein goldner Ring, den er nicht abmachen kann; er verbindet den Finger, aber sein Herr bemerkt den Verband, nimmt ihn den Ring ab und wirft diesen in den Brunnen. Ehe er dann mit dem Rosse flieht, taucht er auf dessen Rat den Kopf in den Brunnen, sein Haar wird golden, und er stülpt eine Kappe darüber.'[2] ('Before the forbidden door the youth found a puddle of gold; he dipped a finger into it and bandaged it over with a piece of cloth. When the dragon woke and caught sight of the bandage he made the youth take it off and, behold, the finger had changed into gold. Whereupon the dragon caught hold of him and dipped him into the puddle until his whole body was golden.' 'In a Moravian variant the youth has the post of watching the horse, and he has to guard himself against a certain well. But he plunged his finger into it and found a ring appear, which he could not dislodge from his finger. He bandages his finger, but when his master sees it, he takes the ring away and throws it into the well. As he then bolts with the (magic) horse he follows his advice and plunges his head into the well, whereupon his hair turns to gold and he claps his cap over it.') The Furious Host of Odin emerges from the hollow of a mountain;[3] those who care for the horses when they are within the mountain receive as a reward the horsedung and hoof-clippings, both of which then turn to gold.[4]

Another allied theme with condensed symbolism is that of the horse's *ears*. To begin with these can be phallic symbols, as with the magic Uććaihcrava, Indra's

[1] Laistner, *op. cit.* Bd. ii. S. 147.
[2] *Id., op. cit.* Bd. ii. S. 147.
[3] Meyer, *op. cit.* S. 241-244.
[4] Jähns, *op. cit.* Bd. i. S. 335.

steed, whose name signifies simply 'erect ears'.[1] Then the orifice of the ear is an unconscious equivalent of the anus, hence the conception of a rich man with horse's or ass's ears (Midas, etc.). It is associated at this point with birth phantasies, as in the legend of the conception of Jesus through the ear.[2] In the following Russian tale there is a combination of incest and homosexual themes, whereby the youth wins the king's daughter. Ivan, the youngest and stupid brother, has the most worthless horse of the stable. He creeps into one ear and out by the other. On this two young riders (= the Dioscori) appear and transform his horse into a wonderful steed with a mane and tail of gold. By its help he performs marvellous feats, and wins the Czar's daughter.[3]

The Wind God was the first of the triad of divine guises in which we met the Horse God, and we have now to investigate the mundane origins of this conception. The emanation of a gaseous fluid from the body is a process which has greatly influenced the imagination of mankind and has stimulated some of the most exalted ideas. On the physical plane it assumes various forms, although there are only two gases emitted from the body —expired air and flatus. There is the breath, the voice and minor respiratory phenomena (sneezing, etc.). The act of speaking becomes identified in the unconscious with that of thinking, and the very invisibility of all these acts strengthens the idea of power with which for more reasons than one they are invested. Nor is the idea of fertility lacking. We need not recount the endless beliefs, from the first chapter of Genesis onward, in which the idea of the Creative Breath or Divine Spirit plays a central part. Now in the course of my psycho-analytical work I have come across the curious phantasy that the act of procreation may consist in the passage of flatus

[1] Gubernatis, *op. cit.* S. 223.
[2] See Ernest Jones, 'Die Empfängnis der Jungfrau Maria durch das Ohr: Ein Beitrag zu der Beziehung zwischen Kunst und Religion'. *Jahrbuch der Psychoanalyse*, 1914, Bd. vi. S. 135. ['The Madonna's Conception through the Ear. A Contribution to the Relation between Aesthetics and Religion', *Essays in Applied Psycho-Analysis*, 1923, ch. viii. p. 261.]
[3] Gubernatis, *op. cit.* S. 229.

from one body to another,[1] and I have elsewhere shown[2] that this notion unconsciously plays an important part in far loftier contexts. The intense repression to which early interest in flatus is later subjected makes it intelligible that it can manifest itself in later life principally in disguised forms, one of the chief being a transference upwards that goes to strengthen the natural interest in respiratory and allied processes. Particularly the notion of action at a distance, or of peculiar powers of searching and penetrating in the manner of a gas, receives much from this deep source.

It is of interest here to note that the Vedic equivalents of the Greek Centaurs were the cloud-maidens called Gandharvas,[3] and it has been thought that the two words are etymologically related.[4] The latter is cognate with *gandha*, which means 'evil smell'. Now evil smells were one of the means of protection against the Nightmare, and certain inferences are legitimately to be drawn from this. Charms against the Nightmare or night-fiend are characteristically symbols of the part of the body where the attack is feared. Most of these charms, therefore, are genital symbols, knife, broom, horseshoe, and the like. The following account has to be read in conjunction with this general law: 'Die Masuren empfehlen als Mittel wider die Mahrte, sich auf den Bauch zu legen: wenn dann die Zmora kommt, den Schläfer nach ihrer Gewohnheit zu küssen und zu lecken, und merkt, dass sie nicht das Gesicht küsst, wird sie ärgerlich und geht davon (Toeppen). Wer die Mura von sich abhalten will, lege sich ein mit Menschenkot bestrichenes Tuch auf die Brust, raten die Tschechen (Grohmann); oder auch, man esse vor Schlafengehen angerauchte Gerichte, am besten angerauchte Milch (Ebt). In diesen Angaben scheint sich der eigentliche Grund zu verraten, warum die Logik des Volksglaubens darauf

[1] Ernest Jones, *Zentralblatt für Psychoanalyse*, Jahrg. i. S. 566.
[2] Ernest Jones, 'Die Empfängnis der Jungfrau Maria durch das Ohr', *loc. cit.*
[3] Cox, *op. cit.* vol. ii. p. 35.
[4] Laistner, *op. cit.* Bd. i. S. 314.

verfiel, stark duftende Blumen oder Kümmelbrot für
ein Schutzmittel zu halten.'[1] ('The Masurians recommend
as a protection against the Nightmare to lie on one's
belly. When the Mara comes to kiss or lick the sleeper
according to her custom and notices that she is not kissing the face, she gets angry and departs. To keep the
Mara away one should lay on one's breast a towel
streaked with human fæces, so the Czechs advise; or before
going to sleep one may eat highly seasoned dishes, best
of all milk with a stench of smoke. We seem to divine
in these data the real reason why the logic of popular
belief came to the idea that strongly smelling flowers or
carraway bread were excellent means of protection.') In
an Oldenburg legend the Alp, instead of sticking his
tongue into the sleeper's mouth or creeping into it in the
form of a snake—two common enough habits—*blows*
into it.[2] The source of his blowing is seen in another,
Hessian belief, according to which 'rühren die Sumpf-
ausdünstungen davon her, dass der Alp fistet'[3] ('the
stenches of marshes come from the flatus of the night
bogey'). We have remarked above on the association
between water and generation, and also called attention
to the connection between the words *marsh*, Welsh
march, and German *Mähre*. It is therefore quite fit-
ting that Odin and Poseidon, the Gods of Horses and
Water, should also be specially Wind or Storm Gods.
The importance of wind for fertility was briefly touched
on above, and I suspect that the infantile theory here
indicated has played a large part in this connection. The
act of passing flatus is so evident with horses that it is
not surprising to find how many beliefs there are about
their being fertilized by the wind. We need only recall
the classical instances of this belief being held in respect
of the mares of Boetia,[4] Cappadocia[5] and Lusitania.[6]
We may also mention that Aeolus, the West Wind who

[1] Laistner, *op. cit.* Bd. i. S. 342, 343.
[2] Strackerjan. Quoted by Laistner, *op. cit.* Bd. i. S. 42.
[3] Wolf. Quoted by Laistner, *op. cit.* Bd. i. S. 314.
[4] Virgil, *Georgics*, iii. 266-276.
[5] St. Augustine, *Civ. Dei.*, xxi. 5.   [6] Pliny, *Hist. Nat.* viii. 67.

impregnated Ocyrhoë, who was also called Hippe
(=mare), had another title Hippodates.[1]

It is well known how often the sexual act is conceived
of as simply a 'finding out' process, and so becomes connected with knowledge and wisdom; one has only to recall the regular Old Testament use of 'to know a woman'
to denote sexual intercourse, and the fact that the snake
is everywhere a symbol of wisdom and other things (cp.
the tree of knowledge in Eden). An instance in connection with horses well illustrates this: 'Nicht selten trifft
das Hervorrufen der Quelle durch Rosseshuf mit dem
Weissagen durch Rossestritt zusammen. Es ist gewisser-
maszen, als beginne der Bronn der Weisheit zu flieszen.
Auf dem Kirchhof zu Bergkirchen trafen einmal zwei
Brüder im feindlichen Kampfe zusammen. Der eine
erkannte den andern und rief ihm zu: "Ich bin dein
Bruder." Der andere glaubte ihm nicht. Aber sein Pferd
traf, als der Zweifelnde zum Kampf ausprengen wollte,
den Stein mit dem Hufe; siehe da sprang ein Quell
empor. Die Warheit war erwiesen und die glücklichen
Brüder bauten zum Andenken Bergkirchen.'[2] ('It is not
rare for the evoking of springs by a horse's hoof to be
accompanied by predicting through the horse's tread.
It is as though knowledge began to flow from the foun-
tain. In the churchyard at Bergkirchen two brothers
once met in a deadly fight. The one recognized the other
and called out to him "I am your brother". The other
did not believe him. But as the doubter sprang forward
once more into the fight his horse struck the stone with
his hoof and, behold, a spring gushed forth. The truth
was demonstrated, and in memory of the miracle the
brothers built Bergkirchen.') Therefore a form of sexual
act that denotes penetration *at a distance* can also be
symbolized as knowing from afar. And in fact we read
of Odin the Horse and Wind God that: 'er fährt in
Augenblicken in die fernsten Länder und weiss, was hier
geschieht.'[3] ('In a moment he travels in the most distant

[1] Jähns, *op. cit.* S. 264-265.
[2] *Id., op. cit.* S. 275-276.   [3] Mogk, *op. cit.* S. 44.

lands and knows what happens there.') This rapid penetration at a distance becomes transferred from the idea
of space to the allied one of time; hence such gods, and
especially horse gods, can read the future. Thus Odin
'besitzt prophetische Gaben und kann die Menschen
Vorzeichen und Zukunft lehren'; 'als geheimnisvoll
flüsternder und auf- und abrauschender Windgott *weis-
sagt* er, ist runen-, zauber- und sangeskundig.'[1] ('pos-
sesses prophetic gifts and can instruct mankind in
auguries and in the future'; 'as the secret whispering
and rustling Wind God he *predicts*, has a knowledge
of runes, of magic and of song.') He could not only
read thoughts, like the clever Hans, but could also
solve riddles; in fact, 'der Rätselkundige' was one of his
titles.[2]

We shall confine our instances of the present topic to
horses. The transference of the ideas connected with
flatus to the subject of breath and voice is peculiarly
easy in the case of the horse, whose neighing is evidently
a sexual process and has hardly any other biological
significance. Jähns remarks:[3] 'Da der Hengst ganz vor-
zugsweise dann wihert, wenn er den Trieb zur Begattung
empfindet, Zeugungskraft und Lebensfülle dem Lichte
aber ebenso eng verbunden sind, wie Unfruchtbarkeit
der Finsternis und dem Tode, so muste auch aus solchen
Gründen das mutige Gewiher als gutes Omen gelten.
In welcher bedeutungsvollen reichen Mannigfaltigkeit
der Volksaberglaube dise Anschauungen weitergebildet,
bis in die Neuzeit bewart und zumal um die heilige Zeit
der Zwölften gruppirt hat, werden wir ausfürlich an
anderen Stellen besprechen.' ('Since a stallion chiefly
neighs when he feels the impulse to copulate, and since
procreative capacity and the sense of life are as closely
associated with the idea of light as barrenness with that
of darkness and death, we have the reason why a lusty
neigh counts as a good omen. In what rich and manifold
significance the popular belief has elaborated this con-

---

[1] Meyer, *op. cit.* S. 233.
[2] Jähns, *op. cit.* S. 299.   [3] *Id., op. cit.* S. 269.

clusion, how it has preserved it into modern times and especially connected it with the holy Twelfth Night, we shall presently show at length.') Though the horse as a whole—and individual parts in particular—has generally been regarded as connected with good luck,[1] evidently on account of his sexual significance, this applies more to his neighing than to any other attribute.[2] The Teutonic races paid the greatest attention to it, *divining future events* from the different intonations;[3] and both the Persians[4] and the Irish decided the choice of their king from the omen thus obtained. The predicting function of neighing is referred to in numerous myths and folk-lore tales.[5] One instance may be given indicating the sexual significance of the act: 'Mädchen reiten wol auf einem Besen(!) bis an die Tür des Pferdestalls und horchen. Wihert ein Ross, da kommt die Magd bis Johannis in die Ehe, hört sie dagegen die laute Blähung eines Pferdes, so musz sie im kommenden Jahre Kindtaufe geben one einen Mann zu haben.'[6] ('Girls ride on a broomstick to the door of the stable and listen. If a steed neighs it means she will be married before Midsummer Day, but if she hears only the flatus of a horse she will bear a child in the coming year without being married.') It is interesting that Brand derived the word 'witch' from the Dutch *witchelen* = neighing, on account of the foretelling capacity of both.[7] This is not strictly true, for witch comes from the Anglo-Saxon *wicca*,[8] which is cognate with Middle Dutch *wicker*, 'a soothsayer', and Low German *wikken*, 'to predict' (allied to *wissen*), but it is possible that the two may ultimately have a common origin.

From neighing it is only a step to speaking. And mythology and history are full of accounts of speaking horses,

[1] Lawrence, *op. cit.* ch. xi.
[2] Grimm, *op. cit.* Bd. iii. S. 442, Nr. 239.
[3] Lawrence, *op. cit.* p. 73, quoting Tacitus.
[4] Grimm, *op. cit.* Bd. ii. S. 549.
[5] Wuttke, *op. cit.* S. 219. Jähns, *op. cit.* S. 423.
[6] Jähns, *op. cit.* S. 295.
[7] Brand, *op. cit.* vol. iii. p. 2.   [8] Skeat, *op. cit.* p. 719.

which need not here be detailed;[1] speaking is also closely connected with prophesying. According to Jähns,[2] 'zunächst war es die wirkliche Stimme des Pferdes, die als weissagerisch galt. Öffentlich lauschte der Priester dem Orakel der Pferde, die dem Volke als Vertraute und Mitwiszer der Götter erschienen, wärend er selbst nur ihr Diener war.' ('At first it was the actual voice of the horse that was regarded as foretelling. The priest publicly listened to the oracle of the horses, for they seemed to the people to be the initiates and confidants of the gods, whereas he himself was only their servant.') Speaking is obviously connected with declamation and oratory, the beginning of poetry, therefore the man with best and finest *flow* of words carried fame. We can now understand why one of the descendants of Odin was called Ruprecht (glittering with fame), and why Odin was the god of song and poetry, which he discovered. 'Daher heisst die Poesie die Gabe, der Trank Odins und der Dichter der Metträger Odins. Denn ein Trunk von dem Dichtermete machte einen gewöhnlichen Sterblichen zum Dichter, und dieser Dichtermet befand sich in Odins Bewahrung. Diese Auffassung vom Dichtermet ist relativ jung: der Lebensmet Odrerir ist zum Dichtermet geworden.'[3] ('Hence poetry is known as the gift, the drink of Odin's, and the poet the mead-bearer of Odin's. For a drink from the poetic mead makes an ordinary mortal into a poet, and this drink was in Odin's keeping. This conception of poetic mead is relatively recent: the life-giving mead Odrerir has become the drink of poets.') This reminds us that it was a horse, Pegasos, who gave Hippocrene to the world on Helikon, the mountain of the Muses.

In connection with the words *Mare* and *Märchen* it might be added that the idea of bringing news is obviously connected with the ideas both of finding out knowledge and of passage through the air.

---

[1] Cox, *op. cit.* vol. i. pp. 247, 391. W. Hertz, *Der Werwolf*, 1862, S. 67, etc. Jähns, *op. cit.* S. 264.

[2] Jähns, *op. cit.* S. 269.   [3] Mogk, *op. cit.* S. 46.

Hermes, often regarded as an equivalent of Odin, was at once the Wind God and the *God of messages*, and it will be remembered that news was daily brought to Odin by two ravens,[1] birds[2] which Laistner has brought into the circle of the sexual Nightmare beliefs.[3]

We may close this section by quoting the following interesting passage from Jähns,[4] which illustrates many of the points brought out above: 'Ebenso spiegelt sich bis heut die Bedeutung des Sonnenrosses in der Sprache. Nicht nur *Schimmel* zeigt genau denselben Stamm wie *Schimmer*, auch das Wort *Mähre* dürfte in lezter Instanz von dem altdeutschen Adjektive *mar*, d.i. "glänzend", abstammen, eine Herkunft, welche der früher gegebenen Deutung durch Bewegungsbezeichnungen keineswegs widerspräche, da auch "glänzen" ebenso wie z.B. "blizen" und "blinken" auf eine Bewegungserscheinung zurückfürt. Jene Etymologie empfilt sich überdis durch eine Parallele mit dem Sanskrit. Wie *mar* hat nämlich die Sanskritwurzel *har* den Sinn von "glänzen". Zwei bekannte Derivata diser Wurzel, *hári* und *harít*, sind aber die gebräuchlichsten Bezeichnungen der Sonnenrosse in den Veden, welche somit genau so gebildet sind wie unser Wort *Schimmel*. Endlich spricht für jene Ableitung des Wortes *Märhe* auch noch der Umstand, dasz das gleichklingende deutsche *Märe* (*Märchen*), das isländische *märd*, d.i. "Loblied", das gothische *merjan*, d.i. "verkündigen", ebenso von dem glanzbedeutenden *mar* zu stammen scheinen, wie z.B. aus der Sanskritwurzel *ark*, d.i. "glänzen," das Wort *arkuh*, d.h. "Licht," aber auch "Loblied", hervorgegangen ist. Auch das althochdeutsche Wort *Hrosa* bedeutet sowol die "Stute" als die "Rumträgerin", die "Fama".' ('The significance of the Sun-Horse is still mirrored in our language. Not only does the word *Schimmel* (= white horse) show just the same root as *Schimmer* (= gleam), but even the word *Mähre* (= mare) must ultimately be derived

---

[1] Mogk, *op. cit.* S. 49. Wuttke, *op. cit.* S. 17.
[2] For the sexual significance of birds that bring news, etc., see Abraham, *op. cit.* S. 29, 30.
[3] Laistner, *op. cit.* Bd. ii. Kap. 51.   [4] Jähns, *op. cit.* S. 248-249.

from the Old German adjective *mar*, *i.e.* shining. This source in no way contradicts the interpretation we gave earlier in terms of movement,[1] since *glanzen* (= to shine) itself, as well as *blizen* (= to glitter) and *blinken* (= to dazzle) go back to the phenomenon of movement. This etymology is supported by a parallel with Sanscrit. Just as *mar*, so has the Sanscrit root *har* the sense of "shining". Now two well-known derivatives of this root, *hari* and *harit*, are the most usual designations of the Sun steeds in the Vedas, so that these are formed in just the same way as the German word *Schimmel*. Finally, in favour of this derivation of the word *Märhe* speaks the further circumstance that the similarly sounding German *Märe* (= tale), from which comes *Märchen* (= fairy-tale), the Icelandic *märd* (= song of praise), the Gothic *merjan* (= to foretell), all seem to come from the *mar* (= shining), just as the word *arkuh* (= light, and also song of praise) comes from the Sanscrit root *ark* (= to shine). The Old High German word *Hrosa* meant "mare" as well as "the bearer of fame".')

C. CONCLUSIONS

The data just brought forward should enable us to solve what is perhaps the most puzzling riddle in this whole group of mythical beliefs, and one which if solved should illuminate the general question of the connection between the Horse and the Nightmare mythology. I refer to the fact, for which ample evidence has been adduced above, that the two attributes of the horse which primarily appealed to the mythopœic imagination are its glistening appearance and its capacity for swift movement. The latter is intelligible enough, for the movement of the horse is not only a striking, but also its most useful, attribute. But what is to be made of the other? The glossy appearance of a well-groomed charger is doubtless a pleasing feature, but that this should have been selected as one of the two most important

[1] See Part III. p. 251.

attributes of the horse, the one that mainly enabled it to be identified with the sun itself, can hardly be called very comprehensible.

Let us first consider the *movement* attribute more closely. Although, as was remarked, the actual fact of movement is important enough in itself, it is easy to show that the idea has been extensively sexualized and that the part it plays in mythology is due to the way it has been exploited in this sense. It is not unnatural that swift movement is in a general way to be equated with the idea of potency; indeed a good part of the ambitions of modern civilization illustrates this truth. But psycho-analysis is able to show the specific manner in which this association is formed. As I have pointed out earlier in a clinical connection,[1] the potency in question is a pregenital one; it is based on a very early association between the ideas of movement and of excrementitial performances, one easily illustrated by the fact that "movement" and "motion" are even in adult years still the commonest phrases used to designate the act of defæcation. This association, of which one gets ample proof in the course of psycho-analytical work, is perhaps most readily demonstrated in cases where the patient is one of those motorists that may be called speed-maniacs, *i.e.* where the act of fast driving is not so much a pleasure as an indispensable necessity the thwarting of which is unbearable.

I have the impression that, although this association is certainly forged with all the three acts of excretion, it is the urinary one that contributes the most characteristic elements. If we study the ideas surrounding the procreative powers of the horse, which we have seen to be the central source of the mythological interest in the animal, we note at once that they especially cluster around the association between Horse and Water, and this in spite of the fact that horse-dung so far surpasses its urine in fertility value as to be still a serious rival to the most elaborate form of artificial chemical fertilizers

[1] Part II. p. 208.

of soil. I am referring here not simply to the obvious features of the erotic centaurs and kelpies, but especially to the fact that the creation of growth, vegetation, etc., is plainly to be equated to the striking of springs; from the horse, particularly from his hoof, spurts forth ambrosial fluid with these magical powers. Now water is everywhere connected not only with fertility, but also with the idea of movement; that the Latin *aqua* and *equus* are both derived from the same Sanscrit root meaning movement is highly characteristic of this group of associations. The three movements of which water is capable are identified with three aspects of the sexual act: (1) undulation with riding and therefore with the movements of coitus, (2) spurting or issuing forth with the emission of semen, and (3) flowing with the pre-seminal, *i.e.* infantile, act of urination.

This dissection of the components of the sexual act may be used as a scheme for purposes of orientation in the mass of data I have presented above. First let us distinguish between the to-and-fro movements of coitus and the final act of emission. The former belong much more to the adult, genital level of development, and they are essentially represented in the horse mythology—as has been expounded above at length—by the act of riding, of course a bisexual act. The emission belongs to both the adult and the childhood stage of development, with the characteristic difference that in the former it is a spurting act (semen) and in the latter much more a flowing act (urine). Movement in general, and riding in particular, thus represent the sexual conception of the horse in mythology, the former more on the infantile, the latter on the adult plane. The former is mainly derived from interest in the horse's very visible and notable excretory performances, perhaps the urinary one most of all. To sum up these conclusions I would say that what attracted the unconscious, and therefore the mythopœic, imagination in the idea of the horse was the pleasure that could be obtained from riding him, and the interest in his procreative powers, especially as exemplified in infantile terms by his remarkable excretory performances which became identified with the general idea of movement.

Let us now return to the other, more enigmatic attribute, that of shining. The etymological data already quoted[1] above suggest an equivalency between the ideas of shining and moving, dissimilar as these are in our consciousness, and in my opinion this is a clue that provides an answer to the riddle. The solution I would propound is that the curiously excessive interest in the supposed shine or gleam of the horse is derived from the same source as that in movement, *i.e.* from interest in the horse's reproductive-excremental performances, particularly that of urination. It is certainly striking that the whitish-yellow colour of horse's urine is paralleled by the colour of the symbolic objects to which the attribute of shining is ascribed: the milk-white magic steed, the golden mane, and the pale yellow rays of the sun, whose equivalency to flowing fire (in the unconscious: urine) was pointed out above. The equivalency of shining and moving is especially clear in the Horse-Sun group of beliefs; 'golden movement' sums up the essence of the conception. Lightning itself, the sexual symbolism of which Abraham has demonstrated, was always regarded mythologically as the rapid 'movement' of the gods.[2] What I regard as a decisively confirmatory piece of evidence in favour of the conclusion just reached is the fact that the same verb in German *strahlen* denotes both the staling of a horse and the process of shining; incidentally, the substantive *Strahl* also has the meaning of 'arrow', 'pike', 'lightning', 'glistening', 'glittering', 'radiating', 'gleaming', etc.; thus being an essentially masculine word. It is hardly possible that this could be so if there were not some instinctive, though unconscious, tendency in the popular mind to forge an association between the two ideas.[3] Both the

---

[1] Part III. pp. 314, 315.   [2] Jähns, *op. cit.* S. 281.

[3] It is curious how the word *Strahl* adheres to ideas connected with horses. *Strahlkrankheiten* means 'diseases of the horse's hoof', the word *Strahl* being applied to the radiating lines of the hoof.

glittering and the swift horse, therefore, fundamentally signify in mythology the potent urinating horse.

By pursuing the various ideas in horse mythology we have been able to establish the closest parallelism between them and those belonging to the night-fiend. We have seen in the extraordinarily rich sexual symbolism of the horse not only that experiences derived from anxiety dreams—transformation of human into animal, flight by night, etc.—run through the whole of horse mythology, but that this mythology is connected point by point with the corresponding myths of the night-fiend. In the terror of the night attack, whether of fiend as such or fiend in equine guise, we find extensive evidence of the dread of castration and of death, the plainest indication of the sensations of coitus and emission, and the characteristic propensity to sex inversion. All the beliefs about the Nightmare, in whatever guise, proceed from the idea of a sexual assault which is both wished for and dreaded. We have seen, in short, that the expression Nightmare signifies something other than a mistake in spelling.

CHAPTER IV

THE HORSE AND MEDIÆVAL SUPERSTITIONS

IN Part II. we investigated the relations between the
Nightmare and certain mediæval superstitions. In the
present Part we have investigated those between it
and the mythology of the Horse. If our reasoning is
sound it should be possible to point out connections
along the third line of the triangle, *i.e.* between the
mythological beliefs about the Horse and those belonging to the superstitions considered in the preceding Part.

A. INCUBUS AND SUCCUBUS

The Incubus and Succubus represent simply one
variety of night-fiend—one modified by religious influences. In essence they are the familiar Alp and Mara.
To detail the resemblances between the beliefs about
them and those of the Night Horse, therefore, would be
merely to repeat the preceding chapters. The same
features recur throughout both sets of beliefs: the
agonizing terror, ultimately of castration and death,
accompanied by the sensation of something pressing (or
trampling) on the breast, the erotic ideas based on
repressed incest wishes, the oscillation between the
divine and the demonic; even the feature so characteristic of the Horse myths, the close association with
water, is found with both, for Grimm[1] has pointed out
the habitual way in which night-fiends, *i.e.* Incubi,
frequent marshes and other watery loci; the name of the
river Marne, for instance, is cognate with the Norwegian
morn, one of the varieties of the *mara* words.[2]

Perhaps the most interesting connection between the
two is the following set of Scandinavian customs and
beliefs. One of the recognized ways of guarding against

[1] J. Grimm, *Deutsche Mythologie*, 1835, Bd. ii. S. 849, 850.
[2] Wolf von Unwerth, 'Eine isländische Mahrensage', *Wörter und Sachen,
kulturhistorische Zeitschrift für Sprach- und Sachforschung*, 1910, Bd. ii. S. 182.

the *mara*, in Mecklenburg, Tirol and elsewhere, was to put a horse's skull on the roof of the house or—if horses were in danger of being 'ridden' by her—in the manger.[1] Now in Jutland it is reported that when this was not effective a horse was buried alive to achieve the purpose,[2] and there is little doubt that this must be a relic of an old sacrificial custom. In olden times, therefore, horses were probably sacrificed both to the Horse-God[3] and to the female Night-Fiend, two beings the close connection between whom we have amply established. It is not long since a horse's penis used to be preserved by Norwegian peasants as a specially treasured heirloom,[4] and this also must belong to the same cult. An old Icelandic legend relates how a particularly terrible *mara*, when exorcised by a bishop, turned into a horse's bone.[5] It is thus clear that originally the equation *mara* = mare was taken literally, so that to sacrifice a horse was to kill the fiend herself and at the same time to propitiate her along the typical totemistic lines.

The belief that the *Mara* was wont to change herself into a mare, usually a white one, when visiting men at night, *i.e.* the belief that the Nightmare *was* a mare, is to be found in various parts of Europe.[6]

B. The Vampire and Werewolf

In the respective chapters on these beliefs we expatiated on the extensive interchangeability of the two, so that they may be considered here together. With them we have the *motif* of transformation into animal that is so prominent a feature of Horse mythology, but which is by definition excluded from the Incubus group. That of sucking, the hall-mark of the Vampire, is in the nature of things absent from the Horse group of beliefs and the

---

[1] J. Grimm, *Deutsche Mythologie*, 4e Ausgabe, 1876, S. 550, 1041.
[2] E. T. Kristensen, *Danske Sagn*, 1892, vol. ii. pp. 105, 251.
[3] See Part III. p. 262.
[4] A. Heusler, 'Die Geschichte vom Völsi, eine altnordische Bekehrungsanekdote', *Zeitschrift des Vereins für Volkskunde*, 1903, S. 24, 28.
[5] Unwerth, *op. cit.* S. 163.
[6] Cp., for instance, F. S. Krauss, *Slavische Volkforschungen*, 1908, S. 148.

oral-sadistic one of biting, which is distinctive of the
Werewolf, plays a less important part—though it does
occur—than might perhaps have been expected; it is the
horse's hoof, not his teeth, that is the feared weapon.
Equally prominent with all these, however, is the part
played by the idea of death. We have laid such stress on
this in the respective chapters that we need here only
bring to mind the psychopompic function of the ghostly
Werewolf and the Hell horse in relation to the close connection between the Werewolf belief and the Wild Hunt
more characteristic of the Horse.[1] The same is true of the
Night-flight theme, on the importance of which in all
Nightmare beliefs we have repeatedly laid stress. Then
the beliefs enumerated earlier[2] which connect the Werewolf with the wind and sun are throughout parallel to
those of the Horse and Wind- or Sun-God.

Apart, however, from the fundamental underlying
themes of incest and terror, it is noteworthy how the
beliefs in question are connected even in minor superficial details. Thus, for example, the evil number seven
—partly connected with the fear of precocious birth, *i.e.*
in the seventh month[3]—keeps recurring in the various
beliefs and stories. The mythical horse of the Hun-
garians, Tatos, was born in the following curious way.[4]
The hero carried a five-cornered black egg under his arm
for seven summers and seven winters; on the appropriate Ash Wednesday the steed came to the world,
without a chin but with teeth. It will perhaps be remembered that a child born with teeth is prone to become a
Werewolf.

If a Kelpie, *i.e.* a Scotch centaur, have intercourse
with a woman, the seventh child will belong to the
water,[5] presumably becoming a Kelpie himself. We have
learnt earlier that a seventh child is likely to become a
Nightmare—an *Alp* if male, a *Mara* if female—a Vampire or a Werewolf.

[1] See Part II. p. 146.   [2] Part II. p. 134.   [3] Eight months' children are rare.
[4] A. de Gubernatis, *Die Thiere in der indogermanische Mythologie*, 1874,
S. 222.
[5] A. Wuttke, *Der deutsche Volksaberglaube der Gegenwart*, 1900, S. 50.

If a woman creeps through a horse-collar so as to secure an easy childbirth, the baby will be a *Mara*.[1] If for the same purpose she creeps through a mare's caul, her child will be if male a Werewolf, if female a *Mara*.[2] If a man creep through a girdle of skin he will become a Werewolf.[3]

C. THE DEVIL

Being male, the Devil is naturally the equivalent of the Horse God rather than of the Night Mare, and in the chapter concerned with him I have dealt fully with the themes of sexuality, incest and castration that we have just seen to underlie the beliefs about the Horse God. Not only so, however, for the mediæval Devil was a direct descendant of the Teutonic Horse God, Odin, and inherited a number of his personal characteristics. Perhaps the best known of these was his horse's hoof, the presence of which betrayed him on so many occasions. In numerous legends and sagas he appears in actual horse guise.[4] Usually this is for the purpose of conveying someone, as, for instance, the famous Dietrich, to hell. Sometimes a troop of black horses carried off the souls of the damned to hell,[5] an idea which is an almost direct representative of the psychopompic Furious Host of Odin. An English demon known as Grant, doubtless a descendant of the Teutonic Grendel, used to appear in the form of a foal.[6]

The Teutonic *Wunschross*, the magic steed who enabled one to fulfil all one's wishes, also contributed a good deal to the mediæval conception of the devil. This of course was in the form of temptation; Jähns[7] gives numerous examples of this, including stories of Charlemagne and Heinrich der Loewe. In a Norman legend there is a neat combination of this theme and the preceding one: a black horse appeared to a priest, on New

[1] Part III. p. 249.   [2] B. Thorpe, *Northern Mythology*, 1851, vol. ii. p. 169.
[3] Part II. p. 139.   [4] Grimm, *op. cit.* Bd. ii. S. 831.
[5] *Ibid.*   [6] *Ibid.*
[7] M. Jähns, *Ross und Reiter in Leben und Sprache, Glauben und Geschichte der Deutschen*, 1872, Bd. i. S. 355.

Year's Day, 1091, and by offering him temptations induced him to mount on his back, whereupon he sprang with him straight to hell.[1]

In these stories we note again the curious interchange-ability of horse and rider. Often the Devil is a horse, often he simply rides on a horse. The women he used to visit during sleep complained that they had been 'rid-ing', or else 'ridden on', the whole night long. In France the concubines of priests turned into mares after they died and were called 'les juments au diable'.[2]

The last trace of the horse identification was the foot, which still remains as an attribute of the Devil. Numer-ous legends end by triumphantly asserting 'And there in the rock is the mark of the Devil's hoof left to this day'. Here again the same interchangeability is in play, for sometimes the mark is left by the Devil himself, some-times by his charger.

D. WITCH

Here also I need not recapitulate the fundamental themes common to the two sets of beliefs, for they are dealt with at length in the respective chapters, and will confine myself here to a few more external considera-tions. To begin with is the striking fact that sexual dreams, with emission, used to be referred to in English both as 'mare-riding' and as 'witch-riding', where the equivalency of Witch and Mara is expressed directly. It is implied also in some of the tests for Witches, which at the same time illustrate the transformation theme (human into animal). Thus when a Witch changes her-self into a mare,[3] and the mare is shod, the woman is found to have horseshoes on her hands and feet.[4] Again a Witch can be detected by burning the shoes of any horse she has bewitched, for this causes her great pain

[1] Gubernatis, op. cit. S. 226.
[2] Part III. p. 250.
[3] A belief still cherished in Baltic countries, notably Mecklenburg (Jähns, op. cit. Bd. i. S. 413).
[4] E. Meier, Deutsche Sagen, Sitten und Gebräuche aus Schwaben, 1852, S. 191.

in the feet.[1] Here the Witch is identified with her victim (on whom she has 'ridden'), and one is reminded of the following interesting totemistic identification in the same context.

In ancient European times, particularly among the Teutonic races, it was customary to sacrifice horses, the sacred animals, to the gods, and hand in hand with this went, as is usual in such rites, the taboo of eating horse-flesh—one which lingers in rationalized forms to this day. Now one of the horrible things of which Witches were accused was the eating of horse-flesh, thus violating this taboo. Boguet,[2] for example, in describing 'qu'il y avait une grande chaudière sur le feu, dans laquelle chacun alloit prendre de la chair', expressly adds, 'que la chair n'est autre que de cheval'. If one thinks of the extensive part played by horses in the same ceremonies, the preliminary rides (men being often converted into horses for the purpose), the making music on horses' heads, the appearance of the Devil in the form of a horse (often carrying the Witch thus), mounted on one, or at least with a horse's foot, the custom of drinking out of horse's hooves (hence harking back to the ancient Aryan source of ambrosia), one must conclude that we have to do here with relics of pagan beliefs of great antiquity in which there is a close association between horses and supernatural beings with alarming nocturnal activities.

One need not again insist on the extensive part played by the idea of riding in the whole Witch superstition, one derived exclusively from experiences with horses. Even the favourite day for the Witches' Sabbath, May 1, was a day sacred to the Horse God, Odin, and one when the nocturnal procession of his army took place. In fact, the ghostly troops of Witches riding and hurtling through the air are plainly descendants, though with partly inverted sex, of the old Wild Hunt and Furious Host.

[1] J. G. Dalyell, *The Darker Superstitions of Scotland*, 1835, pp. 323-324.
[2] Henri Boguet, *Discours des sorciers*, 1603, pp. 82, 83.

CHAPTER V

THE *MR* ROOT

THE mythological data brought forward in the preceding chapters have shown the close parallelism between beliefs about the Horse and those about the Night Fiend, and psycho-analysis has enabled us to penetrate to the common origins of both in the repressed infantile sexuality that is the ultimate source of Nightmare experiences. In this chapter I propose to bring forward an extract of the extensive etymological data bearing on the two words 'mare' and 'mara', the psychological connections of which have been shown to be astonishingly close, and to attempt to show that psycho-analysis can also make contributions which may assist etymologists in the solution of some of their own problems.

The problem I select to illustrate this thesis is as follows. The word ' mare ' is certainly the Anglo-Saxon *mere*, feminine of *mearh* = horse. In Old High German the corresponding words were respectively *meriha* or *merha*, and *marah*, *marh* or *marcha*. The oldest sources of this word actually known are the Teutonic *marhja* (feminine of *marha*) and the Celtic *marka*. The word was thus *mar* followed by either an aspirated or a guttural palatal, which, incidentally, is preserved in the corresponding modern word only in the valley of the upper Adige. Etymologists have, in accordance with known laws, to assume an origin in an Old Teutonic and general European *mark-os*.[1] This root, however, has not been demonstrated in these languages nor in the still earlier Indo-Germanic, and its further connections are therefore a matter for conjecture only. We have mentioned earlier two or three suppositions of Jähns on this point, though apparently etymologists have not

[1] See, for instance, W. W. Skeat, *Etymological Dictionary of the English Language*, 1910.

taken them very seriously. I hope to give reason for thinking that, with certain modifications, his suppositions have a certain basis of truth, and also to show that psycho-analysis can help to solve problems of this order.

Before attempting this, however, I shall have to establish a basis on what appears to be quite different ground, and I propose to do so by turning attention to the etymology of the other word that interests us here, *mara*, the night-fiend who is responsible for the second half of 'Nightmare'. This word can be traced to an extremely ancient Old Teutonic source, and there is no doubt about its being derived from a still older one. The primitive language which philologists have reconstructed under the name of Indo-Germanic (or, better, Indo-European) contains a large number of allied words the ultimate source of which is a primordial *MR* root. The study of the genealogical trees proceeding from this root is a most fascinating one,[1] but I shall here consider only a small extract which is cognate to our present theme.

The consonantal sound *M* was variously combined with five others, all linguo-palatal sounds, *D, R, L, K, G*, so as to create nine distinct roots. From these a very large number of individual words were formed, but we are concerned here only with the roots themselves; the accompanying diagram will make it easier to grasp the various combinations.

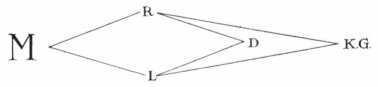

The primordial combination of them was in all probability *MR*, usually as *MAR*, occasionally as *MER*.

[1] The works most useful in this study are: H. Bächtold-Stäubli, *Handwörterbuch des deutschen Aberglaubens*, 1927. P. Ehrenreich, *Die allgemeine Mythologie und ihre ethnologischen Grundlagen*, 1910. A. Fick, *Vergleichendes Wörterbuch der indogermanischen Sprachen*, 3e. Aufl., 1874. Wolfgang Golther, *Handbuch der germanischen Mythologie*, 1895. J. Grimm, *Etymologisches Wörterbuch*, 1854–1911. Merker, *Reallexicon*. A. Schrader, *Reallexicon der indogermanischen Altertumskunde*, 1901. Skeat, *op. cit.* A. Walde, *Lateinisches etymologisches Wörterbuch*, 1910.

This had three chief sets of meanings, here given in order of their antiquity: the first two are to be traced to the Indo-European, the third to the European Division only.

(1) A. To rub on, bray, gall, grind, crush, injure; B. to wear away, exhaust, consume; C. to weaken, soften, soak (*e.g.* to dip bread in a liquid).

From A come the following words. The 'mare' of Nightmare. This, which literally means 'a crusher', is cognate with the Anglo-Saxon verb *merran* (Old High German *marrjan*), to obstruct, impede, vex, and hence to dissipate, exhaust, waste; from it comes also 'to mar'. Its Middle Dutch equivalent *marren* signifies both to hinder, to injure and to bind, to fasten (whence our words 'to moor' and 'marline'), the latter meaning being also that of the Indo-Germanic root *Mu*. Anyone who has had to treat cases of Nightmare or—what is much the same thing— dread of nocturnal emissions will agree that the connotations just mentioned are peculiarly appropriate. In Old Teutonic both the male and female night-fiend were designated by the word *maran*. Further, the words 'mortar' (what is ground or the object in which it is ground), the Greek μάρναμαι, to fight (literally 'to rub against'), and the Latin *martulus* (Teutonic *marta*, a hammer), whence the cognomen Charles Martel, all come from this *MAR* (1) A. root.

From B come, through the Greek, 'amaurotic' (blind) from *marva* = soft, and 'moron', of feeble intelligence (*mara* = stupid).

From C come μαραίνω, to weaken, to wear out; the Anglo-Saxon *mearu*, tender, pliable (also from *marva* = soft); and the Latin *mereo*, I earn (literally, get a share), whence *merenda* and the German dialect *Mährte* (Old High German *meriod*), both meaning an afternoon meal, and our 'merit', 'meritorious', 'meretricious' (harlot-like), etc.

(2) To die, to be ruined. Here we get through Ger-

manic the word 'murder'; through Latin 'mortal', 'mortify', etc.; through Greek 'ambrosia' (= immortal); and the Welsh *maru*, dead.

An interesting group here originates in the early designation—particularly by peoples without experience of tides—of all water other than running water as 'dead'. Hence the Gothic *marei*, sea or lake (the Germans still employ one word, *See*, for both), Sanscrit *mîra*, ocean, Old Teutonic *mari*, sea, Latin *mare*, Welsh *môr*, and the modern words 'mere', 'marsh' (= mere-ish), 'moor', 'marine', 'maritime', etc.

(3) To gleam, *mara*, pure; Latin *merus*, clear, whence 'mere-ly'.

The meaning seems to have diverged in the one direction *via* the Letto-Slavonian *mara*, connoting 'news' (whence the German *Märchen* = fairy-tale), and in another towards such ideas as 'celebrated', whence the title 'Waldemar', the town 'Weimar', etc. Perhaps the difference is simply that between 'known' and 'well known', both of which can—for instance, in the German *bekannt*—be designated by one word. The German *mär*, dear (like *Mär-chen*, from the Middle High German *maere*), presumably comes from the closeness of the ideas of familiarity and loveableness.

MR was readily replaced by *ML*, more often as *MEL*, less often as *MAL*. The inter-changeability of *R* and *L* is very familiar to philologists; examples in the present context are: *marva*, *malva*, soft; *mard-*, *mald-*, to become soft; *marg*, *malg*, to stroke. An amusing example of the reverse process is furnished by the word 'marmalade'; the first part of this comes from *mar* via *med* and Latin *mel*, the word itself signifying 'honey-apple' or quince, but the Portuguese, who first made the concoction (from quinces), changed it back again from *mal* to *mar*. One surmises that the change to *L* denotes a certain softening of the ideas thus conveyed, such as a change from 'grind' to 'pound', etc., but even though this conclusion may be generally correct there are certainly exceptions to it. The words derived from this root may be roughly grouped according to the predominant meaning.

(1) To pound: 'mallet', (Pall) 'Mall' (Latin *malleus*).

(2) To grind: cp. Old Irish *molim*, I grind. 'Mould' (= soil, not 'to mould'). 'mole', 'meal', 'millet', 'muller' (stone used for grinding powder). 'Mill', 'molar', from Latin.

(3) To dissolve: 'malt', 'melt', 'milt', Old Norse *melta*, to digest.

(4) To soften: 'mild', 'mauve' (the colour of mallow), 'mallow', 'mal-achite' 'mulch' (wet straw). Lithuanian *melas*, dear. Russian *miliui*, kind. 'Mildew', 'mellifluous', 'molasses', from Latin *mel* (= honey)—cp. Teutonic *melitha* and Old Irish *mil* = honey.

(5) (As *mal.*) To besmear, to blacken: 'melanotic' (also Christian name 'Melanie') from the Greek. 'Malice', 'malign', etc., from the Latin *malus*, evil. Cornish *malan*, the devil.

The combination with D appears also to exercise a certain softening influence. *MAD* (Sanscrit *madlin*), meant sweet or loveable, and from it (via *medhu*, honey) comes our honey-drink 'mead'. *MELD* correspondingly means 'to soften', 'to dissolve'. 'Mild', from √*mel*, may have been influenced by it, and we have 'mollify', 'mollusc', 'to moil', via the Latin *mollis*, soft. *MARD*, on the other hand, though it also meant to soften, had the harsher connotations of 'to grind,' 'to pound', 'to bite', 'to weary of'. 'Mordant', 'mordacity', and 'morsel', from the Latin *mordere*, 'to bite'. This root was also intensified by an initial *s*, which the Latin lost. Incidentally, the root *mar* was similarly intensified, *e.g.* Sanscrit *smr* = remember, long for; the initial *s* has been lost in our 'mourn' and 'martyr' derived from it, but retained in 'smart', in the German *Schmerz* = pain, and in the Kashube *Zmora* = mara, night-hag. *Mard* is almost certainly an earlier root than *Meld-*, which was probably formed from it by modification.

The fundamental root was also extended by adding one of the posterior linguo-palatals, *K* or *G*. *MAK* meant 'to pound', and via the Latin we have from it the word 'to macerate'. *MARK* proved to have a specially fruitful growth. It has three fairly well defined sets of meanings.

(1) To injure. 'Marcescent' from the Latin *marcere*, to wither.

(2) To grasp: then to stroke, to beat, to punish. From this we get diverse words as 'mulct' (cp. Lat. *mulcere*, 'to stroke'; *mulcare*, 'to punish by beating'), 'morphia', 'morphology', 'merchant', 'market', 'mercenary', and the French *merci*, English 'mercy'.

(3) To stroke, to soften, to soak. Cognate with the Gothic *marka*, border, we get 'margin', 'mark', (Welsh) 'marches' and the 'Merse' division of Berwickshire. The 'softer' meaning changed the form of the root to *malg*, which we shall consider presently. The root *MARG*, or *merg*, closely allied to this group, signified to rub or stroke, and doubtless influenced the form of some of its derivatives, *e.g.* 'margin'.

In accord with a suggestion proffered earlier we find that the root *MELG*, 'to stroke', has blander connotations than those of *MARK* or *MARG*. From it are derived, by very different routes, 'milk' and 'emulsion'.

This condensed extract will be enough to indicate how extraordinarily prolific the *MR* root has proved to be, a feature which in itself, as Sperber[1] has pointed out, is highly characteristic of roots having originally a sexual signification. In the present instance it would not seem too venturesome to divine what this must have been. If one reviews the various groups of meanings mentioned above it becomes fairly plain that the original meaning must have referred to two ideas, that of some act and

[1] H. Sperber, 'Über den Einfluss sexueller Momente auf Entstehung und Entwicklung der Sprache', *Imago*, 1912, Bd. i. S. 405-453.

that of the consequence of it. (1) The act was primarily to rub on, up or against, and this then diverged into a more and a less sadistic group. The former may be described by the words to pound, grind, crush, injure, bite, beat, gall, oppress; the latter by the words to bind together, grasp, stroke. (2) The consequence of the act is indicated by such words—sometimes active, sometimes passive—as to die, ruin, exhaust, weaken, make tender or pliant, soften, smear, dissolve, dissipate, consume. It would be fair to take as representative of these two ideas the words to rub hard and to be softened respectively, which is near to what Fick[1] considers to be the original meaning of the whole root, viz., to rub on, to exhaust, to wear oneself out. We have here an unmistakable allusion to the act of masturbation, one the psychological significance of which is throughout identical with that of the Nightmare experience: incest guilt, nocturnal experiences, sadism, dread of castration or death, and so on.

This conclusion would appear to be so irrefragable that one is tempted to inquire further into the very constituents of the roots in question. Very little work has been done on the psychological significance of individual sounds. The best-known point to be established is the sucking and maternal associations of the consonantal sound M. This is the least variable basis of what we may call the MR roots, for the only circumstance in which it is replaced by another labial, B, is in the reversal of R and its vowel so irksome to philologists. I may cite two examples in the present context, one being the transformation of the Indo-Germanic *mar*, 'to die', into the Greek βροτός, a mortal (the earlier μορτός being still extant in dialect form), and that of the Indo-Germanic *mardu*, soft, into the Greek βραδύς, slow, Latin *bardus*, stupid.

In the set of roots we have been considering the sound M then allies itself to one or another of the linguo-palatals R, L, D, K, G. Of these the most important is

[1] *Op. cit.* Bd. iii. S. 716.

probably *R*, for on its presence or absence would appear
to depend whether the signification arising belongs respectively to the more or to the less sadistic groups mentioned above. That a psychological problem lies here has
been perceived by a recent philologist:[1] 'Was zunächst
den Anlaut betrifft, so wäre es interessant und wie es
scheint, auch bedeutungsvoll, das Verhalten der Sprachen
in Bezug auf den Liquida-Anlaut zu untersuchen. Eine
grosse Anzahl von Sprachen können nämlich entweder
kein *r* oder kein *l*, oder keines von beiden im Anlaut
halten. . . . Jedoch scheint es fast sicher zu sein, dass
derlei Beschränkungen des Anlautes nicht primärer,
sondern sekundärer Natur sind, dass die Sprachen der
älteren Kulturkreise sowohl *r* als *l* im Anlaut an-
standslos gebrauchen.' ('As for the initial sound it would
be interesting, and apparently also very important, to
examine the behaviour of languages in respect of the
liquid initial sounds. For a considerable number of
languages are not able to use either *r* or *l*, or neither,
as an initial sound. . . . Nevertheless it seems almost
certain that such restrictions are of a secondary, not a
primary, nature, and that the older languages un-
reservedly employed both *r* and *l* as an initial
sound.')

One of the Vedic strophes[2] designed to facilitate the
flow of speech when recited has as its theme the ejacu-
latory and fertilizing powers of Indra's twin steeds. The
letter *r* appears in every word of the strophe, which
largely consists of a play on the words *varsh* and *vrish*,
signifying both 'to ejaculate' and 'to fertilize'. In
Piedmont there exists, or did exist until lately, a
drawing-room game at weddings in which each guest
had to describe the gift he intended to make the bride;
but in doing so he had to avoid all words containing
the letter *r*, otherwise he paid a forfeit.[3] In other words,

---

[1] P. W. Schmidt, *Die Sprachfamilien und Sprachenkreise der Erde*, 1912,
S. 289.
[2] *Rigveda*, v. 36, 5.
[3] A. De Gubernatis, *Die Thiere in der indogermanische Mythologie*, 1874,
S. 273.

the *r*-sound connoted something which a guest did not give or do to a bride.

The two instances just quoted are broad hints of how the popular mind unconsciously conceives of the *r*-sound in a sexual sense, and this would seem to be borne out by the non-European meaning of the root *ar* = fire and *Ra* = God. I would suggest, however, that the considerations adduced above, among others, indicate a still more specific original signification of the *r*-sound, namely, a sadistic one and particularly an oral-sadistic one. [Some support for this suggestion is afforded by Jespersen's[1] observation that the sound is connected with the rougher side of maleness, and that it becomes softened when submitted to the refining influence of femininity. He writes: 'There is one change characteristic of many languages in which it seems as if women have played an important part even if they are not solely responsible for it: I refer to the weakening of the old fully trilled tongue-point *r*. I have elsewhere (*Fonetik*, p. 417 ff.) tried to show that this weakening, which results in various sounds and sometimes in a complete omission of the sound in some positions, is in the main a consequence of, or at any rate favoured by, a change in social life: the old loud trilled point sound is natural and justified when life is chiefly carried on out-of-doors, but indoor life prefers, on the whole, less noisy speech habits, and the more refined this domestic life is, the more all kinds of noises and even speech sounds will be toned down. One of the results is that this original *r*-sound, the rubadub in the orchestra of language, is no longer allowed to bombard the ears, but is softened down in various ways, as we see chiefly in the great cities and among the educated classes, while the rustic population in many countries keeps up the old sound with much greater conservatism. Now we find that women are not unfrequently mentioned in connection with this reduction of the trilled *r*; thus in the sixteenth century in France there was a tendency to leave off the trilling and

[1] O. Jespersen, *Language: Its Nature, Development and Origin*, 1922, p. 244.

even to go further than to the present English untrilled point *r* by pronouncing *z* instead, but some of the old grammarians mention this pronunciation as characteristic of women and a few men who imitate women (Erasmus,"mulierculae Parisinae"; Sylvius,"mulierculae . . . Parrhisinae, et earum modo quidam parum viri"; Pillot, "Parisinae mulierculae . . . adeo delicatulae sunt, ut pro *pere* dicant *pese*"). In the ordinary language there are a few remnants of this tendency; thus, when by the side of the original *chaire* we now have also the form *chaise*, and it is worthy of note that the latter form is reserved for the everyday signification (Engl. chair, seat) as belonging more naturally to the speech of women, while *chaire* has the more special signification of "pulpit, professorial chair". Now the same tendency to substitute *z*—or after a voiceless sound *s*—for *r* is found in our own days among the ladies of Christiania, who will say *gzuelig* for *gruelig* and *fsygtelig* for *frygtelig* (Brekke, *Bidrag til dansknorskens lydloere*, 1881, p. 17; I have often heard the sound myself). And even in far-off Siberia we find that the Chuckchi women will say *nidzak* or *nizak* for the male *nirak* "two", *zërka* for *rërka* "walrus", etc.'

There is almost within our own experience a set of considerations in English history which strongly confirms Jespersen's argument about woman's influence on the *r*-sound. As has been well expounded recently by Wingfield-Stratford,[1] the outstanding cultural feature of the mid-nineteenth century was the refining influence that women, among whom the young Queen played a not inconsiderable part, exerted on the Englishman whose coarseness and brutality had been a by-word in Western Europe in the immediately preceding generations. This influence often assumed forms that to us appear grotesque, and one of these concerns the present theme. Some of us are old enough to recall traces of a dying fashion in speech which was admirably represented on the stage in *The Barretts of Wimpole Street*.

[1] E. Wingfield-Stratford, *The Victorian Tragedy*, 1930.

I refer to the taboo that over-refined people put on the r-sound, which had to be replaced by w.[1] Those who witnessed that play will have no doubt about the ultra-feminine, and indeed effeminate, nature of this taboo, and those who were not so fortunate may be convinced by the following passage from the preface to J. M. Barrie's *Dear Brutus*:[2] 'There remains Lady Caroline Laney of the disdainful poise, lately from the enormously select school where they are taught to pronounce their r's as w's; nothing else seems to be taught, but for matrimonial success nothing else is necessary. Every woman who pronounces r as w will find a mate; it appeals to all that is chivalrous in man.']

If we inquire further into the physiological associations of the sound in question, it is not hard to see that they are characteristically those of anger and fear. Trilling was in all probability originally derived from the rumble of a growl, and one feels instinctively the onomatopœic appropriateness of the Teutonic *marren*, to growl like a dog, and the German *murren*, to grumble. Jespersen[3] remarks about palatal sounds, 'it is strange that among an infant's sounds one can often detect sounds—for instance, k, g, h, and uvular r—which the child will find difficulty in producing afterwards when they occur in real words, or which may be unknown to the language which it will some day speak', and one may very well ascribe this phenomenon to the influence of early repression. On the other hand, the snoring and choking rumbles so characteristic of deep sleep disturbed by anxiety dreams both in childhood and in adult life, and of Nightmare experiences in particular, originate equally in anger (repressed sadism) and in fear.

*   *   *   *   *

After this excursion into the ultimate source of the linguistic expressions for the experience of Nightmare, we may return to the question raised at the beginning of

[1] w is naturally the easiest substitute for r, employed, for instance, by children and by those adults—usually women—who never achieve a mastery of the harder sound.
[2] Uniform edition, p. 7.   [3] Jespersen, *op. cit.* p. 106.

this chapter, namely, the etymology of the other 'mare'. The masculine form of this in Old Teutonic was *marha*, in Keltic *marka*, in Old High German *marh*, *marcha*. The feminine was in Old Teutonic *marhja*, in Old High German *merhâ*, the subsequent vowel change to Modern German *märhe* and English 'mare' presumably indicating the feminine gender. A synonym of the *mar* root discussed above was in Old Teutonic *marja*, and the question is whether the word 'mare' ultimately belongs to the *Mar* group or to a separate and entirely unknown root.

The word cannot actually be traced further back than what I have just stated. There is, however, a variety of ways in which philologists obtain help in these difficult problems. Their knowledge of the laws relating to sound change—such as, for example, the well-known laws of Grimm on the shiftings that have taken place between English and German—enables them to infer what form a given word must have taken in another language, even when there is no documentary proof of this. Often, again, comparison with allied or intermediate languages will furnish data of value. An example of this may be quoted from the present context: the fact that the Lithuanian *melzu* means both 'to stroke' and 'to milk' shows the identity of the Old Teutonic *malg*, 'to milk', with the Indo-Germanic *marg*, 'to stroke'. Now the general probability is certainly in favour of the view that the 'mare' word is in some way related to the *Mar* group, *i.e.* that the Old Teutonic *marhja* and *marja* could not be entirely unconnected; the addition of an aspirate, palatal or guttural, to the *mar* stem is so frequent or manifold that one is very inclined to regard the *marcha* (male horse) as one more example of it.

Can psycho-analytical considerations throw any further light on this obscure problem: for instance, by suggesting the unknown point at which the horse word may have broken off from the main group? Jähns[1]

[1] M. Jähns, *Ross und Reiter in Leben und Sprache, Glauben und Geschichte der Deutschen*, 1872, S. 12.

insists, from Celtic and Wallachian analogies, that the idea of movement was inherent in the early meaning of the word, and further, basing himself on Max Müller's Sanscrit studies of the same conception,[1] that the idea of shining (sun = horse's head, rays = mane) was equally implicit, the latter connection going back directly to *mar* No. 3 = to gleam. Against the first argument may be brought forward the fact that, with a very few insignificant exceptions (*e.g.*, Greek μάργος, wandering, and μαργίτης, a tramp), the vast number of words derived from the *mar* group can hardly be said to have much to do with movement in the ordinary sense: to grind or crush does, it is true, imply violent action, as does the trampling of horses, but hardly movement in the sense generally connoted in horse mythology, namely, of swift transit through space. And as to the second argument it brings one against the difficulty, not mentioned above, of understanding how the *mar* No. 3 ('to shine') is connected with the other meanings of the root. It is thought to be the same word as the other *mars*, though this is not absolutely certain, but 'to shine and 'to rub' or 'grind' seem very disparate ideas.

At this point I would recall the detailed considerations adduced in Chapter III which indicated the very definite conclusion that the idea linking the two outstanding equine attributes in mythology, namely, movement and shining, must have been a primitive interest in the horse's urinary feats as signs of an admirable potency. If this conclusion has any bearing on the etymological problem of the 'mare' word, it would be that the point of departure of the word from the *mar* group should be sought rather among those derivatives which denote what we called above[2] the consequences of an act rather than among those denoting the act itself. For urination could only be the consequence of a preceding act, *i.e.* the result of the infantile masturbation that lies behind the Nightmare experience; it is to be equated to the 'softening', 'dissolving' idea. And

[1] Jähns, *op. cit.* S. 249.   [2] Part III. p. 332.

it would follow that the *mar* No. 3 would itself also represent a specialization of this second 'consequence' half
of the total primary conception, as *mar* No. 2 (= 'to
die') evidently did.

If future philological researches confirm the necessarily tentative hypothesis just mentioned, one might be
able to consider a psychological suggestion on the whole
importance of the horse mythology in its relation to
Nightmare beliefs. This is that it ultimately represents
a huge *compensation* for the fears of ' softening' and loss
relating to the Nightmare emissions. For the attribute
of exceptional potency is unmistakable in the horse
mythology. And that ideas of fame, praise and admiration are among the chief derivatives of *mar* No. 3, a
feature Jähns[1] illustrates in connection with the horse
beliefs of both Europe and India, would be quite in
accord with this general tendency.

[1] See Part III. p. 313.

PART IV

CONCLUSION

CONCLUSION

IF by 'scientific' materialism is meant the tendency to discount the significance of mental and spiritual experiences, to displace the psychical by the physical, then the history of the Nightmare affords one of the most impressive examples of its darkening counsel. Until this tendency manifested itself, in relatively recent times, no sharp distinction had been drawn between the voluptuous and the fearful experiences of sleep. Both were equally ascribed to the activity of supernatural beings, and even in medical circles the same names, Incubus, Ephialtes, were used to designate both. Writers had repeatedly observed that the series of voluptuous—voluptuous-fearful—fearful in dream life was of an unbroken gradation, and daily clinical experience amply confirms this. The typical Nightmare is merely one extreme member of this series. It was Freud who first demonstrated the inherent connection between intrapsychic dread and repressed sexual impulses, and we can now understand the Nightmare as an event in which such impulses have been overwhelmed, and shrouded, by extreme fear. The intensity of the fear is proportionate to the guilt of the repressed incestuous wishes that are striving for imaginary gratification, the physical counterpart of which is an orgasm—often provoked by involuntary masturbation. If the wish were not in a state of repression, there would be no fear, and the result would be a simple erotic dream. The real cause of the Nightmare has thus two essential attributes: (1) it arises from within, (2) it is of mental origin, a sexual wish in a state of repression. Except for the repression this statement is true also of erotic dreams.

This formula, however, is accepted nowhere outside the circle of psycho-analysis, neither for the erotic nor for the Nightmare dream, *i.e.* the two extreme members of the series referred to above. The history of the

343

explanations proffered for these two types of dream is instructive. Until the advent of modern science the second feature mentioned above, the mental and sexual origin, was universally accepted as the explanation of both dreams, but the first feature, the endogenous origin, was denied. Since that advent this second feature has been discarded and the first feature installed as the full explanation. I suggest that both explanations are equally imperfect, though I shall give reasons for thinking that the older, popular 'superstitious' one was nearer to the truth than the later 'scientific' one.

The account just given of the history of the matter needs to be slightly amplified to make it more comprehensible. In the popular view erotic dreams were supposed to be brought about by the sexual wishes of lewd demons: in the current 'scientific'—or rather medical—view they are supposed to be produced by excessive physical tensions in the sexual apparatus. In the popular view Nightmares were similarly sexual assaults on the part of lewd demons, strongly resisted by the victim (an attitude corresponding to what we now term 'repression'): in the current medical view they are ascribed to physical disturbances in the alimentary, respiratory or circulatory system, disturbances of either an irritating nature, such as undigested food, or of a mechanical nature, such as a distended stomach. With erotic dreams the medical view dates from the twelfth century, and began to prevail over the popular view in the seventeenth. With the Nightmare it was foreshadowed by classical medical writers (Galen, etc.), but began to prevail over the popular view only in the eighteenth century. The view presented in this book, which fuses the two others, was hinted at by Thomas Nashe in 1594 and Splittgerber in 1860, but was scientifically established by Freud only at the beginning of this century. The sexual origin of the Nightmare, like that of Hysteria, both well known until the knowledge of it was blotted out by the 'scientific materialism'—in its anti-psychological sense—of the past two hundred years.

had to be discovered afresh in the twentieth century—
and, appropriately enough, by the same man.

Both the old popular view and the current medical
one agree in one fundamental respect, namely, in de-
vising an explanation—for erotic dreams as well as for
the Nightmare—that divests the subject of any personal
responsibility for his nocturnal erotic experiences. Both
invoke the mechanism of projection for their purpose:
the one projects the agency on to the outside world of
spirits, the other on to inanimate processes in the body.
Of the two the popular view retained both the psychological and the sexual elements, and was thus nearer to
the truth, particularly in the case of the Nightmare, than
is the present-day medical view. It was an advance to
discard the belief in spirits and demons, but a retro-
gression to discard the psychical and erotic, for the
supernatural beings at least possessed these attributes.
For thousands of years the forces of internal repression,
i.e. fear, made use of the supernatural projection to
guard man against too near an insight into his own
nature. When this defence began to fail 'scientific'
materialism came to the rescue, but this has delayed
the advent of psychological truth only for a couple of
centuries, and the obstacle it interposes will not be so
formidable as the 'spiritual' one.

Turning now to the influence of these nocturnal
experiences on various conscious beliefs, we note a
similar dawning of truth which is at last emerging into
light. Here, however, the institution that retarded
the recognition of the truth was, not the medical profession, but the Church. After broad hints from earlier
times, suppressed by the obscurantism of the Middle
Ages, extensive evidence has accumulated during the
past century that goes to show how potent has been the
influence of dreams, and particularly of terror dreams,
in the elaboration of various beliefs. This is most easily
recognized with such 'superstitions' as the idea of fabulous or disreputable supernatural beings, of human
beings being transformed into animals, of night journeys

through the air, of animals being identified with the spirits of the dead, *i.e.* of ancestors, and of the great *revenant* belief in the return of the departed. Psychoanalysis of dreams in which corresponding ideas occur has shown plainly that they originate in early mental conflicts relating to the parents—notably repressed death wishes and guilt over incestuous impulses, in the primordial struggles between love and hate.

It is not so easy to admit the possibility that various higher beliefs, and among them our most cherished, may have the same origin. Psychologists and anthropologists have brought forward much evidence to show that the belief in à soul that survives death has been extensively influenced by the experience of dreams, the infantile source of which we now know, and have thus opened the possibility of this belief having an altogether subjective origin. Even the second great theological dogma, the belief in a Deity, is becoming accessible to psychological investigation. It is generally recognized that it is bound up with the whole problem of evil, with both the explanation of the evil in human nature and the practical issue of how best to cope with it, and this is in accord with the historical, semantic and psychological considerations adduced in this book which go to show that God and the Devil were originally one Being. The analysis of the belief in the Devil, which may nowadays be classed as a superstition almost as definitely as the four other superstitious beliefs here treated, reveals it to be a derivative of the infantile conflicts over sexual and hostile wishes concerning the parents. This must raise the question whether the other aspect of the same Being, the divine aspect, does not represent merely another line of development from the same source. The whole subject of religion, its meaning and function, is obviously too vast to enter on here,[1] but I would say that in my opinion evidence is rapidly accumulating to show that the concept of the Heavenly Father is a subjective projection of the child's feelings about the earthly Father, and that

[1] [See my *Zur Psychoanalyse der christlichen Religion*, 1928.]

the religious attitude has been evolved from the attempts
to deal with the disturbing 'sinful' wishes concerning the
parents. Psycho-analysis is showing more and more how
the sense of sin—with its corollary in the idea of salvation—is born in the Oedipus complex, and that the
struggle to deal with the unconscious derivatives of this
continuously occupies mankind from the cradle to the
grave.

If this view is true it would certainly go to explain
the story of the superstitious beliefs treated in this book,
and particularly the Witchcraft epidemic, in a way that
nothing else does. The analysis here presented shows—
in my opinion conclusively—the incestuous origin of the
beliefs, and, as related above, the Church fully recognized that the Devil and Witch cult constituted a caricature, even to minute details, of the Christian faith. If,
now, that cult was to Christianity as reverse to obverse,
and if its signification was essentially incestuous, one
can scarcely avoid the inference that its threat to
Christianity lay in the risk of its exposing the incest
origin of the Christian beliefs themselves. It is true that
the process was throughout an unconscious and disguised one, but the threat was undoubtedly felt. The
horrified and panic-stricken endeavours of the Church
signified in essence a specially savage outburst of intoler-
ance against anything that to it represented incest. One
is led to the conclusion that Christianity must itself mean
a sublimation of, and therefore at the same time a
defence against, the primordial Oedipus wishes of mankind, a solution of these fundamental conflicts which was
felt to be vitally threatened by the danger they fought
so desperately against; there is no other way of explaining the intensity of the emotion displayed and the lengths
to which it was prepared to go to stamp out its enemy,
even by pursuing a line of conduct so grossly at variance
with its humane and ethical teachings. Devils and
Witches simply caricatured Christian beliefs, and by so
doing threatened to expose the repressed Oedipus wishes
on which these are based.

A close analogy can be shown to exist between the phenomena here investigated and psychoneurotic symptoms; they are indeed to a large extent identical. Both originate in the repressed sexual wishes of early childhood, which remain scarcely visible until external conditions compel certain sharply defined manifestations of them. The gradual disappearance of the superstitions took place in the same way as a spontaneous recovery does with neurotic symptoms, partly from an increase of the repression, partly from a fresh outlet being provided for the underlying trends. As has been shown in the preceding chapters, both these processes played a part in the disappearance of the five groups of superstitions: increased acuity of scientific thought combined with even more intense sexual repression rendered them unsuitable forms of expression for the buried wishes. These considerations are suggestive in respect of the future development of the processes here treated. The experience accumulated with the neuroses shows that so long as the causative factors are not removed—which has certainly not been done here—the mere disappearance of the symptoms offers no assurance against future disturbances; the tendency of the underlying forces either to recreate the old symptoms or to seek satisfaction by other ways of expression remains intact. The possibility of a relapse into the old superstitions has to be rejected on many historical grounds and would indeed be hard to imagine in our modern civilization, so that another group of outlets has to be found. There is much reason to think that the chief one of these has been the increase in individual psychoneuroses. In making the nice comparison between the amount of neurosis in modern and in ancient times respectively we may venture to guess that the main difference has been not in the actual quantity so much as in the different distribution of the manifestations. By this I mean that in former times in Europe, and still in savage races, neurotic manifestations appear to have been more communally organized and to have enjoyed a more general social acceptance than with us. What, for instance, are now called neurotic or psychotic patients are in a large measure the descendants of the old Witches, Lycanthropes, and so on, together with the people who believed in them. A further consideration of importance, which is usually overlooked, is that the sufferings they endure are perhaps as oppressive and no less widely spread than those due to the analogous processes in the Middle Ages. One may seriously ask whether a patient afflicted with a morbid phobia, *e.g.*, of thunder, suffers less than one who was afraid of the Devil. The latter was in many respects actually in a better position, since his fear was understood by his friends and recognized as being justified. He was not compelled to keep it secret in order to escape the shame and stigma of being so cowardly and weak as to 'give in to his imaginary fears'. A fear that is regarded by both the victim and his environment as reasonable and right is easier to bear than a quite senseless and irrational dread of something harmless, one which is not in accord with the other conscious thoughts and even resists all conscious endeavours to cope with it.

From all this two main conclusions may be drawn, to do with the problems of psychological 'repression', *i.e.* excessive fear of the unconscious mind, and of judgement. We can scarcely occupy ourselves here with the social side of the first of these;[1] I have only tried to show, by one set of examples, what frightful consequences may follow irrational 'repression' of human instincts, *i.e.* dread of them. We have also seen how hard it is, and for hundreds of years impossible, to exterminate these consequences when their real meaning has not been discovered.

The relation of the theme to the problem of judgement is equally important. For anyone who is convinced that his opinion on an emotionally coloured topic, *e.g.*, a social or religious one, is without doubt the only right one there is no sounder exercise than to reflect on the fact

---

[1] [See *Social Aspects of Psycho-Analysis*, 1924, edited by Ernest Jones.]

that the most capable and keen thinkers of the Middle
Ages, men who probably were by no means his inferior
in mental gifts, unhesitatingly recognized the truth of
propositions that now seem to us simply ridiculous. In
discussing a group of minor errors in thinking, brought
about by unconscious influences, Freud[1] made the
weighty remark: 'Ich gebe aber zu bedenken, ob man
nicht Grund hat, die gleichen Gesichtspunkte auch auf
die Beurteilung der ungleich wichtigeren *Urteilsirrtümer*
der Menschen im Leben und in der Wissenschaft aus-
zudehnen. Nur den auserlesensten und ausgeglichensten
Geistern scheint es möglich zu sein, das Bild der wahr-
genommenen äusseren Realität vor der Verzerrung zu
bewahren, die es sonst beim Durchgang durch die
psychische Individualität des Wahrnehmenden erfährt.'
('I leave it to your consideration whether there is not
ground for extending the same points of view to the
more important errors of judgement committed in science
and in life in general. Only the choicest and most bal-
anced minds seem able to guard the image they perceive
of outer reality from the distortion to which it is usually
subjected in its passage through the mental individuality
of the perceiver.')

One of the principal aims of science is to achieve
an objective view of the world, of civilization and life.
The obstacles in the way of this aim that proceed
from conscious inhibitions, for instance prejudices, have
been overcome up to a certain point: we are now
beginning the harder and more important work of dis-
lodging the obstacles that proceed from the unconscious.
The first step in this direction is the endeavour to illuminate the nature and activity of these unconscious
activities that mar and distort our conscious judgements.
Freud has been the pioneer along a path that it is now
possible to traverse; and when this is done mankind will
have in the future less excuse for the dark pages that
disgrace the book of its history as do the forms of superstition we have here examined.

[1] Freud, *Zur Psychopathologie des Alltagslebens*, Dritte Aufl., 1910, S. 121.

INDEX OF AUTHORS

352 INDEX OF AUTHORS

GENERAL INDEX